The Jacobite Clans of the Gl

BY THE SAME AUTHOR

Dundee and its Textile Industry, 1850–1914
From Esk to Tweed
Economic History of Modern Scotland
Integration and Enlightenment: Scotland, 1746–1832
The Jacobite Cause
The Eclipse of Parliament
Chambers Dictionary of World History *(editor)*
England's Colonial Wars, 1550–1688
Britain's Colonial Wars, 1688–1783

with John Gibson
The Jacobite Threat: A source book

ALSO PUBLISHED BY
SCOTTISH CULTURAL PRESS

The Jacobite Risings in Britain, 1689–1746

THE

Jacobite Clans

OF THE

Great Glen

~ 1650–1784 ~

Bruce Lenman

SCOTTISH CULTURAL PRESS
www.scottishbooks.com

First published 1984 in hardback by
Methuen London Ltd

Paperback edition published 1995 and reprinted 2004 by

SCOTTISH CULTURAL PRESS
Unit 6, Newbattle Abbey Business Park
Newbattle Road, Dalkeith, EH22 3LJ, Scotland
Tel: +44 (0)131 660 6366 • Fax: +44 (0)131 660 4666
Email: info@scottishbooks.com
www.scottishbooks.com

BRITISH LIBRARY CATALOGUING IN PUBLICATION DATA
A catalogue record for this book is available from the British Library

ISBN: 1 898218 19 6

Printed and bound by Cromwell Press Ltd, Trowbridge, Wiltshire

In Memoriam

R. M. Ogilvie

CONTENTS

PREFACE

The Jacobite Clans of the Great Glen is the companion volume to *The Jacobite Risings in Britain, 1689–1746*, also recently re-issued by Scottish Cultural Press. That book started as a detailed study of Lowland Jacobitism, and though it subsequently broadened out to survey the essential Highland element in Jacobite rebellions, I remained after its completion anxious to supplement it with in-depth study of a Jacobite region in the Highlands together with its clans. The chance to do this came my way due to the great kindness of Sir Donald Cameron of Lochiel, Kt, who made available to me manuscript correspondence between his ancestors and namesake of '45 fame and Simon Fraser of Lovat.

Though many other manuscripts were consulted later, this original breakthrough ensured that the core of *The Jacobite Clans* is in the study of the Camerons and Frasers. Its geographical spine, the Great Glen, happens to link Lochaber with Fraser of Lovat country in the straight line which only a major geological fault produces, and links these two clans with many others.

Since 1984, when *The Jacobite Clans* was first published, there has been disappointingly little fresh work on the politico-military history of the Jacobite clans, especially during the eighteenth century. Notably, however, John S. Gibson pushed my own original line of investigation much further, with distinguished results, in his biography of Lochiel of the '45 published in 1994. Re-publication of *The Jacobite Clans* therefore can be said to fill a gap in the literature almost as much now as it did in the 1980s.

Bruce P. Lenman

1 The Environment and the Clans

Scotland is in geological terms an extraordinarily varied assembly of bits and pieces of the earth's crust, much of which originated in the southern hemisphere before the drifting of continents carried it into its present position about forty million years ago. A time span of over 2,500 million years separates the oldest from the youngest of Scottish rocks, and it is a fundamental fact of Highland life that the bulk of the rock series in the Highlands of Scotland are amongst the very oldest in the whole sequence. The Lewisian gneiss found in the Outer Hebrides and the north-west mainland of the Highlands, for example, was originally volcanic ash and sand deposited 3,000 million years ago. It was buried, squeezed, melted, repeatedly injected by masses of molten rock magma, and eventually uplifted and resurrected by erosion of covering strata into the pitted rolling landform we now see again. However, such a history necessarily metamorphosed the original soft deposits into the gnarled, grey, tough, crystalline rock which, extensively covered with peat and studded with the dark waters of a thousand little lochans, forms the bleak landscape of central Lewis.[1]

Lewisian gneiss is a Pre-cambrian rock in the sequence of the geological column, and an early one at that. There are, however, many younger Pre-cambrian rocks in the Highlands, and the two great glens which form the stage for most of the events related in this book lie in the midst of a region dominated by masses of younger Pre-cambrian rock known as the Moine series. Originally limestones, sandstones and mudstones mixed with volcanic ash and rock, the Moine series has been metamorphosed over aeons into a complex of schists, granulites and gneisses. These too are hard crystalline rocks which simply do not break down into thick fertile soils like the much younger rocks of sedimentary origin which underlie most of the Lowlands of Scotland. Nor do the later insertions of pockets of originally underground or plutonic rocks of a hard crystalline nature like granites and gabbros modify the hard, unyielding grain of this countryside. What they do is help explain some of the more striking features of the region we shall be studying. At its southern march, for example, the looming mass of Ben Nevis, the highest peak in the British Isles, is composed of an inner and outer ring of granite crowned with a hard lava cap. It is in fact the remains of a collapsed ancient volcano.

If, however, the fundamental rock structures are the most important determining factor in the life of man in the Highlands, earth movements and earth sculpture explain the dramatic topography within which the history of the clans here studied was acted out. They are, quite simply, the clans of the great central dislocation of the Scottish Highlands, the Great Glen Fault, and of its principal eastern approach, Glen Spean. Between the Great Glen Fault and the Highland Boundary Fault (which runs from Stonehaven on the North Sea to the Firth of Clyde at the foot of Loch Lomond) lie the Grampian Highlands. Both faults are still mildly active as earthquake lines. Strong shocks occurred in the Inverness area at the north end of the Great Glen in 1816, 1888, 1890, and 1891, while over 400 shocks have been recorded in the neighbourhood of Comrie, which is on the Highland Boundary Fault.[2]

The Great Glen, or Glen More, to give it its Gaelic form, is a sixty-mile-long arrow-straight fissure extending right across the Highlands from Inverlochy or Fort William in the south-west to Inverness in the north-east. Its strategic importance was immense in the early modern period, for it separated the Hebridean Islands and the north-western part of the Highlands proper from the Grampian Highlands. In a very real sense it is the heart of the Highlands, or rather their strategic pivot. From the west there are several approaches giving access to Glen More. From the south-west the great sea loch, Loch Linnhe runs past the Isle of Mull and the ten-mile stretch of the low and lovely Island of Lismore, a green and fertile haven of rich loam soil on a bed of fruitful limestone, to reach the Corran Narrows and then broaden again to the head of the loch where it communicates with Loch Eil to the west, and receives the waters of the River Lochy which runs down a short distance from Loch Lochy, draining the southern end of Glen More. The site at the mouth of this river, Inverlochy, was destined by nature for an important role in human affairs.

Along the north shore of Loch Eil there has always been an important east-west route which at Glenfinnan, at the head of Loch Shiel, offers access to the coastal districts of Arisaig, Morar, and, down the long narrow waters of Loch Shiel, Moidart. It is no accident that in the late summer of 1745 Prince Charles Edward Stuart, who had come from France via the Hebridean isle of Eriskay, anchored off the shore of Arisaig on 25 July, St James's Day, in Loch nan Uamh, and went on to raise his standard on 19 August at Glenfinnan, after sailing up Loch Shiel to the rendezvous on the level sward of the little delta at its head. Since he had no clear idea of what would happen, he was admirably placed for either an advance or a withdrawal. There are other lochs and glens which, like Loch Eil, link up from the west with the sequence of lochs along the line of the

Great Glen Fault. Loch Lochy, Loch Oich, and Loch Ness, each an ice-scooped rock trench in alignment with the main direction of the fault, have such western approaches.

Few of these are in fact east-west routes comparable to Loch Eil. Loch Arkaig, whose waters drain into Loch Lochy through the short River Arkaig, is a case in point. Cameron of Lochiel, whose original residence seems to have been a defended islet in Loch Eil,* and then a fortalice on a rock knoll beside the River Lochy at Torcastle, moved his home after 1651 to Achnacarry on the River Arkaig. At the western end of Loch Arkaig two glens, Glen Pean and Glen Dessarry give access respectively to south Morar and to north Morar and Knoydart, all on the western seaboard. However, these ways are even now rough bounds rather than well-trodden routes, and this is even truer of Glengarry, much of which is occupied by the length of Loch Garry, and which empties its waters into Loch Oich, the smallest of the Great Glen Lochs, at Invergarry. Heavily wooded in the seventeenth and eighteenth centuries, and ringed by mountains, several of them over 3,000 feet high, Glengarry and its westward extension Glen Quoich, was a fastness rather than a passage way. The same is true of the more northerly of the two great western side glens of Loch Ness, Glen Urquhart, which runs out to the loch near Drumnadrochit. The imposing mass of Urquhart Castle on a promontory jutting into Loch Ness has a long history. As a royal fortress it dates from about 1200. James IV of Scotland repaired it and gave the lordship of Urquhart to John Grant of Freuchie. Plundered in the mid-sixteenth and again in the mid-seventeenth centuries, it was partially blown up in 1691 to deny its use to Jacobites. By 1715 it was a picturesque ruin, so much so that it was reported with some slight exaggeration that 'the Castell of Urquhart is blowen down by the last storme of wind'.[3] Its real function latterly was to control the upper reaches of the twenty three or so miles of deep-water communication represented by the loch and its northern extension known as Loch Dochfour.

The one exception to all this is the strategic Glenmoriston, which drains into the southern part of Loch Ness at Invermoriston. From the head of Glenmoriston there is an excellent route by Loch Cluanie into the sharp defile of Glen Shiel, crowned on its northern side by the glorious mountain ridge known as the Five Sisters of Kintail. The River Shiel runs into Loch Duich whence there is a clear passage by the waters of Loch Alsh either to the Minch, the stretch of sea between the Inner and Outer Hebrides, or more nearly to the Isle of Skye. Alternatively, from Invershiel it is possible to traverse the pass of Mam Rattachan and to reach the township of

*Loch Eil is the correct spelling of the loch. By convention the Cameron chief's territorial designation is spelled as one word and the spelling is the form Lochiel.

Bernera opposite the south end of Skye and adjacent to the old-established crossing from Kyle Rhea on Skye to Glenelg. It is no accident that the decisive battle in the brief Jacobite rising in 1719 was fought in Glen Shiel, as a small army of Scottish exiles and clansmen, reinforced by some regular infantry of the Spanish government which was sponsoring the episode, began rather tentatively to take the track leading *via* Glenmoriston and Loch Ness to Inverness. They were defeated by a force of British troops under General Wightman moving in exactly the opposite direction along the same strategic corridor. General Wade built a small barracks at Bernera on the north side of Glenelg Bay, to keep an eye on the crossing to Skye, though cynics have argued that the only useful purpose this hopelessly weak post ever served was when, as a ruin in the nineteenth century, it sheltered the victims of the particularly ruthless Highland Clearances in Knoydart.[4]

On its eastern side Glen More, in contrast to its northern and southern ends, is remarkable mainly for its long history of inaccessibility, rooted in the topography of the area. The hills soar up suddenly and dramatically, presenting formidable problems for communication from the east. Notoriously, when in the eighteenth century a military road was driven from the east over into the centre of Glen More, it had to climb to 2,500 feet by means of a series of zig-zags at the Pass of Corrieyairack, thereby presenting to the Jacobite army of Prince Charles in 1745 an ideal position for defensive tiers of musketry fire. General Cope, in command of the Hanoverian forces and already deeply demoralised by the absence of any serious support for his troops even among Whig clans in the Highlands, almost certainly spared his men decimation when he decided not to force the position, but to make for Inverness by forced marches.

The conspicuous exception to this general pattern of inaccessibility is the broad, historic corridor of Glen Spean, branching eastward from Spean Bridge and traversed by a river far more turbulent before 1934, when Loch Laggan, which lies east of the glen was dammed and extended by four miles. Here is the main eastern approach to the lands of Lochaber at the south end of Glen More. That the first skirmish of the '45 should be near the strategic outlet at Spean Bridge was not entirely coincidental. The area could not be avoided even by the Royalist army of the Marquis of Montrose in the severe winter of 1644–5 when it escaped from an apparent trap in Glen More between the Earl of Seaforth's army of 5,000 at Inverness, and Argyll's Campbells at Inverlochy by a brilliant flanking march. From the south end of Loch Ness it climbed up Glen Tarff and then down Glen Roy to where it debouched into Glen Spean at Roy Bridge, before its final march across Leanachan towards Inverlochy and bloody victory. In the other direction, Glen Spean broadens out after its own thirteen or so miles into the braes of that district of the Highlands known as Badenoch whence there is easy access to the headwaters of the River Spey and the broad corridor of Strath Spey down towards Moray and the north-east of Scotland. To preserve the clans of Glen More from the great territorial magnates of these two last districts, it was necessary that the principal clans of Glen Spean and upper Strath Spey should act as guardians of the eastern approaches.

As we shall see, that is precisely what the MacDonalds of Keppoch and the Macphersons did. They really belonged by nature to the smaller human groupings characteristic of the extremely dissected mountain terrain of the central and western Highlands, where the forces of earth-sculpture such as glaciation have carved the high-level plateau of 2–3,000 feet in height, still to be discerned over extensive parts of the eastern Highlands, into a myriad of narrow glens and narrower lochs. Where earth movements have left 'shatter belts' in the rocks, glaciers in the ice ages have often scooped out very long and very narrow lochs, of which perhaps the most extreme example is Loch Ericht which lies between Perth- and Inverness-shires, fifteen miles long and never more than half a mile wide. It is a monument to glacial action comparable to the famous 'parallel roads' of Glen Roy, markings of remarkable regularity picked out by the bent grass which grows on them in contrast to the heather and bracken of the main slopes. The 'roads' are in fact successive levels of the shrinking margins of a sub-glacial lake. Even when the last ice age finally cleared from the western Highlands ten thousand or so years ago the area was left exposed to vigorous earth-shaping influences such as heavy rainfall. Very large parts of the territories which were inhabited by the clans which are central to this study have rainfalls well over a hundred inches a year. Theirs was a beautiful, but harsh and deeply divided, natural heritage.

If, however we turn to the clans which inhabited the Great Glen and its principal eastern approach in the seventeenth and eighteenth centuries, we run at once into the difficult question of the nature of Scottish clans. To this there is no simple answer, but the issue must be examined in general terms before any survey of specific clans is essayed. The Gaelic word *clann* has as the English equivalent of its primary meaning the word 'children'. It was also used in Gaelic as a synonym for words like *cinel, tuath,* and *fine,* all of which imply a family group of four generations sprung at least in theory from a common ancestor. Clans of this kind are freely mentioned in the sources for Highland history from the sixth to the twelfth centuries, but it is significant that all these named ones were extinct by the sixteenth century. The clans of the early modern period were the product of a fusion of older tribal and Celtic influences with the incoming structures of Anglo-Norman feudalism. Anglo-Norman families and feudal relationships were deliberately imported into Scotland by the kings of the Canmore dynasty, partly to toughen their realm against risk of attack from Norman England,

and partly to gain access to the techniques of feudalised warfare which would enable them to commit successful aggression against independent communities as far apart as Galloway in the south-west, and Moray in the north. Although feudalisation had to be carried out with tact and without excessive violence to local prejudices north of the Forth Clyde line, it is quite clear that the Highland Line posed no serious barrier to this process whatsoever.[6] The fusion of feudal and Gaelic tribal influences became pervasive in the Highlands. The precise nature of the balance within any given synthesis varied a great deal. In that sense one cannot really talk about a 'clan system', only about specific clans, and though generalisations are possible, exceptions may be found to all of them. For example, it is generally true that the feudal influences were more potent in the eastern Highlands, where a magnate like the Earl (later Marquis and Duke) of Atholl could wax mighty without in any significant sense being a clan chief, and that the tribal influences were more important in the west. Yet the Macleans, often thought of as a united western clan with Maclean of Duart or Dowart as its chief, never functioned as a unit. They were divided into two main branches, the Siol Lachlan (the race of Lachlan) and the Siol Eachann (the race of Hector), each of which was in turn divided into three branches. The race of Lachlan comprised the branches of Duart, Ardgour, and Coll; that of Hector those of Lochbuie, Kingairloch, and Dochgarroch. Apart from the last named, which was isolated among strangers at the northern end of Loch Ness, the heads of the branches often chose to cooperate and intermarry, but always by free choice, for to them their separate identity was as important as tribal solidarity.[7]

Broadly speaking, feudal structures gave a clan chief a valuable set of mechanisms to help him run his clan. Even chiefs like Mackintosh of Mackintosh, whose very name showed that he was originally a pre-feudal royal official with the rank of toiseach, found it useful to adopt feudal forms for the rule of the Clann an Toisich, 'the children of the toiseach'. Above all, feudalism meant feudal courts, starting with the basic baronial jurisdiction, but extending up to the mini-kingdoms known as regalities, normally composed of a group of baronies. A regality was created for the Grants on Speyside after the Glorious Revolution of 1688, which they supported, and we shall witness the glee of a Lord Fraser of Lovat when he finally vindicated his rights to a regalian jurisdiction within his ancestral clan territories. A Gaelic chief with a feudal court could not only discipline his clan but could also use feudal law to move towards a concept of individual ownership of land, and to establish succession by primogeniture in his own family. Both concepts carried within them seeds of tension for an older Gaelic heritage undoubtedly inclined to view the right to control land as residing in the settled community of those who farmed it. The

MacDonalds of Keppoch had no other claim to their clan lands. Equally a female heiress marrying outwith the clan could threaten its survival.[8]

On the other hand, if seventeenth-century people by and large accepted the vicissitudes of heredity as the raw material of politics, they were never as abjectly or automatically at the mercy of indefeasible hereditary right as some of their modern admirers would like to think. It was for men to interpret and rightly apply the often ambiguous opportunities provided by the accidents of succession. The MacLeods of Dunvegan used a royal charter to transfer the estates of an heiress to her uncle, the heir male. The Gordons simply made an heir by marriage called Seton change his name to Gordon, and in all clans it was important that the leading branches should intermarry, and that the marriage plans of a female heiress should be controlled by kinsmen. In the period of this study the Clan Fraser was reduced to turmoil and guerrilla warfare when aggressive outsiders tried, ultimately unsuccessfully, to commit a sort of genetic kidnap of the chiefly authority. Only with the restoration in 1715 of the true heir male of the name of Fraser was the situation normalised again, and that because he was in the last analysis the preferred candidate of the leading Frasers.

Another romantic illusion best confined to coloured 'clan maps' sold to tourists, is that Highland clans necessarily consisted of solid blocks of people with the same surname and, of course, a common descent. Common descent with the chief is a palpable nonsense when the peasantry were of ancient Celtic stock, and the chief of Norman descent, as is the case with a couple of clans important in this study. Besides, surnames were a luxury not much indulged in by the Highland peasantry until quite late. People were identified by patronymics and nicknames. All Highland clans were normally happy to incorporate promising recruits from outside the clan area, and when surnames became commoner in the later seventeenth and eighteenth centuries humbler men, and some not so humble, were in the habit of changing their clan name with their circumstances. People moved around and cooperated across clan lines. For example in 1699, only seven years after the massacre of Glencoe, the records of the Justice Court of Argyll show a Glencoe MacDonald or MacIan forming with a Campbell cousin from Kilmartin a robber band which eventually consisted of four Campbells, two MacIans, and a Cameron, with a view to plundering forays in mid-Argyll. More sobering still is the fact that the judicial proceedings taken against those Argyll men who followed the Earl of Argyll into rebellion against James VII and II in 1685 reveal that only a minority of them at that late date were called Campbell.[9]

For many political purposes clans were their chiefs and the leading clan gentry of his name. Below that level could lie a very mixed and indeed changing population. Clan rivalries could be bitter. If they existed they could be assiduously fanned by the chiefs and their fuglemen, the Gaelic bards, who in the earlier part of the eighteenth century were often performing the sort of public relations exercise for their patrons which Edmund Burke conducted, in prose and English, for the Rockingham Whigs in Westminster politics in the second half of the eighteenth century. However, there is evidence, all of it entirely creditable to the Highlanders of all classes concerned, that the levels of inter-clan bitterness declined sharply in real terms in the later seventeenth and early eighteenth centuries. In order to fully appreciate it, allowance has to be made for the participation of the clans of the central Highlands in the rising organised in 1644–5 by James Graham, Marquis of Montrose on behalf of Charles I and against the government of the Covenanters, who ruled through the Estates, the parliament of Scotland.

It is often said that Montrose's campaigns constitute a 'proto-Jacobite' rising because of the nature of his Highland support, and the way it was drawn mainly from small clans on the fringe of the Campbell empire, clans more motivated by hatred of Campbells than by specifically Royalist ideology. Modern scholarship has reassessed his whirlwind campaigns of 1644–5, coming up with two radical conclusions. One is that the prime responsibility for the remarkable run of battlefield successes which alone made the rising significant rested on that greatest of sword-and-buckler men, his lieutenant Alasdair MacColla (in English Lieutenant-General Sir Alexander MacDonald or MacDonnel). He was Ulster Scot from that part of Antrim conquered in the sixteenth century by a branch of the MacDonalds known as Clan Donald South. Roman Catholic in religion and Royalist in politics, they had been involved in the early and abortive plans of Charles I for a series of concentric attacks on the Covenanting regime in Scotland. The second important conclusion of modern scholarship is that the hard core of Montrose's army and the foundation of its capacity for tenacious, brutal combat was the force of a thousand or so professional infantry from Ulster, despatched by Alasdair MacColla's chief, the Marquis of Antrim, with an eye to recovering the territories of Kintyre and Islay which had fallen under the sway of the Campbells of Argyll.[10]

There was not in fact much enthusiasm for either Alasdair MacColla or for Montrose in the western and central Highlands. Despite having accepted from Charles I at Berwick in 1639 a joint commission with Antrim as royal lieutenants in the Highlands and Islands, Sir James MacDonald of Sleat in Skye refused to join MacColla when he first reached Scotland. From Skye MacColla went to Glengarry where he found 'plenty of beef but few supporters'. The Mackenzies, Sutherlands, Grants, and other Covenanting clans prepared to oppose him. As he moved along Glen More and out through Glen Spean towards the east, MacColla received precious few reinforcements in Lochaber and Badenoch, apart from some

300 Macphersons under their chief Ewen Og. If a reason be sought for this coldness, it can be found in the widespread and accurate view that Alasdair MacColla represented an Irish invasion. Even after his link with Montrose and victory at Tippermuir north-west of Perth, it seems that Glengarry still refused to join MacColla, though some of Glengarry's clansmen under his uncle Donald Gorm did rally to Montrose, as did the Camerons of Glen Nevis. Despite the Royalism of their chief, the Marquis of Huntly, few Gordons joined Montrose before his victory over the Campbells at Inverlochy, and there was plenty of opposition to him still at the north end of Glen More in May 1645 when the Frasers and Mackenzies between them bore the brunt of the 2,000 or so losses to the Covenanting army defeated by Alasdair MacColla and Montrose at Auldearn. There were said to be eighty-seven widows in the Fraser barony of Lovat alone after the battle.

The indiscriminate violence which accompanied even the march of Montrose's men certainly alienated Scottish opinion, Lowland and Highland, as did the sack and massacre his men perpetrated in the traditionally Royalist burgh of Aberdeen, and the virtual massacres with which most of his battles ended. It was a relief to many when Alasdair MacColla was killed in Ireland in 1647. He had tried to bring the genocidal warfare of Counter-Reformation Ireland to Scotland. His policy in Argyll, his real target, was to cut Campbell throats to clear farms for MacDonalds. There is some evidence that in Kintyre, which he physically occupied before his defeat and ejection by a Covenanting army under General David Leslie (the officer who had already routed Montrose at Philiphaugh on the Borders) Alasdair MacColla may have had to apply pressure to some of the MacDonald gentry to join him. They had been allowed to remain if they accepted Argyll's suzerainty, and had begun to intermarry with Campbells. Defection, if followed by defeat, was liable to be followed, as indeed it was in this instance, by retaliatory massacres and ejection.[11]

The bulk of articulate Scottish opinion seems to have been affronted by the masterful egotism of Montrose, trying to impose his will on his country without the support of most of its nobility but with the aid of an alien and terrifying force. Not much wonder that when his second attempt to light the fires of civil war foundered in defeat, in 1650, he was quickly executed. There was much wider support in the Highlands for Charles II than ever for Charles I. In the fighting against Cromwell's armies in 1650–51, the Highland clans were prominent. Many Macleans fell in battle at Inverkeithing, resisting an English invasion of Fife. Clan Cameron was intercepted before it could join the Royalist invasion of England in 1651, and there were few MacDonalds in the army because of the ravages of the Montrose wars, but Clan MacLeod under Roderick MacLeod of Talisker and Norman MacLeod of Bernera suffered huge losses in the final battle at Worcester. Curiously, the MacLeod family bard, Mairi Nighean Alasdair Ruaidh (Mary MacLeod), makes only fleeting reference to the episode. It did not interest her. Wider still was the support in the central Highlands for a Royalist rising in 1654. Aeneas or Angus MacDonell of Glengarry* was the original ringleader of the plotters, backed by Mackenzies, Frasers, MacDonalds of Keppoch, MacNaughtons and Camerons. Glengarry even aspired to lead the rising and he could hardly have done worse than the Earl of Glencairn and General Middleton, who led the rising to futility and defeat.

Highland chiefs shared in the general swing to conservative Royalism which affected nearly all the Scottish upper classes after 1647. The fact is hardly surprising. Ever since the series of agreements between the island chiefs and the Edinburgh government in 1609, which include the so-called Statutes of Iona, the chiefs had been used to making regular visits to Edinburgh to consult with the Privy Council, and they nearly all retained a lawyer to act as their agent in the capital. They were integrated members of the Scottish aristocracy.[12] Apart from a basic commitment to maintain the identity of the clan which was their power base, they were most likely to be moved to vigorous political action by major national issues. Even if they thought, as many did, that the Argyll Campbells had been allowed to expand beyond the limits set by justice and prudence, they responded as Scottish gentlemen, within a framework of Scottish politics. This meant, for example, that they accepted the active cooperation of Lord Lorne, Argyll's heir, during the 1654–5 rising against the Cromwellian occupying army.

Iain Lom, the MacDonald bard of Keppoch whose hymns of hate are among the great verse celebrating the Montrose wars, is here a misleading figure, unrepresentative of his own clan. Royalist and Roman Catholic, he was one of the few, even in his own overwhelmingly Catholic clan, to embrace the genocidal strategy of Alasdair McColla with zeal. His favoured method of dealing with fellow countrymen who differed profoundly from him was mass slaughter, and when such a policy could not be applied this warped genius was not above regretting the fact. When, however, in 1663 the unpopular Alasdair MacDonald of Keppoch was murdered, partly because of feuds with MacDonald of Inverlair and Alasdair Buidhe, former Tutor (i.e. guardian) of Keppoch, nobody stirred despite the rage of Iain Lom at the deed. The clansmen suspected that the late chief was contemplating a deal with their would-be landlord, Mackintosh, at their expense. Iain Lom brought in outside help in the shape of Sir James

*Contemporaries were not exact or consistent in spelling this name. Either MacDonald or MacDonell is acceptable in modern usage for Glengarry but the latter form is here adopted to distinguish him from MacDonald of Sleat or the Antrim MacDonnels.

MacDonald of Sleat and Aeneas of Glengarry, had six alleged killers executed, and characteristically gloated over their severed heads in verse.[13]

The clan showed what it thought by making Alasdair Buidhe, whose sons were alleged to have been involved in the killing but who escaped, their chief. Iain Lom was an isolated figure. And it is to the credit of his kinsmen that this was so. With Alasdair MacColla's defeat and death the Irish invasion really was over for everyone but Iain Lom. During the spectacular defeat of the Earl of Argyll in 1685, when he rose against James VII and II, the Marquis of Atholl led a royal army into Argyll, of which he had been made Lieutenant. Sir Ewen Cameron of Lochiel joined him with 300 of his clansmen. Atholl from the start suspected Sir Ewen of complicity with Argyll and after the notorious affair of Ard Rannach, where a night patrol of Camerons accidentally killed some of Atholl's Perthshire horse, he would have liked to arrest all the Camerons. He was dissuaded by a council aware that Macleans and MacDonalds were preparing to help the Camerons resist. That Lochiel was accused of giving information to Campbell spies may tell us nothing about Lochiel, but it tells us a lot about how contemporaries viewed his relations with Clan Campbell.

Intelligent Scottish politics, not tribal blood-lusts rooted in wars of religion, were the guiding principles of most Highland chiefs. We shall see later that in 1715 the chiefs of the central Highlands tacitly refused to embark on destructive inter-clan warfare in Argyll at the behest of the Earl of Mar.[14]

What then were the clans of Glen More, who with their allies and outposts in Glen Spean and Badenoch made up a sort of political system both isolated from, and integrated into the world of Scottish politics? It is most convenient to start at the north end of the Great Glen and work south, for the most northerly of the clans, the Clan Fraser of Lovat, has a history which more than most brings out certain key points about clan structure and development.[15]

The clan territory, though never totally fixed, remained roughly constant from 1422 to 1746. It fell into two parts divided by the line of Glen More. To the west the Frasers held land to the south and west of the Beauly Firth and in Strathglass, whilst they also held the whole of Strathfarrar to a point just east of Loch Monar. Near the settlement of Struy in Strathglass a spur of Chisholm territory containing Erchless Castle, a seat of the Chisholm, intruded into Fraser territory, though the main Chisholm lands lay in the two western 'feeder' glens to Strathglass, Glen Cannich and Glen Affric. (The original Highland Chisholm seems to have come north to serve as keeper of the royal castle of Urquhart on Loch Ness. His was never a major clan and much of his historic importance lay in his influence with surrounding Fraser gentry.)

The landward glens were thoroughly Highland and heavily wooded, but in the coastal area and in particular in that wedge of territory west of Inverness known as the Aird, the Frasers controlled a warm lowland with low rainfall and, thanks to till deposited by glaciers on the underlying Old Red Sandstone and the raised beaches produced by post-glacial changes in sea level, a soil which ranged from being sandy and self-draining to deep loam. It was one of the few Highland areas capable of producing a cereal surplus, and seventeenth-century observers noted that the density of gentry seats there was striking.[16] One of them was Castle Downie situated a mile from a key ford on the Beauly, a river not bridged before 1810. Castle Downie was burned by Hanoverian soldiery in 1746.

The other part of the Fraser lands resembled the first only in being about thirty miles long and, on average, under ten wide. It lay on the east side of Loch Ness (with some smaller holdings on part of the east bank). Known generally as Stratherrick (strictly the southern part is Abertarff), this was a far wilder and less accessible stretch of countryside starting from the alder, rowan and oak-fringed sides of Loch Ness and soaring up as much as 2,000 feet to the Monadh Liadh, the 'Grey Hills' of the Grampians, which formed its eastern rampart. There was some arable land, but this was primarily pastoral country where the chiefs went to hunt.

The Fraser chiefs, like those of the Chisholms to the west, or the Grants and Roses to the east, were in fact of Norman stock. Settling first in England, they had moved to southern Scotland, and then moved north as part of the expansion of the kingdom of the Canmore dynasty. The chief was using the Gaelic patronymic of MacShimidh or 'son of Simon' before 1416, and seems early to have adopted the Gaelic practice of fostering his children with his tenants. The element of magic in Celtic tribalism and leadership persisted late in the Fraser country. For example, the Aird Frasers cut their lucky sprigs of yew as war badges on the magic knoll of Tomnahurich while their Stratherrick kinsmen cut theirs from a venerable yew on Beinn a'Bhacaidh above Loch Ness.[17] Nevertheless, the chiefs were careful not to marry a MacDonald, a Maclean, a Cameron or a Mackintosh, for fear of conflict of interests driving them into trouble with the Crown. Only latish in the seventeenth century did they marry into the notably prudent MacLeods of Dunvegan. Mostly they intermarried with fellow Anglo-Norman houses, and their success as a clanned power was largely due to the way in which they established cadet branches of the chiefly house in their clan territory.

The basis of land tenure for these junior branches was usually either a tack, wadset, or a feu. A tack was a lease. A wadset was the Scots term for a mortgage. It was often converted into a feu, which meant virtual ownership in exchange for a lump sum plus a small annual payment to a feudal superior who retained certain powers of control. Even a wadset normally gave security of tenure for several generations. Fraser of Phopachy's wadset from the then Lord Lovat in 1599 was only redeemed by the current lord around 1740. The rise and fall of Clan Fraser as a political reality can be measured by the fact that in 1544 there were five cadet branches; in 1650 there were twenty-six; in 1745 there were as many as thirty; in 1802 the number was thirteen; and by 1952 it was a derisory three in an age when Clan Fraser was no more than a romantic memory.

Without the assistance of these vitally important middle management groups, the chiefs could neither discipline nor mobilise their clans. The true political history of these Highland clans of any size would have to be written off the papers of the clan gentry, often known generically as tacksmen, because many of them held leases for long periods on easy terms over extensive areas. Their sub-tenants were not expected to have opinions on matters such as religion and politics, where they simply followed the lead of their superiors. Bardic verse usually tells us about the doings of the chiefly dynasties, and the personal foibles of particular bards. Tacksmens' papers have so low a survival rate that the historian is often reduced to scraps of indirect evidence, but it can be suggestive. For example, towards the end of the period examined in this book Simon Fraser Lord Lovat responded to the '45 rising with a degree of apparently irresolute and devious wavering first to one side, then to the other, which was remarkable even for Simon Fraser. What contributed to his indecisiveness towards the end, when he would probably have been prepared to take violent action on behalf of the Jacobite cause, was the way in which the Fraser gentry of the Aird, strongly encouraged by the carefully equivocal Chisholm, dragged their feet when Simon's chamberlain tried to persuade them to bring out their men.[18]

On the opposite shore of Loch Ness, Glenmoriston and Glen Urquhart were a substantial but detached part of the territory of Clan Grant. The main seat of the Grants lay outside Glen More altogether on Speyside, where this Anglo-Norman family, starting out literally with half the barony of Freuchie, had gradually built up what by 1653 could be described as 'ane great hudge estait'. In 1509 James IV of Scotland had bestowed Glen Urquhart on John Grant second of Freuchie, to 'police and edify' its lawless inhabitants. To help with the process, two of his sons were given the neighbouring lands of Glenmoriston and Corrimony. In theory the Grants were supposed to be a spearhead of an offensive against the likes of the Camerons of Lochiel and the MacDonalds of Clanranald and Glengarry. In practice, Glen Urquhart and Glenmoriston were so vulnerable to counter-attack that the increasingly Gaelicised Grants settled down as a sub-unit in the clan structure of the Great Glen. Grant of Grant, a staunch hereditary Whig, could not control two such remote territories, and they were really in the hands of the resident cadet branches.* Even when the clan chief stepped in after Jacobite activities led to post-1715 forfeitures, and bought control of the lands, it was still the case that in the intricate game of the '45, the local Grant lairds were able to call most of the shots.[19]

Both Glenmoriston and Glen Urquhart were deemed fertile in corn land and blessed with good grazing, not to mention extensive fir woods which were commercially important because of the existence of a natural transportation system by which 'the river doeth transport big gests and butts of timber to the fresh water Loghnes'.[20] Of Glengarry, the vastly bigger glen which came out in the centre of the Great Glen in the area known as Achadrom, reckoned by contemporaries as being the geographical dead centre of Scotland, all of this could also be said, and more, for it was 'verie profitable and fertill of corne fish and milk'. In addition to grain, salmon, and cattle Glengarry was endowed with a notable forest of fir on the south-west side, and with 'a faire Oakenwood' on the northern side.[21]

The chiefs of Glengarry were descended, like those of the MacDonalds of Clanranald, from Ranald, a younger son of John, Lord of the Isles. From Alasdair, chief of Glengarry, the family took its Gaelic patronymic 'Mac 'ic Alasdair', and by the seventeenth century they were recognised as important figures, holding their lands by direct crown charter. They were also considered something of a problem because of a long history of conflict with the Mackenzies, on to whose territories they abutted on the west. Ennobled at the Restoration after a difficult couple of decades during which he had at one point taken refuge in Ireland, Aeneas Lord MacDonell can be found in 1673 entering into a contract of friendship with Duncan Macpherson of Cluny, binding themselves and their successors to 'honoure, owne, aide, fortifie, concurre with, assist and defend' each other and their followers. Active on the Jacobite side in 1689 and 1715, the chiefly house of Glengarry was much more equivocal in the '45, and after a final romantic blaze of glory under Alasdair, lively wastrel and close friend of Walter Scott, they plunged into bankruptcy and the dissolution of the estates.[22]

South of Glengarry lay Lochaber, the domain of the formidable Clan Cameron, led by the Camerons of Lochiel. Like the Frasers, the Camerons were, by the standards of the Great Glen clans, a biggish unit. There is no point in pretending that we know with any degree of precision what the populations involved were, but their order of magnitude may be suggested. There are repeated statements, for example, that the Keppoch

*The chiefs were Grants of Freuchie before February 1694, but with the grant at that time of the regality of Grant they changed their title to Grant of Grant. For the sake of simplicity here he is often referred to, in a usage which is technically correct, as Grant.

MacDonalds were composed of 160–170 households, which has led to informed guesses that the whole clan on the Braes of Lochaber amounted to a little under a thousand people. From what we now know about the size of early modern nuclear families in Britain, that would appear to be a reasonable estimate. Smaller units which feature in our story could be much smaller. The MacDonalds of Glencoe seem to have been scattered over 30–40 households, suggesting a population of a few hundreds.[23] Bigger clans like the Frasers and Camerons, given the area of their territory, say in the case of the Frasers 500 square miles at the very most, and that of very mixed character, cannot have been more than a few thousands strong. A population base of 6–7,000 followers made a chief a major power in the Highlands. Once, however, populations reached these proportions, they tended to lack homogeneity. Simon Fraser, reigning Lord Lovat, would in the 1730s and 1740s actually reward tenants with a meal if they would adopt the name of Fraser, in order to manufacture a sense of solidarity and kinship among his followers.

Clan Cameron was the product of a broadly similar process of integration. The precise origin of the chiefly family is itself obscure. They take their Gaelic title from a fourteenth-century character called Donald Dubh, from whom is derived the patronymic Mac Dhomhnuill Dhuibh (son of the black-haired Donald). Whether that gentleman was connected with the Anglo-Norman family of the Camerons of Ballegarno in Fife is ultimately a matter of opinion. What is clear is that in the thirteenth and fourteenth centuries the most important tribal groups in Lochaber were the Clan Donald, the Clan Chattan (itself a confederacy), and the Maelanfhaidh, a group consisting of three main tribes; the MacMartins of Letterfinlay, the Macgillonies, and the MacSorlies of Glen Nevis. By marriage to a MacMartin heiress, the redoubtable Donald Dubh began to emerge as a successful overlord in Lochaber. After the triumph of Robert the Bruce in establishing the independence of the Scottish kingdom in the early fourteenth century, he rewarded one of his faithful followers, Mackintosh, chief of Clan Chattan, with lands in Badenoch, thereby setting in motion an emigration of Clan Chattan from around Loch Arkaig; from Glen Gloy (to the east of Loch Lochy); and from Glen Spean. Camerons moved into Loch Arkaig and Glen Gloy, while Keppoch MacDonalds occupied 'Brae Lochaber' in Glen Spean. So despite unquestionable charter rights to these lands from first the MacDonald Lords of the Isles, and then the Scottish monarchs, successive Mackintoshes grappled with an insoluble squatter problem.[24]

By the second half of the seventeenth century, with the Camerons led by the formidable and long-lived Sir Ewen Cameron of Lochiel, there was little prospect of Mackintosh re-establishing himself in Lochaber. In 1665 he accepted monetary compensation from Lochiel, who was offered a loan for the purpose by the Marquis of Atholl. In fact Sir Ewen preferred to borrow the money from Argyll. After 1665 the only question at serious issue between Lochiel and Mackintosh was how far away Mackintosh power could be pushed by means of the Keppoch MacDonalds and the Macphersons.

It is difficult to say which of these two was more offensive to Mackintosh. Egged on by successive Lochiels, and also by the Marquis of Huntly, who in 1684 became the first Duke of Gordon, Cluny Macpherson, the chief of the Clan Mhuirich, had produced the remarkable theory that Mackintosh was not the rightful head of the Clan Chattan, that great confederacy of sixteen or so clans of which the Macphersons were members. The official Macpherson argument for some time held that Cluny himself was the rightful head of 'Old Clan Chattan' (whatever that might be). This theory had a new lease of life after 1688 when the Keppoch MacDonalds defeated Mackintosh in battle at Mulroy. It achieved its fullest and most sanctimonious form in *The Loyall Dissuasive* written in London in 1701 by the elderly Jacobite lawyer and laird Sir Aeneas Macpherson of Invereshie, who was lurking in the English capital for some years before Queen Anne's proclamation of indemnity of 1702 allowed him to return safely to Scotland.[25] In fact the Duncan Macpherson of Cluny who reactivated this old quarrel in the late seventeenth century was a fine one to speak, for he seriously tried to transfer his estates to his son-in-law Archibald, a second son of Campbell of Cawdor. The Macpherson gentry, as determined defenders of the clan identity as the contemporary Fraser tacksmen, solemnly pledged themselves in 1689 to resist this nonsense, on behalf of the heir male, then William Macpherson of Nuid. In 1722 Lachlan Macpherson of Nuid succeeded peacefully to the chieftainship. Keppoch had accepted, on agreed terms, a tack of his lands from Mackintosh in 1700, a tack which was renewed in 1722. In 1724 the new Macpherson of Cluny reached an agreement with Mackintosh, and was confirmed in his lands under the virtual ownership of a feu, subject only to feu duties, court service, and a recognition of Lachlan Mackintosh as head of Clan Chattan.[26]

The Glen More clans and their outliers had by that date evolved into a stable system held in place by resistible tensions. Balance was the key to the survival of clan identities, which were effectively a form of local self-government. After the final forfeiture of the Lordship of the Isles in 1494, no great power threatened from the west. They could live with Clanranald and the Stewarts of Appin. To the south the menace of the Campbells of Argyll balked at such tough rival warlords as the Lochiels. To the north the Frasers wrestled with the southern thrust of Clan Mackenzie. To the west Keppoch and Cluny checkmated Mackintosh. Even within the Great Glen the clans and the British Army lay in balance.

2 The Clans and the Wider World

Though physically remote, and speaking a language which was largely confined to the western parts of Scotland and to rural Ireland, the clans of Glen More were in no sense isolated from the wider world around them. On the contrary, the very marginality of their economic and geographical position ensured that the members of these clans often had to look for employment and opportunity outside their ancestral culture. This was particularly true of the men of the chiefly and tacksman families, who started with the advantage of bilinguality in English and Gaelic and familiarity with these two cultures. Study at one of the Scottish universities was perfectly normal for the Highland aristocracy. Simon Fraser, the Lord Lovat of the '45, for example, first developed the literary tastes which lasted all his life at King's College, Aberdeen. Other chiefs patronised the University of St Andrews, a conservative and Jacobite-tainted institution slowly declining from its great days in the early seventeenth century when it had been the aristocratic university *par excellence* in Scotland. One must also remember that the central Highlands, because of their qualified autonomy from government control, very often reflected a wider range of the political and religious options available in any period than areas more subject to governmental pressures for conformity to some particular creed or position.

Of no field was this truer than the religious. Like the state, the established church had difficulty in building a capability for control and discipline in these parts. The problem long pre-dated the Reformation-revolution of 1560. Medieval parishes in the Highlands were impractically large, priests were few, religious houses were scarce and scattered, while bishops were often non-resident or unconsecrated, or both. The Reformed Kirk tended to continue along the same ineffectual lines as its medieval predecessors. John Carswell, superintendant of Argyll and later the second post-Reformation Bishop of the Isles did, it is true, make a highly significant attempt to express the Reformed faith in Gaelic publications, but only a small elite of Highlanders were literate in the esoteric classical Irish-based tradition of scholarship favoured by Carswell, a trained Campbell bard as well as a bishop.[1] In any case, with the solitary exception of Bishop Andrew Knox under James VI and I, Carswell's successors more than upheld the pre-Reformation tradition of inadequate episcopal leadership.

Most Highland parishes had no resident minister of the Reformed Kirk until after 1600. The island parish of North Uist did not have one before 1626, and South Uist followed suit only in 1633. It was this sort of situation which enabled a handful of Counter-Reformation emissaries to secure a series of island and western seaboard enclaves for the Roman Catholic faith. These missionary priests were Franciscans, and from 1626 they operated out of the friary of Bonamargy in County Antrim. The Bonamargy connection may help explain both the success of the missionaries and its limits. Bonamargy lay within the sphere of influence of Clan Donald South, the Scottish MacDonalds who had carved out a small empire of conquest in Ulster. Their chief, ennobled as Earl of Antrim, schemed to use his Ulster lands as a springboard for the reconquest of MacDonald lands in Kintyre and Islay which had been lost to the expanding might of the Campbells of Argyll. Since separating religion and politics in the seventeenth century was unthinkable, there is no doubt that the Earls of Antrim saw in the Counter-Reformation a possible ideological preparation for their own long-pondered plans for a military offensive.

Significantly, Bonamargy became the 'traditional' burial place of the Earls of Antrim in the 1620s. Their pipe-dream of revenge became an appalling reality after 1644 when Alasdair MacColla, that Achilles of the Gael, led a force of Antrim's infantry into Argyll and, after linking up with Montrose, opened Scotland's veins in his unimaginably violent campaigns. Both Presbyterian ministers and Roman Catholic priests tended to regard the other side of the confessional divide in battle array as Amalekites to be smitten hip and thigh before and after victory. However, Alasdair and his men made of genocide a daily practice in Argyll, and after he died fighting in 1647 in County Cork he left behind him in the western Highlands of Scotland a vivid memory of his Counter-Reformation crusade which was a formidable obstacle to any further Romanist evangelisation.[2]

The region tended to relapse into the multi-polar pattern of religious loyalties which had emerged in its previous state of blessed deadlock. The Roman Catholic church survived in specific enclaves, but had neither the resources nor the appeal to spread beyond them. Scottish Catholicism was under the jurisdiction of the Cardinal Prefect at the head of the *Congregatio de Propaganda Fide* established by Pope Gregory XV in 1622 as a secretariate for the non-Catholic world. That this body was not willing to make more resources available to the Scottish mission has been sometimes blamed on the attitudes of Will Leslie, agent in Rome for the Scottish secular clergy during the long period 1653–1707. This is probably unfair to a man who was also a priest in the entourage of Cardinal Barberini, and archivist to *Propaganda Fide*. His duty involved balancing a world-wide effort against chronically inadequate resources. Besides, after being named first archivist to the Congregation in 1660, he had to wrestle with the steady growth of archives which a modern Portuguese historian characterised as 'intricado, complexo e vasto'.[3] *Propaganda* could see clearly enough that the West Highlands of Scotland was not a particularly promising area.

The extent of Romanism in that area in the late seventeenth and early eighteenth centuries is something which can easily be established from sources such as a report which Will Leslie himself submitted to *Propaganda* in 1681 after a visit to Scotland, and a report on the problem of Popery in Scotland submitted to the Church of Scotland in 1705. What is remarkable is the degree of agreement they display. The southern parts of the Outer Hebrides from Barra through South Uist were Roman Catholic as were the small islands south of Skye, Rum, Eigg, and Canna, partly because of the Catholicism of the biggest landlord chief in the area, MacDonald of Clanranald. Clanranald's mainland territories showed similar tendencies, and the presence of other landlord-chiefs of similar persuasion ensured that successive coastal regions north of the Firth of Lorne, such as Morvern, Moidart, Morar, and Knoydart, were preponderantly Catholic. North of Knoydart lay Mackenzie territory, where the story was different. Obviously Glen More and Glen Spean were nothing like as isolated as these Counter-Reformation, or rather Pre-Reformation enclaves, but it was generally considered that Glengarry was untouched by the Reformation. Catholicism was also very widespread in Keppoch's country on the Braes of Lochaber. Indeed, the vast parish of Kilmonivaig, which stretched from Spean Bridge just north of Inverlochy to Glenmoriston and was in fact larger than eleven Scottish counties, was as unmanageable as might be expected, with many pockets of Catholicism in it. Nor was the north end of Glen More a source of comfort to the established Kirk in 1705, for in the Fraser country of Stratherrick, and in the other Fraser stronghold, the Aird, (and more especially in Strathglass) Popery was preponderant amongst the people.[4]

If the purely Presbyterian settlement of the Church of Scotland in 1690 was inevitable (as politically it was, being carried through by a monarch who did not want it but could see no alternative) it was also deeply divisive. North of the Forth the great majority of the nobility and gentry retained strong Episcopalian sympathies, and the Episcopal clergy who ministered to those sympathies themselves tended increasingly to Jacobite views of a very violent kind.[5] All of this would have mattered less had the state thrown its full weight behind the Church of Scotland. In the Western

Highlands, for example, the religious situation was still so complex and fluid, and ordained clergy of any kind were still so thin on the ground, that had William of Orange meant what he said about being determined to effect a real Reformation in the Highlands and Islands there would probably have been at the least a significant swing in the confessional balance there. The new Presbyterian establishment was anxious to train and deploy Gaelic-speaking ministers in the Highlands, to distribute copies of the Irish Bible which it had secured from Ireland, and to conduct a vigorous campaign against 'seminary priests, Jesuits and trafficking Papists'. In practice very little happened, because intentions could not become realities without the active support of civil authority, which was not forthcoming. The Roman Catholic communities, which had been looked after by Prefects Apostolic before 1698, acquired in that year a Vicar Apostolic in Episcopal orders in the shape of Bishop Thomas Nicolson. In 1732 Scotland was divided into separate vicariates for the Highlands and Lowlands, with Bishop Hugh MacDonald as Vicar Apostolic of the Highlands.

The Catholic experience was normally one of ineffectual harassment rather than active persecution. The Church of Scotland experienced from the state gusts of panic-based enthusiasm rather than steady positive support. A good example is the incorporation of the Society in Scotland for the Propagation of Christian Knowledge (S.S.P.C.K.). This body probably originated in an Edinburgh prayer group in the 1690s. It was deeply influenced, through a displaced Episcopalian minister who had gone to England, by its English counterpart and especially by the English society's ideas about education of the young as a key to tackling social, political, and religious problems. From an early stage S.S.P.C.K. supporters were anxious to establish charity schools in Highland parishes. Even if those parishes honoured their legal obligation to set up one parish school, the exercise hardly impinged on most parts of a vast parish like Kilmonivaig which was bigger than some counties, and Kilmonivaig was matched as an example by the parish of Ardnamurchan, which was ninety miles long and entitled to one school. Yet it was only the panic among the political establishment after the abortive French invasion of 1708 which enabled the S.S.P.C.K. to obtain letters of incorporation.

Its schools were ostensibly the spearhead of an offensive against 'Barbaritie, Jacobitism, and Poperie'. Though they did not teach Latin, some of the masters were scholars of repute like the theologian John MacDonald who taught at Bunloit near the mouth of Glen Urquhart. The real problem was that by its constitution the S.S.P.C.K. was allowed to spend only the interest on its limited capital (plus of course any donations). It was supposed to be granted additional funds from the sale of forfeited Jacobite estates after the '15, but the money never reached it.

Handicapped by their refusal to teach in Gaelic until after 1766, the S.S.P.C.K.'s schools peaked in numbers at over 180 in the 1750s before falling to 146 by 1760. Their impact was necessarily limited. In 1718 there was one of these schools in Lochaber, but lack of funds ruled out a similar foundation in Ardnamurchan.

In 1724 the General Assembly of the Church of Scotland set up, partly as a result of steady prodding from the Synod of Argyll, a new Synod of Glenelg, designed to bring fresh vigour and effectiveness to the work of the established church in the Western Highlands and Islands. It did encourage the S.S.P.C.K. to establish schools in Glen More. However, it found General Wade, Commander-in-Chief Scotland, less helpful than he might have been in dealing with Roman Catholic priests and disaffected episcopalian ministers. Worse still was the quiet but steady opposition and obstruction which the synod faced from the heritors (the landlords), whose approval and financial support were indispensable if vitally needed new parishes were to be established. Some financial assistance did reach the synod from the Committee for the Reformation of the Highlands (the so-called 'Royal Bounty' Committee), which administered a gift of £1,000 per annum from George I, announced in 1725 but only effective from 1728. These funds were, however, clearly designated for the support of itinerant Protestant preachers, preferably men possessed of the Gaelic. The value of the bounty was not great and it was eroded by inflation. Despite its public commitment to the cause of Reformation in the Highlands, the London government was basically indifferent, except when frightened, and it regarded the Church of Scotland with a detachment bordering on contempt.

The extent to which the locals were resigned to their arbitrary mosaic of inherited denominational allegiances by 1744 may be demonstrated by the fact that in that year Vicar Apostolic Hugh MacDonald voluntarily testified before the Presbytery of Mull in a case against one of his own priests.[6]

The Synod of Glenelg remained a place where eccentricity could flourish. There was the brief but colourful ministry of the Reverend Daniel MacLachlan in Ardnamurchan, a ministry which did not long survive MacLachlan's pamphlet *An Essay upon Improving and Adding to the Strength of Great Britain and Ireland by Fornication.* He died in Jamaica. Then there was Robertson of Lochbroom who in the 1750s ran a shebeen from which he dispensed illicitly-distilled whisky to his flock.[7] Brigadier Maitland, the governor of Fort William, was prepared to throw enough weight behind Mackintosh to expedite the compromise settlement between that influential man and MacDonald of Keppoch in 1700, but his response to appeals to assist by military action a drive against popery and especially 'trafiqueing Jesuits', appears to have been minimal. Of course, it was difficult to be convinced of the need for rigorous anti-papistical courses in a countryside where someone like the Reverend James Fraser, Minister of Wardlaw and late seventeenth-century historian of the Frasers, made no bones about having served in the Papal Guard in Rome to fund an extended youthful holiday there. This amiable and undoubtedly Protestant Episcopalian clergyman of the Church of Scotland summed up in his person and writings the dialogue between the Great Glen clans and a wider world. He was cosmopolitan, but he wrote of his clan in the happy days before Mackenzie aggression threatened its very being, and he knew full well that when the heir was a minor no Tutor (or guardian) could safely be allowed to function save in close cooperation 'with the leading men of the name of Fraser', of whom the Tutor was one.[8]

What marked out this particular part of Christendom from more favoured regions was not its lack of civilisation, for it was the seat of an ancient and intricate Gaelic culture; nor its lack of governance, for there was as much as people wanted or needed and they were freer from the irresponsible tyranny of kings or political bosses than most; nor yet even a lack of sophistication in its highest ruling class, for that class was cosmopolitan and men like the Lord Lovat of the early eighteenth century moved between religious denominations with the same deft footwork which helped him to move between rival royal courts. It was simply that because of inescapable factors of geology and climate, this agricultural society was poorer than most. Furthermore, the clan structures usually presupposed quite a dense settlement of lairds or tacksmen under the main chief, who was not by any means free to treat his people as an expendable factor of production, or his land as his own private property, even though from the sixteenth and seventeenth centuries he held it under forms of law which gradually replaced older Gaelic concepts of communal holding by individual right. The second Duke of Argyll pioneered the technique of squeezing out his tacksmen in order to engross rent himself, raising the rent on his estates from £5,000 per annum when he succeeded, to £6,687 by 1743, the year of his death. But this was at the cost of weakening the cohesion of Clan Campbell as the '45 demonstrated. Of course, individual lairds like Archibald Campbell of Knockbuy on Lochfyneside could and did try to increase productivity, and Highland rents were probably greatly increased between 1715 and 1745. Despite this, the Highland aristocracy as a whole never had a chance of matching the envied wealth of, say, the aristocracy of the Home Counties around London.[9]

Apart from a steadily increasing export of black cattle, the main mobile economic surplus of the glens, chiefs could try to exploit natural resources such as timber. Chiefs such as Lochiel and Glengarry, among others, ran their woods as commercial enterprises. In 1727 shortage of the charcoal fuel needed for the production of iron in blast-furnaces drove the Backbarrow Company from the north of England to open a furnace at Invergarry, near MacDonell of Glengarry's own castle and principal seat. Skilled workmen were imported from the Lowlands and from England, and roads and wharves were built to bring the ore in via Loch Linnhe and Loch Lochy. First blown in 1729, the furnace ceased working in 1736[10] and, in fact, Lochaber never developed into a major centre of manufactures. In 1769 the traveller Pennant remarked that though Lochaber exported more than 3,000 head of black cattle annually, worth perhaps £7,500, the area had to import at least £4,000-worth of oatmeal every year to cover its chronic cereal deficit. Since rents consumed some £3,000 per annum, the balance remaining could hardly sustain a high standard of living for the peasantry, whose wattle-walled, sod-thatched houses struck Pennant as miserable.[11]

His figures may be doubtful, but his conclusion must have been broadly correct. Let us move forward to the last decade of the eighteenth century and examine the information supplied to the *Statistical Account of Scotland* by the Reverent Mr Ross, who says of the parish of Kilmonivaig that:

> the inhabitants may be divided into two classes: the tacksmen, and the lower rank of tenants and cottars. The latter are extremely poor, and must remain so, unless they emigrate, or some such thing as a woollen manufactory be established at Fort William.

The *deus ex machina* of instant industrialisation was unlikely to materialise, so it is even more interesting to note that the same author believed that 'the tacksmen, in general, cannot be said by any means to be opulent'.[12] Rents, of course, had gone up since 1745, but so had prices, and if tenants or tacksmen were better off in real terms at the time of the '45, it cannot have been by a margin calculated to make them prosperous by the standards of Lowland Scotland or England.

One result of this was that in the early eighteenth century, when it came to influencing central Highland chiefs, a little money went a long way. In the reign of Queen Anne the London government paid regular pensions to the tune of £360 annually to certain Jacobite-inclined chiefs to buy their good behaviour. This was important to men like Stewart of Appin, or young John Cameron of Lochiel, or Glengarry.[13] Shilis na Ceapaich (Sileas MacDonald), a female bard who was a daughter of a chief of the MacDonalds of Keppoch and herself a fierce anti-Union Scottish patriot and Jacobite, was to taunt the Highland chiefs, just after the death of Anne, (when payment of the pensions was terminated) for having sold their principles for very little gold, and that no longer chinking in their pockets. She was a little hard on them. Their principles remained their principles: it was just a question of how actively they chose to pursue them.[14]

These were sophisticated men, most of whom were carried away by a fierce surge of national emotion to support the '15, but who otherwise tried to maintain a balance between Jacobite ideology and the facts of life. The arrival of Prince Charles Edward Stuart in person in the Highlands in 1745 was in many ways a blow, for though he came unsupported he could apply enormous emotional blackmail in face-to-face interviews. Even so, equivocation characterised many families in 1745–6. The record is possibly held by Roderick Chisholm of Chisholm, whose youngest son and namesake led the clan out for Prince Charles, and died at Culloden. Confusion with his father because of their similar names forced the older man to go to some lengths in 1748, with the aid of his lawyer John Mackenzie of Delvine, to establish that he had sat at home and had not repeated his open Jacobitism of 1715.[15] It was suspicious that the clan had risen behind a younger son, but the Chisholm could point to two other sons who had fought for Hanover at Culloden in the Royal Scots Fusiliers, as well as one who was a surgeon in the British Army.[16] It is certainly the case that a surprisingly high proportion of those chiefs who committed themselves unequivocally to Prince Charles in 1745 can be shown to have been in a parlous state financially.

One of the few surplus products, other than timber and black cattle, which the central and western Highlands had over the years sought to market internationally was a supply of young adult males to serve as mercenarary soldiers. The first big market for these Highland mercenaries had been among the Gaelic princes of Ireland, who found in the heavily armoured Highland infantry wielding two-handed battle-axes an effective counter-measure to the armoured *blitzkrieg* of the Anglo-Norman knights on horseback. These Highlanders, whose military techniques owed so much to the Viking element in their ancestry, rolled back the tide of Norman conquest in Ireland after 1300. Known as galloglasses, and with names such as MacDonald, MacDougall, MacRory, and MacSweeney, these mercenary soldiers often received land grants and settled in Ireland.[17] In the sixteenth century, as the Dublin government embarked on a serious attempt to render its authority effective over all Ireland, another huge market for Scottish Highland mercenaries opened up. These were more lightly armed troops known as redshanks. Mostly they served with the Gaelic rulers against Queen Elizabeth, and they were prominent in the climacteric Ulster war between Elizabeth and the Earl of Tyrone, a war which was finally concluded in 1603. Before, the war was over, however, James VI of Scotland, who had intrigued with Tyrone, ostentatiously made preparations to raise Highland troops to assist Elizabeth in Ireland, calling on Grant, Lovat, Lochiel, Glengarry and Keppoch, among others, to raise men who were never needed.[18]

When James succeeded peacefully to the linked crowns of England and Ireland in 1603, a Highland military frontier closed in Ireland. However, alternative opportunities offered themselves to the east rather than in the west, as great European wars began to create fresh markets for mercenary soldiers. The beginnings of a successful Dutch resistance to Philip II of Spain go back to the seizure of the port of Brill by Dutch 'Sea Beggars' in 1572. Before that year was out Scotsmen were fighting for the Dutch, and the Scottish Privy Council was already trying to relieve famine in Edinburgh by encouraging 'idle men and soldiers' to pass 'to the wars in Flanders or other foreign countries'. In the long run there emerged in the service of the United Netherlands a Scots Brigade which was only finally disbanded as a distinct unit during the War of American Independence in 1782, when the Dutch allied with the Americans. The service appealed, naturally, mainly to strongly Protestant men from the Lowlands, but there was always a sprinkling of MacDonalds, Frasers, Macleans, Camerons, and Macphersons in the ranks of the Scots Brigade, while younger sons of chieftains like Malcolm MacLeod of Raasay can be found holding commissions in it in the early eighteenth century.[19]

With the outbreak of war in Bohemia in 1618, a war which set off a chain reaction engulfing most of central and western Europe in the Thirty Years War, Scotland became an important reservoir of troops for the Danish, Swedish, French and Imperial services. Military entrepreneurship became an important economic activity for many Scottish aristocratic families, and not least those in the Highlands. North of Inverness, Clan Mackay became the source of a regiment famous for its role in the armies of Gustavus Adolphus, King of Sweden and perhaps the greatest commander in all this terrible cycle of war.

To avoid clashes of interests the Scottish government was normally prepared to allocate different regions to different regimental recruiting officers. Thus in 1627 the central and northern Highlands were reserved for Spynie's Regiment.[20] Despite the deep sectarian roots of the conflict in the Holy Roman Empire, Scottish regiments could be mixed in religion, and they moved easily from one employer to another. Hepburn's Regiment, raised in 1633 by Sir John Hepburn to fight for Gustavus Adolphus, became the Douglas Regiment in the service of France by 1638. In the late seventeenth century, when the Regiment oscillated between the French and British services, Adam Gordon, a Roman Catholic priest who had served with it, remarked that 'it is 1200 strong 700 wherof ar Catholics'.[21] It was from overseas service that much of the professional military talent displayed in the mid-seventeenth-century civil wars was derived. After the Revolution of 1688, of course, successive British governments looked askance at the Jacobite tendencies of so many Highland clans. They were most unwilling to allow the chiefs to recruit regiments, for fear that they might forget which side they were on in the crunch of a Jacobite rising.

It was still the case that many members of the Highland upper classes had careers as professional soldiers, and their Jacobite proclivities made it easier for them to gain experience in the foremost of all eighteenth-century armies – that of the great military monarchy of France. The family of the chiefs of Glengarry was involved in both serving and recruiting for Louis XV, with paradoxical results for their role in the '45. It cannot be over-emphasised that the Jacobite army which invaded England in 1745 was not a rabble of 'bare-arsed banditti' but a properly regimented force organised in a Lowland Division and a Highland Division and commanded by men familiar with the standard routines of contemporary armies.[22]

In a sense the clans of the Great Glen lived apart. Even Inverness, so important to them as a market and port, and the only town of consequence in their local world, was not integrated into their culture. It used, but did not speak, Gaelic and in 1671 its Town Council saw itself 'lyand in the mouth of the hylands quhair thair ar many disaffected personis subject to povertie and givin to thift and roberrie'.[23] On the other hand, the chiefs were impelled by that very poverty to try to use political structures well outside the Highland orbit as the vehicles for their more vaulting ambitions. Locally, by the mid-seventeenth century, they had gradually developed a sensible, viable community of self-governing units, more or less adjusted and resigned to living together. It was a great, if unrecognised achievement, based on generations of challenge, response, and adaptation. But in 1745–6 commitments to a wider world conspired to destroy it and it could not be reconstructed. The chiefly families could only only look for a way back for themselves.

Sir William Alexander, the Scots politician who in the early seventeenth century tried to establish a New Scotland in what was to become the Maritime Provinces of Canada, suggested in his propaganda that instead of going to die on foreign battlefields Scots should seek advancement in North America. Due to withdrawal of support by Charles I, New Scotland foundered, and it was still pretty marginal when re-established as Nova Scotia. The Scots kept trying to create a place in the Americas for themselves,[24] but it was really only from about 1756 that the aristocracy of the central Highlands finally pulled all the threads together.

Residual patriarchal authority, the dire necessity for acceptance by the central British political elite, and the traditions of military entrepreneurship and of looking beyond the Highlands even into America, were integrated into what proved indeed the way back, for a few. It is the central paradox of this study that the last active role of the clansmen it studies was to be as British soldiers, in America. That paradox also explains why, except on the Braes of Lochaber, where the '45 enabled the Mackintosh and the Duke of Gordon to assert effective ownership over lands long claimed but denied them by the Keppoch MacDonalds, the chiefs of 1651 were, broadly, the landlords of 1785, though in 1746 a whole regional world had foundered.

3 The First Forts – From Inverlochy to Fort William

The civil wars of the 1640s, especially after they had broadened out into what has been called 'the war of the three kingdoms' involving simultaneously England, Ireland and Scotland, had underlined the enormous strategic significance of the Irish Sea, and of the western sea approaches to Scotland. They formed in many ways a continuum, and constituted the 'inland sea' of the British Isles. As soon as the English Parliament had emerged triumphant from the bitter Second Civil War of 1648 it was able to transfer a formidable expeditionary force under Oliver Cromwell to Dublin in August 1649. There followed the bloody storming of Drogheda and Wexford, where the garrisons paid the full penalty for making the besiegers suffer the casualties involved in an assault. Cromwell's subordinates were equally successful. Lord Broghill (Roger Boyle, later 1st Earl of Orrery), an Irishman who was later the principal administrator of Cromwellian Scotland, gained control of Cork and the other Munster ports. Colonel Venables late in 1649 relieved Londonderry and gained control of the court towns of Ulster. Sea power made the margins of Ireland extremely accessible. Land was the barrier, not water, and Oliver Cromwell was moved to report to Westminster that 'though God hath blessed you with a great longitude of land along the shore, yet it hath but little depth into the country'.[1]

Bitterly fought campaigns in 1650 and 1651 under Cromwell and his successors deepened the effectiveness of parliamentary power in Ireland. However, the North of Ireland was in many ways part of a 'sea-province' which transcended the boundaries of any one kingdom and was remarkable for the way in which the territories on its perimeter were penetrated by water communication. This natural unit formed a circle bounded in the north by the Hebridean islands of Jura and Islay. Its southern limit was set by the Isle of Man, which was proud of belonging to none of the three kingdoms. To the west lay the coasts of Ulster, and to the east the shoreline of north-west England and the west of Scotland. At their closest Scotland and Ulster were so near to one another that even in the seventeenth century a man from Galloway thought nothing of making a day trip to County Down to attend a market, and Scots families in County

Down would regularly attend communion in their ancestral kirks in Ayrshire. What is not so often appreciated is that similar practical links survived into the twentieth century between the Inner Hebrides and the north of Ulster. The most convenient market for many a modern Islay farmer was for long Coleraine in County Antrim.

The origins of the medieval Scottish state can be tracked back to the sea-united kingdom of Dalriada which from the fifth century A.D. comprised part of north Antrim plus parts of the Inner Hebrides and Argyll in Scotland. Appropriately, historical geographers have christened this sea area around St George's Channel, the Dalriadic Sea. The term would have meant nothing to Lord Protector Oliver Cromwell and his Council in 1654, but the practical reality which it expresses was familiar indeed to men who had wrestled with the conquest of both Ireland and Scotland in the early 1650s and who were in August 1654 busy tidying up the loose ends left after Glencairn's once-frightening rebellion in the Highlands had collapsed. On 29 August of that year the Protector's Council confirmed that as part of their negotiated surrender terms the Earl of Glencairn and the Laird of Lugton were not only to be confirmed in the revenues from their estates but were each also to be free to raise and transport a regiment of 1,000 foot within six months into the service of any foreign prince or state at amity with the republican Commonwealth which had replaced all three Stuart kingdoms.[2]

It was an elegant exercise in using the Scottish tradition of military entrepreneurship to rid the Commonwealth of two potential nuisances of a high order, but it left the underlying problem of control in the dangerous central areas of the Highlands still to be resolved. For once, however, power in London was in the hands of a ruler who was a professional soldier with considerable experience of the Irish Sea as a strategic highway. Using Liverpool as the primary naval base, the Lord Protector had already been deploying light naval units to assert control over freebooters and pirates in the waters between the Isle of Man and the Hebrides, and also to outflank the formidable physical barrier of the Highland Boundary Fault by sustaining an English striking force 'at the back side of Scotland' in Lochaber at the north-east corner of Loch Linnhe, an arm of the sea. The officer designated for command at this new fort, (to construct which a thousand men were drafted from the English army in Ireland) was Lieutenant-Colonel William Brayne, whose regiment had played a prominent role in the conquest of Scotland in 1651. It had been stationed at Perth, where it had helped to construct on the North Inch one of the massive citadels which were symbols of the might and resolution of the Commonwealth regime in Scotland. They were sited in strategic positions such as Leith, the port of Edinburgh; Perth, the key to access to that vast area of Scotland north of the Tay; Ayr, an ideal point from which to monitor the life of the south-western parts of Scotland; Inverness at the head of the Great Glen; and Inverlochy in Lochaber at the southern end of the Great Glen.

The physical problems involved in establishing a permanent garrison at Inverlochy were formidable, and were much graver than the military opposition which Brayne faced. In December 1654 he reported that enemy opposition was not considerable and all possible diligence was being used to break up their levies, if necessary by amphibious operations against concentrations on Hebridean islands. Captain Nutton's ship, the *Satisfaction,* was being detained for that specific purpose. Brayne felt that his own garrison was perfectly secure, but the pressing need was for reinforcements and supplies. Mainly these were shipped in from garrison centres like Carrickfergus, in Ulster, and Chester, the ancient English bulwark set against the northern parts of Wales. Sailors like Captain Nutton were endlessly occupied shuttling up and down the narrow waters of the western seaways, falling back on the already important port of Liverpool as their main victualling base, but always liable to be detained at Inverlochy where Lieutenant-Colonel Brayne's demands on the naval service were loyally backed by the formidable commander-in-chief in Scotland, General George Monck.[3] A ship such as the *Advantage,* commanded by Captain Edmund Thomson, was stationed for six weeks at Inverlochy, where it unloaded ammunition and stores for Colonel Brayne before being despatched to the Isle of Skye to help foil an attempt to build up royalist forces on the island. The task was not, militarily speaking, a very serious one.

Lieutenant-Colonel John Middleton, the singularly unsuccessful royalist captain-general, was in effect a hunted fugitive. The man-o'-war which had brought him from the Netherlands to take command of the rising in the Highlands had been captured. When he tried to ferry his few remaining troops to safety in Skye he discovered that Sir James MacDonald of Sleat, the chief who controlled that part of Skye most accessible from the mainland, was a staunch supporter of the Commonwealth. Beaten off Skye, Middleton's dispirited band doubled back towards Lochaber, while the *Advantage* refurbished Sir James's supplies of powder and shot. Cromwell had frigates patrolling off Orkney to try to capture Middleton if he cut and ran for the Continent through the gap between Orkney and Shetland, a route well known to in-going and out-going Dutch shipping.[4] Despite these precautions an English spy at the Dutch court of the exiled Charles II was reporting by the early summer of 1655 that 'Middleton and his gang were brought in from Munster in state'. Middleton had in fact managed to reach the German port of Emden. In the Highlands he had become more of an embarrassment to his friends than his foes.[5]

Colonel Brayne's main difficulties related to shortage of shoes, clothes, medicines, and building materials. His men remained aboard ship during the early stages of building a fort at Inverlochy. Eventually, Captain Nutton felt the need for a forecastle – a short raised deck at the fore part of his ship – to shelter the men from inclement weather. He managed to extract timber for this purpose from the Marquis of Argyll.[6] Argyll was in no position to disoblige, as his heir had been prominent in the recent royalist rising. Inverlochy was just outside the edge of his own clan territory and if he wanted to keep the English soldiery at arms length, he needed to be helpful. In any case, the garrison also secured him from attack by Royalist clans.

The fortification at Inverlochy represented an impossible military problem for the surrounding clans, even if they had had the spirit after 1654 to try to destroy it. They could not cut off its supply lines, for these were maritime and Cromwell's navy was infinitely more formidable in the British seas than the Navy Royal of Charles I. The physical problem of the defences teased Highland fighting men with no tradition of siege warfare. Though not as massive as the other citadels, Inverlochy was a bastion-defended, up-to-date fort whose walls were guarded by ditches, a bog, a river and Loch Linnhe. The line of the landward walls was swept by cannon mounted on the bastions. In August 1654 the Admiralty Commissioners were ordered to send to Inverlochy 12 pieces of ordnance, each with field carriages, ammunition and other necessaries; as well as 300 spear pikes, 200 snaphance muskets, 200 bandoliers for the musketeers' ammunition, and a mass of tools and stores for pioneers, carpenters and a smith. Three 'whole culverins' firing 17–20-pound shot, six demi-culverins firing 10-pound shot, and three of the smaller sackers commonly used for raking the decks of ships with anti-personnel fire could have made any mass-assault on Inverlochy a murderous business. Even the muskets were an early form of flintlock, more reliable and faster-firing than the firelocks which had hitherto dominated British battlefields.[7]

Nevertheless, it is as important to grasp the limitations of Inverlochy as it is to understand its strengths. It was tied to the sea. Its reach was limited. In theory it was supposed to master the nearby clans, but in practice it could only mount shallow hit-and-run amphibious operations which very seldom managed to catch their intended victims. In May 1655 Captain Edward Tarleton, whose ship plied regularly between Inverlochy, Chester, Liverpool and Dublin, gave the Admiralty Commissioners a report on two of these strikes. On 29 April he had marched ten miles inland with a military force stiffened by 40 of his own men, only to find that the 'delinquents' he was seeking to surprise must have had notice, for they were gone. Tarleton burned some houses and brought off the not very extensive booty of 150 cows and sheep with no opposition beyond desultory sniping. On 5 May he embarked 250 men for an amphibious search-and-destroy operation, but his pilot's ignorance of a tricky coast led to delay and the flight of all his proposed victims. Tarleton's victory consisted in killing some cattle and burning some houses. Deep penetration was much too dangerous and hit-and-run raids could not achieve surprise.[8] It was really a stand-off situation.

Inverlochy was impregnable, but expensive. It sat at the foot of the mighty mass of Ben Nevis, a symbol of English power but also something of a stranded Leviathan. Deadlock, often the mother of common sense in ideologically charged situations, worked its beneficent magic. All Brayne could hope for was an acknowledgement of the *de facto* power of the Commonwealth from former Royalist clans, which were then bound to retain the effective autonomy guaranteed by geography, and their own elusive fighting power. From the point of view of the clans, it was no bad compromise. Hence the paradox that just when Tarleton's operations were achieving so few concrete results, Highlanders were beginning to come into Inverlochy by the hundred to 'take the engagement' to the Commonwealth.

The position of Inverlochy made service in the fort there intensely unpopular. The troops drafted from the Irish command to build the fort had objected to serving more than three or four months there. In a letter to the Lord Protector, General Monck argued passionately in July 1654 that the importance of the site justified keeping them in that station for at least a year. Pressing his case, he contended that:

> truly the place is of that consequence for the keeping of a garrison there for the destroying of the stubbornest Enemy wee have in the Hills (that of the Clan Cameron's, and Glengaries, and the Earle of Seafort's people), that we shall nott bee able to doe our worke unless we continue a garrison there for one yeare. For in case wee should withdraw that garrison towards the winter from thence, those 3 Clans doe soe over awe the rest of the Clans of the Country that they would be able to inforce them to rise.[9]'

Even allowing for the high hopes of 1654, these arguments were far-fetched, and the suggestion that Inverlochy could curb Seaforth's Mackenzies presumed (no doubt correctly) that the Protector had but a hazy notion of Highland geography. The idea of 'destroying' the Camerons was impractical. Lochiel quite naturally decided not to go on living near Inverlochy, in close proximity to the new garrison, but he only moved a few miles north to Achnacarry, where Loch Arkaig drains into Loch Lochy. His clansmen offered a spirited resistance to the not very effective sallies of the English troops, killing about seventy of those brought in from Ireland. Fighting was not protracted. Mutual respect between two hard-hitting groups of fighting men led to a rapid compromise settlement embodied in a treaty with Lochiel which was finalised in May 1655.

It was very much what it said it was: 'Articles of Agreement' between 'his Highness the Lord Protector of England, Scotland, and Ireland' and 'Ewen Cameron, Laird of Loughyell, alias Macon Aldowy', concluded through their respective representatives, General George Monck and Lieutenant-Colonel Campbell. Within twenty-four hours of the signing of the agreement Lochiel and his friends and associates agreed to repair to the 'old Howse of Inverloughy'. There 'all Englishmen, Lowland Scotts, Irish and all others (except Highlanders)' were to surrender their arms to the garrison of Inverlochy. By definition Lochiel's Camerons kept their arms 'for theire owne defence'.

Lochiel and his principal Highland associates were to give bonds as guarantees that neither they nor their tenants would disturb the public peace. The Cameron chief engaged himself to produce for justice any of his servants or tenants who committed robbery, or to pay compensation to the victims. On the other hand, Lochiel's uncle Donald Cameron was guaranteed compensation for damage to his lands by the garrison of Inverlochy, and the garrison pledged itself to a cessation of punitive strikes against the inhabitants of Lochaber. The Commonwealth regime even undertook to pay up to £500 to 'keepe the Laird of Loughyell free from any by gone duties to William MacEntosh of Tirecastle out of the lands pertaining to him in Loquhaber'.[10] From the Camerons' point of view, it was, all in all, a good deal. They retained their armed local autonomy. The Inverlochy garrison was able to impose an absolute veto on any further meddling by the Camerons in Lowland politics, a veto symbolised by the surrender of arms by any outsiders in Lochiel's entourage, though arguably the principal victims of the terrible century of repeated armed Highland eruptions into the Lowlands between the 1640s and the 1740s were the Highlanders themselves. Above all, the treaty ensured an end to English punitive columns and guerrilla warfare in Lochaber, as long as Lochiel accepted the political *status quo,* which he did faithfully until the Restoration of 1660.

Service with the force of nine or ten companies of foot which constituted the regular garrison of Inverlochy remained so unpopular that the garrison was constituted by lottery, to avoid charges of discrimination or favouritism. Companies were picked by drawing lots among the individual companies of each of the infantry regiments of the army of occupation. The disadvantages of the service were remoteness, shortage of fuel, and miserable weather endured in barracks buildings which always seemed to be in need of repair. Relations with the Camerons and Glengarry's people were excellent, and Inverlochy simply drops out of the records of the

Protector's Council after 1655 because nothing was happening there.

Its original commander, William Brayne, spent most of 1656 organising drafts of troops and money from Scotland to reinforce the Lord Protector's aggressive 'Western Design' against Spanish power in the Caribbean. In January 1657 Major-General William Brayne actually arrived in Jamaica, after a terrible voyage and with a shaken, decimated army, as head of the government in this, England's lately conquered colony and naval base. His regime before his early death in September 1657 was high-handedly authoritarian and centralised. In a sparsely inhabited, dangerously exposed advanced base, such methods were understandable in a commander anxious to push 'plantation, fortification, annoying the enemy'.[11] His achievement at Inverlochy was totally different. There he had come to terms with old-established and unshakeable local social and political structures. His sensible policies were ably continued by his successor Major John Hill who, on 5 October 1658, proclaimed Oliver Cromwell's son Richard Lord Protector of the Commonwealth at Inverlochy with no little pomp. Seven companies paraded before Hill, the Sheriff and his law clerks, and a party of local lairds and gentlemen headed by Lochiel and Glengarry. The official report concluded that: 'All the heritours and gentry seem'd very hearty in their expressions of joy, who were all upon the concluding of that daies solemnity invited by the Governour to a very liberall colation or banquet.'[12]

It was the same story all over the British Isles. Not a dog barked at the accession of Richard Cromwell. Royalists everywhere were in despair. Their hour was to come, but not because of their own actions or merits. The Commonwealth regime collapsed from inside. Until the last few months of its life, it was its apparent stability which impressed observers, and men like Lochiel would clearly have been quite happy to coexist with it for ever. Their mental reservations were of as little interest to Hill as they were of importance to anybody. The simple fact was that no previous government had ever looked so formidable, or behaved so reasonably from a position of strength in Glen More.

Inverlochy was only its southern *place d'armes*; an even mightier citadel was raised at the same time in Inverness, to control the northern part of Glen More, and to look out over Seaforth's Mackenzie country to the north and west. Inverness was, of course, far better known to the merchant shipping of the era than the waters of Loch Linnhe. With its old-established harbour in the River Ness and its position at the focus of the Moray Firth, which is bordered by exceptionally fertile coastal plains, Inverness was an obvious seat of command for a naval power with considerable amphibious capabilities. The early English occupation had nervously dug itself in behind earthen ramparts across the streets, and had concentrated on such traditional sites as the old castle on its hill beside the Ness, and on the nearby bridge.

Soon, however, the garrison bought a substantial plot of land beside the Ness, known as the Carseland, and started building in May 1652 a quadrilateral, moated, bastion-defended artillery fort of stone and brick, designed on the most ambitious lines. Supplies of hardwood for the fort, which had a whole complex of interior structures, came by sea from England, but the fir used extensively in building was bought locally from a Fraser chieftain, Hugh Fraser of Struy. The Minister of Kirkhill alleged in 1655 that he had seen Struy receive single payments of up to 30,000 merks* (£20,000 Scots). It was still a formidable amount of money. So was the shilling sterling a day offered for digging the ditches and counterscarps, which accounted for the rush of countryfolk to the work. Most of them probably never received a higher daily wage in the course of their labouring lives. The ashlar masonry used in the lower courses of the fort's building was plundered from the many ruined medieval monastic and cathedral sites accessible by sea from the Moray Firth, a fact which led the incumbent of Kirkhill to believe that a work of such impiety built by English sectaries could scarce be expected to stand. It stood well enough, however, partly because his fellow Scots, from labourers to skilled masons, helped to build it sound and solid. A sally port threatened the town while on the other side a great formal port approached by a massive drawbridge flaunted the arms of the Commonwealth with the motto '*Togam tuentur arma*' (armed might protects the civilian). Like the fine garrison church, or the 'brave great clock with four large gilded dials and a curious ball', the armorial display was baroque propaganda designed to impress the observer with a sense of massive power.[13]

The garrison was quite modest in size. Colonel Fitch's regiment, which fluctuated between 400 and 700 effectives, was in post from 1652 to the Restoration. It was unevictable and tied to the sea lanes for supplies, which arrived in quantity. During the later part of their Scottish campaign Cromwell's troops had repeatedly outflanked Scottish water defences like the Firth of Forth with amphibious landings from craft such as shallops, big heavy boats mounting at least one mast with fore-and-aft or lug sails and usually one or two cannon. They had room for many infantry over a short crossing, but a shallow enough draught to allow them to work inshore and let their men wade into action. Many shallops had been used to invade Fife, the peninsula across the Forth from Edinburgh. One of them 'the 38th double shallop for landing English forces in Fife', whose master

*A merk was 13s. 4d., i.e. two-thirds of £1 Scots. By our period, the exchange rate had stabilised at £12 Scots to £1 sterling. (Unless specified to the contrary, all sums of money in this book refer to £ sterling.)

was Roger Hall, was certainly then sent to Inverness, dragged the five or six miles to Loch Ness by means of rollers, and used to give the garrison access to the twenty-two mile stretch of Loch Ness, which in turn meant that they could move swiftly along the shores of an important part of the Fraser country, and past the entrances to Glen Urquhart and Glenmoriston.[14] In practice, after the shock of Glencairn's Rising, the military government of Scotland showed exactly the same conservative swing that characterised the government of contemporary Ireland under Oliver Cromwell's able younger son, Henry Cromwell. Every effort was made to conciliate the local ruling class and govern through them. In the central part of the Highlands the policy was to pursue malefactors by writing to their clan chief, ordering him to bring them to justice. The system made the chiefs accessories to the Commonwealth regime, but it also recognised them as local rulers with jurisdiction over their own people and police powers based on possession of armed force.

It was certainly a very curious situation in that some of the most conservative aristocrats in the British Isles had to cooperate with an army which represented a new, rationalised and much more powerful central state, run by men of disconcertingly unusual origins and views. Several leading figures in the administration of Cromwellian Scotland were in fact Americans, returned New Englanders come to help run an Old England which was now both radical and surprisingly tolerant of Protestant dissent. Harvard alumnus George Downing was head of the intelligence staff, or 'scoutmaster-general' in Scotland. His father, Emmanuel, co-founder of Salem, Massachusetts, was chief clerk of the Scottish Council, on which another New Englander, Samuel Desborough, waxed powerful. New England officers soldiered in the army in Scotland. A good example is George Fenwick, who at various times commanded in Berwick, Edinburgh and Leith. An even more famous New England name represented in Scotland is that of Winthrop. Young Major Stephen Winthrop was plagued by ill-health during Glencairn's Rising, but he survived and returned to hold major commands in Scotland. He was the son and grandson of governors of Massachusetts, and a cousin of George Downing. Spending most of his time in Scotland between 1654 and 1656, he was a JP for Aberdeenshire and was elected for the burghs of Banff, Cullen, and Aberdeen to the parliament of 1656.[15]

The long history of the relationship between the forts and chiefs of the central Highlands therefore exhibited at a very early stage some of the rhythmic tendencies which were always to characterise it. Waves of hostility and conflict between the chiefs and the British Army would be followed by a trough of exhaustion and then by a steadily swelling wave of coexistence and even cooperation. Rather satisfyingly, the Americans, who were to provide the occasion for the final reconciliation of the chiefs with, and their incorporation into, the Westminster-centred British ruling class, were also around at the very start of the permanent involvement of the British Army* with the Highlands. In the 1650s the returned New Englanders were trying to drag the Highlands into the future. By the 1780s the gentry of Glen More and Glen Spean were endeavouring ruthlessly to ram the revolting colonies back into the deferential mould of the past. The initial synthesis between the chiefs and the British army was surprisingly cordial, but brief. It lasted from 1655 to 1660 when the whole Commonwealth experiment foundered, taking down with it not only the union of the three kingdoms, but also the British Army itself. Always an English army in personnel, the army of the Commonwealth, with its more widely recruited officer corps, was expensive and unpopular with the traditional élites who could not control it and who in the end refused to pay for any indefinite extension of its life. If the Restoration meant anything, it meant the abolition of an army full of stubborn, skilled military workmen who read pamphlets and occasionally took industrial action against their betters.

For Lochiel the sudden nature of the Restoration was something of an embarrassment. He had indeed resisted the Cromwellian forces with spirit until 1655, but thereafter he had made a good thing of English rule. The occupation government paid off his arrears to Mackintosh and tried unsuccessfully to persuade the latter to abandon his claims to superiority over the Cameron lands. After 1660 Mackintosh denounced Lochiel as a collaborator, and he was not alone, for Glengarry complained bitterly that in 1659 the Camerons had accepted a commission from the English to take punitive action against the Glengarry MacDonells, who were accused of riot and robbery. The upshot was a Cameron occupation of Glengarry's lands. At the Restoration Glengarry, with a much more sustained record of resistance to the Cromwellian forces, was rewarded with the title of Lord MacDonald and Aros. Lochiel received no such mark of favour. From a Royalist point of view he did not deserve one but his family managed with the passage of time to persuade themselves that they had a grievance on this score. This idea underlies the 'Memoirs of Sir Ewen Cameron of Lochiel' compiled by his son-in-law Alexander Drummond of Balhaldy (really a MacGregor) in the eighteenth century. These memoirs make much play of episodes like the skirmish in which Sir Ewen literally bit the throat out of an officer of the Inverlochy garrison. Even so, they cannot conceal the cordiality of subsequent relations between Lochiel and

*During the period of the Cromwellian Union the army of the state was technically 'British' though English in personnel. In 1660 a distinct Scottish army re-emerged with the re-establishment of the Scottish state. After the 1688 Revolution that army was merged into a British establishment, though the Scottish state survived until 1707.

Monck, and indeed between Lochiel and John Hill. The pious Governor Hill not only helped Lochiel to select a minister for the Cameron country, but also helped to find some of the funds for his stipend. The Camerons were the only clan in the area officially authorised to carry arms, having ceremonially laid them down in the name of King Charles, and picked them up in the name of the Estates (i.e. the Cromwellian regime). They naturally made the most of the political advantage this gave them over other clans, just as they seem to have taken advantage of the market for their produce represented by the Inverlochy garrison. From a Cameron point of view it was a pity that that garrison could not be indefinitely sustained, but it could not.[16] Always a minor structure compared with the great citadels of Cromwellian Scotland, it was literally to vanish in the years after 1660.

The Protectorate regime in Scotland had always run at a loss. A defeated and depressed country could hardly afford so substantial a military establishment. Since even in England, which had to subsidise the Scottish garrisons, the Protectorate showed unmistakeable signs of fiscal exhaustion, it is clear that the long-term financial problem was insoluble. The Restoration cut this Gordian Knot with one blow. The forts and garrisons, and indeed all but the shadow of a standing army vanished forthwith. Between 1661 and 1666 the Scottish standing army consisted of a mere handful of horse and foot. A troop of mounted Life Guards was raised in 1660 for police and ceremonial duties. It participated in the ceremonial re-interment of the scattered body of the Royalist martyr, the Marquis of Montrose, in May 1660, a ceremony all the more ironic in that the Earl of Middleton, Captain-General of the Scottish forces 1661–3, and principal mourner, was an ex-Covenanter whose old father had been brutally slaughtered by Montrose's men. Apart from his Life Guard cavalry troop Middleton had his own troop of horse, plus five companies of Foot Guards and an Independent Company which garrisoned Edinburgh Castle. Garrisons were once more restricted to the traditional seats of royal power – Edinburgh, Dumbarton and Stirling Castles.[17] Due to politico-religious turmoil after 1666, there had to be considerable augmentation of the forces. During the Dutch war of 1665–7 (which was unpopular in Scotland), the forces rose to 3,000 foot and 8 troops of horse. However, a moderate school of Royalist politicians led by Sir Robert Moray persuaded Charles II that this establishment was both expensive and ineffective. A partial disbandment from 1667 reduced it to a couple of troops of Life Guards, with a few supporting infantry companies. When the King needed forces, he relied on a newly reorganised county militia mobilised by the safely Royalist nobles of the kingdom. Since nearly all nobles north of the Tay were staunch royalists, the scheme worked well. It also balanced the government's budget.[18]

By definition, in this conservative world there was no place for the citadels of Cromwellian Scotland. The government had neither the troops nor the funds necessary to sustain them. In the Lowlands it was quite anxious that the citadels be quickly demolished, both as symbols of a hated rival regime, and as potential strongholds which subversive elements like religious dissenters, or worse still religious dissenters cooperating with Dutch landing-parties, might seize and fortify. In December 1661 the Earl of Lauderdale, Secretary of State for Scotland in London, wrote to the revitalised Scottish Privy Council reminding them of the royal anxiety that the important work of 'the slighting of the garrisons' be pushed forward, with the one reservtion that in sites like Leith and Inverness stonework might remain if it was needed 'for keiping out the sea from the houses'. Early the next year there were complaints that very little progress had been made with slighting the Inverness citadel (and not much more at Perth or Ayr) and that this was delaying evacuation of the English forces. In the summer of 1662 the government had reached an agreement with James Grant of Freuchie that he would send labourers to expedite the demolition of the Inverness fortification. The snag was that money was still due on the construction of the Inverness citadel when attempts were being made to dismantle it, which led to desperate attempts by the government to sell timber and stone from the site to clear the debt.[19] The whole business eventually lost its sense of urgency. Quite a lot of the citadel was still left by the early eighteenth century. Long before then servants of Charles II were able to refer casually to storing timber purchased for warship construction in Inverness Citadel.[20]

The policy of the Restoration government in the Highlands, garrisons apart, was much the same as that of its predecessor: it summoned chiefs of clans and branches of clans, and landlords to appear in Edinburgh to give caution for keeping their followers in order. Most of the leading men of Glen More and Glen Spean either just failed to turn up to do this before the Scots Privy Council in Edinburgh in 1661 or, like Lovat, Lochiel, and the baillie of Stratherrick, sent written excuses.[21] Absence of troops undoubtedly led to a weakening of the central government's grip on men like John Grant of Glenmoriston, who after failing to turn up in Edinburgh in 1661 to give caution (in excellent company, be it said, with such as Cluny), subsequently posted a bond to keep the peace, only to rather tarnish his 'good-boy' image by 'gangsterous' conduct towards William Robertson of Inches, one of his creditors. The Robertson family complained in 1664 that John Grant had turned a 'friendly tryst' to discuss the debt question into an ambush, where he assaulted and kidnapped William Robertson and spirited him along Loch Ness to the fastnesses of Glenmoriston where he held him prisoner in the hope of forcing him to forego the debt, which threatened Grant's grip on his estate. Grant was 'put to the horn' as a rebel. The experience was only marginally inconvenient for him.[22]

A clear distinction must be drawn between different kinds of violence which occurred in this area between the Restoration of 1660 and the Revolution of 1688. At no time in this period before 1688 was there large-scale organised violence designed to challenge the basic political order of the state. In that sense Charles II was totally justified in agreeing to a partial disbanding of his Scottish standing army. He did not need a big army, least of all to protect his Edinburgh government from the chiefs of the central Highlands. Disaffected areas there were, of course, but he could and did control them by using forces raised in the far more extensive areas which were loyal. The classic example here is the so-called Highland Host of 1678 which consisted overwhelmingly of militia units from the eastern Highlands and from the eastern Lowlands north of the Forth. Commanded by local nobles, these forces were poured into disaffected shires in the south-west of Scotland to overawe and bully the inhabitants.[23]

To their credit, the chiefs of Glen More and Glen Spean were not prominent in such episodes. Political violence for them was primarily a device of last resort used normally for conservative purposes to stabilise the intricate power-balance which was the local *status quo.* Anyone foreclosing on a major Highland estate could threaten the very life of a clan, and in a sense Robertson of Inches was sailing too close to the wind. He could squeeze a creditor like Glengarry, who had to service existing debt to maintain any kind of credit facility, but he could not appear directly to threaten the grip of a major chief on his ancestral estates. That was physically dangerous, though political violence was normally used to check rather than to obliterate such a threat.

A good example of this was the way in which Lochiel in the Restoration period blocked a renewal of age-old threats to his position. Taking advantage of Lochiel's lack of favour with the government, Lauchlan Mackintosh of that Ilk returned to the offensive in Lochaber. Lauderdale, the principal Scottish minister at the English court of Charles II, was clear that the Scottish Privy council would do best to mediate some sort of agreement between the rivals.[24] However, Mackintosh had secured from the sheriff court of Inverness, which was susceptible to his influence, a decreet of removal against the Camerons in the disputed lands of Loch Arkaig and the barony of Glenloy. Faced with armed resistance from Lochiel, Mackintosh was able to secure letters of fire and sword against the Camerons from a Privy Council to whom they were technically rebels. What followed was a protracted politico-military duel which came to a head in 1665 when Mackintosh swooped down with 1,500 men, coming south down Glen More.

Lochiel faced him within the natural redoubt formed by Loch Arkaig,

Loch Lochy, the river Lochy, and Loch Eil. It could be outflanked only by a tactically hazardous and lengthy march through the rough country of Glen Dessary and Glen Pean to the west of Loch Arkaig. Direct assault from the north required a fleet of boats, or the forcing of one heavily guarded ford. It was a tactical stand-off which became a political one when Glenorchy's heir, John Campbell, the future Earl of Breadalbane, arrived with a force which he promised to throw against the first party to attack. The Campbells did not want the Cameron buffer removed, but they did secure a measure of control over it when Argyll helped Lochiel by lending him some of the cash needed to seal the agreed compromise whereby Mackintosh accepted financial compensation for his Arkaig and Glenloy pretensions.

The inevitable flux and change of clan relationships was becoming confined to quite narrow limits at the southern end of More by the end of the seventeenth century. Lochiel could not stop Argyll's conquest of Maclean of Duart's lands in Mull, despite the fact that Lochiel's wife was of the Duart family, but Lochiel could refuse to become another Campbell satellite. In any case, by 1684 Argyll himself had been convicted of treason by the Stuart regime and had fled abroad, whence he returned to lead an unsuccessful rising in 1685. Argyll's defeat, arrest, and execution inevitably created a high level of insecurity in Lochaber. Mackintosh, equipped with new letters of fire and sword, and royal troops, tried to do to the Keppoch MacDonalds what he had failed to do to the Camerons. At the battle of Mulroy in 1688, the last big clan battle, Keppoch trounced the invaders, with massive Cameron assistance. If Mackintosh could have asserted effective superiority over Keppoch, Lochiel would have been the next target. In fact, nobody wanted a major Scottish magnate to acquire the immense additional muscle he could build by digesting the Cameron empire. When, in the confusion of Argyll's temporary eclipse, the Marquis of Huntly, high in royal favour and lately created Duke of Gordon, emerged with what had once been Argyll's financial claims on Lochiel for loans needed to secure territory from the Mackintosh, steps were taken to eliminate this new threat. The government simply refused to let the Duke of Gordon try to foreclose on Glenloy and Loch Arkaig. Lochiel had to make a trip to London, but King James knew at once where the line had to be drawn.[25]

The Scots Privy Council was liable to be swayed by the tongue or influence of one party to a dispute, which is why a man like Lochiel normally negotiated safe conducts for himself and his principal advisers before he would turn up before the Council when locked in dispute with someone like Mackintosh.[26] It was a sensible safeguard against arbitrary incarceration in Edinburgh Tolbooth. The Privy Council always sobered up when faced with military facts, and usually reverted to an honest-broker role, negotiating a compromise without undue loss of face for either party. The tendency amongst modern historians to see interstitial violence between major Highland power blocks simply as 'anarchy' is unfortunate. Provided the rival groupings were reasonably balanced in relative power, force was often calculating, conservative, and capable of modifying the iniquities which Edinburgh lawyers, then and later, were happy to condone, in the name of Justice, and for substantial fees. By 1674 Ewen Cameron of Lochiel was being nominated a justice of the peace for the shire of Argyll, by the influence of the Earl of Argyll himself.[27] Mediation was in fact the only sensible policy for the Privy Council in most Highland disputes. For example, when in 1670 the Council heard that there had been a dispute involving bloodshed between Camerons and Glengarry's men at Inverlochy, its immediate response was to try to hold Lochiel and Lord MacDonald and Aros (i.e. Glengarry) responsible for their respective 'Names', and to set up a sub-committee to mediate between them. The problem was exacerbated by the fractured nature of Clan Donald, so Sir James MacDonald of Sleat was summoned to Edinburgh to assist the negotiation. He was a MacDonald, but hostile to Glengarry's pretensions to clan leadership.[28]

High dudgeon could, of course, be taken over the results of such mediation. In August 1665 there arose an 'unhappy tumult' between a large group of MacDonalds from Moydart, mainly followers of Glengarry, and local burgesses at a fair and market in Inverness. Eventually several hundred armed burgesses led by provost Alexander Cuthbert, sword in hand, drove the MacDonalds out, killing several. The Privy Council reached the sensible conclusion that, on balance, the burgesses were to blame, but that the riot was more an unfortunate accident than anything else. Inverness was told to pay the MacDonalds £4,800 Scots (£400 Sterling), plus surgeons' fees for the wounded, and both the burgh of Inverness and Lord MacDonald and Aros were to find caution under penalty of 20,000 merks to keep the peace between their people. In September 1666 the town council of Inverness passed an act only repealed in 1675 that those who had helped the MacDonalds to sue them before the Privy Council (John Forbes of Culloden, his brother Duncan, William Robertson of Inches, Thomas Watson, Alexander Forbes, Alexander Chisholm, and William Cunningham) should be deemed incapable of election to the burgh council. Tempers cooled with time and the Culloden interest again grew potent in eighteenth-century Inverness. In all fairness, it is difficult to see what else or what better the Privy Council could have done abut the 1665 tumult, and it did assoilzie or free Inverness from all further legal harassment over the issue.[29]

There was a great deal of mobile wealth, especially in the shape of cattle, around in the Restoration Highlands. Such wealth tends to attract criminals in any society, thugh it is quite clear that losses due to crime never seriously slowed the huge expansion of cattle-droving in the late seventeenth- and eighteenth-century Highlands. Where there were sustained complaints about crime, as in a petition presented in 1681 to the Duke of Albany and York, the virtual viceroy of Scotland, by 'the gentlemen heritors and freeholders of the Lowlands of the Shyre of Inverness and others near and about the Burgh thereof', there can usually be found a political conflict just under the surface. The petitioners appealed for garrisons in their area at points such as Inverlochy, but the reality behind their generalisations seems to have been a dispute between the Forbes of Culloden family and the Frasers about the estates of Ferintosh and Bunchrew, which the Forbes family had bought from the Frasers.[30] The Restoration regime simply could not afford to pour troops into the Highlands on a sufficient scale to make any difference. When unusually provoked in 1664, the Scottish Privy Council's idea of firm action was: 'a garison to be planted in Braemar of fourty musketters of the Kinges forces, and another garison in Innerlochy and Riven of Badzenoch of fourscore musketters'.[31]

The many companies of foot of the Cromwellian era could not police Lochaber. Only the local chiefs could do that, and as long as they were prepared to accept the authorities in control of the central state, those authorities were wise to try to exercise control through the chiefs. The chiefs were mostly men of property with no desire to condone mere lawlessness. The rare exceptions, such as MacDonald of Keppoch who was virtually a professional bandit, were known and distrusted by other chiefs, who alone could do anything to check them. Groups such as the MacGregors gave endless trouble precisely because they had no generally acknowledged chief capable of disciplining them. In the last analysis, there was no serious alternative to cooperation with the local elites. Plodding government infantrymen, as such, had been proven incapable of catching anyone in the face of a hostile countryside. Cooperation offered both state and chiefs great benefits. The state increased its effectiveness, while decreasing its costs. The chiefs could participate in a Scottish social and economic system which for most of the Restoration was buoyant and satisfying, while retaining vast local autonomy.

The one set of circumstances which this sensible system could not cope with was a deep, active political cleavage between the central state and the regional élites. A union of hearts was not essential. The Protectorate had shown that the central Highland chiefs could and would work with a regime they did not much like in theory, but which deployed sufficient power at local level to compel their respect, and then treated them with common sense and respect. An ineffective government which the chiefs disliked was, however, a recipe for disaster, and that was precisely what emerged after 1685. The death of Charles II in that year was a calamity. There was quite enough support for his successor, James VII of Scotland and II of England and Ireland, to be able easily to put down a rebellion in 1685 in Argyll. Led by the exiled Campbell chief, the Earl of Argyll, the rebels were defeated when they tried to enter the Lowlands, and Argyllshire was occupied by Royalist militia troops, many drawn from Atholl. By his tactlessness, ineptitude, wooden arrogance and unpopular (if often defensible) policies James threw away a position of immense strength. He alienated the Scots nobles whom he had wooed successfully as Duke of Albany in the early 1680s. His English subjects were in fact so alienated that they called in his son-in-law William of Orange with an army which overthrew James bloodlessly in the Glorious Revolution of 1688.

In Scotland a resolute minority was able to carry through a similar revolution, with the bulk of the ruling class standing sullenly aside. War was written on the face of these events, war with France and in the British Isles. The eventual outcome in the Highlands was to be the re-establishment of the Inverlochy garrison, but fully to grasp the reasons for that decision, one must see how far they parallel the motives for establishing it in the first place in 1654. As in 1654 there was a background of warfare in the Highlands and in Ireland, warfare in which the Irish Sea and Hebridean waters played a key logistic and strategic role. That remarkable man William Blathwayt, who has been described as the 'imperial fixer' *par excellence* of the late seventeenth and early eighteenth centuries was the civil servant who more than any other, as Secretary at War, co-ordinated the Williamite military effort against James II in Ireland in 1689–90. Blathwayt sweated out the siege of Londonderry by the forces of James II. He was given repeated demonstrations of the erratic impact of changing weather conditions on the naval units based in Liverpool, which were trying to bring succour to the beleaguered Protestants of Derry.[32] Though at one point it looked as if the Revolution of 1688 might cost Blathwayt his tenure of his quasi-ministerial secretaryship, he survived like the great bulk of the English bureaucracy built up by Charles II and James II, and served William of Orange with that same dedication he had offered to the Stuarts. From 1692 until his death Blathwayt was Secretary of State. However, the immediate effect of the events of 1688 was to make military administration much more difficult. The armies of James II were disbanded, mutinous or given to large-scale desertion while Blathwayt had to mobilise forces for war in Ireland, Flanders, and America.[33]

So, far from being able, like the military administrators of the Commonwealth in 1654, to draft substantial resources from Ireland to help control the restive Highlands of Scotland, Blathwayt was most anxious early in 1689 to increase Scotland's extremely inadequate contribution to the general war effort of the Williamite kingdoms. He was working on a proposal that four new regiments be raised from the politically reliable parts of the west of Scotland, a proposal endorsed by three leading generals of the period.[34] It was the Scottish Jacobite rebellion which burst out in 1689 under the leadership of John Graham of Claverhouse, Viscount Dundee which alone made it possible for enough military force to be concentrated in the Highlands to make the idea of leaving a garrison at Inverlochy practical. Left to his own devices, William of Orange would probably have preferred simply to drain Scotland of troops and taxes to fight the Continental wars in which his heart really lay.

The Jacobite rising in Scotland was fought mainly in the eastern Highlands. It was not widely supported, but as was to become commonplace in future risings there was a disproportionate showing from the smaller clans of the west-central Highlands, from the territories just north of the Campbells' Argyll. On 26 July 1689, Claverhouse won, at the cost of his own life, a spectacular victory over the Williamite commander General Hugh Mackay, at the battle in the Pass of Killiecrankie. The attempt by the Jacobite army to burst into the Lowlands was checked by a quarter of their number in bitter fighting in the old episcopal centre of Dunkeld. A regiment of militant western Presbyterians, the Cameronians, stood firm under repeated attacks, one of which cost their commander, the young Colonel Cleland, his life. With a disconsolate Jacobite host wandering round the eastern Highlands, King William had at least temporarily to agree to build up the decimated regiments of Mackay. That stout fighter, though hopelessly outgeneralled, had led a proportion of his forces in an ordered retreat across the fords of the River Garry and away from Killiecrankie. In the long run his cavalry was to charge over the Jacobite army and disperse it on Speyside at the Haughs of Cromdale in May 1690.[35]

On 1 March 1691 a sub-committee of the Scottish Privy Council, headed by the restored Earl of Argyll, pressed upon the London authorities the need for funding for two operations. One was the embarkation of 600 men on a frigate squadron whose arrival 'we mightily long for'. These troops were to cooperate with the Earl of Argyll's Campbells in sweeps in the Hebrides which would not only disrupt the flow of possible reinforcements to the Jacobite army, but might also with luck draw Jacobite strength over to the west where the general consensus was that it could do little serious harm. On the other hand, the very remoteness of the western Highlands and Island posed the usual problems for central government control. The Cromwellian precedent was, however, there to cite, and cited it was. The committee urged the adoption of the 'great design' whereby Cromwell had brought the western clans under obedience. It was a simplistic view, but it had substance, as had the supporting argument that only by thrusting a garrison into Inverlochy could the Jacobite

Highlanders be deprived of the perpetual privilege of operating on internal lines against government troops forever labouring round an extensive periphery. Mackay wanted 3,000 foot, beside his amphibious 600, for the operation. Argyll and his colleagues wanted £4-5,000 at once for funding the plan. They added engagingly that it would have to come from England, for the Scottish Treasury would be exhausted by paying for the 600.[36]

The last remarks cannot have come like sweet music to the ears of the government, but at least it was being presented with a concrete policy in the middle of an incredibly confused situation. The next reference to the matter in the papers of the English Privy Council refers to 'Colonel Hills, Governor of Inverlochy alias Fort William' as an accomplished fact, but only to contradict a rumour that he was dead. Another rumour – that the Jacobite commander Colonel Cannon was dead also – was denied in much the same breath as a report was accepted that the New England expedition against Quebec, capital of New France, had had to be abandoned by its leader, Sir William Phipps. The fog of war could hardly be more palpable. Even the report of the climacteric Williamite victory in the Irish campaign at Aughrim was reported with the caveat that further confirmation would be needed for certainty.[37]

What the Revolution of 1688 did finally achieve in the sphere of military structure was the formation and consolidation of a British Army. Though Scotland remained a quite distinct kingdom through to 1707, there was no Scottish Army after 1688. The official return of the land forces of William and Mary in 1692 makes this abundantly clear. It provided for a distinct Irish Establishment of 1 regiment of horse, 2 of dragoons, and 15 regiments of foot. There was no separate return for Scotland (though there were separate returns for Danish and Dutch forces in William's service). Scottish regiments such as the Coldstream Regiment of Foot Guards and Their Majestys' Regiment of Scots Guard were scattered through the general British establishment, and might never cross the Tweed in generations of service. Most significant of all: no Scottish fort was returned amongst the principal guards and garrisons of the Crown.[38] Scottish garrisons did exist, but they were not regarded as of sufficient significance to warrant the commitment of a major element of the military power of a Crown waging war on several fronts. A list of the places in Scotland where bodies of troops were stationed in 1690 was quite lengthy, for it included Inverness, Aberdeen, Blair Atholl, Abergeldie, Ruthven in Badenoch, Finlarig, and Fort William. It is a measure of the financial resources available to sustain these garrisons that their commanders were told to secure fuel by threatening their neighbourhoods with military retaliation if fuel was not 'voluntarily' sent in, and the officers in command were all ordered to supply candles to their men upon their own credit against a very dubious promise of future reimbursement by the state.

Only the governors of Fort William and Inverness were exempted from the forced candle loan,[39] and it is clear that these two points of strength were regarded as being in a different category from the others. General Mackay, in advising the Lords of the Privy Council, argued bluntly: 'that Fort William being a post of great importance for the security of the peace be provyded of necessary supplyes of money and other things, particularly meat and fyre, preferable to all other posts.'[40]

Obviously, in a war during which Jacobite forces operating in the Highlands received significant reinforcement from Jacobite Ireland, Fort William was a far more important site than Inverness, because it lay athwart some of the more significant lines of communication between the two kingdoms. Nevertheless, Inverness was rightly seen as an essential complement to a garrison at Inverlochy, since a firm grip on the central line of Glen More was widely recognised as the only sensible basis for a policy of strategic guards and garrisons in the Highlands. Mackay was anxious that the defences of Inverness be brought up to date with wooden palisades and a counterscarp round the town. By counterscarp he meant the outer edge of the ditch whose long, sloping inner side or glacis supported the palisades. Mackay was convinced that, provided the government could supply some money, tools, and a military engineer to oversee the exercise, Inverness could easily be brought into a defensible state, for the timber required could be cut in Mackintosh of Borlum's woods within three miles of the town.[41] What kept ambitious schemes such as this in the realm of the hypothetical was the complete lack of the political will to implement them.

Ardent Williamites were full of schemes for reverting to the policies which had once enabled Cromwell to control the Highlands. They offered sound local advice. A plan which came out of the Forbes of Culloden circle, for example, urged that between Inverlochy and Inverness minor posts should be established at the entrance to Glen Spean; at Invergarry 'which opens the way to the Shires of Inverness and Ross' by a series of westward routes; and 'at Erchelish [i.e. Erchless Castle] in Strathglass (14 myles from Inverness and 12 from Invergarry); that being upon the pass from Seafort and Lovat's Countreys to Lockaber'. A neater guide to the geo-politics of the Great Glen would be difficult to find. Its fatal flaw was its assumption that 300 men would constitute the permanent garrison of Inverness, and no less than 1,200 troops would be found to hold Inverlochy.[42] Nothing could have been more remote from reality. Whereas the Cromwellian regime regarded the unity and defence of the British Isles as its first priority, the new Dutch king who sat on the thrones of the three kingdoms of the same Atlantic archipelago in 1690 saw it merely as a springboard for his re-entry into the Great Game of Continental power politics. After the main force of Scottish Jacobitism had been scattered at the Haughs of Cromdale, William was primarily interested in finding a man who would show him how to wind down military operations in the Highlands quickly and cheaply. In the Earl of Breadalbane, he found him. Sir John Campbell of Glenorchy, Earl of Breadalbane and, in Gaelic, MacCailein 'ic Dhonnachaidh, known to his clansmen as Ian Glas or Grey John, was heir to a tradition in which forceful double dealing was elevated to an art form. It was also combined with an underlying prudence which ensured that, unlike Simon Fraser Lord Lovat, his contemporary, he never finessed the head off his own shoulders.

Enobled by the Restoration regime, and allowed by it to enrich himself by the sword as he asserted territorial claims in the Highlands, Breadalbane nevertheless sat tight at the Revolution of 1688. He lurked in his castles, supporting neither Claverhouse nor Mackay, and bearing the ravaging of Glenlyon and the burning of his house of Achallader by the rascally MacDonalds of Glencoe with the outward appearance of composure. By the spring of 1690 he was dealing openly with the new King William, and covertly with the Jacobites still in arms in the Highlands. To William he suggested that the Highlands might be a reservoir of military manpower, even for use in foreign wars. It was to prove a prescient suggestion, but it was understandably not acted on in 1690. More marketable was a plan whose details Breadalbane largely filched from George Mackenzie, Viscount of Tarbat, whereby persuasion and bribery were to be substituted for arms in bringing peace to the Highlands. William had no illusions about Breadalbane. A confession in a London prison by Lord Annandale had shown Ian Glas also to be actively correponding with the Jacobites. Perhaps that was why William authorised him to negotiate for the new government in 1691.

The negotiations which followed are notorious in Highland history. They were held beside Breadalbane's recently burned seat of Achallader at the head of Glen Orchy, not far from the Moor of Rannoch, that bleak central recess in the mountains. It was made clear that William would move troops in, and unleash the frigates that were already in Hebridean waters if a settlement was not forthcoming. On the other hand, the absence of immediate coercion enabled touchy, proud men like Lochiel, Glengarry and Keppoch to insist that any settlement be reached in a manner calculated to spare them any loss of face. The almost mandarinical obsession with face, to this day a conspicuous aspect of Highland culture, has perhaps never been so publicly indulged as in those late June days of 1691 at Achallader. The Jacobite chiefs turned up with Major-General Thomas Buchan and Sir George Barclay, the commanders of what scraps were left of the forces of King James in Scotland. King William offered pardon and indemnity, the latter in the shape of possible cash payments, in exchange for submission. A truce was agreed within a week and more or less kept. It was enshrined in the Treaty of Achallader of 30 June 1691.[43]

These proceedings were highly contentious. Many Williamites distrusted Breadalbane intensely. Among them was Major-General Hugh Mackay, who thought Scotland plagued by prevaricating and devious politicians. Mackay also thought Cromwell had been right to subsidise his Scottish garrisons from English revenues, on the ground that a stabilised Scotland was a direct English interest. Mackay's solution to the problem of such awkward Jacobite chiefs as Lochiel, Glengarry, or Keppoch was to pin them down with powerful garrisons. Inverlochy he considered to be the lynchpin of effective Highland policy, pointing out how effectively a small but active Williamite garrison at Inverness had neutralised potential local Jacobite supporters like the Frasers, and the Mackenzies. Mackay stressed the need for adequate backing for Colonel Hill. The latter predictably shared his former commander's views, and especially the distrust of equivocal wheeler-dealers like Breadalbane.

What Hill was able to pounce on was the alarming nature of the so-called 'secret clauses' in the Treaty of Achallader. They were astonishingly ill-kept secrets, for when Hill forwarded a copy of them to the Scots Privy Council via its President, the Duke of Hamilton, it emerged that another member, the Earl of Kintore, had a copy. So had the Forbes of Culloden family. Presumably, most interested nobles had access to a copy. The clauses in question allowed the Jacobites to send emissaries to James to ask permission to conclude the treaty. They also allowed the Jacobites to rise in the event that King William withdrew his forces from Scotland, or King James managed to mount an invasion from outside. Finally, Breadalbane promised to join the Jacobites with a thousand men if William breached the treaty. All these concessions were meaningless. James could hardly refuse permission to conclude the truce without alienating his few remaining active Scottish friends. In the event of a French invasion, or Williamite withdrawal (both unlikely), the Jacobites would have risen anyway, regardless of any solemn pledges. Breadalbane was William's plenipotentiary. Provided he delivered a cessation of arms, he knew William would regard this as a victory, which is what it was. Besides, the threat of a French invasion, which was very real in the aftermath of the defeat of the English Channel fleet by a French fleet in the Battle of Beachy Head of 1690, was fading. 1691 saw an unmistakeable resurgency of English naval power, and in May 1692 French plans to transport King James and an army to the South of England were utterly shattered by the virtual annihilation of an outnumbered French fleet at the Battle of La Hogue.[44]

Breadalbane, no stranger to the Continental headquarters of William of

Orange, seems to have been confident of his master's approval throughout, and after La Hogue he must have felt vindicated by events. The Jacobite chiefs had been paralysed from the summer of 1691. King James delayed his unavoidable acquiescence in their peacemaking until early December. The news of his decision only reached Scotland towards the end of that month. By the spring of 1692 La Hogue had destroyed any hope of another serious Jacobite rising. However, Hill and Mackay were still right in insisting that if William wanted a secure grip on the Highlands he had to pay for it with adequate garrisons, preferably with a significant proportion of local men capable of obtaining and using local information. Things were never quite what they seemed to be in the Highlands. Seaforth, the chief of Clan Mackenzie, was nominally for King James in the Revolution of 1688, but when he faced a significant Williamite force at Inverness he sent word to the Williamite command that though honour compelled him to make Jacobite gestures, he would make sure they were ineffective.[45] Power was essential in the Highlands, and ruthless power was respected there even more than in most places. The Treaty of Achallader was useful to King William mainly because it won time for events to run his way. It still needed to be followed up with adequate garrisoned force. The attempt to exert authority cheaply and unscrupulously, which William's Scottish government made in 1692, was to lead not to respect but to infamy.

4 *The Nadir of Government*

The weakness of Williamite government in the Highlands of Scotland immediately after the Revolution of 1668 can hardly be exaggerated. The town of Inverness had found it necessary to buy off MacDonald followers of Claverhouse who had threatened to burn it to the ground. The principal miscreant was predictably MacDonald of Keppoch, known as 'Coll of the Cows', whose feats as a cattle-reiver were legendary. An angry Claverhouse had reached Inverness in time to check Coll's clansmen, but the town still had to pay part of the 4,000 merks ransom demanded (Claverhouse had to give Keppoch a bond for the balance). In 1689 the Privy Council was being dunned by Inverness for compensation for the ransom, and for powder and shot removed to Stirling Castle, whilst at the same time it was reduced to bargaining with Sir John Maclean of Duart, the leading Jacobite chief on the Isle of Mull, for the release of Williamite prisoners whom he held, as if he were an independent power. None of this was compatible with an image of strength, least of all when the Council ruled flatly that it could not possibly refund the cost of the Inverness ransom, or the cost incurred by that burgh in throwing up fortifications.[1]

In the summer of 1690 Lochaber was effectively a foreign land where Major-General Buchan and Brigadier Cannon could sulk after their debacle at Cromdale and insist that the council of Highland chiefs in the Jacobite camp would not hear of releasing Williamite prisoners held in duress in Duart unless their own relatives captured at Cromdale were released in exchange.[2] The long arm of naval power might in theory have compensated for the inaccessibility of Maclean, but here too the shortage of cash which had precluded any generous treatment for Inverness reared its head. Two frigates and a sloop were commissioned to cruise off the west coast under Captain Edward Pottinger, but there was no assurance that money would be forthcoming from England to pay for them, nor was there money in Edinburgh. The staunchly Whig merchants of Glasgow were presumably among the keenest supporters of this naval force, yet even their partisan zeal must have been a fraction dulled when it became clear that the Privy Council wanted them to pay for the enterprise. The ruling magistrates of Glasgow, who were corporately tacksmen or leasees of the excise of the six western shires of Scotland were ordered to give Pottinger six weeks' provisions for his flotilla on credit, in exchange for a hazy promise to try to recover the money from the English Lords of the Admiralty. Walter Gibson, late provost of Glasgow, and his brother James Gibson were put under considerable pressure to agree to furnish and provide for King William's service a ship which they had just finished building at Greenock.[3]

Pottinger's squadron included HMS *Dartmouth*, a sleek fine-lined frigate mounting thirty-six guns, and technically ranked as a fifth-rater in the line of battle. She had been completed by John Tippets at Portsmouth in 1655. As Sir John Tippets he became Surveyor of the Navy in 1672 and in between he had been associated with the radical developments in the construction of smaller British warships which produced the first frigate, the *Constant Warwick* in 1646. These fast vessels with fine underwater lines were inspired, according to Samuel Pepys, by 'the Dunkirk frigates, which outsailed all other ships in the seas'. The *Dartmouth* had a lengthy sea career behind her and had undergone a drastic overhaul, including a renewal of her keel, in 1678 before she moved to Hebridian waters in 1690. Based on Greenock from March she was committed at once to a gruelling programme of patrol work which Pottinger complained was leading to progressive deterioration in such vital equipment as anchor cables. In October 1690 the *Dartmouth* sailed into the Sound of Mull in company with two smaller ships, bent on forcing Maclean of Duart to come to heel by signing the Articles of Allegiance to William and Mary, as well as surrendering his unfortunate prisoners. As the ships sailed down the Sound they were threatened by bad weather, so they made an emergency anchorage in Scallastle Bay, five miles from where Duart castle perched on its rocky headland. A violent storm broke the *Dartmouth's* anchor cables. She drifted two miles before striking on the rocky islet of Eileen Rubha an Ridire where, according to local tradition, 'The waves beat on her until she went to pieces there, to the great rejoicing of the Macleans'. There were only six survivors from the crew of about 130. The fate of the *Dartmouth* epitomised the policies of the post-Revolution government in the Highlands. Where the natives were unfriendly its authority hardly extended beyond a musket-shot length from Mackay's encampment, or a cannon shot from the rampart of one of its few forts. Its attempts to take masterful action hovered between farce and fiasco, with a strong element of personal tragedy, as with the seamen who died in the storm-lashed, icy waters of the Sound of Mull.[4]

However, William's government was as stubborn about adhering to unsuccessful policies as had been its predecessor. Indeed, many sincere Whigs who had supported the Glorious Revolution out of principle were shocked by the extent to which William was happy to be served by men who had served James VII and II. Prominent among these was Sir John Dalrymple, Master of Stair, son of a very great jurist, the first Viscount of Stair. The father had been driven into exile under James VII. The son stayed in Scotland waiting to be bought for the sake of his formidable abilities, which James could see made him a better ally than foe. In due course Sir John Dalrymple was reconciled to his sovereign with the post of Lord Advocate (the principal state prosecutor in Scotland), and had risen just before the Revolution to the position of Lord Justice Clerk, which made him head of the principal criminal appeal court and a Senator of the College of Justice. None of this prevented him from coolly abandoning his inept royal master at the Revolution, in time to play a prominent role in the convention parliament and commission which offered William and Mary the crown of Scotland. Rewarded with his old post of Lord Advocate, and graced with the style of Master of Stair following the elevation of his returned father to the dignity of a viscountcy, he became joint Secretary of State for Scotland with George, Earl of Melville early in 1691. To ensure his ascendancy in that unequal partnership, the Master of Stair stayed close to King William in England, or in his camp in Flanders, transmitting his sovereign's will by letter to Melville and the Scots Privy Council. There can have been little doubt in the Master's mind that William considered the presence at one point of seven troops of horse and thirty-nine companies of foot in Scotland, at an annual charge of nearly £50,000, as a scandalous waste of assets. The fact that they were being paid so irregularly as to reduce several units to near-mutiny weighed in the balance not at all.[5]

The obvious policy for a man anxious to have the good will of William of Orange was to try to secure a formal submission of the recalcitrant and conspicuously Jacobite Highland chiefs, as a precondition for the transfer of troops from Scotland to Flanders. In practice, the withdrawal of some of the best Scottish regiments such as the Cameronians preceded any satisfactory settlement in the Highlands. It became essential for the government to play a weakening hand boldly. The Earl of Breadalbane had, at Achallader, offered the Jacobite chiefs very reasonable terms. Lochiel, who was related to Breadalbane, appears to have been an early supporter of the terms, if indeed he was not also part-author of them. There were however infuriating delays in securing the public adherence of the Jacobite chiefs to the Achallader terms, mainly because of the mischievous manoeuverings of MacDonell or MacDonald of Glengarry. Egged on by Breadalbane's political enemy Atholl, he tried to exploit the proposed settlement by denouncing Breadalbane as a traitor to King William. To set a deadline, insisting that the Jacobite chiefs swear an act of allegiance to William by the first day of January 1692, was perfectly sensible behaviour on the part of the government, and everyone knew that it would have to unleash a general offensive if its deadline was widely spurned. Any other course would have earned universal contempt. In fact, as soon as it became clear that the government meant what it said, the chiefs fell into line. Their outrageous behaviour in previous months had largely been the result of their shrewd appreciation of the lack of means and will on the other side. Glengarry's submission was particularly gratifying to the new regime, which correctly identified him as the arch trouble-maker.

It seems to have been the Master of Stair who single-handedly resolved not to leave well alone, but to try to rub in the government's success by an act of exemplary frightfulness against a small clan which had technically failed to meet the requirement for an oath of allegiance by 1 January. The clan was that of the MacDonalds or MacIans, of Glencoe, whose aged chief had tried to take the oath before Colonel Hill at Fort William on the last day of December 1691, and had discovered too late that he needed a civil officer of the Crown rather than a military one. Finding an appropriate and willing officer in the shape of a sheriff-depute, Campbell of Ardkinglass, required another week. Sir John Dalrymple, Master of Stair, had become the sole secretary of state responsible for Scotland in December 1691, but he was under heavy criticism for the way his policies were working out, and the Glencoe people seem to have become the focus of his mounting paranoia. They were no angels. Even by Highland standards they had a bad reputation as thieves and plunderers. Rightly or wrongly, for the matter was and is controversial, then and now, Dalrymple regarded them as papists as well as desperadoes. This may explain his lack of similar animus against the equally cheeky Macleans of Duart, but the real attraction of the MacIans was that they were small, weak and accessible.

Glencoe, lying as it did just south of Lochaber and accessible from the seaward side *via* Linnhe and Loch Leven, as well as on the landward side *via* the Moor of Rannoch, was, with its towering mountain ramparts to the north and south, more a potential trap than a natural fortress. It was lethally close to Fort William. Troops from Colonel Hill's Regiment and from the Earl of Argyll's Regiment, under the command of Robert Campbell of Glenlyon, who had been ruined by the depradations of the MacIans, closed in during the bitter weather of February 1692. Disgracefully abusing the hospitality they had been offered, the soldiers rose against their hosts in the early hours of 13 February. The massacre was a botched affair from which the bulk of the clan escaped. Breadalbane was appalled when he heard of the business, seeing clearly that it was likely to prove entirely counter-productive. The Master of Stair was widely recognised to be the principal perpetrator of the crime, though Sir Thomas Livingstone, Mackay's successor as Commander-in-Chief Scotland, clearly knew all about the plan. Hill must have known what was afoot, though that pious and devoted soldier probably had little relish for it, and King William must have had more than an inkling of the implications of papers he signed. They were all protected by a traditional British whitewash job which dragged on until 1695. Though this was neither the first nor the most serious of Highland massacres, it was politically the most expensive, a pure gift to Jacobite propagandists.[6]

On the ground in the key area of the central Highlands, the massacre totally destroyed government credibility. So far from being intimidated, Lochiel, the nearest chief threatened by the gesture of massacre, sent immediate orders to his people to drive out any soldiers quartered on them. Neighbouring clans followed suit and a defensive alliance was discussed. The surviving MacDonalds of Glencoe, led by the late chief's two sons, gave an example to all. Far from being daunted, they sent their women and children to safety, and stood to arms, actually rallying additional supporters to their war parties. In the words of an early eighteenth-century writer who had direct access to the family traditions of the Camerons of Lochiel:

> The detestable authors of this barbarous massacre were so scandalized and affronted by the general voice of mankind, that they thought fitt to proceed no further, and evacuated the Highlands of all their troops except such as were posted in strong houses and other garrisons; whereby, the chiefs finding themselves secure, proceeded no further in their intended confederacy.[7]

The immediate results of the massacre of Glencoe were thus very paradoxical. Attempted genocide proved the prelude to a not unreasonable accommodation based on the Jacobite chiefs withdrawing their open challenge to the regime, and on the government pulling its troops out of their country. The commander of Fort William, with his regiment in garrison, kept an eye on Sir Ewen Cameron of Lochiel to make sure that he did not go back on the Achallader agreement. Lochiel kept an eagle eye on the garrison, to make sure that it accepted the minimum mobility which was the price of the Master of Stair's incompetent villainy. The balance was extremely fragile. Lochiel was known to have had extensive and amiable dealings with the Duke of Perth, James VII and II's principal servant in Scotland, and his main contact man with the Highland clans. Perth was exiled by the Revolution. His son Lord Drummond returned to Scotland, appearing before the Privy Council in February 1695 to give £1,000 sterling security for his own good behaviour. As he had come from the Jacobite court in a France currently at war with the three kingdoms of the British Isles, the attitude of the Privy Council was quite reasonable. Then in 1696 came the exposure of the deadly serious Jacobite plot to assassinate King William at Turnham Green near London, as a prelude to a French invasion of England, and an English Jacobite rising. The exiled James had certainly infiltrated a number of predominantly Roman Catholic professional soldiers from his service into London, to stiffen the expected rising, and some of these were involved in the plot, though it is clear that James himself never countenanced the murder of William.[8]

The natural result of the exposure of the plot was a massive surge of popular sympathy for William of Orange. Probably to the surprise of the reserved little Dutchman a red-cockaded General Association for King William sprung up. It was widely supported in England, and also in the American colonies where American Englishmen took the Principles of the Glorious Revolution vastly more seriously than the cynical wordly-wise wheeler-dealers of Westminster or the Court of St James. Jacobites were virtually an extinct breed in New York or Rhode Island by 1690, but in Britain the hunting of Jacobites, Tories, and papists became for a spell a popular passion. This heightening of the levels of ideological awareness, and by implication of ideological conflict, in British society was extremely unwelcome to a realistic pragmastic like Sir Ewen Cameron of Lochiel. He was trying to work out a tolerable pattern of co-existence with the second-occupation regime at Inverlochy in his lifetime. He had never really tried to drive out that garrison by main force. Indeed his biographer says that when Colonel Brayne first came in 1654 to Inverlochy, with his very formidable force and very adequate supplies to sustain his beachhead, Lochiel had decided within twenty-four hours that the main English position was already too strong to assault.[9] More than forty years later, in the aftermath of the massacre in Glencoe, Lochiel had even less interest in a head-on clash with the garrison at Fort William.

He retained his own political preferences, but the fact was that the odium and embarrassment created by the massacre put Westminster heavily on the defensive in dealing with its subjects, and this, as usual, produced a far more realistic and reasonable style of government. The Scots Privy Council, for example, allowed various individuals who were included in General Buchan's final surrender terms to remain in Scotland without taking the requisite oaths to the new regime because Grant of Freuchie interceded for them on the grounds that the oaths presented insuperable psychological and moral problems for them, or in the language of the time that they were 'not clear to swear'. There was nothing Machiavellian in Grant's intercession. His Williamite loyalties were of the deepest dye. Moderation in fact achieved what massacre had not. Glengarry judged it expedient to surrender his house at Invergarry without a struggle to a government force, while even Sir John Maclean of Duart went to London, where he found favour and looked like becoming a real adherent of the Revolution government, until a sudden swing in his emotions carried him across the English Channel and into the exiled Jacobite court at Saint-Germains.[10]

Little wonder that in the aftermath of the unsuccessful assassination plot Lochiel bent over backwards to be on good terms with the elderly governor of Fort William. Colonel Hill did not retire until 1698, but his final years were eased by presents of game from Lochiel, not to mention invitations to hunt in Cameron territory, and the regular presence of the Cameron chief at festivities in the fort. There is absolutely no need to assume that Sir Ewen's presence at the officers' drinking parties was a super-subtle device to cover heightened levels of plotting for his beloved King James. Precious little such plotting was going on, and as the war between the British kingdoms and the France of Louis XIV ground down towards a peace of temporary exhaustion in 1697, only a fool, and few Highland chiefs came into the category, would have imagined that plotting stood much chance of success.[11] Lochiel was trying, successfully, to preserve a post-1692 situation which suited him well, and which gave to the chiefs of Glen More a very large measure of local autonomy.

The use to which that autonomy was put at the southern end of the glen was eminently sensible, and even the puckish Glengarry behaved himself in the central part of the glen in the 1690s. The northern parts of Glen More were, however, entering a period of extreme turmoil in the same period, because they lacked the underlying stability in land ownership and political ascendancy without which it was extremely difficult for these communities to stop the outside world from interfering in their daily lives. As it happened, it was not the English government which was the aggressor, but a leading figure in the magnate politics of a still nominally autonomous Scotland.

The succession to the extensive and strategically placed estates of the Lords Fraser of Lovat had become a bone of contention because of what amounted to a genetic crisis in the main line. Hugh Fraser had succeeded as a minor less than three years old when his grandfather died. His own father had died shortly after his birth in March 1643. The estates were managed for the youngster by his uncle Colonel Alexander, Tutor of Lovat, who prudently made submission to the triumphant Cromwellian regime in the Great Glen. The Tutor of Lovat came into the fort at Inverness with his brothers Captain Thomas Fraser of Beaufort and Captain James Fraser, a mercenary soldier fresh from the wars in Germany, and gave guarantees for the behaviour of all his clan. In so doing he was only going along with the policy adopted by Seaforth, MacLeod of MacLeod and Glengarry. Like all these clan leaders, the Lovat Frasers managed to turn themselves back into loudly loyal royalists after the Restoration in 1660. The young heir, finding it difficult after he returned from St

Andrews University to make the Tutor surrender his powers and give due account of his stewardship, consulted the rising and rascally young lawyer Sir George Mackenzie of Tarbat late in 1659. It proved a fatal step, for Tarbat decoyed the immature youth of sixteen into a grossly unequal match with his own sister, Anne Mackenzie, who may have been fully twenty years older than her new spouse. The Fraser gentry, who had every reason and right to be consulted on so grave a matter, had been effectively cheated.

The marriage proved unhappy, but did produce offspring of whom only one was a son, born with a large black birth mark on his upper lip, and called in Gaelic Mac Shimidh Ball-dubh, the black-spotted son of Simon.* In Lowland parlance he was Hugh, Master of Lovat. His mother's death in 1670 might have cleared the way for his father's remarriage and the procreation of more sons to render the succession stable, but in fact the unhappy young lord himself died in 1672, and his funeral was generally recognised as the beginning of a most difficult period in the history of his clan. Its cadet branches were in an equally parlous condition, as it happened. The Tutor had no male heir, while the Frasers of Philorth, Strichen, Inverallochy, and Durris were all reduced to one son apiece. Hugh, the new Lord Fraser of Lovat therefore succeeded to his estates as a boy, virtually a prisoner of his Mackenzie relatives. His uncle, Sir George Mackenzie of Tarbat, soon to be ennobled as the first Earl of Cromartie, assumed the status of guardian, moved the boy to his own stronghold of Castle Leod in Strathpeffer north-west of the Aird, and transferred the active management of the Lovat estates to his own chief, the Earl of Seaforth. Seaforth's factor saw to the day-to-day running of the property – to the unconcealed fury of Thomas Fraser of Beaufort, James Fraser of Brea, Simon Fraser of Inverallochy, and Thomas Fraser of Strichen, all of whom knew that by normal custom they should have been consulted as to the arrangements made for Hugh, and that they should certainly have had the local management of the estates during the minority. A major struggle between the Fraser gentry and the expansionist Mackenzies was virtually inevitable.

Since the gentry were for decision-making purposes the clan, the Frasers were probably right in seeing Tarbat's sustained hostility to their kindred as a threat to the very survival of Clan Fraser. What made the situation worse was the poor physical and mental calibre of the current Lord Lovat, allied to the systematic asset-stripping on his estates which became the Tarbat policy. As it was, Tarbat could not but acknowledge considerable debts to his nephew, so he reached out for an alliance with

*Mac Shimidh, meaning son of Simon, had become a fixed patronymic for the Frasers of Lovat.

another powerful magnate house which might lend its political and military muscle to the Mackenzie side in the great game being played out on the Fraser lands. He was able to exploit his control over Lord Lovat's marriage plans to secure just such an alliance when in 1687 he arranged for the young Hugh Fraser to marry Lady Amelia Murray, daughter of the Marquis of Atholl. The lady's brother was to become the first Duke of Atholl, and by any standards the Murray Earls, Marquises and Dukes of Atholl were a magnate house of the very first rank in Scotland. They were the holders of the mighty Regality of Atholl, which dominated Highland Perthshire. Normally resident in Dunkeld, where the River Tay breaks through the southern edge of the Highland Boundary Fault, they possessed as their principal fortress the great castle at Blair Atholl, which dominated access to Deeside through Glen Tilt, as well as a major route north to Inverness by the passes into Speyside. The Regality of Atholl, which like the other major Scottish regalities traditionally excluded the royal authority for most matters other than high treason, had as its *caput* the small village of Logierait. Here, in an iron-age fort, met the Council of Atholl, composed of the holders of the baronies which were the basic building blocks of such bigger political units as regalities. After the Revolution of 1688 Lord John Murray, later Earl of Tullibardine, heir to the Marquis of Atholl, stood high in favour with William of Orange, being both King's Commissioner to the Scottish parliament and a Secretary of State.

Hugh Fraser, caught between two extremely assertive families like the Mackenzies of Tarbat and the Murrays of Atholl, would appear to have been by common consent, including his own, a man of weak will and feeble body. His marriage was unhappy, produced only daughters, and was terminated by his own premature death, hastened by dissipation, in 1696. In his contract of marriage, signed when he was about eighteen years of age, Hugh Fraser had consigned his estates to his issue male, in default of whom he consigned them to his daughters, with a proviso that they go undivided to an eldest daughter marrying a gentleman of the name of Fraser. With an Edinburgh advocate like Tarbat as the principal curator of the youthful bridegroom, it is hardly surprising that this arrangement was duly confirmed by royal charter in 1694. However, it went clean against the original rights and feudal conditions of the lordship, which had always been held in strict male succession, basically in order to ensure that if the main chiefly family died out, the lordship would be taken over by one of the cadet houses of the name. By a deed dated 26 March 1696, Hugh in fact repudiated his former arrangements for the succession, on the ground that they had been extorted from him by unscrupulous relatives exploiting his ignorance and over-compliant nature to violate the fundamental law of his inheritance. He now assigned the succession to the true Fraser heir male, disponing the estates, failing heirs-male of his own body, to his grand-uncle, Thomas Fraser of Beaufort, and his heirs-male. Thus the succession in 1696 was disputed. From the point of view of Clan Fraser, that was a far more desirable situation than simple acquiescence in a Mackenzie putsch reinforced by the Atholl interest.

Thomas Beaufort promptly adopted the title of Lord Fraser of Lovat, and his remarkable second son Simon, because of the assumed death of his elder brother Alexander, simultaneously adopted the style of Master of Lovat. Alexander probably led a group of Frasers who rallied to the standard of John Graham of Claverhouse, Viscount Dundee in the first of all the main Jacobite risings proper in 1689. The sources are not wholly reliable for the composition of Dundee's small army, and Fraser of Foyers is recorded as commanding the Stratherrick men. They cannot have been very numerous, for they are not recorded as one of the bigger units, such as the 600 Camerons under old Sir Ewen and his son John, or even Glengarry's 2–300. They were presumably one of the smaller groups from Glen More, like the 100 men led by Grant of Glenmoriston. In any case the Lovat tradition which places Alexander at the battle of Killiecrankie does not suggest that it was this escapade which led to his subsequent disappearance. The Treaty of Achallader closed the Jacobite campaign in such a way as to secure most participants from legal harassment by a Williamite regime. It appears to have been a subsequent unlucky homocide which forced Alexander to flee to Wales, where he died childless. It was therefore Hugh Fraser, and Simon, Master of Lovat, who not only asserted their rights to the titles, but also, far more significantly, seized control of the estates with the active cooperation of the resident Fraser gentry. Their Mackenzie and Murray rivals claimed the succession to both title and property for the child Amelia Fraser, eldest daughter of the previous holder. The Earl of Tullibardine had the gift of the child in marriage and physical control of her person in one of his Atholl strongholds, to which she had been rapidly moved when it became clear that the Beauforts meant to play their moves without too nice a respect for Edinburgh-based law.[12]

Some sort of compromise might have removed the danger of open violence, but it would have had to have involved marrying Amelia to the aggressive and articulate Simon of Beaufort, a man with a precocious genius for making enemies. Tullibardine seems to have abandoned plans for marrying the girl to his own son, but he was damned if he would marry her to Simon. He selected instead of his own son the son of another Fraser peer, in the hope of splitting the groups backing the Beauforts by offering them 'a true Fraser'. The lucky man was to be the Master of Saltoun, heir to Lord Saltoun. It was a shrewd move, as well as an emotionally satisfying one. Tullibardine and Simon hated one another. Simon had accepted in 1695 a commission in Tullibardine's regiment. As a lieutenant of grenadiers and later a captain in King William's army Simon was hardly, despite a great deal of subsequent effort to talk the episode away, a youthful martyr for Jacobitism. Nor did he make any public protest, as several of his brother officers did, when required to take the oath of abjuration denying allegiance to James VII and II after the assassination plot of 1696. All his life, Simon was good at swearing cartloads of oaths, if he needed to. The real point of conflict between him and his colonel, Tullibardine, was not political allegiance, but property. Simon quite rightly repudiated with scorn and some threats of personal violence an attempt to cajole, bribe and bully him into renouncing his inheritance. Simon Fraser did indeed harbour Jacobite sentiments, among many others. Since he also leaked like a sieve both in conversation and in correspondence, Tullibardine had tried to break Captain Fraser with a court-martial for treason, but it was so widely known that personal venom lay behind the charges that Sir Thomas Livingstone, the Commander-in-Chief Scotland, quashed them. Compromise was simply not possible between Simon and Tullibardine. It had to be a fight to the finish.

Tullibardine's next move was ill-considered. He persuaded Lord Saltoun to tour the Fraser country in company with a younger son of the Marquis of Atholl, Lord Mungo Murray. They visited the dowager Lady Lovat at her seat at Castle Downie, but their main aim was clearly to rally supporters and win over waverers among the Fraser gentry. They needed an escort big enough to frighten off the Beauforts, who had already warned Saltoun not to come. As it was they were kidnapped by Simon and a party of Stratherrick men at Bunchrew near Inverness, and immured in the castle of one of their own supporters, Fraser of Fanellan. The Scottish government dared not move against Simon, for fear of what he would do to his prisoners. In Edinburgh the Lord Advocate was talking about threats to burn them alive. This was the sort of thing which Spanish *conquistadors* did do to unfortunate Inca opponents in Peru in the sixteenth century, but Simon Fraser was no such cold-blooded sadist. On the other hand, he was a hot-blooded megalomaniac, and profoundly insensitive to all emotions other than his own, to which of course he was hypersensitive. Saltoun was shown a vast gallows outside the window of his prison and told he had forty-eight hours to live. He was upset; very upset. Though Simon probably never seriously intended to kill him, Saltoun swore blood-curdling oaths renouncing all interest in the Lovat estates. After a further period of confinement on an islet in the Beauly River, Lord Mungo and he were released. Curiously enough, Lord Saltoun had lost all interest in marrying his eldest son to young Amelia. The Beauforts had done what they had to do, at the price of leaving themselves open to serious legal charges.[13]

However, there was no reason for the Beauforts to despair. If convictions were secured against them, pardons could conceivably be obtained cancelling any such convictions, and everybody knew that both convictions and pardons depended on the game of high politics. Tullibardine's Atholl interest was only one amongst four major magnate interests; Atholl, Argyll, Hamilton and Queensberry. Within the Scottish ministry Tullibardine was rather isolated, and by 1696 was deep in a power struggle with Queensberry and Argyll. The bitter competition between these interests has been adduced as evidence of the total unworkability of Scottish politics between the Revolution of 1688 and the Act of Union. Judged by a standard so deprecating of all faction, the Westminster parliament of the day would have qualified for the scrap heap, and the fact is that viewed from the grass roots of the Scottish counties, the divisions between the top politicians were essential to the preservation of anything like an open political dialogue between the centre and the localities. To put it crudely: if you quarrelled with one you could always appeal to another. As we shall see when we turn to the political frustrations of Grant of Grant in the 1730s and 1740s, the total ascendancy of the Argyll interest at one stage in the politics of post-Union North Britain bred extremely dangerous tensions in the body politic. Yes, Tullibardine could use the central courts in Edinburgh to some extent to serve his own ends. They were, and are, highly susceptible to the deepest desires of the political masters who appoint them, but at least in the seventeenth century nobody had any illusions about this. The central civil court, the Court of Session, with its enormous potential for good or ill over property rights, was very sensibly regarded as far too potent to have its membership dictated by a single political faction. Efforts were normally made to 'balance' its composition and the deadlock over the exceptionally influential position of Lord President of the Court of Session (because of widespread opposition to Tullibardine's candidate) kept it vacant between 1696 and 1698.[14]

Nor were the Beauforts and their supporters in any doubt as to where to look for succour. At the height of the crisis of 1697 a letter purporting to come from Thomas, Lord Fraser of Lovat, but from its bombast clearly from Simon's pen, was despatched to Argyll. Apart from Lovat, it was signed by Thomas Fraser of Struy, William Fraser of Culbokie, William Fraser of Foyers, William Fraser of Erchit, Alexander Fraser of Culduthel, John Fraser of Little Garth, and Thomas Fraser of Gortuleg. These holders of lands in the Fraser country repeated the allegation that Tullibardine was of a mind to marry the heiress to his own son, and insisted that rather than be so subjected to a stranger, they would fight. They appealed to Argyll implicitely to stop the excessive aggrandisement of a rival dynasty, and explicitly to contain a threat of civil war at the north end of the Glen More, and to ensure the attachment to the Argyll interest of 'his old relations, faithful friends and dependents and sword vassals' the Frasers. All in all it was not an unintelligent gambit which might eventually have succeeded but for an episode coyly referred to in the letter, where there was mention of 'a considerable advantage by my eldest son's being married to the Dowager of Lovat'.[15]

That unfortunate woman had fallen into the Beaufort net at the time of the seizure of Lords Mungo Murray and Saltoun. Though Simon's ideal matrimonial catch at this point in time would undoubtedly have been the young Amelia, his agile mind rapidly grasped the tactical advantages which would flow from a match with the mother if the daughter remained unattainable. The real question, from that day to this, is whether the lady was ultimately willing, or whether he achieved his ends by what amounted to forcible rape. There are arguments on both sides of the question. Those well disposed to Simon point out that there are reports of him living as man and wife with the Dowager Lady Lovat after the marriage ceremony was performed by a local minister, and even reports that she showed some reluctance to return to her own family afterwards. According to this school of thought the well-documented antics on the wedding night, such as one of Simon's henchmen slitting the bride's stays with his dirk while a piper played lustily to drown any protests, were simply an extreme form of the suggestive horseplay common when the wedding party performed the traditional rite of bedding the newly-weds.

On the other hand, there is a case to be made for the worst interpretation of the evidence, which is abundant and largely undisputed. The manhandling of a lady of such elevated birth caused a sensation, and the subsequent sustained legal offensive mounted by her family against Simon Fraser gave opportunity for even the humblest female servants to be summoned to give evidence before the High Court of Justiciary in Edinburgh as to what actually happened in the bedchamber. Translated out of Gaelic, the words of a young woman like Christian Maclean, servant to James Fraser of Reelig could become valuable copy for the considerable industry devoted to the publication of sanctimoniously salacious pamphlets. The key evidence, however, was probably that of 'Amelie Rioch, late Serviterix to Lady Lovat'. This sixteen-year-old was summoned at two in the morning to help undress the swooning Lady Lovat, who was already undressed partially. Her hair was down and her dress must have been stripped off for Amelie to see Fraser of Kinmonavie hold her up while Simon Fraser pulled down her petticoats. The pantomine over her buckram stays was not a preliminary to undressing her. Modern underwear had not been invented, and she was as mother naked below the waist when stripped of her petticoats as one of Simon's clansmen was when stripped of his kilt. Lady Lovat was sexually fully exposed in a room full of servants and Fraser lairds. When they turned her face down on the bed and held her arms above her head to facilitate slitting the laces on her stays, she was being placed in a more modest position than previously, and the final operation thus accomplished merely showed that Simon was a man for a comfortable ride. For the rest of his life he was to be haunted by the charge of being a rapist, and the balance of the evidence is against his furious denials.[16]

In any case, the whole episode, however interpreted, was political suicide. The Atholl family moved swiftly to put the machinery of the Scots Privy Council in motion against the Beauforts, and though opponents of the Atholl interest, like Argyll, were clearly sympathetic towards the offenders, they could hardly stand up for them in public. 'Letters of intercomuning' were issued in November 1697, forbidding any loyal subject to deal with the errant Frasers, for whom, dead or alive, a reward of 2,000 merks was offered. Simon had retired to the well-defended islet of Eilean Aigas in the Beauly River, where he held his bride. The heralds who acted as messengers of the Privy Council were reduced to sneaking in by night to leave their summons in a cleft stick on the bank opposite Eilean Aigas, or to uttering their legal threats at the safe distance of the market cross of the burgh of Elgin. Politically, however, Simon's isolation was crippling. Old Colonel Hill at Fort William told Forbes of Culloden that he thought Simon had taken leave of his senses.[17] Powerful figures in the Laigh of Moray, neighbours with whom Simon simply had to be able to live, like Campbell of Cawdor and Rose of Kilravock, interceded for the lady's release. In the end Simon had to give way. The evidence as to her emotions when she returned to her family is conflicting, and all sources are tainted with partiality. In the end, her feelings hardly mattered, for her family were bound to make sure she never saw Simon again, and with his last hostage gone, Simon was open to physical attack. It was not slow in coming.

As Lord John Murray, Secretary of State in Scotland, the Earl of Tullibardine had long been concerned with security problems in the area of the Great Glen. In January 1694 James Stewart of Ardvorlich had written to him, complaining of the prevalence of theft and blackmail, and proposing two solutions. One was that commissioners be appointed to administer justice in special circuit courts, held in the region. The other was that a new regiment, at least half of whose men were locals, should be added to the garrison at Inverlochy, and devoted primarily to police duties.[18] Colonel John Hill certainly agreed that justice courts sitting in Fort William might enable him 'to break the neck of theft', but the wise old colonel came to recognise by 1697 that the area he was supposed to keep watch over had settled down after the disturbances of the Revolution and was really pretty peaceable. The main threat to order lay in the quarrels of powerful men like Keppoch and Mackintosh. As for letters of fire and sword issued by the Edinburgh Privy Council, Hill was convinced that they were destructively anachronistic and almost always the result of political machination. He was right.[19]

With the seizure of Saltoun and Lord Mungo, the Earl of Tullibardine concerted plans with the Chancellor of Scotland, the Earl of Marchmont, for military moves against the Beauforts. Marchmont was in possession of letters from Simon Fraser, forwarded by Colonel Hill, in which Simon furiously charged his enemies with conspiring 'if God and good friends doe not prevent it, utterly to extirpet not only my fathers famillie, but the wholl name of Frazer'. He then made it clear that as long as he held hostages 'they would certainly suffer befor me or myne'.[20] However, there was a general conviction that, stripped of his human pledges, Simon was vulnerable in a way that Keppoch was not, even when Mackintosh did secure letters of fire and sword against him. February 1698 saw a significant force of perhaps 800 Atholl men, commanded by the Marquis himself, invade the Fraser country along with five troops of dragoons and 2–300 of Colonel John Hill's best infantry. It was clear that they could hardly be faced in open battle, and the Beauforts at one point fled to Skye. Since the father had married Sibylla, daughter of John MacLeod of MacLeod, Simon was moving into his mother's old home when he took refuge in Dunvegan Castle. There his father died in May 1699. Simon commemorated his chiefly virtues with a momument and inscription in Dunvegan kirkyard, and assumed the title of Lord Lovat. It was some slight compensation for his occupied estates, not to mention further legal humiliation in Edinburgh in September 1698 where father, son and twenty leading men of the clan were convicted of high treason, being sentenced to death and forfeiture of estates.

Such a trial, in the absence of the accused, was almost certainly technically illegal. The chieftans, tacksmen and other gentry of the Clan Fraser were being attacked by a characteristic combination of the two most aggressive, predatory, and unscrupulous groups in late seventeenth- and eighteenth-century Scotland – the peers and the Edinburgh advocates. Greedy for power, anxious to reverse the shift of economic power towards the middling groups in Scottish landed society in the late sixteenth and early seventeenth centuries, and on the whole profoundly unpatriotic and anxious to assimilate with the political and social style of the English peerage, the Scots peers found in the Edinburgh men of law their ideal 'doers'.

For the advocates, who were themselves overwhelmingly of landed extraction, the rewards for cooperating in the aggrandisement of the noble politicians were twofold. They made a lot of money out of legal fees. Secondly, they could the more conveniently pursue their campaign against the private jurisdictions which limited their influence. Their own particular sub-imperialism, rooted in the fact that they monopolised the appointments to the position of sheriff and to the bench of the central appeal courts, was to receive a massive boost with the Act of Union of 1707, and was to achieve final victory with the abolition of nearly all heritable jurisdictions after the '45. It was the misfortune of Clan Fraser that Mackenzie of Tarbat was a rival clan leader who was also both a peer and an Edinburgh advocate. George, Viscount Tarbat recognised that in the 1690s there were still physical limits to the reach of the politico-legal system he was so skilled at manipulating to his own advantage but, as he shrewdly observed, virtually all land which was worth appropriating, even in the Highlands, was open to pressure from the central government. The most cunning and elusive of clan chiefs could usually be stripped of his lushest estates before he fell back on the barren mountains where he was safe from pursuit. As Tarbat pointed out, chasing a skinned fox still capable of biting back was hardly worth the bother.[21]

The Atholl occupation obviously involved a systematic attempt to ravage the properties of those Fraser gentlemen well disposed to Simon's cause. The resulting resentment helps to explain the scale of support shown for Simon when he returned from Skye. When the Marquis of Atholl sent some 300 men led by his sons Lord James and Lord Mungo Murray to try to capture Simon in Stratherrick, the tables were turned when the local people rose against the invaders. They were surrounded and captured. The triumphant Simon was with difficulty dissuaded from mayhem – it would merely have confirmed his political isolation. The Lords James and Mungo were released while Simon threw himself on the mercy and support of Archibald, tenth Earl and after 1701 first Duke of Argyll, a fierce rival of Atholl and a man high in favour with William of Orange. On the advice of Sir James Stewart of Goodtrees, the Lord Advocate (or principal state prosecutor) in Scotland, Argyll eventually sent Simon Fraser beyond the effective jurisdiction of the Scottish central courts by dispatching him to Northumberland in the north of England. There at Chirton near North Shields, Argyll had a more or less permanent home where he lived with a lady friend at a safe distance from his estranged Duchess Elizabeth.

Argyll had had no great difficulty in persuading King William that there was a case for granting a pardon to Lovat for his 'political' offences. Everyone knew that he simply had to fight back as best he could against the offensive of the Murrays of Atholl. The stumbling-block to total rehabilitation was the rape charge. Allied to Tullibardine's considerable influence over a bench of judges in the High Court of Justiciary, many of whom had been appointed during Tullibardine's period in high office, the rape enabled the Atholl family to pin Simon on the judicial ropes and to hammer him with spirit-sapping blows. His 'marriage' was of course annulled. Then in February 1702 the Privy Council issued Letters of Intercommuning or a Commission of Fire and Sword against him, in much the same terms as it had in 1697. The death of William and the accession of Queen Anne early in March 1702 were decisive buffets of fortune for Lovat. Under Anne the Atholl interest rode high, and by failing to turn up to face trial in Edinburgh Lord Lovat had confirmed the popular opinion that he was guilty of rape. His financial resources were becoming strained. A spell abroad, both Argyll and Lovat agreed, would best suit Simon Fraser.

Before he left, that crafty man confirmed the loyalty of many Fraser lairds by granting them bonds for significant sums, payable in the future only if in the meantime they had remained true to his interest. Two of these bonds, one to Thomas Fraser of Struy, and another to Hugh Fraser of Kinmonavie, for 10,000 and 1,000 merks respectively, were dated 7 March 1702, the day before the accession of Queen Anne. Just before the '45, at a time when Simon was up to his neck in ambiguous dealings with Jacobite plotters, the Fraser lairds pressed for payment of the outstanding bonds. Their debtor then produced the wonderful argument that he had been in the grip of criminal insanity when he issued them. So deluded had he been, Simon wailed, that he had actually been plotting in favour of the exiled dynasty. The bonds were part of his preparation for the criminal folly of a Jacobite rising. Fortunately, now restored to pure pro-Hanoverian sanity, Lord Lovat could take advantage of the fact that the law did not allow for the collection of debts incurred for criminal purposes. It was upstaged by his final exit line (*dulce et decorum est pro patria mori*) on the stark proscenium of the scaffold in 1747, but on the date he produced it this flight of Lovatic forensic eloquence was probably the old thespian's best effort so far.[22]

His departure from London in May 1702 appears to have been a reluctant business. There was never much doubt as to where he would go if forced into exile, for his inability to bide his time patiently meant that he was almost bound to head for the government-in-exile at the Jacobite court at Saint-Germains in France. War having broken out between Queen Anne and Louis XIV, he could only approach Saint-Germains by a circuitous route through Holland and the southern Netherlands. Behind him he left a harassed but still defiant Fraser gentry and a triumphant Atholl interest. Families like the Frasers of Culduthel, known to be ardent Simonites, were hauled before Edinburgh courts for two or three months every year by vexatious actions raised by the Atholls. Though legally inconclusive, these cases were, as they were meant to be, financially ruinous for their victims. Interestingly, the Culduthels tried to secure support from the Duke of Gordon, the feudal superior of some of their lands, and he and his lawyers did what they could. However, the extent to which the Duke of

Gordon was out of political favour at the time when the Culduthels approached him may be deduced from the fact that he was then a prisoner in Edinburgh Castle. For such a one as he, it was like being in a bad, expensive hotel, and though it did not preclude political activity, it did not suggest that he had the ear of government.[23] Meanwhile the Atholl family had discovered another match for the Lovat heiress, Amelia, in the shape of Alexander, son of Sir Roderick Mackenzie, and grandson of Sir John Mackenzie of Tarbat. Sir Roderick had a judicial title – as a Senator of the College of Justice he was Lord Prestonhall; and he was also the brother of the first Earl of Cromartie.

The new suitor's father thus combined Mackenzie aggression and legal guile. Buying up certified debts against Lovat, he was able to secure legal judgements which conveyed the Lovat estates to himself, and the title to Amelia. Simon was not around to offer any defence. In the meantime, Prestonhall entailed the estate on his son whom he persuaded to adopt the name and style of Alexander Fraser of Fraserdale. Amelia was styled Lady Lovat, while their son was designated Master of Lovat. By 1706 Prestonhall's conceit and satisfaction at having stolen an ancient family's estate was so overweening that he executed a second deed of entail dismissing the need to adopt the Fraser name as one of several 'limitations and irritancies' which he wanted to sweep away. The Mackenzies were openly moving to establish another branch of their clanned power.[24]

Simon could do nothing to stop this, having over-reached himself yet again in the bizarre episode known as the 'Scotch Plot'. His arrival at the Jacobite court in 1702 plunged Simon Fraser into a depressing atmosphere ridden by faction. James VII and II was dead. His son James Francis Edward Stuart, 'James VIII and III', was a boy. Power, if that be the word, lay with the ultra-pious Queen Mother Maria Beatrice. The female members of the exiled royal house had always been particularly convinced of its private ideology: that they were martyrs for the Faith, and that despite the tendency of successive Holy Fathers to take refuge in fence-sitting and clouds of pious platitudes when pressed on the issue, the cause of Holy Church and that of the Stuarts was one. Quite serious steps were being taken towards having the late King James canonised,[25] and the Earl of Middleton, Secretary of State and head of the moderate 'compounder' faction had found it appropriate, shortly before Lovat's arrival, to be converted to the Roman Catholic faith by a vision of his late royal master. The episode carried the Queen Mother into transports of enthusiasm, confirmed Middleton's grip on the seals, and enabled him to pass an important adverse judgement on the new arrival. Simon Fraser struck the Secretary of State as a slippery rascal.

Not to be outdone, Simon who in any case had gravitated to the extreme and ultra-Catholic faction led by Middleton's rival Lord Perth, suddenly developed an intense interest in the state of his soul, and announced, in due course, the conversion which won the heart of Maria Beatrice and a passport from the dank and powerless piety of Saint-Germains to the court of the mighty Louis XIV at Versailles. There, schemes of invasion to restore the Stuarts to their three thrones had been debated for years. The more pious members of an ageing court were particularly keen on a dynasty they identified with the cause of Catholicism in Britain. Simon's main contribution seems to have been to direct this general enthusiasm towards Scotland, and to suggest breezily that what was needed was a Jacobite rebellion in his native land, timed to coincide with French intervention. What nobody could be sure of was how seriously the French would support a rising, but Simon clearly reckoned he had nothing to lose. Sent back to Scotland in 1703 to test the temperature of the water, he seems to have found much less enthusiasm for a rising than he had expected. Never at a loss, Simon then turned round and with a little doctoring of the letters he carried from the courts in France, tried to make something out of the trip by peaching on the hated Atholl dynasty, on the specious grounds that they were at the very core of a web of Jacobite intrigue. Whether the Scots politicians who appeared to swallow his bait so gullibly really believed his story is by no means clear. Argyll and Lord Leven, who first sponsored Lovat's 'revelations' to Queensberry, were as hostile to Atholl as Queensberry was, and they may well have been operating on the adage that any stick would serve to beat a dog. From Lovat's point of view the immediate advantage he gained was protection and support from Queensberry, and that was no small matter for a man against whom the Scottish Privy Council, under Atholl's influence of course, was busy launching punitive action. Besides, his ancestral estates must have seemed irredeemably lost, for MacLeod of MacLeod, head of Simon's mother's family, was about to marry a sister of Fraser of Fraserdale's wife, and this meant that even Simon's relatives were accepting the new claimants to the Lovat titles.

Nevertheless, Simon Fraser was inherently unlikely to succeed in his new role as a double agent, despite his appropriate lucubrations about the evils of Jacobitism and popery. He had broadened his charges to cover Atholl, the Duke of Hamilton (Atholl's brother-in-law), and the Duke of Gordon (who had once snubbed Simon). That some of these noblemen had indulged in improper correspondence is clear, but so had a high proportion of active Scottish politicians. With the capture of Sir John Maclean, who had acted as sponsor to Lovat at the Jacobite court in France, and who rashly tried to slip into England in an open fishing boat, in which his wife contrived to give birth, alternative sources of information became available. A committee of the House of Lords was set up to probe the whole business of what was known as the 'Scotch Plot'. Captured

Jacobites blabbed freely. Atholl defended himself with vigour. The final report, while endorsing the idea that there had been some sort of plot, emphatically cleared all the accused. By this time Simon Fraser had read the signs of a coming storm with sufficient shrewdness to deem it prudent to retire to the Continent. The Atholl interest had had no difficulty in depicting him as an unbelievably disreputable character and a totally unreliable witness: rapist, papist, Jacobite spy, and unscrupulous slanderer. That he had originally been deeply wronged by his enemies had to be concealed by saying that he was a landless opportunist, but since everything else was true, the first big lie slipped down easily.[26]

Atholl was made a Privy Councillor and Lord Privy Seal in April 1703, and by a diploma dated 30 June of that same year he was granted a ducal title. The new Duke of Atholl was created a Knight of the Thistle early in 1704. The sun of royal favour truly shone upon him, yet despite his staunch loyalty to Queen Anne, he fell out of favour in October 1704, being deprived of all his offices for conscientious opposition to proposals for an incorporating union between England and Scotland. Even in 1704 unconditional subservience to the Queen's ministers was what Westminster meant by 'loyalty'.[27] Simon Fraser was, however, in no position to try to wrest advantage from the turn of events, as he no doubt would have tried, despite in his heart sharing Atholl's views on any incorporating union. He had tried to worm his way back into favour at Saint-Germains and then Versailles by a great display of concern for the Catholic faith, but his track record over the 'Scotch Plot' nonsense more than justified the decision of Louis XIV and his Secretary of State Jean-Baptiste Colbert de Torcy to clap him in preventive detention.

The French were considering playing for such high stakes that they could not afford to have an arch double-crosser like Lovat loose, the more so as he had suggested the invasion plan with which they were toying, and its most influential exponent, Colonel Nathaniel Hooke, a future Baron Hooke in the Jacobite peerage, had acted as Lovat's principal contact in French official circles when Simon originally set off on his mission to Britain. Hooke had himself reconnoitered the Scottish scene. By 1705 he was assuring his French masters that there was plenty of support for 'James VIII' in Scotland and that the Kingdom was poorly defended, with only four significant fortresses – Edinburgh, Stirling, Dumbarton, and Inverlochy. He also had tales about the readiness of Lochiel and Glengarry to rise, but they were all at second hand. Lochiel had talked a lot about meeting Hooke, but somehow never turned up, no doubt, said Hooke, because of his great age.[28] By 1707 Hooke was proposing a remarkably shrewd policy. The youthful James should be spirited into Scotland by a force of fast Dunkirk frigates. Raising the kingdom, he should then repeat the tactics which had given the Scots victory over Charles I in the Bishops' Wars of the 1630s. In Hooke's words, once the Scots had risen: 'Nothing could hinder them from making themselves masters of the town of Newcastle, and of its coal mines, which are so necessary for firing in London, that the inhabitants of that place could not be deprived of them for six weeks without being reduced to the greatest extremity.'[29]

As it happened, this brilliant conception, capable perhaps of bringing England if not to its knees then certainly to the negotiating table, and of restoring the ancient independence of the Kingdom of Scotland, was completely botched in execution by the French in 1708. The naval and military commanders had doubts about the commitment of Louis XIV to anything more than a spoiling attack designed to tie up British resources for a limited period. When the fleet did reach the Firth of Forth, after several delays, it fled northwards at the sight of a Royal Navy squadron, despite the pleas and tears of James Francis Edward Stuart, who begged to be landed on the shores of his ancient kingdom, if necessary alone. The evidence is that that would probably have sufficed to give him control of Scotland.[30]

However, the background planning for this enterprise goes far to explain the determination of the French court to keep Lovat out of the way in Bourges, Angoulême and then Saumur. His voluminous correspondence shows him frantically trying to make interest with Jacobite worthies such as the Marshal Duke of Berwick (the bastard son of James VII and II) and Cardinal Gualterio, Protector of the English Nation at Rome and pensioner of France. Always his aim was release. Little wonder that in 1707–8 his friends were urging him to have patience and keep quiet, for attracting attention at that point was counter-productive. The passing of the crisis of 1708 brought no change. The only consistent ally Simon won was the not very prosperous Marquis de la Fréziliére who chose to recognise kinship with the, originally Norman, Frasers. He died in 1711 leaving a son who hoped Lovat would help him rather than offering aid to Lovat himself.[21]

Clan Fraser was in fact slowly sinking. It had maintained a spirited guerrilla war against the Mackenzies in the sense that Simon had been able to collect the rents on most of the Lovat estates, and so to terrorise the chamberlains of the rival claimants that they could not lift any rent from their respective areas. When he left the country his brother John carried on the battle, moving around Stratherrick with a group of thirty or forty 'loose and broken men', and maintaining a garrison of young men at Beauly, 'the heart of the country of Aird'. He collected cattle, sheep, and meal in place of cash rent. He constantly harried a small military force sent to protect Hugh Fraser and Captain John Mackenzie, 'conjunct bailie and chamberlain' to his arch enemy Alexander Mackenzie of Prestonhall, thinly and temporarily disguised as Fraser of Fraserdale , and he handed out rough treatment to gentry like Fraser of Eskadale, who were tempted to defect to the Mackenzie interest. However, the Scots Privy Council eventually poured substantial troop reinforcements into the area, so when John elected to share Simon's exile, and indeed imprisonment, he was not so much demonstrating brotherly love as admitting that he had lost a war and had nowhere to go.[32]

It was the quite exceptional set of circumstances generated by the 1715 rising which alone enabled Clan Fraser to make a come-back. The Fraser gentry, like everyone else in Scotland early in 1714, knew that a Jacobite rising was in the wind. For long they had assumed the rightful Lord Lovat to have died in a French prison, but John Fraser had returned in 1713 to tell them that Simon lived. Alexander Fraser of Phopachy and Major James Fraser, a younger brother of Fraser of Culduthel, called together four other heads of families: Alexander Fraser of Culduthel, Hugh Fraser of Foyers, Hugh Fraser of Struy, and Major Fraser of Castle Leathers. Together they resolved to send John Fraser to Skye for his own safety, and also, one suspects, to have a fall-back position if they could not resurrect Simon as their chief. They knew Queen Anne was dying and 'they were persuaded upon King George's accession there would arise some disturbance in Britaine, and if Simon could be stolen out of France, he might come to fish in drumly waters.'*

The point was that the Mackenzies, from Seaforth himself to the *soi-disant* Fraser of Fraserdale, shared the general revulsion of the Scottish ruling class from the Act of Union and the House of Hanover. They went into the rebellion when the Earl of Mar finally triggered it off, and of course they paid the penalty of failure. It proved not to be an obliterative penalty. Nobody really wanted to break the pattern of polycentric balance between the major clans, and Seaforth was able to make his peace with the government by 1726. Nevertheless, any question of further Mackenzie expansion was ruled out, if the Frasers backed Hanover, and Hanover won. The Fraser lairds who decided to wheel Simon back on stage despite the fact that he was 'very low in his person', must have known this, for before they sent Major Fraser to France, they made contact with Sir Peter Fraser of Durris in Aberdeenshire, a man personally known to King George by reason of his three years' residence at the court of the Electorate of Hanover. When Simon Fraser broke out of his not very rigorous imprisonment at Saumur and returned first to England with the dauntless Major Fraser, he was coming back to do a job.[33]

Despite his own deep-seated political ambiguity, that job was to jump on the Hanoverian bandwagon, if it was rolling, and finally repel the Mackenzies from the north end of Glen More. By a mixture of luck and

*'Drumly' means troubled or muddy.

skill he achieved his purpose. The paradox was that after the '15 the area was more stable than it had been for a long time, in that the last great predatory assault by an outside clan had been repelled. Westminster, itself the source of endless mischief in the central Highlands, reverted to its only legitimate task – ensuring that the clans did not interfere in Lowland politics by the use of force. As for government, in day-to-day terms there was enough of it, but it was mainly in the private sector, for the clans were perfectly capable of governing themselves. That Lovat himself was by 1721 trying to bombard George I with long complaints about the systematic persecution of himself and his ultra-Hanoverian clan by a diabolical combination of the Scots law officers of the government and rebel Jacobite plotters, was merely a manifestation of Simon's paranoia, and a reminder that if the Fraser gentry saw Simon as a means to an end, he saw them as a springboard from which he should vault into prominence in British politics. So far the tension between Simon and his most important followers had been creative. In the very long run it was to turn destructive.

5 *The 'Disaffected Clans' from the '15 to the Era of General Wade*

That Scotland was seething with unrest in the period immediately after the Union of 1707 is abundantly clear. The Scots had been hi-jacked into an unwelcome political embrace by a conspiracy between Westminster and their own venal and self-regarding aristocracy. The new structures did not work to the immediate economic advantage of the Scots. Scottish national pride was offended by an undisguised endeavour, in the long run largely successful, to extinguish Scottish identity. They violated even the most moderate hopes for continued political development in the tradition established in Scotland by the Revolution of 1688–90. Neither in intent nor in practice were the forty-five MPs or sixteen so-called representative peers from North Britain serious representatives of the regions and burghs of Scotland. The vast majority of them throughout the eighteenth century went to Westminster to better themselves by selling their political acquiescence to English politicians in exchange for pecuniary and political favours. None of this would greatly have mattered if the Scottish ruling classes had maintained a united front in favour of the Union. If Westminster consistently offered them gratifications inconceivable in a purely Scottish context, so much the worse for Scotland. The leading Scots politicians were on the whole not very interested in the impact of the new common market and common political institutions on the bulk of Scotsmen, provided that their own privileged existence and standards of living were assimilated with those of the ruling élites of South Britain, whom they so much envied.

By 1714 it was quite clear that this process of assimilation had failed to occur on a sufficient scale. The magnates of Scotland had assumed that they would enter the House of Lords by either holding English peerages, or by obtaining peerages of the United Kingdom after 1707. To their fury, in a key case involving the Duke of Hamilton in 1711, the House of Lords refused, quite improperly, to allow Scots lords to take their seats on the strength of such peerages. The sixteen places for representative peers, which the magnates had assumed would be consolation prizes for second-raters, suddenly became the only way to Westminster for a Scots peer. Notoriously, the elections for the sixteen places were totally manipulated by Westminster through the device of the 'King's List'. Backed by government patronage and pressure, the list was irresistible, and inclusion on it a virtual licence to be elected. In 1719 the leading English politicians of the day, Stanhope and Sunderland, proposed a Peerage Bill which would have deprived the sovereign of the power to create peers except to replace extinct titles. It would have replaced the sixteen Scots elected peers by twenty-five hereditary Scots members of the House of Lords. Robert Walpole, then out of office, led a chorus of opposition which destroyed the bill, which was seen as a partisan measure, but in 1721 John Duke of Argyll and Greenwich was unabashed about his record of support for the measure. He pointed out to Lord Grange that all the peerage elections in Scotland achieved was a facility for the Court interest to bring in whoever it pleased.

The Scots nobles were also offended when the Scots Privy Council was abolished suddenly in 1708 for purely electoral reasons. It was a body which not only provided places for the aristocracy, but which was also quite essential for effective executive action, especially on security, in North Britain. Gentle and simple alike tended to resent the new Customs and Excise service introduced into Scotland after 1707, and the resentment often assumed violent forms. Scots Episcopalians were disgruntled over the Presbyterian settlement of 1690 in the Kirk by Law Established, while Presbyterians resented the restoration of lay patronage by parliamentary statute in 1712. Scots of all shades of opinion were shocked to find that Westminster could and did breach the Act of Union with impunity. It may be that the immediate economic impact of the Union was uncertain, but it was bound to disappoint expectations because such unreasonable, not to say absurd expectations had been encouraged by pro-Union propagandists like Daniel Defoe, the novelist.[1]

By 1714 it was clear that the Union had been a political boon to the Jacobites. Only they were prepared to use the force which alone could break it. The question was not so much whether a rebellion would break out, as when. With the accession of the alien Hanoverian dynasty, and the virtual Whig *putsch* in central government which accompanied it, political tension mounted to unendurable levels in the Highlands. The Duke of Atholl wrote to the Secretary of State, the first Duke of Montrose, in July 1715 pointing out that Highland Jacobites had made no secret for some time of their expectations that their king James Francis Edward Stuart, then still a young man, but doomed to be known in history as the Old Pretender, would be with them soon.

Atholl was appalled to think how little was being done by the government either to encourage Hanoverian supporters or to discourage Jacobites in the Highlands. He analysed Jacobite support in a very interesting way, dividing it into two main power blocks. There were the magnates like the Marquis of Huntly (heir to the Duke of Gordon), the Earl of Seaforth and Lord Drummond. All of these Atholl saw simplistically as papists. They would field perhaps 4–5,000 men for the Pretender. Then there were 'the disaffected clans'. Atholl described these as lying around Inverlochy and being capable of raising as many men again. The duke was particularly vexed about the state of the garrison at Inverlochy, which he believed held but a single regiment. He was in correspondence with the governor and was clear that unless reinforced Inverlochy would be in a poor state to face a crisis. As well as reinforcements for Inverlochy, Atholl wanted to see two regiments of foot and one of dragoons sent to Perth, whence they could march rapidly to almost anywhere in mainland Scotland.[2]

His Grace's views were far too realistic to have much chance of adoption by His Majesty's Ministers. As if that were not irritating enough, Atholl had known since January 1715 that there was serious talk of the return to Scotland of Simon Fraser, whom Atholl regarded as a political enemy, rapist, and general trouble-maker, not just for his violent handling of an Atholl female, but also for his machinations in the 'Scotch Plot'.[3] Atholl's fury was, however, not enough to delay Simon's return to the neighbourhood of Inverness. Neither end of Glen More was conducive to lowering the ducal blood pressure much in the summer of 1715. Montrose's awareness of the weakness of Hanoverian supporters in the Highlands was no doubt sharpened by the correspondence he maintained with Lord Reay, chief of the northern Mackays. Lord Reay had had to sell Strathnaver to the Earl of Sutherland as early as 1624. (Eric, the seventh Lord Reay (1797–1847) completed the process of land-selling which by his death left him with no land at all.) In 1715 the then Lord Reay was a fine example of the middle point of this process of decline and fall. His letters breathed financial embarrassment. He had bought arms for his clansmen at the death of Queen Anne, to guard against a Jacobite rising, but he and they were so impoverished that he had to sell them, with the result that at the end of 1715 he was asking to be given 200 stands of arms to make up the deficiency. He brightly suggested that to rescue him from bankruptcy, if a pension could not be produced, he should be given command of Inverlochy, to which he would lead a regiment of his Highlanders. The thought of Inverlochy as a form of outdoor relief for Clann Aoidh (as the Mackays were known in Gaelic) and its scapegrace chief Lord Reay was not acceptable to those in authority. It would, of course, have guaranteed instant trouble between Lochiel and his Camerons and these undeserving poor cousins from northern parts.[4]

In the event, the spark of rebellion did not break out in the tinder-box of the Central Highlands. Due entirely to the personal and political frustrations of the Earl of Mar, that architect of the Union and early sycophant of George I, the Jacobite standard was unfurled in the north-eastern margin of the Highlands, and as it snapped defiantly in the breeze on the Braes of Mar on 6 September 1715, it signified the start of much more than a Highland rising. Mar performed what subsequent British politicians christened a U-turn. He publicly announced that he had been mistaken in pressing the Union. That statement plus the still potent emotional appeal of Scotland's ancient exiled dynasty placed him securely at the head of something suspiciously like a national rising. The Duke of Argyll, the Whig commander who was to save the day for Hanover, believed that north of the Forth Jacobites outnumbered Hanoverian partisans by nine to one. Certainly Lowland burghs and Lowland lairds in the areas over which Mar's Jacobite forces rapidly asserted their control were just as inclined to active Jacobitism as the Highland areas. With a supportive rising in the north of England, the '15 was a deadly serious threat to the Hanoverian succession, even if the monstrous ineptitude with which the rebellion was directed eventually turned it into a priceless opportunity for precisely those unscrupulous Whig politicians who had done so much to provoke it, and so little to pre-empt it.

The crux of the crisis lay in a duel between two great Scots magnates, Argyll and Mar, for control of Stirling, the strategic key in the middle of the Lowlands without which a Jacobite army could not open the door to cooperation with its numerous sympathisers in southern Scotland and northern England. Inverlochy just was not near the vital heart of the '15. Mar had indeed been in touch with the chiefs of the Central Highlands before the rising, but in a manner calculated merely to add confusion to their counsels when he (literally) changed his coat and left London on a collier to lead a Jacobite rising in Scotland. Late in August 1715 Mar sent George I a fawning letter in which, after recounting the services rendered by himself and by his ancestors to the Protestant Succession, he assured the royal Guelph that 'your majesty shall ever find me as faithful and dutiful a subject and servant as ever any of my family have been to the crown'. Mar also let it be known, with characteristic modesty, that he just happened to be in possession of an address signed by many of the most powerful Highland chiefs, many of whom later rallied to the Jacobite standard in arms, in which they asked him to assure the government of 'their loyalty to his sacred majesty King George'.

There was nothing bogus about the address, apart from the sentiments it expressed. Mar really had organised such a document. The Duke of Montrose certainly knew about it. He also knew something about its fate as it was circulated in the Highlands. His information came through the regimental commander at Fort William, Sir William Gordon, a political soldier who doubled up as spy for Montrose in the hope that he might secure preferment through the Montrose interest. The height of Sir William's ambition was to be appointed Governor of Fort William, with all the power and perquisites normally going with the job. He knew that so elevated a position was normally reserved for one of higher social rank than himself, but he hoped that if the whole joint was not available, he might be allowed to carve off some of the perquisites. At first the news Sir William* had of the address was entirely reassuring. Campbell of Glendaruel had beavered his way round the Highlands north of Fort William securing signatures from virtually all the well-known chiefs and was in January 1715 believed to be on his way to Mull to secure the signature of some island worthies. The tone of local chiefs in dealing with the garrison commander was nothing if not deeply respectful; Lochiel and Keppoch both expressed appreciation of the 'clemency and goodness' with which George I had treated them and insisted that they meant to prove their appreciation by a dutiful and peaceful behaviour under his government. Within a fortnight Glengarry had written two letters to Sir William singing the same song. Apart from the fact that Rob Roy MacGregor *alias* Campbell, notorious Jacobite and *bête noire* of the Duke of Montrose, was known to have been in company with Lochiel and Glengarry before he moved to Badenoch, everything in the garden was lovely.[5]

Even more deceptive was the outcome of the election for the Westminster parliament which occurred early in 1715. The smooth succession of the Hanoverian dynasty to the twin thrones of Great Britain and Ireland had been followed by something very like a clean sweep for Whigs in central government. The Tory party had fatally alienated George I by its policy of making a separate peace with France in 1713, effectively ditching Britain's European allies, such as the Electorate of Hanover, to do so. In addition there was a stench of Jacobitism hovering over the Tory ranks, despite the fact that most Tories were not committed Jacobites, and it had been Tory leaders as much as Whigs who had organised the transfer of the crown to Hanover. The Duke of Montrose, who had been dismissed from office as Keeper of the Privy Seal by the Tories in 1713, and who was promptly reinstated as Secretary of State for Scotland by the Whigs in 1714, had as his first major task the management of the North British elections. Their outcome was deeply gratifying to him. The election of the so-called 'Representative' Peers was a farce. It was a nomination process organised round a government list of acceptable candidates. The odd mutiny did break out amongst the otherwise subservient noble electors, but no such unseemly fracas disturbed the bland proceedings of 1715. Montrose was even more pleased with the results in the forty-five Scotch

*This would appear to be Sir William Gordon of Dalpholly and later of Invergordon Bart. He was the son of a moneylender and had a not very reputable career as an MP attached to the Squadrone, which was the party of Montrose, and the rival party to the Argyll of Argathelian party in Scotland.

constituencies for the House of Commons. Those who had been at all unsound on the Protestant Succession in the previous parliamentary session fared badly. By normal reckoning forty out of the forty-five MPs returned were marked by zealous enthusiasm for the reigning dynasty and government.

It was all slightly too good to be true. That the very success of the Whigs in manipulating the excecutive and electoral processes to their own exclusive advantage was creating widespread resentment was clear. What Whigs counted on was the inability of anything short of armed force to reverse the process, and they could not see the Pretender hazarding his life at the head of a rising in Britain without substantial foreign support, which they knew was unlikely to be forthcoming, least of all from an exhausted France.[6] Sir William Gordon was a preoccupied man as he gazed out over the ramparts of Inverlochy in the spring of 1715, but his preoccupation was not with an impending Jacobite rising. He was vexed because Sir Robert Pollock had been promoted to the governorship of Inverlochy over his head, and because the new governor meant to pocket three-quarters of the perquisites in exchange for roughly a quarter of a working year actually on the job. Sir William, who counted on having to spend half his time in residence, and counted this unto himself for a virtue, thought his quarter cut of the perks a miserable deal.[7] The rumours which had been circulating among the clans in late 1714 and early 1715 about the coming of the Pretender with French troops and arms were in fact dying away, in part because they were so obviously unrealistic. Indeed, Sir William did not think it necessary to forward to the Secretary of State the detailed reports he had received about a conference between Lochiel and Struan Robertson, held somewhere in the peaty vastness of Struan's thieves' kitchen, the Moor of Rannoch. Both participants were known for their Jacobite proclivities, and General Wightman, the military officer immediately responsible for the Central Highlands, had been informed of the episode, but the general view was that nothing of any consequence or novelty had emerged from the talks.[8]

By the summer of 1715 a new current of unease began to stir in government correspondence. Sir Robert Pollock began to agitate about the ruinous state of his new command, Fort William, and the grossly rundown condition of its garrison, which nominally consisted of two full regiments, Hill's and Hamilton's. In practice a significant number of men were scattered in a series of outposts at places like Duart in Mull, where they were supposed to keep an eye on the local Macleans, notorious for not sharing the Whig views of their Campbell lairds. The forty-eight men on Mull were enough to be provocative, but too weak to be effective. Other outposts were at Invergarry, to keep an eye on the glen's MacDonells, and Eilean Donan Castle in Mackenzie country in Ross-shire. All were indefensible. None had even a secure water supply within them. They amounted to little more than a series of sacrificial Hanoverian lambs surrounded by Jacobite or potentially Jacobite wolves. Even the troops packed like sardines in the cramped unhealthy quarters of Fort William, with its decaying wooden shack dignified by the title of a garrison church, were better placed. Death and disease had reduced Hill's to a mere 162 effectives in Fort William, with another 48 in Mull. Hamilton's effectives numbered 178 in Fort William, with 37 in outposts. Two regiments of nominal establishment therefore amounted in practice to 340 men in the one defensible position. Nor was there any serious chance of reinforcement, for with post-war reductions in the British military establishment whole regiments were being spirited away to Ireland, to be hidden by transfer to the Irish establishment. Montrose urged the governor of Fort William to make up by his zeal and vigilance for the weakness of his garrison. It was a typical politician's reply, admirably designed to fob off anything except the harsher forms of reality.[9]

By July the government intelligence network in the Highlands was producing the most alarming reports. Pollock knew that the Jacobite gentry of the region were almost constantly in cabals with no good intention towards the government, but the rising tide of expectation amongst the 'vulgar' Highlanders at first rather puzzled him. They had some knowledge of rioting against the Whig regime in England, but that hardly seemed enough to buoy their hopes so high. Then came a spate of letters from correspondents, spelling out what were clearly signs of a coming rebellion. Sir John Maclean of Duart, that landless Jacobite intriguer, was known to have moved through Lochaber and Glengarry, where he conferred with Lochiel and Glengarry before moving on to Inverness to meet Seaforth. Before he left Glen More, crossing the Grampians to go to Blair Atholl, he was known to have devoted a great deal of energy to trying to swing the allegiance of Clan Fraser back to the Stuarts. It was generally believed that the leading men of the Frasers had been won over to Hanover by means of the interest and assiduous attention of the Duke of Argyll. Arms and ammunition were being bought, smuggled in, or made by Highland gunsmiths on an unprecedented scale. Emissaries of the Earl of Mar were known to be active in the Central Highlands, and rumours of the Pretender's impending arrival were ten a penny. Very real doubts were felt in Whig circles about the 'soundness' of the Duke of Atholl. His big hunting parties were feared to be what Mar's great hunting party later in the year did indeed turn out to be – a cover for the start of a rebellion. On the third of August, the very month when he resigned as Secretary of State, the Duke of Montrose wrote a frightened letter from Whitehall to Sir Robert Pollock at Fort William ordering him to put his troops on the alert, and promising that if he could hold his own for a short period one of three regiments being recalled from Ireland would be rushed north to reinforce him.[10] It was too late. Before the month of September was seven days old, the long-awaited, widely publicised, and eagerly expected rebellion was a reality.

Its centre of gravity lay in the eastern parts of the Highlands, and in the eastern Lowlands north of the Tay. There we have the testimony of the Hanoverian Commander-in-Chief in Scotland at the crisis of the rebellion, the Duke of Argyll, that Jacobite sympathisers were in an overwhelming majority. Jacobite support was notably widely based, ranging from Highland chiefs to Lowland peers and lairds. It was also very strong in the disgruntled and depressed trading burghs of the east coast. Argyll very sensibly moved to the key position around Stirling where the Firth of Forth and the extensive bogs and mosses around the headwaters of the river Forth constricted the southward path for a northern army to a space of narrow dimensions dominated by the mighty royal fortress of Stirling Castle, perched on its percipitous volcanic crag. Mar rapidly assembled an army far larger than that of his Whig opponent. From his camp at Perth on the Tay, he was well placed to move out for the encounter with Argyll which alone would do his business. He did not even need to win the action. Outnumbered by 10,000 to 3,300, Argyll knew full well that he could not hope to replace the casualties incurred in a hard day's fight. The Jacobite host would have simply ground the government force into dust, winning by default with the assault on the morning of the second day of battle. For the first few weeks of the rising this strategy seemed so obvious that it was natural to assume that Mar would concentrate almost exclusively on a rapid build-up of the forces under his personal command before using them as an irresistible battering-ram against the Whig barrier between him and the many Jacobite activists in the south of Scotland and the north of England.

Pollock was handicapped by the swift snapping-up of his detached outposts by the Jacobite clans around them, for this deprived him, as he had long foreseen it would, not only of troops but also of information, but he began to suspect that all the Jacobite chiefs of Lochaber and other neighbouring regions would simply assemble their men and march east to join Mar. The Fort William garrison was too weak to stop them: nor was it a target they needed to waste powder, shot and lives in assaulting, ill-provided though it was. Pollock had to watch as MacIan of Glencoe and his followers moved past the fort. Glengarry marched with several hundred men from Invergarry, carrying with him the Hanoverian regulars he had captured. Most humiliating of all was the report Sir Robert Pollock had to make on 28 October 1715, that Lochiel had ferried the bulk of his fighting strength across the waters of Loch Linnhe in the neighbourhood of the Corran Narrows, a little over eight miles south of the Fort

William garrison which was in no position seriously to trouble his lands in his absence.[11]

In fact Mar had thought of the chiefs of the Central Highlands at an early stage in his rising. On 1 September 1715 he sent a message 'to the Lairds of Glengary, Lochiel, Clanranald, Keppoch, Apin, Glenco, McDougal, and Glenmoriston', *via* the hands of Glengarry. In this letter he made his twofold appeal to loyalty to the ancient dynasty of Scotland, and to pure Scottish anti-Union patriotism. Only by restoring the Stuarts, he argued, could the thraldom of the Union settlement be broken. He then urged the chiefs to raise and arm their men and march immediately to join 'the Gentlemen of Argyleshire in the King's Interest'. From thence the assembled Jacobite western forces were to march on Glasgow, maintaining strict discipline so as not to alienate the countryside by uncontrolled plundering.[12] Mar did not fail to write to John Cameron of Lochiel, Younger, the acting head of Clan Cameron, expressing regret at the absence of John's father, Sir Ewen, from the main Jacobite camp. Sir Ewen was much too old and frail to play any active role in the rebellion, though he lived until 1719, and the flattery which Mar so smoothly conveyed was clearly designed to remind John Cameron of the ultra-royalist public image of which his family was so proud. What John Cameron needed was not so much hints of future honours as a decisive military lead from Mar.[13]

It was not forthcoming. As Mar dallied, confusion set in in Jacobite counsels in the west. Between the Jacobite Earl of Seaforth north of Inverness, with his warlike Mackenzies, and Huntly and his tepidly Jacobite Gordons in the north-east, a wedge of stubborn Whiggery was emerging. It comprised the followers of Forbes of Culloden and Rose of Kilravock, the Grants of Speyside, and even the notoriously equivocal Frasers at the northern end of Glen More. Clanranald was confused when he heard that some Jacobite MacDonalds, Mackinnons, and MacLeods had been ordered to march north to link up with Huntly and Seaforth.[14] Young Lochiel was soon being bombarded with requests to intervene in the extremely ambiguous politics of the Campbells of Breadalbane, where no man knew exactly where the aged, slippery and cunning chief himself stood.[15] Towards the end of September, Mar repeated his original orders for a march on Glasgow, orders which overlooked such small details as the opposition of the Argyll Campbells and the great government fortress of Dumbarton barring the direct route.[16]

Fort William undoubtedly did act as a minor deterrent to Clan Cameron, but it was itself in a sorry state. Bits of it fell down. After a bastion collapsed the commander had to devote most of the energies of his 400 effectives to building a ten-foot wall across the breach. The fort was effectively under blockade. Whereas at the time of the Glorious Revolution the Jacobite clans had been extensively harassed by amphibious attacks (as they were again in 1745), few ships of the Royal Navy showed in west Highland waters in 1715. Almost all the small boats on Loch Linnhe were in Jacobite hands. The Fort William garrison was disgusted when one of the few naval vessels to break through the Jacobite blockade not only failed to bring any supplies, but also depleted their own reserves by its demands for victuals. A couple of short-range sallies which involved staving in a boat or two and capturing a pair of locals was the limit of the fort's offensive capability.[17] Yet despite anguished appeals from his brother Allan, who was in Mar's entourage, young Lochiel was reluctant to commit the bulk of his fighting men.[18] The fort seems to have been more an excuse than a decisive threat.

Mar eventually sent a professional soldier, General Alexander Gordon of Auchintoul, to try to pull the military effort of the western clans together. His orders were to lead an invasion of Argyll by marching on the Campbell capital of Inveraray, ostensibly in order to clear his western flank for a march on Glasgow. Both John Cameron of Lochiel and Stewart of Appin seem to have suspected that the march on Inveraray was a military irrelevance dictated mainly by Mar's personal feud with Argyll. General Alexander Gordon was a professional trained in the French service, when he had progressed into the Russian army, where his relative General Patrick Gordon of Auchleuchries held high rank. After service against the Poles on behalf of Peter the Great, he retired as a major-general in 1711 to return to his inheritance in Scotland. Despite being hardened in so tough a school, he entirely failed to raise the tempo of local conflict.

As his forces moved towards Inveraray, they encamped 'at Strathphillen about sixteen miles from the Head of the Loch'. The loch in question was Loch Lomond, and Strath Fillan was equally suited as a point of departure for Inveraray, or for a march by Glen Falloch to the head of Loch Lomond. The latter manoeuvre would have made sense only if the Jacobites had held naval supremacy on the loch, a supremacy which would have allowed them to bypass Argyll. Presumably, it was because of this high strategic significance that Glengarry had early established a Jacobite camp there, reinforced by MacGregors and Glencoe men. In practice, General Gordon found Loch Lomond closed to him. The Jacobite MacGregor groups on the east side of the loch had seized the opportunity of a rising to launch hit-and-run raids on the staunchly Whig west bank. This provoked a decisive riposte. The Whigs had significant naval forces in the Clyde, covering the approach to Glasgow, and the water route to Inveraray up Loch Fyne. From the men o'war four pinnaces (shallow-draught vessels using both oar and sail) and three longboats, were provided. From the Clyde towns came four more boats. All were dragged by horses from Dumbarton to the shores of the loch. Once launched, this little armada, with its complement of light cannon, enabled the Whigs to launch a deeply satisfying punitive strike into MacGregor country. John Campbell of Mamore, uncle to Argyll, headed a group of Campbell gentry and a force of vengeance-bent Lowland townsmen. They were reinforced for the occasion by the Whig Sir Humphrey Colquhoun of Luss and his clansmen, not to mention Colquhoun's son-in-law James Grant of Pluscarden, son of that prominent north-eastern Whig chief, Grant of Grant. The demonstration against the MacGregors was bloodless. What suffered most was their few boats, and the fact is that the closure of Loch Lomond as a Jacobite option was the principal achievement. General Gordon, some weeks later, moved on into Argyll.

He came before Inveraray with perhaps 2,400 men, including Lochiel Younger and a few hundred Camerons. With him also were detachments from most of the western Jacobite clans, such as the Stewarts of Appin, the Macleans, the MacDougalls of Lorne, and even some Campbells of Breadalbane. Leaving Strath Fillan on 17 October, they had reached Inveraray by the 19th. The tiny burgh on Loch Fyne, still clustered round the old castle dating from about 1520 and finally demolished in 1770, held some 1,000 Campbell fighting-men. The hard-bitten Campbell lairds who would have had to lead them in any action rapidly formed a very low opinion of their nominal commander, Argyll's brother and heir the Earl of Ilay. He was to emerge as an outstanding machine boss in the seamily corrupt politics of the Scottish Westminster constituencies, but as a soldier he struck them as a conceited and incompetent fusspot. Fortunately, nothing really happened. There was a deal of huffing and puffing, and some enormously protracted Highland palavering. On the 24th the Jacobite host marched off by way of Strath Fillan to join Mar's main army after a week's march to Auchterarder.[19]

These events strongly support two conclusions. One is that though clan loyalties were still a very important element of any Highland magnate's 'tail' of followers, the great days of internecine warfare between clans were certainly over. No government of any conceivable complexion was likely to allow the aggrandisement of a major Highland clan by means of the systematic slaughter and dispossession of a rival group. A large part of Inveraray was burned by Montrose during his obliterative offensive into Argyll in 1644. In 1715, when the Campbells were poorly led and heavily outnumbered, there was no sign of a lust for rapine and slaughter on the part of the Jacobite chiefs facing them, and this was to be reciprocated by Argyll himself in his hour of triumph at the end of the rebellion. They were all Scottish gentlemen arguing about British politics, and this trait was to be even more marked in 1745 when anti-Campbell emotions amongst the social and political élite seem to have been rooted primarily in resentment towards the working of the Argyll political machine.

The second conclusion is to some extent a corollary of the first; most of the Highland chiefs before Inveraray in October 1715 felt that they were in the wrong place. The Earl of Mar had plenty of military clout. What he lacked was the will and capacity to use it in the only relevant place – in a major battle against Argyll in the centre of Scotland. His hesitation had already largely negated the achievements of his subordinate, Brigadier William Mackintosh of Borlum, who had crossed the Forth with 2,000 men in a brilliant outflanking manoeuvre, but had then been left at a loose end to wander off to join the small northern English Jacobite rising. Much too late, Mar eventually advanced from Dunkeld, only to withdraw again after the indecisive action at Sheriffmuir or 13 November 1715. The next day Borlum and the English Jacobites surrendered at Preston. Since contingents from most of the clans of Glen More and Glen Spean had reached Mar's camp before Sheriffmuir, the failure to win the decisive victory which alone would have served the Jacobite cause was widely appreciated in the central Highlands by early December, and Jacobite morale there naturally slumped. The arrival of 'James VIII' in person in Scotland at the very end of the year did little to boost the flagging spirits of his followers.

Mar had a talent for pushing paper, even in defeat. The orders reaching Lochiel by early 1716 had changed to urgent instructions to march north on Inverness where the Jacobite garrison had been overwhelmed on the very day of Sheriffmuir by the comic-opera assault of local Whig lairds, including the returned chief of the Frasers, Simon Fraser, Lord Lovat.[20] There was no flicker of zeal for such a counter-attack in the bosom of John Cameron of Lochiel, Younger. The fall of Inverness was itself a commentary on the increasing lack of credibility in Mar's public position. No doubt relying on information from Allan Cameron, Mar had tried to open a correspondence with the Deputy Governor of Fort William, endeavouring to seduce him from his loyalty by exploiting his resentment at being superseded by Pollock.[21] It might have worked with a disgruntled fellow-politician in the Palace of Westminster, but the gambit was no substitute for battlefield achievement. Pollock was never threatened with mutiny. His main worry was that the local Jacobite chiefs would retreat with their armed followers into a last redoubt in Glengarry's woods. No such Highland suicidal last stand occurred. The latter stages of the rebellion were marked by a steady movement of Lowland Jacobite peers and lairds towards the western isles, whence they sailed into convenient exile. Some Highland chiefs went abroad, among them John Cameron of Lochiel, who returned only in 1719. Even Keppoch went abroad for a spell before returning to his impenetrable country, whence he penned characteristically impudent letters to the Governor of Fort William, blaming his recent Jacobite capers entirely on improper pressure on him from his two feudal superiors, Huntly and Mackintosh, men whom he habitually held in much the same sort of contempt as he reserved for London politicians.

Sir Robert Pollock was convinced that only ruthless burning of houses, killing of cattle, and general disarmament would really bring the local chiefs to heel. They probably agreed, but in practice Pollock had only 450 men in his garrison, many of them sick and half of them very raw recruits. General Cadogan wanted him to detach 300 men to reinforce Colonel Clayton's 500 men, who were moving into position for a possible punitive strike into the heart of the Great Glen. Pollock was clear that he regarded this as a risky ploy, for it would leave Fort William disgracefully undermanned and easy meat for local dissidents just as soon as the punitive column moved off.[22] That the end of the Jacobite rising was by no means an indication that the underlying discontents which had caused it were at an end, was commonly acknowledged even by staunch Whigs. The second Earl of Stair – head of a fanatically Unionist house, one of Marlborough's generals, and British Ambassador-Extraordinary to the King of France from 1715 to 1720 – was emphatic that 'our friends in England' must:

> . . . think of doing without loss of time, what is necessary to make the Union not greivous to Scotland, and to make it a real strength and security to Great Britain, and to themselves. They have an opportunity now in their hands to settle themselves upon such a foundation of solid strength, as will be very hard to shake, which if they neglect tis very probable the whole nation of Scotland discontented, will one day joyn with the Tories and overturn the Whiggs and maybe the Constitution at the same time.

Stair went on to point out that had the rebellion shown more staying power, France would have been tempted to intervene. As it was, Stair reckoned that the French court had begun to fit out ships and move troops towards suitable ports. The Whig regime, sitting on a disgruntled Scotland and based on the systematic proscription of the Tories, was almost as much of an unpopular minority as the regime of James VII and II in 1688. The main difference was that France after 1688 was reluctant to intervene in force. No Bourbon, after all, could hope to emulate the feat of William of Orange in ascending the British thrones.[23]

That the minority of committed Whigs in the central part of the Highlands were obsessed with security problems is therefore hardly surprising. They were naturally concerned about their own personal security, being rightly convinced that their Jacobite neighbours would almost automatically start any rising by trying to kidnap leading local Whigs. Duncan Forbes of Culloden was to spend a good deal of the '45 fending off Jacobite attempts to snatch him from Culloden House. Sir Robert Munro of

Foulis, a staunchly Whig chief from the area north of Inverness, was very anxious during the 1715 crisis that the government recognise the advantages it would derive from stationing a regiment at Inverness. Partly, it is true, he saw this as a means of enhancing the personal security of local Whigs, but more significant was his argument about the strategic significance of Inverness. He pointed out that during 'the late happy revolution' an under-strength regiment of 400 men in Inverness had played a crucial role in the latter stages of the Claverhouse rising, because they sat on the narrow land bridge between the Laigh (or Lowlands) of Moray and Ross, the Mackenzie country north-west of the burgh. The Jacobite commanders, Buchan and Canon, were thereby deprived of the option of linking up with the Mackenzie chief, Seaforth, whose men were in arms and who might have been galvanised into positive action by the arrival of what was left of the Jacobite army after Dunkeld. As it was, Buchan and Cannon were confined to Moray where Mackay eventually caught and scattered their forces.[24]

Despite the lucidity of the geo-political arguments being advanced by the local supporters of Westminster, the chances of their strategic plans being put into practice depended on the less than clear-cut will of Westminster to take the steps and face the expense necessary to make its power effective in the area. When Sir Robert Munro of Foulis wrote to the Duke of Montrose from Inverness at the end of January 1716, urging that a remission from the legal charges outstanding against him be obtained for Lord Lovat, in exchange for his participation in the Whig seizure of the town, he underlined the need to back those who had backed King George.[25] A combination of a discriminating use of patronage, plus the permanent deployment of significant numbers of seasoned regulars in adequate fortifications was the minimum programme capable of guaranteeing results, but forts and soldiers cost money, while Lovat was a wonderful example of the fact that it was not always easy to tell just whose heart was given to King George. Nor was there any guarantee that the Highland problem in 1716 would look so grave from London as to justify a resolute and drastic attempt to change the whole tone of Highland society, despite Scottish Whig demands for 'clearing this country of Jacobitism and of hereditary nonsense'. The '15 was played out mainly in the Lowlands. Nobody could describe the central Highlands as a storm-centre. The clans there were mostly Jacobite, but they neither attacked Dumbarton nor stormed Fort William. Along with the Earl of Southesk 'the heads of the Clans' were among the very first Jacobite commanders to offer submission to the Duke of Argyll after it became known that the Pretender and Mar had cut and run from Montrose to France.[26] Lovat's spies reported that Glengarry, Keppoch, Clanranald and other Jacobite chiefs were conferring together on an agreed course of action in March 1716. There were momentary doubts on the other side of the military hill as to whether they were agreeing to surrender, or coordinating further resistance.[27] Whig anxiety was soon allayed.

There was no serious resistance as government forces moved into the heart of Glen More. General Cadogan had replaced the Duke of Argyll as commander of government forces. An officer of his staff went to Inverness where he was promptly kidnapped by some Camerons and taken to Glengarry. There the officer met a disconsolate group of Jacobite leaders, including the laurel-less General Gordon. Glengarry indulged in some huffing and puffing with a view, as he himself said, to upping the bid from the other side of the card table, but after two days he dismissed Cadogan's staff officer with the message that it was not so much the wise and merciful King George he objected to, as the Westminster political bosses, 'King Townshend, King Stanhope, King Walpole etc'. So much for the single-minded devotion of an archaic Gaelic patriarch to the father figure of his rightful Stuart monarch! By the spring of 1716 the Hanoverian military were beginning to suspect that the detailed accounts of Jacobite conferences reaching them from Lovat's spies told them more about Lovat's animosities than about what was going on in Jacobite circles. Far more significance was rightly attached to the 'hard' news the Colonel Clayton had occupied Lochiel's house with 750 men. Sir Robert Pollock had been forced to disgorge 250 men, but his weakened garrison was in no serious danger. The Camerons did not intend to fight.[28] Politically it was an extraordinarily sensible decision. Glengarry and Keppoch both surrendered themselves, their men, and their arms, at Inverness. General Cadogan's progress by water on a naval pinnace, mounting sail but using oars, as it moved along Loch Ness towards a portage on Loch Oich, and thence by land to Inverlochy and Fort William, resembled nothing so much as a lap of honour.[29] Apart from the usual flutter of lunatic rumours about French landings on Skye, the game was over.[30] Glengarry's card-playing analogy was truer than he imagined. The other side might deny it was playing political ombre, but of course it was. Glengarry was a gambler who lost gracefully, and it is difficult to be very strict with a man who loses his gold with grace.

Cadogan had been selected Commander-in-Chief Scotland on the strength of conspicuous hard-line views. He ordered Sir William Gordon, who had condescended to take up command at Fort William, to proceed with fire and sword against any locals who failed to submit to the House of Hanover within a finite time. Sir William's main interest was a quick transfer to command of Edinburgh Castle. He complained that by the time he had detached 300 men to reinforce Colonel Chomley's garrison of 200 at Glengarry's house so that it could move into Clan Ranald's country, he would not have the force to do much locally. He also wanted to admit to mercy the Cameron commoners who applied for it, including one or two who had been commissioned by Lochiel, despite the fact that King George's proclamation excluded officers and heritors (i.e. landowners) from the easy terms offered to commoners. Sir William was no doubt correct in believing that it never entered the royal Hanoverian head, nor that of the Whig oligarchs who drew up its proclamations, that a commoner could possibly be an officer.[31]

Some leading Scots Whigs had hopes of substantial profit from the forfeiture of Jacobite estates and their purchase by the 'holding' organisation using the title of the London York Buildings Company, possibly with financial backing from the Bank of Scotland. That bank had been accused of Jacobite sympathies by the rival interests which lay behind the chartering of the Royal Bank of Scotland in 1727, and could therefore be relied upon to go out of its way to support unmistakeably Whig ventures, such as speculating in forfeited Jacobite estates.[32] The York Buildings Company had been incorporated by an act of parliament of 1691, in the reign of William and Mary, under the name of 'The Governor and Company of Undertakers for raising Thames Water in York Buildings'. They were originally part of an attempt to cope with the difficult matter of the water supply for early modern London. During the hectic speculative boom in London in the period 1719–20 the company was bought cheaply for its charter, corporate personality and common seal, and its power to buy and sell lands and hereditaments. That it was from the start a crooked business may be deduced from the fact that its stock shot up from a £10 par to £300 as a result of assiduous puffing. From the Commissioners of Inquiry into the forfeited Jacobite estates the York Buildings Company purchased eventually a vast sweep of properties, which due to ineptitude and worse on the part of the company proved in the long run disappointingly unprofitable, and nearly all of which lay in the more accessible parts of the Lowlands or at least on the east of the country. In what was presumably a fit of insanity, the company also bought Rob Roy's small estate at Inversnaid on the west side of Loch Lomond.[33]

Rob Roy's estate was never likely to pay much rent to anyone save Rob. Indeed, that distinguished MacGregor cateran always had a penchant for using it as a base from which to collect rents due to other people, and notably the Duke of Montrose, with whom he had quarrelled bitterly over money matters. When forfeited, Inversnaid turned out to have an extremely complex debt-structure. Inevitably, the Duke of Montrose had claims on it, and his right-hand man, Mungo Graham of Gorthie claimed in a document issued on 6 October 1722 in Edinburgh that Rob Roy owed him £2,135 Scots or £178 sterling plus back interest to 1713. (Rob had, however, also borrowed from a wide range of people, including Glasgow businessmen.[34]) Montrose had long wished to see measures taken 'for curbing the insolence of that insupportable crew of McGregors'. He regarded extirpation as the ideal but impractical solution, and was encouraged by the idea that the '15 would force the government to take some action.[35]

Rob Roy was much too formidable and well supported in his own territory for the local Whigs to dare to challenge him.[36] What Gorthie and Montrose hoped was that the decision to build forts in disaffected areas after the failure of the '15 could be exploited by ensuring that a post was erected at Inversnaid. This proved easier said than done, for the Board of Ordnance, which decided on the sites for building, proved extremely jealous of its professional autonomy. Besides, when Inversnaid was discussed a force of 100 men rising to 150 'upon occasion' was all that was envisaged. Montrose was clear that this was not enough.[37] So a small barracks, rather than a fort, was built in 1718–19 at Inversnaid. It was the first of four new posts, the others being Ruthven in Badenoch, Bernera on the mainland oppposite the Isle of Skye, and Fort Augustus in the Great Glen. Though kept in repair until the late eighteenth century, Inversnaid proved little more than a hostage to fortune. The Montrose interest would really have preferred to have several companies of government troops told off to do nothing but chase Rob Roy through the Highlands. The idea appealed to military hawks like Lord Cadogan, but was never practical politics.[38] As it was, Inversnaid proved unmanageable.

If the attempted takeover of Rob Roy's estate by the York Buildings Company makes any sense at all, it makes sense only as a response to pressure on the company from the Duke of Montrose, who had both financial and political influence over it. When the full scale of the fiasco became apparent the Duke may have been compelled to do the decent thing, for that would explain why his henchman Mungo Graham of Gorthie bought the albatross of Inversnaid from the company. However, Inversnaid was merely a single example of the horrendous difficulties involved in trying effectively to forfeit a Highland estate after the '15, in the face of physical resistance backed up by obstruction on the part of the Scottish legal profession, from local solicitors to the highest courts in Edinburgh. It proved, for example, quite impossible to forfeit the vast estates of Seaforth, the Mackenzie chief. His factor collected the rents and forwarded them to his exiled master, while government representatives venturing near them were regularly run out of the county. Little wonder the government was prepared to return the estates as part of a political deal with Seaforth in the 1720s.

Young John Cameron of Lochiel's forfeiture was a non-event, apart from his exile. Ownership of the estates was complicated immensely by the fact that his old father, Sir Ewen Cameron of Lochiel, was still alive at the time of the '15. Indeed, he did not die until February 1719. The Commissioners for the Forfeited Estates did solemnly set about gathering 'Particulars of Claims on the Estate of Lochiel'. They collected the usual host of debts, bonds, and claims for damage, all of which the Crown had to take seriously for fear of alienating large numbers of people by effectively forfeiting their assets. However, two of the claims recorded were of an inherently different nature. Ludovick Cameron claimed on the strength of the terms of his marriage contract 'Part of the Estate of Lochzeil'. Even more disconcerting was a communication from Donald Cameron, John's heir and Sir Ewen's grandson, the future 'Gentle Lochiel' of the '45, which simply claimed 'the whole Estate'. Ludovick Cameron was the only son of Sir Ewen and his third wife, Dame Jean Barclay, a daughter of the Aberdeenshire laird Colonel David Barclay of Urie. He alleged that Sir Ewen, with the consent of his eldest son and heir John, had pledged himself to 'Dispone heretably and irredeemably' certain lands from his estate to any heir male procreated of the marriage. By 1718 Ludovick's apparently impeccable claim was on file. So was Donald Cameron's flat demand that he be recognised as legal heir to the barony of Lochiel and lands of Loch Arkaig and Glen Loy. The claim spelled out the argument that successive Cameron contracts, including the one between Donald's father John and his spouse Isobel Campbell of Lochnell, had turned Sir Ewen into a pensioner on part of his own estates, and had made John the active manager, but that as early as 1706 John had transferred his own legal rights to his heir male, reserving only a life-rent. The ever-optimistic Duncan Forbes was trying simultaneously to make more of Argyll's feudal superiorities in the Cameron lands, but estates could scarcely be taken from a John Cameron Younger who was not technically their owner. Apart from compiling a rental in 1718, the Commissioners achieved little, and after 1719 the Cameron lands were effectively free of the threat of forfeiture.[39]

The estate of John Grant of Glenmoriston had a different, but not less fascinating history in forfeiture. Unlike the powerful Mackenzies or Camerons, the Grants in that particular glen were a weak and isolated section of their essentially Speyside name. Accessible by water from Inverness, the glen could not count on the Frasers to act as some sort of political buffer between them and authority, because the Frasers had been divided during the rebellion, and Simon Fraser, the man who had snatched most advantage from the confusion of events, was making much of his new-found enthusiasm for the House of Hanover. John Grant of Glenmoriston was therefore legally forfeited, but enforcing the forfeiture by collecting the rents proved impossible. The Commissioners for the Forfeited Estates did appoint two gentlemen to act as factors on the forfeited properties, William Ross of Easterfearn and Robert Ross, baillie of Tain. When the Commissioners finally settled accounts with them for the period 1715–22, they had sadly to admit that their efforts had been futile 'by the

Opposition given them by an armed fforce in the Execution of their Trust (which unavoidably prevented them from receiving the rents of the said estate)'. Like most Highland estates forfeited after the '15, this one was clearly more trouble than it was worth.[40]

As with Inversnaid, the main problem was to find a way in which the Commissioners could both retreat and at the same time save their face. A theoretical rental of £57 13s. 0d. per annum was hardly worth dying for. In 1722 the Commissioners put the estate up for sale, 'by an half Hour Glass, and the highest Bidder, at the outrunning of the Glass, to be preferred to the Purchase'. It was put up for sale at a starting price of sixteen years' purchase, but no satisfactory offer could be obtained. Eventually, in 1730 the estate was sold to 'Mr Ludovick Colquhoun of Luss advocat', a younger son of Grant of Grant, who had changed his name on inheriting the Luss estates. The death of an elder brother turned him into a Grant again, in time to be the ambiguous Grant of Grant of the '45. In 1730 he was a solid enough Whig, but he had to be given the estate. The nominal price of £1,086 was covered by debts on the estate which had been validated, and which he paid off, but which he was allowed to deduct from the sum due to the government. When the final balance was struck in 1732 it became clear that the chiefly house of Clan Grant had simply taken over the estate, including the debts, of Grant of Glenmoriston.[41] It was less able to control the locals because they were physically separated from the regality of Grant on Speyside. Besides, the list of debts confirmed the position of the middling gentry on the estate. Alexander Grant of Sheuglie is an excellent example. Despite having played an active role in the '15, he was not subjected to any prosecution. On the contrary, he was recognised as a major creditor of the Glenmoriston estate, and the sums owing to him for such advances as 2,000 merks Scots were amongst the assigned debts which Ludovick Colquhoun of Luss undertook to pay. Sheuglie had occupied the grazings in Glenfad as security as soon as the act of attainder against Glenmoriston was passed, so the new proprietor found him literally sitting pretty on the estate. Since he had married in 1713 as his second wife Isabel, daughter of John Grant of Glenmoriston, it could be said that Sheuglie represented the surviving Glenmoriston interest.

This story was typical of the Grant gentry in the area. In Glen Urquhart the most prominent family was the Grants of Corrimony, holders of a barony confirmed to them by a charter of James IV dated 1509. It was burdened with debts to Grant of Grant around 1715, and Corrimony himself was an old man nearing the end of his life, but his second son William was an officer in the company of Grants from Urquhart who fought alongside Glengarry's men at Sheriffmuir when the main Jacobite army finally committed itself to battle on 13 November 1715. His elder brother John, who cleared the problem of debt due to

Grant of Grant, was retoured heir general to his father in 1724 (not necessarily the date of his father's death, for the retour was a technical feudal confirmation of ownership rather than actual succession to property). John died in 1726. His son and successor Alexander, laird of Corrimony, played an extremely unstable part in the '45, partly under the influence of the much older and more committed Jacobite, Alexander Grant of Sheuglie. Corrimony was attracted by Prince Charles, but repelled by the devious crypto-Jacobitism of Lord Lovat. Despite the disapproval of Grant of Grant, he committed himself to the '45 at the last minute, was severely wounded at Culloden, and after a period of hiding emerged to enjoy his property until he died in his bed in Nairn in 1797 aged eighty-one. Nobody could possibly have foreseen in 1716–17 the antics of these two lairds in 1745–6. On the contrary, the whole point was that the Grants of Glenmoriston and Glen Urquhart settled down surprisingly quickly and peacefully after the end of the '15.[42]

This settling down of the central Highlands after the '15 rising was not seriously disturbed by that most bizarre of Jacobite rebellions, the '19. It had no serious local roots, being almost entirely the product of a diplomatic estrangement between the British government and the Spanish regime dominated by that extraordinary Italian adventurer, Cardinal Alberoni, the son of a gardener who rose to be a prince of the church and first minister of Spain. Alberoni was originally hopeful of good relations with Britain, but he was also determined to reassert Spanish control over extensive areas of Italy transferred to the Austrian Habsburgs by the Treaty of Utrecht of 1713. When the British checked a massive Spanish invasion of Sicily by destroying the Spanish supporting fleet off Cape Passaro in August 1718, Alberoni fell back on the Jacobite card as one of the few expedients available to him that was capable of embarrassing the Westminster government. His plan for 1719 was for a major descent on the west of England by several thousand regular troops headed by the Tory and Jacobite hero, the Duke of Ormonde. The armada carrying this expedition was made ready in Cadiz with much publicity, though the British could not work out whether its objective was Britain or Ireland. It mattered not, for it was blown to pieces by a tremendous gale off Cape Finisterre in March 1719. The British ambassador in Paris, the Earl of Stair, had sent ample warning of the armada's departure. All military officers and governors of castles in Britain and Ireland were ordered to their posts early in March, and General Wightman was sent to ginger up the military establishment in Scotland.[43]

Paradoxically, Wightman was the only commander to have the satisfaction of a crack at the invading Spanish regulars. It had been Ormonde who had insisted that there be a purely diversionary attack on the Highlands of Scotland. George Keith, hereditary Earl Marischal of Scotland, sailed to the Hebrides with two frigates. Embarked on them were some 500 unfortunate Spanish infrantrymen. At Stornoway he was joined by a 25-ton boat from le Havre carrying his brother James Keith; Seaforth, chief of the Mackenzies; and the Marquis of Tullibardine, exiled heir to the enormous Atholl territorial empire in the eastern Highlands. From the start there was division among the leaders. Marischal was for landing on the mainland and dashing for Inverness, which he believed to be held by a wholly inadequate force of 300 regulars. Tullibardine and another exile who had come from le Havre, Campbell of Glendaruel, were for waiting in Lewis until they heard of the fate of Ormonde's expedition. Theirs was an eminently reasonable point of view. The Scottish expedition was neither designed nor equipped to be more than a minor diversion. Contact with mainland Jacobites showed that they were deeply unwilling to move until they were sure Ormonde had landed. John Cameron of Lochiel, Younger, who had been living in poverty in Bordeaux after the '15, made his way to Scotland on 20 April, with Ranald MacDonald of Clanranald, joined the Jacobite force. By then it had sailed across the waters of the Minch and, due to adverse winds rather than policy, had ended up on the shore of Loch Alsh, over from the eastern extremity of the Isle of Skye. Its leaders were still arguing and Lochiel and Clanranald were among those who were for caution, until firm news of Ormonde's fate was to hand.[44]

Loch Alsh led into Loch Duich, from whose head Glen Shiel provided a route eastward to Glenmoriston. Unfortunately, it also provided a speedy route in the other direction for the forces General Wightman was assembling at Inverness. They could move down to the foot of Loch Ness to Cillechuimein, a place later better known as Fort Augustus, and then through Glenmoriston. Marischal sent his ships home, just in time to avoid their destruction by the Royal Navy, and marched east. As early as 21 April the Duke of Montrose was writing to Scotland to say that London had just heard simultaneously of Seaforth's landing, and 'the good news of the Spanish fleet being disperst'.[45] By early June people in the Highlands were well aware of the fiasco which had sent Ormonde back to Spain. Lochiel went to his own country to raise recruits, but came back with only 150 men. Apart from the 500 Spaniards James Keith reckoned they assembled 'not above a thousand men, and even those seemed not very fond of the enterprise'. On 10 June at the battle of Glen Shiel this unenthusiastic force dissolved, pounded out of position by the grenades and mortar fire of the massively reinforced Inverness garrison commanded by Wightman.

The Jacobite leaders escaped, among them the irrepressible Roy Roy, but the debacle was total. Lochaber had hardly stirred. Given the speed with which the Great Glen clans had abandoned the semblance of a military resistance after the failure of the '15, the cooperative or discreetly evasive behaviour of their chiefs, and the fact that London politicians were not interested in an area which they tended to think of as dreary, remote and unprofitable, it is conceivable that the government profile in that part of Scotland might have settled at a very low level indeed within a few years of the 1719 rising. Then Simon Fraser started to stir the pot. His aim, as ever, was to extract advantage from the fears of others. More precisely, he hoped to become King's Lieutenant of Inverness, and to acquire a command in a revived system of independent Highland companies. These last were essentially a rural gendarmerie, and had a considerable history behind them by 1724, when Lovat seriously suggested their reconstitution. They had been raised in the Restoration period to wage war on cattle thieves and blackmailers. Crown commissions to raise companies would be granted to favoured noblemen or gentlemen, and by the late seventeenth century they seem to have adopted the neutral dark green tartan which was to earn them the name of the Black Watch. They survived the Revolution, there being four independent companies in 1689, increasing to five in 1691, and going on to the regular army pay roll in 1693, though remaining part-time soldiers based on their own farms. By 1703 Captain Alexander Campbell of Fonab and Captain William Grant commanded the only two surviving companies. A third was commissioned in 1704, but none of these units did useful service in 1715, so it is hardly surprising that they were all abolished in 1717, when official faith in any kind of Highlander was at a low ebb.

Lovat in 1724 favoured George I with an extensive memorandum bewailing the deplorable state of law and order in the Highlands. Cattle thieves and blackmailers undermined property rights in the lucrative black cattle trade. The Disarming Act passed after the '15 had been a farce in practice. Weapons were abundant and regular soldiers, clumsy and ignorant of Gaelic were no answer. Reliable men were not being appointed JPs in the Highlands (where there were few JPs of any kind). What was required, said Lovat, was high county office for deserving and loyal men, like himself, as well as commands in revived independent companies for able, respected local magnates, like Lord Lovat.[46] It was an archetypal Lovat memorandum. So much was this the case that the government discerned just a glimmer of self-seeking, and despatched a tough professional soldier to form an independent judgement of the situation. George Wade was a Protestant from Ireland who had seen long and active service on the battlefields of Flanders, Portugal, and Spain in the War of the Spanish Succession. In 1715 he had executed a commission to enforce home security measures in the west of England around Bath. His reputation as an internal security specialist was confirmed by his command of the operation when in 1717 the residence of Count Karl Gyllenborg, the Swedish minister to London, was ransacked by British troops, in order to secure evidence of Swedish intrigues with British Jacobites. It was therefore a senior figure in the British ruling élite whom George I ordered to the Scottish Highlands in 1724 to report, in Wade's words: . . . how far the Memorial delivered to Your Majesty by Simon Lord Lovat and his Remarks thereupon are founded on Facts, and the present Practices of those People; and whether the Remedies mentioned therein may properly be applied for preventing the Several Grievances, Abuses, and Violences complained of in the said Memorial.

Wade's first report was submitted in 1724. It estimated the total fighting manpower of the Highlands at 22,000, of which it considered not more than 10,000 to be well affected to the House of Hanover. Most of the remaining 12,000 were in Wade's view 'ready, whenever encouraged by their Superiors or Chiefs of Clans, to create new Troubles and rise in Arms in favour of the Pretender'. He confirmed that the disarming act had been ineffective, wasting public money and making the disaffected more formidable. Wade alleged that blackmailing of 'almost all the Low Country' was a feature of Highland life, the principal offenders being the Camerons, Mackenzies and 'the McDonnell's of Keppoch, the Broadalbin Men, and the McGregors on the Borders of Argyleshire'. Obviously there was an element of exaggeration in the general's assessment. To him the majority of Highlanders were, as his report said, disloyal savages living in chaos and anarchy. Justices of the peace were few and far between, while three of the deputy sheriffs in the shire of Inverness had actually been in arms against the government during the '15.

Wade was particularly disgusted that in the past four years the Lords of Justiciary when sitting on assize at Inverness (as the main criminal court for most of the Highlands) had only managed to hang one man, for murder. To a Hanoverian soldier it was disgraceful that the Camerons were reputed to have assassinated two of their own number for attempting to accept money in exchange for denouncing fellow clansmen as cattle thieves, when assize judges were failing to string a regular dozen or more on the gallows annually. Wade was aware that Scottish national sentiment, and not just Highland 'barbarism', lay at the root of much that offended him. Donald Murchison, Seaforth's factor, collected the rents on his attainted master's estates, but he went to Edinburgh with complete impunity to arrange for them to be remitted to France. Indeed Wade seems to have developed a positive interest in Highlanders and Highland culture, for he paid to have Gaelic poetry translated into English, and he even tried, alas unsuccessfully, to persuade Keppoch to write an autobiography.

In 1724, and in a scheme delivered to George I in April 1725, Wade produced his positive recommendations. He wanted to revive the Highland companies. Three commanded by captains were each to have 60–70 men, while three commanded by lieutenants were to have half that complement, making up a total of 300 men in all. Wade insisted 'that a Redoubte or Barrack be erected at Inverness' sufficient to house a body of troops capable of blocking the passage from the north to the lowlands of Moray of any rebel force. He had viewed the barracks erected in 1716 at what he called 'Killihniman' (cille-chuimein in Gaelic, meaning the cell or church of Cumin), at the southern end of Loch Ness. Built on a peninsula beyond the village, between the rivers Oich and Tarff, it was curiously isolated from the loch, its main lifeline to the north. Wade wanted a redoubt by the lochside, plus connecting works to the barracks. From 1727 to 1730 he laboured to create a new square structure capable of holding 300 men (three times the force which the 1716 barracks housed). It had bastions at each angle, a ditch, a covered way where defenders could move under the protection of the parapet, and a glacis or gently sloping field of fire below the parapet. Twelve six-pound guns were mounted on the structure. For the galley which Wade said he needed on Loch Ness, and which he secured, there was a small harbour on the nearby Tarff. She was a 30-ton ship mounting half a dozen light guns known as 'patteroes'. Despite all this work the fort, named Fort Augustus after William Augustus Duke of Cumberland (a child in 1730), lasted two days when besieged in 1746. Wade undoubtedly envisaged it in an active rather than a passive role, as a great place of arms, from which defending troops would sally out, as in 1719, to crush rebellion in the bud. He saw it as 'the most Centrical part of the Highlands', equidistant from Fort William and Inverness, where 1,000 men could be concentrated from these garrisons at twenty-four hours' notice.

By definition, therefore, Wade's forts had to be seen as a well-garrisoned whole, as a dynamic system, and not as isolated strong points. He assumed that Fort William would hold a full regiment, from which detachments would hold the small barracks at Bernara on the main route to Skye, and at Ruthven in Badenoch on Speyside away to the west. Both were listening posts. Ruthven was left to a sergeant's guard in the '45, though a very resolute sergeant survived a first Jacobite siege in August of that year. When they came back with artillery in 1746 Sergeant, now Lieutenant, Molloy surrendered. Wade's other big fort, Fort George, was built from 1726 on the Castle Hill at Inverness. Graced with a royal name, it was an idol with feet of clay, or rather of gravel, for the hill threatened to collapse under it before it was finished, and its running gravel base made it an eighteenth-century military engineer's dream for practice with mines. Scarce besieged, it fell in February 1746, or rather blew up, taking with it the over-zealous French artillery sergeant who had laid the mines under its bastions.

When he moved north on a permanent basis in June 1725, carrying his commission as Commander of the Forces in North Britain (a reward for his first report), Wade was therefore far from obsessed by roads. The only reference to them in his April 1725 scheme was an item in his list of activities requiring funding which said that provision of money would be wanting 'for mending the Roads between the Garrisons and Barracks, for the better Communication of his Majesty's Troops'.[47] The man's heart was in a vision of massive military sweeps by a force of several regiments, with a view to systematically daunting and disarming politically recalcitrant groups. Unexpectedly, the first such operation which he led was against the Malt Tax rioters in the city of Glasgow in July 1725, but he soon returned to his original objectives – the Jacobite clans, starting with the Mackenzies. By the time he had worked his way, much later, as far south as Menteith and Dunbartonshire in the extreme south-west of the Highlands, he had collected 2,685 weapons, which seems a poor bag from 12,000 supposed hostiles, but Wade was pleased with it.

Hardly had Wade settled down to his self-appointed mission in the Highlands than there was in 1727 yet another scare about possible Spanish intervention. Jacobite agents were moving about in the west Highlands as a result of a renewed, and ill-founded, Spanish surge of self-confidence rooted in what proved to be a short-lived alliance between Spain and the Empire ruled by the Austrian Hapsburgs. The first treaty of Vienna of 1725 proved evanescent. Nevertheless, a couple of Jacobite busybodies bustled round addressing letters to, among others, Lochiel, Glenmoriston, Keppoch, Glengarry, Chisholm of Strathglass, and Cluny. An approach to Lovat was considered. When taxed by Wade, whose spies seem to have penetrated the plot early on, the chiefs did not deny the approaches, but simply said they were not so daft as to commit themselves to such obviously unreliable and irresponsible schemes. The whole episode left as its principal impact the making-up of the captain's companies in the Highland companies from 60 to 100 privates, and the lieutenants' from 30 to 60. With officers, the companies formed a potential battalion of 525 men.

In reporting on the Spanish plot Wade added that: the great Road of Communication extending from the East to the West Sea, through the middle of the Highlands, has been successfully carried on upon the South side of the Lakes from Inverness to Fort William, being near 60 miles in length, and is made practicable for the March of Artillery or other Wheel Carriage . . .[48]

So the concept of a central road designed mainly to link the three forts of the Great Glen was still uppermost in his mind, to the point of being executed well ahead of the new structure at Fort Augustus, on which little or no progress had been made by the time of the 1727 report. However, once that road was in position, the road-building programme assumed a life of its own. Between 1725 and his departure from Scotland in 1740 Wade claimed to have built 250 miles of road. Apart from the 60 miles from Fort William to Inverness, Wade had by 1730 constructed two fairly obvious routes running into the Highlands from Perth and Stirling respectively, and reaching right up to Inverness. Here was the long-desired means of rushing government reinforcements by land from the Lowlands to the main urban centre in the Highlands. Wade had by 1731 established a pattern whereby he received an annual grant of £3,000 for road construction by parties from the regiments he commanded. The money was partly strategic spending on defence, partly cloud-cuckoo optimism that building roads would automatically introduce commerce and banish Highland 'barbarism' (defined roughly as any distinctive feature of Gaelic culture).

In 1731 he embarked on the simple but ambitious plan of linking his two road systems. From Dalwhinnie in the central Grampian Highlands a new road struck off ambitiously westwards across the headwaters of the river Spey and climbed by a series of zig-zags to 2,500 feet at the Pass of Corrieyairack, before it plunged down to Fort Augustus. Here was the route which General Cope wanted to take late in 1745, only to find the Jacobites ahead of him and ready to line the zig-zags with musketeers in the coming battle. Cope's bolt for Inverness was understandable, but it left the bulk of Wade's road construction available for the only army it ever decisively helped towards victory – the Jacobite army led by Prince Charles Edward Stuart.[49]

This was the central paradox of Wade's achievement in Scotland. It all pivoted on the maintenance of an adequate force in the Great Glen forts. Adequate meant not less than a couple of seasoned infantry regiments with supporting artillery, at least some horse for scouting purposes in the field, and the Highland companies full of Gaelic speakers acting not only as a rural gendarmerie, but also as the eyes and ears of their regular colleagues. After being augmented in 1727 the Highland companies cost £9,140 17s. annually. Wade was well aware of the need to secure value for money. He knew that one reason why the similar companies active in King William's reign had eventually been dissolved was that they had been abused by the rascally Highland lairds who commanded them on the assumption that their commissions made them licensed free-loaders on the British taxpayer. The first commanders of the companies raised in 1725 were carefully picked. Hence the preponderance of impeccably Whig names like Campbell, Grant, and Munro. The captains were Grant of Ballindalloch, Lovat, and Campbell of Lochnell. The lieutenants were Campbell of Skipness, Campbell of Carrick and Munro of Culcairn. Even so, Wade was by 1731 enraged to find that as soon as he himself left the

Highlands the thrifty commanders of these units stood down their men, while pocketing pay and allowances as usual. A stiff dressing-down from Wade at his annual review of the companies at Ruthven in 1731 seems to have had some effect, for he was reported much better pleased at the 1732 review. The shiftiest rogue of all the captains was naturally Lovat. It was not so much surprising that he was finally stripped of his company in 1739, as amazing that he lasted so long.

By then the Westminster government had embarked on a series of steps which rendered most of Wade's achievements worse than useless. By 1739 it was drifting into the hostilities with Spain later known as the War of Jenkin's Ear. In October 1739 there were issued letters of service from the Court of St James, ordering that the six existing companies be expanded to ten, and that the whole body be formed into a regular regiment of foot under the command of John Earl of Crawford. The officers' commissions were dated from October 1739. War Office records make it clear that the 43rd regiment (later the 42nd), or Black Watch, was regarded as an embodied unit by January 1740.[50] Its name, in the Gaelic form Am Freiceadan Dubh, was the nickname attached to the former Highland companies, with their sombre government tartan of blue, black, and green set, to distinguish them from the Saighdearan Dearg, the 'red soldiers' of the red-coated regular infantry. After three more years of service in the Highlands, which was specifically what the original companies had been enlisted to do, the Black Watch were moved south with a view to feeding them into the British line of battle in Flanders. The cost of the embodied Black Watch was over £15,000 per annum, and Westminster by 1743 saw Scotland simply as a source of money and men needed to sustain His Majesty's Government's pretensions on the European stage. By depleting Highland garrisons and removing vital local scouting and intelligence forces in the shape of the companies, Westminster did not reverse the tide of defeat in Flanders. It merely facilitated a rebellion in Scotland which cost upwards of half a million sterling. Depriving the Great Glen forts of all offensive capability proved an act of irresponsible folly.

6 *The Alienation of Grant of Grant and its Consequences*

The stability of the political system which was emerging as a recognisable unit along the central axis of the Great Glen was always precarious. In the first place it was itself in a perpetual state of flux, though these fluctuations became less violent in the 1730s and 1740s as the chiefs stabilised both their own grip over their clans and their relationships with the other chiefs. By the early 1740s confederal agreements of a loose but significant kind were being signed between clans. Secondly, these interlinked local magnates were in no way a self-contained society, even if they were an increasingly distinct one. On the contrary, they were exposed to the sometimes traumatic impact of forces beyond their control, forces which at the highest political level emanated from not one, but three royal courts: the British, the French, and the exiled Jacobite courts. Thirdly, the internal stability of this regional system was itself a complex affair dependent not on one, but on a whole series of balances. There was the military balance between the Hanoverian garrisons and the armed clans; there was the economic balance between expenditure and income for each chief; and there was the political balance between local power and access to central government favours. The last two balances were themselves intimately inter-connected. As the 1730s merged into the early 1740s two major influences began to change their nature. Firstly, relationships between the three courts changed and, secondly, several of the internal balances in the Great Glen area became unstable. Political disgruntlement and unrest increased.

No chief displays the nature of the political problem more spectacularly than Simon Fraser, Lord Lovat, and that all the more clearly because of his umbilical relationship with one of the pillars of the Hanoverian regime in the north. Lovat's love-hate relationship with the family of Forbes of Culloden is one of the major themes of his life. It had begun in a fit of opportunistic euphoria during the '15. By 1722 it was veering towards hatred, due to fierce local rivalries over the three seats in the Westminster parliament which fell within the sphere of the political ambitions of John and Duncan Forbes. In April 1722 Duncan Forbes himself had been elected MP for the Inverness district of burghs, comprising Inverness,

Fortrose, Nairn and Forres. His brother, the laird of Culloden, fought Sir James Grant of Grant for possession of the seat for Inverness-shire, and lost. Prudently, John Forbes also offered himself as a candidate for Nairnshire, a seat which he eventually gained and held until 1727, though not by a simple victory at the polls. There he lost, but the election became the subject of petitions to the House of Commons. Such election petitions were commonplace in the eighteenth century and until Grenville's epoch-making act of 1770, which eliminated the worse abuses and ensured a more-or-less honest trial of election cases, they were notoriously decided on purely partisan grounds.[1] John Forbes made enough interest to secure a vote of the House which cancelled in his favour the indenture returning his rival. It was all very wearing. On top of these traumas, the price of having fought Lovat's brother-in-law for Inverness-shire was, inevitably, the bitter resentment of Lovat, to whom a brother in the hand was clearly worth far more than a brace of Forbes brothers in the bush.

More important from the point of view of the young Duncan Forbes were the cordial relations he established almost at once after his election with the brains of the Argathelians (or followers of the Duke of Argyll), the Earl of Ilay, relations which go far to explain his nomination as Lord Advocate in 1725. One of the rare occasions after the passage of the Septennial Act when a parliament did not run for the best part of seven years occurred in 1727 with the death of George I. The monarch was still not only an important working part of government but also in a very real sense the primary lever of government. Parliament was his parliament. In no way was he a mere convenience for the political class, a device for stimulating deferential instincts in the general public, or for distracting attention from the real exercise of state power. He *was* state authority, and therefore his death automatically involved a general election. A new king needed to summon, personally, his own first parliament. At the polls in Inverness-shire, Grant of Grant yet again fought and drubbed 'Bumper John' of Culloden. Lovat's relationship with the Culloden family was not improved by what he was bound to see as wanton aggression against his family interest. The cost of contests inevitably rose after the Septennial Act and anyone who forced a fight in a county constituency cost his opponent a lot of money, win or lose.

However, there was good reason for the wily Simon to rein in his emotions when dealing with Duncan Forbes in the late 1720s. With the death of George I in 1727, Lovat lost the pension from the Hanoverian dynasty by which he set great store. Apart from its financial value, it was an indicator of political favour which was eclipsed just when Lovat's long campaign to reverse the Court of Session decree of 1702 in favour of Amelia, Baroness Lovat, was coming to a head. The issue of the title was settled early in 1730, with Duncan Forbes arguing the very convincing case against the view that the fief was or could be a female one. Lovat was well aware of the advantage he derived from the advocacy of a great lawyer who was also a great speaker, and Culloden himself was soon in receipt of Lovat letters expressing admiration for and gratitude to Duncan Forbes. When eventually, on 2 July 1730, Simon Fraser was adjudged the only rightful holder of the title 'Lord Lovat', the successful litigant wrote at once to John Forbes saying that gratitude for the generous behaviour of the Culloden family would bind him to them for ever.

For ever is a long time. Besides, the legal result was less decisive than it sounded and extended only to the title. The vital sinews of power in the shape of the estates were still a matter of ambiguous complexity. Only a legislative sword could have cut cleanly through that particular Gordian knot, and Simon had none of the political clout which was essential to secure access to the legislative weapon. This fact is the essential background to the steady deterioration in Lovat–Forbes relations which occurred during the approach to and aftermath of the general election of 1734, a general election which in retrospect marked the beginning of a decade of acute political and economic stress for the inter-connected clan chiefs of the Great Glen, culminating in quite unexpected fashion in the dramatic events of 1745–6.

Duncan Forbes was returned for Inverness burghs, a seat which he continued to hold until 1737 when he left parliament for the high dignity of Lord President of the Court of Session. His brother John was a dying man by 1734, able to stand by Duncan in the electoral battle in Inverness and fight Grant of Grant in the shire, but dead by the end of November. Both in the burghs, and in Inverness-shire, there were savage struggles between rival groupings of lairds and nobles for control of the seats. For the third time, Sir James Grant of Grant faced a Forbes challenge to his grip on Inverness-shire. He was to beat it off, but as it developed he became distinctly nervous. The ideological content of all these rivalries seems to have been in reality nil. It was a period of some considerable political confusion. 1733 had seen the tremendous political crisis provided by Walpole's excise scheme, denounced as an intolerable interference with the liberties of free-born Englishmen, and eventually withdrawn before it reached the House of Lords. Scottish foes of the Argathelians, like Lords Marchmont, Montrose, and Stair, came out clearly against Walpole and were deprived of office for their pains. Argyll himself pursued a typically high-handed course, voting against Walpole in the Lords in May 1733 and effectively forcing Sir Robert to buy his disdainful neutrality with further concessions. Ilay continued to cooperate very closely with Walpole. Duncan Forbes was always careful to advertise his total devotion to Sir Robert Walpole, but there does seem to have been a passing phase of coolness in his relations with Ilay which, in the general air of confusion of the day, encouraged local lairds (who aspired to replace him as 'sycophant fiscal' to the Argyll interest) to manoeuvre against him. The utter cynicism which inspired the smear campaign which was an integral part of this game may be best illustrated by the fact that Brodie of Brodie was at one point seeking support from Ilay for an attack on Duncan Forbes and his 'Jacobite Popish friends'.[2]

Trouble over the general election in Inverness-shire was brewing long before 1734. Simon Fraser was particularly sensitive about keeping his lines of access to the seat of political power clear, because of the increasingly grave nature of his financial commitments. In November 1729 he lobbied Grant of Grant, urging him, if in Edinburgh, to put in a good word for Lovat's case with any Lords of Session of his acquaintance and, if in London, to try to secure for Lovat the restoration of the pension he had held in the later years of George I. The money, said Lovat, was essential to his family.[3] Of course, all Lovat's demands were in Lovat's eyes selfless to a degree, but he had a point. The Beaufort Frasers needed money desperately to assert their rights and to hold off other landed families in the endless testing of the parameters of local power whereby they regulated their status. For example, Lovat was committed to finding half the cost of a prosecution he was mounting with Grant of Grant, against the murderers of one of his Fraser clansmen, who had been a tenant of Grant's in Aviemore.[4] Mackintosh was by early October 1729 closeted with Duncan Forbes at Culloden House and Lovat was convinced that Mackintosh, among other ploys, meant to intercede for the murderers. Whether this piece of paranoia was justified was less important than the valid assumption behind it – that failure successfully to prosecute would weaken Simon's drive to emerge as unchallenged head of the Name of Fraser.[5]

But of course the essential foundation of effective clan leadership – control of clan territory – was still far from safely in Lovat's clutches. Although he was to be successful over the title dispute in 1730, he knew some time before that that he would have to buy final victory on the ground. All he lacked was money. By 1727 he was trying to buy up any outstanding debts secured on the Fraser lands, and had indeed come to terms with the creditors of Amelia Lovat's late husband Lord Prestonhall for a substantial sum. The marriage portion which Brigadier Ludovick Grant of Grant had promised him with the hand of Margaret Grant was not entirely paid, so Sir James Grant was soon being bombarded with Lovatic missives urging him to hand over the balance of the money.

Sir James not unreasonably hesitated, since the marriage settlement committed Lovat to permanent financial provision for his wife, and a prudent brother might well hesitate before sinking his sister's funds in what amounted to the highly speculative purchase of debts. Lovat naturally insisted that Prestonhall's debts were perfectly good security for Margaret Grant's jointure, and even if they were not, Simon thundered, he would expect Sir James to venture the sum involved with him as part of the campaign to save the Fraser estates for his nephew Lovat's son young Simon.[6] However, even Lovat realised that rhetoric was more convincing when reinforced with logic, so he also secured a memorandum from Patrick Grant, the lawyer Lord Elchies, in which Elchies argued that the point at which the Grants could afford to hold back from commitment to Simon Fraser was past.[7] The latter had already laid out over £2,000 of his own money in buying debts owed on the security of the Lovat estates, and Elchies was clear that the Prestonhall debts were a perfectly good negotiable asset. The real hazard was that once he had the balance of the Grant money in his hands, Simon Fraser would be beyond any effective control by Sir James. Elchies very sensibly suggested that the money be deposited with a third party in Edinburgh pending a final settlement between Grant and Lovat lawyers over the problem of Margaret Grant's jointure. Lovat himself accepted the idea, urging Sir James to instruct his chamberlain to leave the money with a 'sure hand' in Edinburgh while their lawyers quickly came to a final agreement about Margaret's settlement. He was for once in a position to play a forceful hand. As Elchies wryly reminded Sir James, by giving Lovat his sister, Brigadier Grant had doomed his family to some extent to sail 'in the same bottom' with Simon.[8]

Far more important and expensive was the busines of buying off the main rival claimant to the Lovat estates, Prestonhall's son, now Fraser of Fraserdale. Losing the battle over the Lovat title was a sign to Fraserdale that he would be wise to allow himself to be bought out. Lovat already had leverage over him in the shape of Prestonhall's debts, but it was not decisive leverage. It remained a very nice question how much Simon could be made to pay for final victory. The exact price was likely to depend partly on the amount of political influence the respective parties could muster. Lovat went straight for the post of sheriff of Inverness-shire, which in fact Grant of Grant, the sitting MP, regarded as at his own disposal, and was thinking of bestowing on his lawyer son Ludovick. Through a friend in London, Lovat approached Ilay, who was already being plied on the subject by Sir James Grant. Lovat wrote to Ludovick a letter breathing injured innocence and full of protestations that the interests of the Grants would be closest to his heart, especially at election time when the sheriff acted as returning officer. Inevitably, Sir James was annoyed by Simon's deviousness and pretensions. Indeed, the latter eventually complained that Sir James was being bloody-minded about a job scarce worth sixpence to the Grants, but of inestimable potential value to the Beaufort Frasers.[9] Simon had his way. It was he who presided over the decisive battle between the rival candidates, as the newly-appointed Sheriff of Inverness.

That battle was not the election itself. The election result depended entirely on the names on the duly accredited list of freeholders. The number of voters was not very large, fluctuating between thirty and eighty, and no one was under the illusion that the majority were in any way free agents. They were mere tools of the ambitions and egos of the half-dozen or so men who fought over the representation of the county. Nor did anyone think for a moment that the purpose of the election was to represent independently the views of the county community, however defined. Everyone assumed that the MP would use his position to bootlick such ministers as he could gain access to with a view to obtaining favours for himself, his family and his friends. Opposition to ministerial views almost always meant that bootlicking had failed to produce the desired concessions over a long period. What the election was about was persuading the ministry that the winner and his supporters were the men in that shire to whom any favours and concessions should be made.

Lovat reported before the election that the Culloden brothers had 'hooked in' Norman MacLeod of MacLeod to assist what was to be the dying challenge of John Forbes to Sir James Grant. MacLeod mattered because he could throw into the battle his estates and influence as chief of the Skye MacLeods. In practice this meant that with the legal assistance of Duncan he could manufacture votes by creating 'parchment barons'. The process was corrupt and improper, but standard, and became progressively worse as the eighteenth century went on and the Westminster legislature failed to exercise effective control over electoral malpractice. Votes hinged on a freeholding of lands 'of old extent', i.e. mentioned in a medieval valuation as worth forty shillings. Major landowners involved in a contested election regularly manufactured 'faggot votes' or 'parchment barons' by a nominal transfer of an appropriate piece of land to men who were completely subordinate to them and sure to vote according to whatever orders they received from above. Lovat feared that Sir James would go down under a hail of anything from twelve to twenty MacLeod parchment barons. If this happened, wailed the Fraiser chief, 'what will the ministry think of his interest and mine in the shire'.[10]

Hardly surprisingly, Sir James Grant himself began to display distinct signs of alarm, which provoked his mercurial correspondent-in-chief into characteristic huffing and puffing, for once largely justified. It was absurd, Lovat declaimed, to think that a man with friends like those around Sir James could possibly be beaten. If it was to be a duel in manufacturing 'parchment barons' Simon was determined to set his own lawyers to work to churn them out with a will. Twenty was the number Lovat had in mind.[11] In a straightforward competition in unscrupulousness he had little to fear from any normal man. What even Lovat found difficult to stomach in this particular drawn-out election struggle was the damage it inflicted on his financial position and the threat posed by its inevitable personal vendettas to relationships he was most anxious to cultivate.

He was enraged to find that Fraserdale was being advised to stand out, in the final arbitration with Simon over his interest in the Lovat estates, for a full £12,000, which was £3,000 more than the sum Lovat thought would have secured a final settlement before the election. MacLeod of MacLeod and Lord Seaforth, chief of the Mackenzies, were Fraserdale's principal confidants, along with most of the principal figures in the Culloden electoral camp.[12] So incensed was Lovat when it became clear what the election was likely to cost him that in an angry face-to-face confrontation with Duncan Forbes he screamed that there were circumstances under which he would not hesitate to slit the latter's throat. Even by Lovat standards threatening to murder the principal state prosecutor in Scotland was going a little far.[13]

Equally alarming to Lovat were what he saw as the fiendish intrigues whereby his political opponents tried to undermine his credit with the prime minister and his Scottish managers. There were Westminster party divisions in Scotland, fossilised since the union of 1707. Those politicians not in the Argathelian camp were loosely organised in the Squadrone. Whatever Lovat was or claimed to be, he never even wanted to be deemed a Squadrone man. As he told Mackintosh at one point, only Ilay and Argyll could do their busines for them.[14] It has been suggested that in England the militant Whig and Tory parties of the reign of Queen Anne somewhat dimmed their glories after 1720. The Tories survived as a distinct, though reduced, party until at least 1754, with a minority Jacobite element coexisting with a Hanoverian Tory majority element organised in the Cocoa Tree Club. However, in practice the Tory opposition more often than not was to be found working with the so-called 'Country Whigs' in an alliance opposed to the Court interest in charge of government.[15] In this over-riding 'Court–Country' antithesis Lovat could not even be considered a Country man.

Lovat had worked out that, under normal circumstances, as long as Sir Robert Walpole retained the support of the monarch, that premier was irremovable, despite the fact that he tended to be unpopular with the electorate. This particular problem he minimised by having as few elections as possible but, even so, his record in general elections was poor. By 1734 it had become obvious that his supporters fared badly in 'open' constituencies where the electorate was big enough or independent enough to reflect in some measure the views of the political nation. He survived mainly because of the way in which government influence, direct and indirect, could sway the decision in the numerous more 'closed' constituencies where the result hinged on a small number of men susceptible to government patronage and pressure. In many ways it was a markedly offensive racket in a political system which was supposed to have some elements of principle and representation built into it for ever by the Glorious Revolution of 1688. Country politicians naturally waxed indignant about the pillars of the system – the Septennial Act, the large standing army, the alien dynasty with its continuing commitment to Hanover, and the pervasive use of patronage. Lovat positively relished the sight of Walpole holding off the opposition with a high and arrogant hand. Simon cackled with glee at the thought of the opposition 'patriots'' inevitable defeat early in 1734 on a motion to return to triennial parliaments.[16]

Lovat did not wish seriously to challenge the Walpolean racket. He wanted to be cut into it. Hence his splenetic ire when Brodie of Brodie, the Lord Lyon King of Arms and an active intriguer in the politics of Moray and Nairn, assumed the air of Lord Ilay's minister in the north. Brodie openly tried to impress his importance on Lord Elchies and the laird of Luss. Lovat could not permit a rival to posture unchallenged as the main channel of access to power and profit. He raved at Brodie as a social inferior with whom he had no kinship ties, as well as a liar and a cheat.

The two men who had been with Lovat when Brodie struck his sub-imperial attitudes were important, Luss as a son of Grant of Grant, and Patrick Grant, Lord Elchies as a law lord holding a high place in the counsels of the Grant and Colquhoun lairds. In a letter of Janury 1733 Lovat recounted yet another howling row in which the 'King of Beasts', as he was wont to call Lyon, had snarled that he possessed the power to destroy Lovat's credit with Ilay – no doubt by revealing some fraction of the devious Simon's intrigues with the Jacobite camp, whilst incidentally trying to sow dissension between Lovat and the Grants by suggesting that, whilst publicly supporting the candidature of Sir James Grant, Simon and his Frasers were secretly in league with Grant's opponents. Swearing that all the Brodies on earth allied to all the devils in hell were not enough to wreck his credit with Ilay, Lovat claimed later that he only restrained himself from killing Brodie on the spot because it would have harmed Ilay's electoral interests. All this was unctuously reported to Sir James Grant, no doubt in the hope it would reach Ilay, along with the final threat that after the election was ovver Simon would seek satisfaction of Brodie, even if he had to crawl to the duelling-ground to face a lion as stout as any in Arabia. It was all splendid stuff, but underneath the rhetoric the two men were in deadly earnest as they quarrelled over the right to gnaw the meat off the bones cast aside from my lord's table.[17]

Lovat's neuroses were not improved by his inability to use Sir James Grant as a direct means of communication with Ilay and Sir Robert Walpole. It was the old story: the more Lovat bombarded Sir James with scores of wild, whirling and very, very demanding letters, the more that cautious MP drew back from his terrifying correspondent. By the fifth of January 1734 Lovat was openly upbraiding Grant for his excessive reserve and pointing out that despite his extensive conversations and conferences with Ilay and Walpole – opportunities for which Lovat would presumably have given his right hand – Grant had conveyed not one syllable of strategic information to his over-eager ally. Simon was convinced that as an 'old courtier' he was capable of giving tactical advice to Sir James. He was also desperately anxious some how to secure from Ilay recognition of his position as an established client. Unfortunately Lovat's devices to this end tended to be transparent and offered no real incentive to Ilay to participate in the game. Though Lovat had obviously decided to grit his teeth and pay the sum of £12,000 demanded by Fraser of Fraserdale to buy out his interests in the Lovat estates, he made a great show of only doing so in response to the representations and advice of Sir James Grant's son and Lord Elchies. Lovat also fished, shamelessly, for a letter from Ilay, and he moaned and snorted at his lordship's inability to find a few minutes to write a note of counsel to so devoted a slave and supporter as himself.[18] Of course, had Ilay as much as put pen to paper on the topic he would have guaranteed himself a lifetime's supply of garrulous communications from Simon, all starting on the first page with extravagant oaths of fealty allied to reminders that the writer had made the greatest financial sacrifice of his life purely on the advice of, and for the sake of, Ilay. By the second page Simon would have reached the stage of asking for some mere trifle of a favour by way of partial recompense.

If Ilay saw that snare too clearly under a thin coating of dust, Lovat by no means abandoned all hope for the future. He did have a very bad moment when he heard that Sir James Grant had been thinking of moving into opposition. Lovat wailed that he would rather flee to Spain than remain in the north knowing that his arch enemies had been given such a handle wherewith to engineer his downfall. Simon added his usual bitter complaint about the failure of the Duke of Argyll adequately to reward him. He muttered with ominous foresight that another 1715 would show up the folly of such conduct. In the same note to Grant, Lovat enclosed a copy of a letter he had sent to Sir Robert Walpole, of which he was rather proud, for it asked for nothing, despite its author's deep sense of grievance at being excluded from a seat in paliament.[19]

Any Lovat letter not asking, begging, or demanding something of its recipient is, of course, a rarity. However, the letter in question fits into the commonplace category of letters addressed to prime ministers simply to act as a sycophantish reminder of the existence of a humble, devoted, loyal and obedient worm unworthy of continuous notice, but touchingly grateful for an occasional glance, especially if accompanied by a suitable crumb of patronage. It was a New Year greeting to a Sir Robert whom Lovat assumed was surrounded by hosts of well-wishers, all devoted, like Lovat, to Walpole's life and interests. Among these, of course, would be Lovat's good friend my lord Ilay, serving Sir Robert even at the hazard of his life. An ever-so-slightly discordant note crept in when Lovat remarked that under Sir Robert's administration he himself was excluded from a place among the favoured sixteen 'representative' peers, who were effectively nominated by a government list, despite his 'Great Services', high birth, and extensive influence in the county. Quite how Lovat squared his statement to Grant that he had asked Walpole for nothing with the final part of this letter, which complained that he needed money, had received no gratification since the late King's death, and said he would be grateful for any pension Ilay could fix up, is difficult to work out. Perhaps the point is that no specific sum was mentioned.[20]

Lovat genuinely believed that he had more experience of court intrigue than any other person in Britain. His beady eye invariably spotted an occasion when favour with the central government could be turned into local advantage. Thus, in his ideal world a tight network of local alliances would exploit its leverage with the central executive to obtain favours for Lovat and his friends. The dying days of 1734 saw Simon writing to Ludovick, second son of Sir James Grant, who had succeeded to the name and estates of the Colquhouns of Luss in 1719. His father had married Anne Colquhoun, heiress of Luss, but on becoming chief of his own Name was compelled by an entail forbidding the merger of the Luss and Grant inheritances to convey his wife's estates to his own younger son. To Ludovick Colquhoun Lovat underlined his deep anxiety to see Sir James Grant reconciled with the administration.[21] About the same time he was begging Sir James directly to resume his court to the Earl of Ilay, on the ground that he had received intelligence from Edinburgh to the effect that the Lord President of the Court of Session was dying. With strategic patronage such as the Lord Presidency about to come on the political market, the very idea of disagreeing with the government of the day obviously filled Simon Fraser with pain and anguish.[22] What filled his acquaintances with something like despair was Simon's counterproductive crudity of approach, and his chronic inability to adjust his expectations to a realistic assessment of his own political weight, which was limited. His attempts to magnify his influence by manipulating his friends and relatives tended simply to lead them a dance of frustration and embarrassment.

For example, Lovat was clearly in favour of Sir James Grant adopting an attitude of subservience to Ilay and Walpole, come what may, since in no other way would Grant be able to obtain favours for Lovat. Endless baits therefore had to be dangled before Grant to ensure compliance with the ministry. The legal amibitions of Ludovick Colquhoun, who had been admitted to the Faculty of Advocates in April 1728 were for some time a standard theme in Lovat letters. Lovat was always receiving intelligence that law lords were on the point of death. In November 1734 it was the Lord Justice Clerk (who subsequently was inconsiderate enough to recover) whose place Ilay would have to give to young Ludovick, due to the pressing solicitations of friends such as his father and Lovat.[23] By December, of course, Lovat was harping on the Lord President's decline as a reason for not breaking with Ilay.[24]

Both Sir James Grant and Sir Robert Munro became heartily sick of the egregiously self-interested and abysmally tactless advice which Lovat habitually showered on them when they were attending parliament in London. He even had to apologise for his antics in November 1734, though at the end of an atypically chastened note excusing himself on grounds of over-eagerness due to passionate affection for his two friends Grant and Munro, he reiterated his point that Ludovick's future hung on the demise of one of the old men on the Session.[25] In fact Ludovick never achieved this legal apotheosis. With the death of his elder brother Humphrey in 1732 he had become heir to the Grant estates. As there was a legal bar on a laird of Grant holding Luss, that property had to go to Ludovick's younger brother James, whereupon Ludovick reverted to his original name and effectively reproduced his father's mediocre career. Nor were Sir James Grant and Sir Robert Munro, the staunchly Presbyterian and Whig MP for the Northern burghs, convinced that the tidal wave of uninhibited letters which Lovat sent after them was at all safe. One letter in the wrong hands might blight their careers as well as his. Again Lovat had to eat relatively humble pie. Typically, at the same time he tried to use the letter of apology to Sir James Grant to open a secret correspondence anent his endless grievances over his independent company. He cheerfully assumed that if Grant contacted Colonel Guest, the latter could be relied upon to take Lovat's side in a quarrel with Wade.[26]

Altogether, the outcome of the furious legal and political activity which Simon Fraser indulged in between the late 1720s and the end of 1734 was disappointing, though he had his triumphs. He must have enjoyed the meeting of the head court of the shire in September 1733, which determined the freeholders (i.e. the voters) roll. Grant of Grant had just conceded the much-desired sheriffdom to Lovat, so MacShimi was in the chair when the chief of the Grants made a series of bland but outrageous proposals, naturally upheld by the sheriff, which had the effect of crushing the Culloden interest. Lovat and Grant made up a roll which included all the thirteen fictitious votes manufactured by their faction but which excluded nine of their oponents' supporters despite the fact that their names had been on the previous roll. The Forbes brothers raised an action against Grant, but it failed.[27] Yet victory in a parliamentary election, when he was not a candidate, could only be a means to an end for Lovat and he knew well that elections cost him a great deal of money and more good will.

The few top political managers at Westminster who paid any attention to the in-fighting in the northern Scottish constituencies do seem to have sensed at quite an early stage that the savagery with which the local Whig magnates were fighting one another over their shares of a grossly inadequate political cake was dangerous. Not content with doing battle in Inverness-shire, Sir James Grant was considering standing for Morayshire, to the rage of Francis Stewart, seventh Earl of Moray, a man who had been among those summoned to surrender on suspicion of disaffection to the House of Hanover during the '15. No evidence was adduced to support this charge and both he and his son and successor James, eighth Earl of Moray, who succeeded in 1739, proved loyal supporters of the established regime. John Stewart of Pittendreich, second son of Earl Francis, who was himself MP for the Fife constituency of the Anstruther Easter burghs between 1741 and 1747, seems to have acted as his father's contact man with Ilay and also as the principal mender of fences in the Moray interest in the north-east. Pittendreich was a captain in the 54th Foot, the Earl of Loudon's Highlanders, and was captured by the victorious Jacobites at Prestonpans in 1745.[28] it was therefore very significant when he wrote to Robin Urquhart of Birdyards urging him to make up his quarrel with Brodie of Brodie, in the context of the need to keep a solid Argathelian phalanx together in the area.[29] Doubly significant was the reaction of Birdyards, who promptly wrote to Lovat, enclosing Pittendreich's letter and saying two things. One was that he himself regarded the suggestion that he come to terms with Lord Lyon Brodie of Brodie as virtually an order from Ilay. The other was that he thought Lovat really should submit his own notorious and violent quarrel with the Lyon to Pittendreich's arbitration.[30]

In a political world where patronage from the great was the sole object of ambition, the suggestion was a perfectly rational one. By implication Lovat was being urged not only to stop abusing Brodie, but also to at least curb the vaulting ambition of Grant of Grant. The snag was that the volcanic egotism of Simon Fraser, once roused, was not susceptible to dousing. Such efforts merely produced dense clouds of superheated steam. Simon's rhetoric was always capable of rendering bad inter-personal relations worse. Anyone who could express unholy glee at the news of the fatal illness which was to kill John Forbes of Culloden in December 1734, and add by way of pleasantry 'I piss upon MacLeod', to stress his current hostility to the Skye chief, was not one of nature's peacemakers.[31] Some might even feel that his exchange with Sir James Grant in which the two men jested amiably about the possibility that the irrepressible Simon would copulate with Grant's daughter-in-law and sisters when they paid a visit to Beaufort indicates that neither character was notably sensitive to the finer feelings of others.[32]

The irony of it all was that Lovat could and did see the appalling consequences of personal quarrels when they involved other people. Long before the end of 1733 he was desperately unhappy about the coolness clearly developing between Grant of Grant and Ilay. The harsh truth was that Ilay was paying Grant, year after year, with fair words and prevarication.[33] With the one hand, during the protracted run up to the election, Lovat was whipping men like MacDonell of Glengarry, Fraser of Foyers, and Fraser of Dunballoch into line, mainly by pressure of debts due to Lovat, to vote for Grant.[34] With the other, much less successfully, he was trying to persuade Ilay to find a Lord of Session's gown for Sir James Grant's son Ludovick Colquhoun. Despite the fact that Simon persisted grimly in his attempt to make Ilay disgorge a gown, Ilay never seems to have understood the seismic implications of not making some gesture. The election campaign of 1734 left the Whig interest in Inverness-shire fissured, if not cracked.

The MP was victorious, but deeply soured. His principal backer, the most abrasive and paranoid man in the county, was left financially pressed and on foul terms with leading figures in the Argathelian camp – from the Culloden family, whom Simon openly despised as upstarts, to General Wade, whom Lovat accused of deliberately trying to engineer incidents which would enable him to strip the Fraser chief of his independent company. Even at a lower level, many existing tensions had been heightened. Mackintosh of Mackintosh, for example, had an historic feud with the chiefs who guarded southern Glen More and its approaches, but the 1734 election also sharpened his rivalry with the guardian of the northern approaches of Glen More. Lovat was desperately anxious that no political machinations by the chief of Clan Chattan should detach leading MacDonalds like Glengarry and Barrisdale from his own pro-Grant alliance. The challenge was held off successfully, but Lovat obviously bitterly resented repeated attempts by Mackintosh to come to terms with Glengarry and Barrisdale in cabal at Culloden House.[36]

Underneath all this turmoil the regional economy was exhibiting its recurring tendency to subsistence crises, endemic in the nature of its agriculture and of its population patterns but unkindly juxtaposed in the '30s and '40s with political tensions of an unprecedented nature. That Lovat should object violently to being ordered into camp in Badenoch in 1734 by General Wade is hardly surprising. His reasons, however, have more than personal significance. Badenoch, said Lovat, was a bare country in good years, but in March 1734 there was a famine in the area, and he could only feed himself, his company, and the horses with expensive imported meal and fodder.[36] Starving peasants meant low or no rents. No rents made for restive power-hungry landlord-chiefs even more desperate for political pickings to supplement their incomes.

The most insatiably power-hungry of them all, Lovat, was caught in a cruel dilemma after Sir James Grant was declared victor at the polls on 16 May 1734. On the one hand, he still needed the support of the Grants because Fraser of Fraserdale was creating a good deal of trouble about the adequacy of the securities Lovat was offering for the phased series of payments necessary to compensate him for surrendering his claims on the Lovat estates. Simon was genuinely frightened that the greatest object of his life ambition would be snatched away, just as it appeared to lie within his grasp. He begged Sir James Grant to stand by him as guarantor of the sums involved.[38] On the other hand, the MP for Inverness-shire was ultimately of little use to Lovat unless he was on excellent terms with His Majesty's Government. Sir James Grant had consistently behaved as a model North British MP. He voted for the government. He never made speeches. The solitary recorded exception was, characteristically, on behalf of his relative Sir Archibald Grant of Monymusk, MP for Aberdeenshire, who was expelled from the House of Commons in 1732 after it became impossible to conceal the fact that he and a knot of Whig MPs had been systematically embezzling the funds of the Charitable Corporation 'for relief of industrious poor by assisting them with small sums upon pledges at legal interest'. Funds destined for the poor, and partly derived from confiscated Jacobite estates, were simply being stolen by members of the ruling clique. The fact that Sir James appealed for leniency for his scoundrel of a relative gives the key to his attitude after 1734 – he did not object to the ruling racket; he was just frustrated by his inability to have himself cut in, even in a minor way.

The 'hereditary commoner of Inverness-shire' was not even particularly anxious for spoils for himself. He wanted advancement for his son Ludovick, of whom he was sufficiently fond to make over his estates to him in 1735, subject to an allowance to himself of £600 per annum. The trouble was that Ludovick, laird of Luss had fallen foul of Ilay at an early age by marrying as his first wife Marion, daughter of Sir Hew Dalrymple, Bart of North Berwick, Lord President of the Court of Session and a man who can only be described as *persona non grata* with the Clan Campbell. Lord President Dalrymple, in scarcely veiled collusion with his kinsman, Lord Advocate Sir David Dalrymple of Hailes, had led the highly successful campaign of prevarication and obstruction by means of which the Scottish legal establishment had defended the estates of convicted Jacobites after the failure of the 1715 rebellion. The Duke of Argyll, than whom no man did more to preserve three thrones for the House of Hanover in 1715, was in favour of relatively mild treatment of the vanquished, but even he jibbed at the outrageous devices solemnly condoned by the Lords of Session, devices so transparent that the government body set up to administer estates forfeited for treason during the rebellion actually published violent criticisms of the decisions of that august court.[39] The resultant feud between the Dalrymples and the Argathelians was sustained and notorious. While a law student at Edinburgh in 1727, Ludovick Grant, who could count on family interest to back him in Dunbartonshire, had seriously thought of standing for Glasgow burghs, a group of burghs dominated by two interests – the town council of Glasgow and the Argyll Campbells. However, after his marriage Ludovick realised that he was now out of favour with Lord Ilay and through him the government of Sir Robert Walpole, so he abandoned his immediate political ambitions.

Naturally, he hoped that time would efface this unfortunate early impression. Like so many other Highland lairds, he was only too anxious to display grovelling subservience to the reigning political boss in North Britain, provided he could secure some sort of pay-off for his pains. He actually offered the Campbells his Dunbartonshire interests in 1734, when the Glasgow burghs obediently returned William Campbell, a first cousin of the Duke of Argyll and a man who displayed such monstrous arrogance towards his constituents, as well as a studied indifference towards their interests and needs, that it was deemed expedient to replace him for the general election of 1741 with Neil Buchanan, a London merchant who originated from Glasgow and was a staunch adherent of Argyll. Not content with facilitating the creation of a prime example of an elected but quite unrepresentative and irresponsible British MP, Ludovick went even further in 1734 to parade his anxiousness to curry favour with Walpole's election manager in Scotland. Lamed for life by a riding accident, he nevertheless hobbled, or perhaps one should use the Scottish term and say hirpled, round the voters of the northern counties and burghs, earnestly beseeching their countenance for my lord Ilay's candidates.

It was a touching performance which might have extracted blood from a stone, but which failed even momentarily to disturb the pendulum motion of the swinging brick which seemed to serve as Ilay's substitute for a heart. Ludovick reverted to the name of Grant in 1735, when the family estates were made over to him. He tried very hard to cling also to the Luss properties, but lost them to his own younger brother James after a malodorous legal wrangle which confirmed in 1737 that the entail barring any union of the Grant and Luss properties was valid and enforceable.

Losing so vital a case in the Court of Session merely sharpened Ludovick's appetite for a seat on its bench. Yet with a sustained petty-minded personal hostility Ilay dashed every chance of preferment to a Scotch gown for the professionally qualified and well-connected Ludovick

Grant. The original cause of offence, Marion Dalrymple, died in January 1735. In October her bereaved spouse married again, this time with impeccable political taste. His second wife was Lady Margaret Ogilvie, daughter of the Earl of Findlater and Seafield, a peer believed to be in no way obnoxious to Ilay and his political cronies. Astonishingly, such seemly nuptials appeared to make no difference. Lovat was in despair. He wrote to Lord Findlater begging him to use his influence to help Ludovick to a gown and eliciting an elegant and infinitely wise reply in which Findlater said that though he thought the world of the young man, he himself was no courtier, and could do nothing to help him with what were clearly political problems.[40] By January 1737 Lovat was reduced to writing bluntly to Ilay. Ludovick Grant was known to have been disappointed of two gowns; a third was now at the disposal of His Majesty's Government. Simon Fraser for once in his life argued a reasonable case in moderate terms. Here was a suitable candidate who had flown signal after signal to the effect that he would toe whatever line Ilay chalked on the floor of the political arena. He was married into an acceptable family. Were he to fail a third time, his mortification, and that of his friends would be immense. It was. Ludovick abandoned the bar in disgust. He retired to live frugally on his estates, hoping thereby to clear some of the family debts. That these were largely due to unrequited services to the Williamite and Hanoverian interests in the Glorious Revolution and the '15 made the situation all the more galling.[41]

To Lovat the consequences of these endless rebuffs for Ludovick were doubly vexing. Firstly, they progressively destroyed his ability to manipulate and use the Grants. He had begged them not to quarrel with Ilay. He had even followed their advice, or so he said, in plying Ilay on their behalf in modest, guarded language. In quite unguarded language, he had assured Sir James Grant that Sir Robert Walpole was truly anxious about young Ludovick.[42] All this turned to dust and ashes. It was palpably false. Simon Fraser spent much of his life trying to weave together local alliances to which he would give the name of an 'honourable confederacy'. They were designed to serve the mutual interests of the parties involved by enabling them to stand together to secure concessions from government which singly they lacked the power to extract. Using his marriage into the Grants as a base, the Fraser chief had put a great deal of energy into what can be described as a 'Western Design', and the root of his quarrel with Lord Lyon Brodie of Brodie was his allegation that Brodie had 'ratted' on such an alliance between Lovat and his western neighbours.[43] Now another vital bond within that union was wearing away, for Sir James Grant began to move into opposition to Ilay and the ministry of Sir Robert Walpole.

This was the second disastrous consequence of the rebuffs to Ludovick.

It meant that, despite his endless extravagant protestations of commitment to an indissoluble alliance between the Grants and the Frasers, Simon began to lose interest in his Grant relatives. Men on bad terms with the ministry could not serve their friends and kinsmen as Lovat would be served. For example, as he was quick to point out, his difficulties in making the payments he owed to his kinsman Fraser of Foyers could easily have been sharply reduced had he had the political clout to be able to offer Foyers a military commission as part of the deal.[44] Simon still needed the Grants as guarantors of his debts to Fraser of Fraserdale if he was ever to escape from the claws of the Mackenzies by securing a settlement from which neither side could renege or 'resile', to use the Scots legal term. He seems to have been genuinely grateful to Ludovick Grant, who used his best offices to secure such an agreement between the contending parties. In the end it proved necessary for Lovat not only to call on friends and relatives, but also to accept the need to borrow in 1737 £4,000 from the Royal Bank to settle the affair. His credit with his banker was healthy enough, for he had borrowed sums of up to £1,000 already, and had no difficulty in repaying the principal.[45]

It is true that the Fraser chief managed to survive in a hand-to-mouth fashion between 1735 and 1737, but his mind was sharp enough to appreciate the depths of his own political humiliation. Whilst other Highland lairds speedily secured commissions, Foyers (the man whom he would have been so relieved to see furnished with one), remained unprovided for. On top of that dose of wormwood Lovat's quarrel with General Wade, whom he compared to a Turkish bashaw, proved a source of humiliation. Wade alleged that the commanders of the independent Highland companies were almost without exception incompetent and corrupt, embezzling their mens' pay and stealing their clothing allowances. When these observations were laid before King George II, a Teutonic martinet who regarded the army as his particular province, the result was an explosion of Hanoverian anger and demands that some of the commanders be broken. Sir James Grant warned Lovat very plainly that the royal rage was real and that the days were gone when a smart turn-out at one annual inspection would maintain a commander's reputation. Lovat knew that the link between the Culloden family and the Duke of Argyll was too close and too old ever to snap. His own hopes had rested on the semi-detached nature of the relationship between Argyll and his brother and heir Ilay. For long periods the brothers communicated only by note, yet managed to work remarkably well together. Lovat assiduously courted Ilay both directly and indirectly through the Grants. Neither route yielded any satisfaction. Gentlemen willing to assure my Lord Ilay that they were pleased to see him crush the 'Patriot' opposition at the polls were two a penny.

At much the same time Lovat's prestige suffered a further blow in the burgh of Inverness. It was a Culloden citadel politically but the Frasers were a potent country power around it, so it was natural that Simon had a kinsman like Baillie William Fraser to act as his spokesman in the town. The physical assault on that worthy in January 1736 was a slap in the face to Lovat, as Lovat knew.[47] His political activities had left him with no effective leverage at Westminster. His career as a captain of an independent company had been a fiasco. This was partly due to political feuds spawned in elections, partly due to improper behaviour on his part, and partly it must be said because of a clash of ideas rooted in a generation gap. Simon was an old man who claimed that under King William III captains of independent companies were treated as having the quasi-proprietorial rights of colonels of regiments. Wade and George II undoubtedly saw these captains as rogues leading savages, rogues in need of severe disciplinary control.[48] Lovat knew that Sir James Grant could do little for him, and that Grant largely ignored his advice. Nobody except Lovat regarded this accumulation of failures as a public problem. In March 1735 Lovat had gloomily remarked that he seemed to have brought his hogs to a bad political market and that all his life if one interest failed him, he would turn to another. Lost in screeds of Lovatic verbiage, the remark was in fact a significant one.[49]

The trouble was that Lovat wrote so much so wildly. In retrospect, it is easy enough to pick out of his letters sentences which show a remarkable capacity to forecast the trend of events. For example, in yet another letter to Sir James Grant he enclosed a copy of a letter he wrote in January 1737 to Sir Robert Munro of Foulis in which he said that Ilay's refusal to oblige the Grants undermined the alliance with Ilay's most essential interest on the far side of the Grampians, for not only the Grants but also their associates were mortally insulted.[50] In Lovat's eyes the further news that Duncan Forbes of Culloden had been raised to the dignity of Lord President of the Court of Session to replace the deceased Sir Hew Dalrymple was an additional offence. Lovat saw the Grants and Frasers as the ancient houses of his native region, and the Culloden family as bourgeois upstarts puffed with conceit.[51] For Duncan Forbes he amiably suggested ear-cropping and castration as suitable treatment for one who so presumed beyond his social standing.[52]

Oddly enough, 1737 saw Lovat display more violent animus against Ilay and Duncan Forbes, whom he predictably blamed for Ludovick's disappointment, than against the Grants themselves. Partly this was because of the much wider range of pressures on Lovat's mind. The Grants, pushed to extremes, could not consider much beyond low-profile support for the Hanoverians allied to sulking at home. Lovat found the transition to Jacobitism no emotional problem at all, and his financial dealings were on a far bolder, more hazardous scale than those of the Grants. While some of his speculations were modest (such as raising £300 credit for Duncan Grant, a friendly Inverness merchant, for building cruives, or fish traps, to improve his river fishings), others involved quite large bonds, such as the £5,000 which the Royal Bank of Scotland granted him on the security of the Grants. Creditors like Mackenzie of Fraserdale were themselves debtors whose own creditors threatened them with a debtors' prison should they fail to dun Simon relentlessly and successfully.[53]

Lovat's correspondence with Sir Robert Munro and Sir James Grant was so full of resentment that that cautious pair again took fright and warned the Fraser chief that theirs was an age when wise men moved cautiously and spoke ambiguously. What Lovat actually said, or roared, at home in his Highland fastness defies imagination, so it was hardly surprising, though deeply ironic, that when he quarrelled with two of his former supporters, they should in the spring of 1737 raise the charge of Jacobitism against him. These were Major Craiks of Castleledders (otherwise known as James Fraser of Castleleathers) and his son. The latter was erstwhile factor to Lovat, who saw himself as having raised the ungrateful pair from beggary. They might have replied in similar vein. Instead, they denounced him as a Jacobite to the government. Certainly, the rumours they started did Simon no particular good. He heard that Ilay had been informed that he meant to send the Master of Lovat to France to be raised in Jacobite principles, which rumour provoked Lovat into placing his unfortunate heir totally at the disposal of Ilay as far as his education was concerned. Prejudiced hearsay cutting little ice with professional lawyers, the storm blew over, nor can it seriously be said that it left Simon with a stained reputation. Even in 1737 his moral reputation was no more vulnerable to staining than a leopard's skin is to spotting.[54] Most people regarded him as unreliable in his allegiance to either Stuart or Hanover, on top of which his instinctive Scottish nationalism kept exploding over such matters as the drastic Bill of Pains and Penalties against the city of Edinburgh which Walpole's government tried to pass in 1737, to punish the city for the episode known as the Porteous Riot.

Briefly, the city mob had demonstrated noisily during the execution of a notorious smuggler, provoking the unpopular commander of the city guard, Captain Porteous, to order his men to fire, with fatal results. Arrested and convicted, Porteous was clearly going to be reprieved due to government influence, so he was taken from prison and lynched by a highly organised crowd. A furious government pushed through the Lords a bill disabling Provost Wilson of Edinburgh from public office and imprisoning him, as well as abolishing the town guard and demolishing one of the town gates. Lovat saw the proceedings of the Lords as almost as offensive as the bill. Leading Scottish judges were summoned to London and made to stand at the bar of the Lords while they gave evidence, whereas English judges in a similar situation either sat on the woolsack or advanced to the table. Lovat regarded the whole business as a deadly affront to Scotland's national honour, and said so. The Duke of Argyll, by now in semi-formed opposition, was hostile to the bill, so Duncan Forbes, his principal spokesman in the Commons, played an important role in the fierce opposition in that house, which watered down the measure to the disabling of Wilson from public office, and the fining of Edinburgh.[55]

The reluctance of Sir James Grant and his friend Sir Robert Munro to become involved in the web of passionate and changing likes and dislikes which Lovat continually wove round himself was understandable in simple human terms, but it also made sense politically, for personal feuds could easily turn into political challenges. By late 1738 rumours were already circulating that Sir James would be challenged at the next election in Inverness-shire by MacLeod of MacLeod, and that the Skye chief would have the full backing of the Forbes interest. Lovat, whose bonds Sir James Grant was still signing, duly reported these moves to Grant, blaming Lord President Duncan Forbes for the expected political offensive, and stressing that Sir Robert Munro would stoutly support the Grant interest in the county.[56] By December 1737 Lovat was trying to persuade Grant to support him in a political counter-thrust against the magistrates of Inverness, a corporate body firmly in the Forbes interest. Simon alleged that his own kinsmen and those of Grant in that burgh were systematically discriminated against by its authorities. Those authorities were, however, vulnerable, for their finances were sustained by the right to level a tax of 2d. Scots – a boddle* – on every pint of ale sold in the burgh. The right ran out in 1738, and needed parliamentary renewal. Quick to allege extensive financial malpractice on the part of the magistrates, Lovat saw in a parliamentary campaign against the renewal of the grant a chance to bring his political enemies in Inverness to their knees. He bombarded Grant with proposals and even organised 'spontaneous' petitions to Grant by Inverness merchants. All the agitation proved vain, partly because of Grant's natural caution and partly because, to Lovat's chagrin, Ilay refused to condone the proposed filibuster. By April 1738 Lovat was brought down from his zest to fight over tuppence literally to the point of saying he cared not a farthing for the affair.[57]

By the spring of that year Lovat was in quite remarkably bad odour politically. His two sons had virtually to be surrendered as hostages to the Hanoverian camp. After much shilly-shallying the eldest one was consigned to London into the hands of Ilay. The younger one, nicknamed the Brigadier (or simply the Brig) by his father, was fostered with the household of the Grants of Grant, a family which might be sulky, but which was

*A boddle was a coin worth the equivalent of a third of an English ha'penny.

incapable of Jacobitism.[58] Some psychological consolation there was for the Fraser chief in October 1738 when he received the charter confirming his grip on the Lovat estates, after it had duly been authenticated by passing the Scottish exchequer and the necessary seals of authority. As the charter secured not only the lands but also Beauly as a burgh of regality (a grant secured for Fraserdale in 1704), Simon chose to make of his infeftment, or formal receipt of heritable honours, a great public occasion to which he summoned his kinsmen, vassals and friends. This solemn entertainment, he archly told Grant, was reported to the periodical press of the day solely because his gentlemen guests insisted it should be. As usual, Simon was backing modestly into the spotlight.[59] His financial position was less parlous than his political one, which is not to say it did not pose problems. He was proud of clearing a £4,000 sterling debt to the Royal Bank within two years, but the only way he could then keep going was promptly to borrow another £5,000, which meant that his interest burden was considerable. While the bank probably did not take every farthing he made, as he later claimed, it certainly removed a lot of spare cash from his coffers.[60] At the legal maximum of 6% the charge would have been £300 per annum.

Lovat's eye remained, in the last analysis, fixed on the royal court. His illusion was that if he could only impress the court with his own importance in Inverness-shire, it would eventually choose to act in that county through him.[61] In a sense, the court eventually paid heavily for freezing the slippery Simon out of favour. He was a man to reckon with in his county, and he had an unerring eye for the realities of Highland power politics. As early as March 1737 he was warning Ludovick Grant of Grant that the Grants of Glen Urquhart were a crazy band totally out of control. If Castle Grant wanted to be able to give effective orders on the west side of Glen More, Simon was clear that it would have to follow his own example and try to nip insubordination in an unruly clan in the bud.[62] The reason for Lovât's early perception of the highly detached relationship between the Grants of Glenmoriston and Glen Urquhart and the main Grant regality on the Spey was not far to seek. The undisciplined western Grants continually raided Fraser territory, to the point where in late 1738 Lovat was threatening the laird of Glenmoriston with a massive law suit, and Ludovick Grant of Grant had to work overtime successfully to arrange an amicable out-of-court settlement between his semi-detached clansmen and his choleric uncle. Lovat was amazed at his own moderation.[63] In a man who sincerely considered his personality to verge on the angelic, this was a measure of the provocation he had received.[64] It was nothing to the provocation which the same uncontrollable Grants were going to offer to the British government in 1745–6.

During the Jacobite rising which began in August 1745, the Camerons and MacDonalds of the region, early supporters of Prince Charles Edward Stuart, lost no time in applying pressure to the men of Urquhart and Glenmoriston to join them. In Urquhart three men of substance at once threw their weight behind the Jacobite cause – Alexander Grant of Corrimony, his namesake of Shewglie, and Alexander Mackay of Achmonie. Of these Shewglie was, according to local tradition, both the ablest and the most committed. Had Sir John Cope been able, as he originally intended, to march his troops from the Lowlands to Fort Augustus, the cajolery and threats of the Camerons and MacDonalds might have been less effective. As it was, Cope never reached Fort Augustus, and Lord President Forbes' hopes that Ludovick Grant of Grant could or would control the western branch of his people proved ill-founded. Jacobite sympathies were widespread in Urquhart and Glenmoriston. They were even shared by the minister of the parish, the Reverend John Grant. The crucial discussion as to what to do took place after divine service in Kilmore kirkyard on an August sabbath. The advice of the factor from Castle Grant that the men stay peaceably at home was ignored. Corrimony and his allies argued that Grant of Grant was only superficially pro-Hanoverian, and that his 'secret will' was Jacobite. It was not true, but it was a view which did not entirely clash with the evidence of his behaviour. Two of Shewglie's sons led a first contingent to the Jacobite army, being joined at Invermoriston by the laird of Glenmoriston, Padruig Bui or Yellow-haired Patrick. Enthusiasm for the Jacobite cause seems to have been at its most intense at the laird or tacksman level. Among the tenantry there was endless debate, in which Ludovick's factor played an active anti-Jacobite role, and more waiting on events. In particular the Urquhart men were reluctant to 'come out' until they saw how the Frasers meant to jump.

At an early stage, Corrimony was deep in converse with Lovat at Castle Downie but the sustained ambiguity of MacShimi dampened the potential zeal of the Grants. Even when the Master of Lovat marched south with a strong reinforcement of Frasers, as well as the Chisholms of Strathglass and Buntait under the Chisholm's youngest son Roderick, the Grant tenants held back. Padruig Bui had signed a bond of manrent as early as 1735 with John MacDonell of Glengarry, for mutual cooperation and protection, so it was natural that the Grants of Glenmoriston fought alongside the Glengarry MacDonells under Angus Og in the Jacobite army which reached Derby, but it was the misfortune of the commons of Urquhart and Glenmoriston that they flocked to Prince Charles's standard only late in the campaign, when the Jacobite army fell back on and occupied Inverness and most of Glen More. Theirs was the thrill of routing and chasing the northern Whig clans organised by Lord Loudon and Duncan Forbes. Indeed they chased them to Skye, but then those late Grant recruits to the Jacobite standard came back to meet defeat and death at Culloden, where thirty of them fell.[65] Culloden was the prelude to savage punitive action by units of the British army in Urquhart and Glenmoriston. Men were shot down in the fields, houses were burned and cattle were driven off. So bad was the situation that a measure of guerrilla resistance was provoked as the locals sniped at and otherwise harassed detached parties of redcoats.

Yet, as informed contemporaries were well aware, the whole saga of the detached Grant estates made sense only in the light of the attitude of Grant of Grant himself. When he abandoned the bar and retired to his estates in 1737, Ludovick wrote to his father in July of that year saying that the family's former services seemed to be a positive drawback in trying to win the favour of the ministry. He added that: '... no disappointment shall ever alter my zeal for the present family on the throne, although I shall not regret to see some change of our Scots ministers, if they behave to us no better than they have done.'

Towards the end of 1737 Ilay does seem to have sensed the dangers of totally alienating the Grants. He offered Ludovick the consolation prize of a sinecure worth £400 a year. It was accepted. Being incompatible with membership of the House of Commons, the pension had to be nominally transferred to one of Ludovick's kinsmen when the Grant chief decided to re-enter the political stage in 1741.

Put up as government candidate for Elginshire (Morayshire) in that year, Ludovick had to beat off an opposition candidate in the shape of John Stewart, brother of the eighth earl of Moray. The seventh earl of Moray had been hereditary sheriff of Elginshire, but had been implicated in the Jacobite rising of 1715, a fact which seriously undermined the power of his family in the county. The only other potential rival for the seat, William Duff of Braco, was persuaded not to stand by Sir James Grant, who effectively reminded Braco of a gentleman's agreement whereby the Grants backed the Duffs in Banffshire, in exchange for an acknowledgement that, politically speaking, Elginshire was a Grant preserve. All worked out very satisfactorily for Ludovick. He won and held the seat without anyone daring to contest his grip on it before the accession of George III in 1760.[66]

Unfortunately everything turned sour for the laird of Grant when he entered the House of Commons. It was the old story. He could not contrive to establish a good relationship with Ilay, who in 1743 succeeded his brother as Duke of Argyll. Around the time of the outbreak of the '45 Ludovick Grant was so disillusioned about his inability to extract any satisfaction or profit from his parliamentary career that he was willing to resign his seat if Argyll would provide for him an appointment as a baron of the Scottish exchequer. There was therefore nothing surprising about the laird of Grant's performance during the last Jacobite rebellion. It was a logical commentary on his relationship with the Hanoverian political ascendancy, and more particularly on his relationship with Ilay's machine in North Britain. Ludovick offered no assistance whatever to the Commander-in-Chief Scotland, General Sir John Cope, when he marched into the Highlands in an abortive attempt to nip the rebellion in the bud. As Cope at one point passed within ten miles of Castle Grant on his forced march to Inverness, the inactivity of Ludovick Grant was pointed, though of course no more so than that of many other substantial Highland landlords known to be Whig in their political sympathies. As Ludovick found it prudent to submit a formal defence of his actions, after taking legal advice, it is possible to examine his conduct in late 1745 and early 1746 in some detail. Nor is the modern observer entirely at the mercy of the story which the laird of Grant's lawyers thought would serve their employer best. There survive accounts of the same sequence of events, or part of it, from witnesses far from well disposed towards Ludovick, and the whole web of testimony was repeatedly probed by loyal English supporters of the Hanoverian dynasty, who cordially distrusted all the Scotsmen involved.

Ludovick and his father Sir James were used to a local political world in which men as important as MacDonell of Glengarry and Cameron of Lochiel naturally interceded for kinsmen to whom the Grants could offer favours. Glengarry told Ludovick bluntly in 1740 that he was always very tender in his dealings with anyone connected with the Grants, 'and do look for just returns'.[67] Ludovick's brother-in-law, James Lord Deskford, articulated clearly in 1741 a broadly similar view of the moral economy of Westminster politics. He remarked that a recent dispute between the Tories and the 'Patriot' (i.e. opposition) Whigs in parliament would divide and therefore weaken the opposition to Walpole's court Whig regime for: 'if you do not often neglect your own interest in order to support that of your friends, your friends will never neglect theirs to support yours, and you will become a single insignificant individual which can never have any weight.' As a paradigm of eighteenth-century British politics, the statement could hardly be bettered.[68]

When the news that Prince Charles had landed in the Highlands reached Ludovick Grant in August 1745 through the agency of the Lord Lyon Brodie of Brodie, it did so in a manner calculated to remind Ludovick of the realities of contemporary life, for in a letter written the day before the raising of the Jacobite standard in Glenfinnan Brodie reported that: 'Lovat will stir of no side, but chooses to do it on our side, provided the King indemnifys him of his losses by [i.e. as a result of the] taking away his company.'[69] Such modified rapture for the illustrious House of Hanover was not far removed from the spirit which beat in Ludovick's breast. Whig politics were the politics of interest. The laird of Grant quite reasonably felt that the time was overdue when a loyal Whig family like the Grants of that Ilk should be able to make a little interest on its own account. He was clear what he wanted. His objectives was as well-known to his brother-in-law as to himself.

James Lord Deskford, a son of James, fifth Earl of Findlater and Seafield, was also well informed about the realities of patronage distribution in the complex governmental situation of August 1745. The Westminster government was split between the Pelhams, Henry and his brother the Duke of Newcastle, and a group of ministers attached to the interest of John, Lord Carteret, who became Earl Granville in 1744. The Pelhams forced Granville out of office in November 1744, but he retained the sympathy of George II, and on the Regency Board which governed Britain until George II returned from abroad late in August 1745, Lords Bath, Tweeddale and Stair were followers of Granville. Ludovick Grant, having failed again and again to secure preferment through the medium of Ilay, now third Duke of Argyll, regarded it as prudent to correspond with the Marquis of Tweeddale, who was after all Secretary of State for Scotland. Baron Dalrymple, a baron of the Scottish Exchequer, having recently died, Ludovick Grant aspired to his place.

The difficulty, as Deskford pointed out, was that in distributing Scottish patronage Henry Pelham was almost entirely under the influence of his potent adherent, the Duke of Argyll. The latter was unlikely to favour Grant, and his stiff-necked pride would make him even more reluctant to concede anything in the face of a rebellion, when it might appear that he was buying loyalty. Cynics might reply that in a rebellion there are few commodities so inherently worth buying, but Deskford's final advice to Ludovick Grant was to adopt the humblest possible posture in applying direct to Inveraray, the seat of His Grace of Argyll. Suitably sycophantic phrases were suggested in which to hail the Campbell chief as 'head of the Whigs in Scotland', and Deskford felt that his brother-in-law should offer to withdraw from parliament if he secured the post he sought. Even so Deskford ended ominously: 'You certainly have no chance for succeeding if you do not do this; perhaps not much tho' you do. Liven, Strichen, John Maul, and Scots Tarbet, are the candidates, as I hear.' He heard right. Ludovick Grant never did become a baron of the Scottish Exchequer.[70]

Nor did he exactly strain himself in defence of the Best (i.e. Hanoverian) of Kings and a Perfect (i.e. Whig) Constitution. Lord President Duncan Forbes, who hastened north on receiving news of the outbreak of the rising, and who coordinated government efforts in and around Inverness, soon had proof of Ludovick's lack of zeal. Inverness was a quite crucial position; the key to the north-west Highlands, the apex of the Glen More sequence of garrisons, and not least a sally port calculated to dampen

Jacobite enthusiasm among the Frasers. It was very weakly held by a small garrison in Inverness castle (Fort George) commanded by Ludovick's uncle Major George Grant who later in the rising was to distinguish himself by surrendering his command after a two-day siege, for which martial performance he was subsequently drummed out of the British army. Fortunately, the Jacobite army's dash for Edinburgh at first drew it well away from Inverness, to which on 10 October 1745 came Lord Loudon, the Campbell soldier who had been appointed commander of all government troops and garrisons from Inverlochy to Inverness, and of all other Highland units raised on behalf of the Hanoverian cause, including a proposed twenty independent companies, to be raised by Whig chiefs and gentry. In actual fact Loudon brought only 150 men of his own regiment, plus a little cash, to Inverness. Duncan Forbes knew as well as anyone that lack of money had hindered pro-government activity in the Highlands in 1715, and that if the friends of government had then been few, they had at least been armed, whereas in 1745 there was an acute shortage of weapons among Whig clans. Nevertheless, his position was desperate and he could but demand of men like Ludovick Grant that they prove their principles by raising soldiers. To be precise, Forbes offered Ludovick a company.

The offer was very coolly received. Companies were plums in Highland politics. One such plum out of twenty was scarcely commensurate with the self-esteem, or indeed the real power, of the Clan Grant among the Whig clans. After the rebellion was over Ludovick Grant deliberately exaggerated the early dangers to his Speyside estates by alleging that the Mackintoshes and Macphersons were from the start in concert with the Jacobite forces, and that with the Jacobite Duke of Perth raising men for the Pretender on the Braes of Mar, and the veteran Jacobite Gordon of Glenbucket doing the same just across the Hills of Cromdale from Strathspey, in Strath Avon and Glen Livet, the Speyside Grants were in a virtual state of siege from the start. This was just not so. Cluny Macpherson was active on the Hanoverian side until well into September 1745, when he made a somewhat traumatic transition to Jacobitism. The Duke of Perth was only briefly in Braemar before returning to Perthshire, and the Mackintoshes made a shamblingly indecisive entry on to the stage of the '45.[71] Aeneas Mackintosh of Mackintosh held a captain's commission from George II, but he was not a man of strong character, and he was married to a Jacobite spitfire of a wife, Anne, daughter of John Farquharson of Invercauld. Mackintosh during the early stages of the rising seemed on the surface to be pursuing an ambiguous course. However, it is clear in retrospect that his main aim was to hinder the raising of recruits for the Jacobite army by potential rivals for the leadership of the Clan Chattan, and that he was throughout hand-in-glove with Duncan

Forbes of Culloden. When, under the influence of the Lord President and MacLeod of MacLeod, he finally made it clear that he would not raise his clan for Prince Charles, his formidable lady raised it herself, making free use of force on reluctant tenants and earning the immortal title of 'Colonel Anne'. Notoriously, later in the campaign the Jacobite colonel captured the Hanoverian captain who happened to be her husband.[72]

Ludovick Grant was in one way much more of a free agent in August 1745 than he later chose to admit. In another way, he was severely limited in his range of options by the position of his family and clan. Both he and the gentry of his name were convinced that they had been systematically discriminated against by the post-1688 Whig political ascendancy which they and their fathers had done so much to instal and maintain in power. It was galling that what they saw as bloody-minded refusal to treat them with minimal courtesy persisted into a major internal security crisis. They sent Lord Deskford to Culloden to explain to the Lord President two simple facts. One was that the Grants expected four companies, and would regard their acceptance of as few as three as a sign of their self-sacrificing patriotism. By implication, fewer than three constituted in their eyes little better than deliberate offensiveness. Secondly, having failed, generation after generation, to secure compensation for their chiefs' heavy financial losses in previous civil wars, they bluntly stated: 'that the whole clan should on all occasions be ready to act in the government's service, only that it would be necessary to give them pay during the time that they should be employed, because Mr Grant's private fortune could not bear so great an expense.'

Neither message appears truly to have penetrated the minds of Loudon and the Lord President. Short both of arms and of credit, they chose simply to bombard Castle Grant with letters insisting that an independent company be formed and sent to reinforce the garrison of Inverness. Ludovick nominated Grant of Rothiemurchus to the captaincy, and when this unit did eventually march into Inverness Forbes had to admit that it was of high calibre.[73] Promptly he asked that the Grants raise just one more. He had already been told that the principal gentlemen of the clan could scarcely be catered for at under four. Most unfortunately the demand for the second company reached Castle Grant just when it became common knowledge in Strathspey that Norman MacLeod of MacLeod, a major ally of Loudon and the Lord President, had been assigned four companies. The result was predictable.

Ludovick Grant kept a guard of about a hundred men around Castle Grant, to discourage any Jacobite hit-and-run raid. Whenever he heard of a substantial number of Jacobite clansmen approaching the boundaries of his regality, he rapidly mobilised something like a full clan regiment of 7–800 men, and moved out to meet them. The technique was enough to outface the Macphersons who prowled on Ludovick's perimeter, but could see no point in risking a bloody clan battle. The laird of Grant made it clear to Loudon that his bold front masked a chronic shortage of muskets for his men. In vain he asked for 400 firelocks. When Lord Lewis Gordon, the Jacobite Lord Lieutenant of Aberdeenshire and Banffshire, first tried to establish a correspondence with Ludovick Grant, his theme was that if Ludovick was not prepared to rise himself, he should not oppose the raising of his clan for Prince Charles. By December 1745 Lord Lewis had grasped that nobody was going to be allowed to meddle with the Speyside Grants, and indeed gave orders to his subordinates that no men were to be raised, even from detached portions of Ludovick's estate held of the Duke of Gordon, over which Lord Lewis as third son of Alexander, third Duke of Gordon (who had died in 1728) regarded himself as having natural claims.[74] When Norman MacLeod moved from Inverness towards Aberdeen late in December 1745 he was chagrined to find that Ludovick Grant refused to move with him.[75] On 23 December 1745 MacLeod was defeated at Inverurie in Aberdeenshire as he approached the river Don just north of Aberdeen. The victor in that engagement, Lord Lewis Gordon, was left master of all the country between Aberdeen and the Spey, thus clearing the way for the eventual retreat of the main Jacobite army towards Inverness after its successful delaying action at Falkirk in January 1746.

Ludovick Grant did not try to bar the advance of Prince Charles on Inverness. Loudon himself evacuated the town rather than try to make a stand there. The Grants would have been swiftly overwhelmed if they had been so foolish as to take the field in February 1746. Instead, Ludovick looked hard at the forces converging on his territory, to see how he personally could break out of the ring. His castle he knew was indefensible if the Jacobites could drag a couple of field guns to its doors, and he knew from his scouts: 'that the Macphersons, some of the Athol men and the Menzies were in a body in Badenoch above him, that Glenbucket with about 300 men were in Strathaven and Glenlivet and that another party was marching by Murray to enter Strathspey by the lower end of it.' Choosing to brush aside Glenbucket's force, the Grant chief moved south until he was out of danger, when he sent the bulk of his men home 'to take care of their cattle and houses'. He himself then went to Aberdeen to join the Duke of Cumberland and the advancing Hanoverian army. The solitary independent company furnished by the Grants was part of the garrison of Fort George which surrendered so ignominiously shortly after the Jacobites occupied Inverness.

With so prudent a chief, who clearly meant to stay in his Speyside lair as long as he could, the men of Urquhart and Glenmoriston were not exactly given a strong lead during the confused months of the rebellion.

On the contrary, they were endowed with something like home rule by default. Exactly what went on in these areas in late 1745 and early 1746 is still difficult to say, because of conflicting evidence. For example, Mr John Grant, minister of the gospel in Urquhart, was arrested after the collapse of the rebellion and shipped off to London, on charges which included expounding the Young Pretender's manifesto to his parishioners from the pulpit in Gaelic. He stoutly denied the charges against him, produced testimonies from two presbyteries as to his inviolable attachment to the person and government of King George, and wrote a defence of himself in which he ascribed his arrest to the personal malice of Ludovick Grant, with whom he had a long-standing feud because the laird of Grant, though principal heritor or landowner of the parish, failed to furnish the minister with an adequate manse let alone a glebe or holding of land, as required by law. After testifying on his own behalf in London in August 1746 John Grant was discharged on bail, to stand trial in Edinburgh. In December 1746 in Edinburgh he was again discharged. The Church of Scotland itself, though officially passionately pro-Hanoverian, handled its Highland clergy and elders accused of Jacobitism in the '45 gently, disciplining only one minister, Thomas Man of Dunkeld, whose offences were blatant and partially confessed, and him only with a five-month suspension from duty. Local tradition in Urquhart is emphatic that throughout the rising the parish minister was a strong Jacobite.[76]

Alexander Grant of Shewglie or Sheuglie poses similar problems. He never came to trial after the '45, for he was shipped to Tilbury where he died of jail fever on 29 July 1746. His reputation was that of a very active Jacobite indeed, but after Culloden he strongly denied having encouraged his tenants to enlist under the banner of Prince Charles. One of the few sources of contemporary information on Urquhart and Glenmoriston during the rebellion is a sequence of letters sent from the area to Ludovick Grant in Castle Grant. They hardly clear away the fog of doubt. In the first place, it is clear that the position of Grant in the two glens west of Loch Ness was still an uneasy one which exposed them to considerable local pressures in an emergency. The Grant connection went back two hundred years, but Grant of Glenmoriston and others of his name still had to contend with many inhabitants with other names and with loyalties to chiefs other than the chief of Clan Grant. That the Grant chiefs followed whenever possible a policy of turning off 'strangers' in favour of Grants when holdings fell vacant seems, naturally enough, to have sharpened local animosities which on occasion boiled over into inter-personal violence.[77] During the rising John Grant, Ludovick Grant's baillie or factor in Urquhart, sent regular reports to Castle Grant of what was going on in his area. He was clear enough about the Jacobite commitment of men like Corrimony and Glenmoriston himself, but even the factor was baffled by the position of Shewglie, whose actions and words were usually at odds with one another. Shewglie's sons went off to join the Jacobite army, but Shewglie then told Grant the factor that they had broken their father's heart by doing so.[78]

Ludovick Grant did issue bluntly worded manifestoes in which he ordered his dependants in Urquhart to stay peaceably at home awaiting his own orders. He added, and he clearly meant what he said, that he would regard disobedience in this matter as a personal insult to be revenged when the occasion offered itself.[79] None of this constituted a rousing call to arms under the Hanoverian standard. The laird of Grant wanted his tenants to sit tight. Alexander Grant of Corrimony wrote to him on 15 October 1745 excusing his own Jacobite behaviour on the ground that it was a necessary humouring of the people around him and the only way a Grant laird cut off from the support of his chief and clan could ensure peaceable possession of his land and cattle. In other words, Corrimony argued that sitting tight was not an option, though he tortuously tried to argue that he was doing the best he could to adhere to the spirit of Ludovick's instructions.[80] John Grant the factor did not agree. He was clear by December 1745 that Corrimony was a violent Jacobite who was determined to run the factor out of Urquhart by threatening his life and property.[81]

All these correspondents repeatedly made the point that if the chief of Clan Grant really wanted to enforce his will west of Loch Ness, he had to go there. In retrospect Ludovick claimed that he had seriously considered moving across with 700 or so men, but that he had been discouraged by the pusillanimity displayed by Loudon, Duncan Forbes, and the considerable Whig militia forces which built up at Inverness. There were reasons for the reluctance of the Whig forces to strike down Glen More. By and large, the clans north of Inverness were Whig. The essential qualification of this remark is that the greatest of them all, the Clan Mackenzie, was just a trifle ambiguous in its loyalties. Its chief, Lord Fortrose (who had lost the legal right to his hereditary title of Earl of Seaforth due to Jacobite proclivities in 1715), stood firmly by the government of George II, mainly it would seem because that regime had chosen to overlook not one, but two acts on his part of treasonable rebellion against it, in 1715 and in the small Jacobite rising of 1719. A rival Mackenzie chief, the Earl of Cromartie, masked his own Jacobite convictions at the start of the '45, but then came out in an open bid to rally the clan behind Prince Charles. Cromartie did raise some men, but his success was very incomplete. Loudon therefore was able to put together a composite force of his own troops plus Munros, Grants, Gunns, Mackays, Sutherlands, and Mackenzies. Inverness was a town dominated by the Culloden interest and formed a snug billet for a Whig host. Its leading clergyman,

Alexander Macbean, 'the John Knox of the North' and minister of the first charge of Inverness, 1727–62, was a militant anti-Jacobite activist in 1745–46. What seems to have given the Whig leaders pause was the thought that a march by a large force of alien northern clans south from Inverness might well provoke the Jacobite mass rising which they were anxious to discourage. So, far from being willing to supplement or substitute for Loudon's troops in his own western territories, it is clear that Ludovick Grant preferred to draw what men and money he could from them over to reinforce himself in Speyside.[82]

Major Grant even had difficulty passing a small non-provocative detail of troops from Inverness to Fort Augustus, with essential money supplies for the pay of the Fort Augustus garrison. Comically, the trouble came from his own militia troops who threatened to mutiny rather than march south. It was their harassed commander's last warlike triumph to talk them into going. To arrest one old man, Lovat, a few miles from Inverness Loudon led out 800 men.[83] It was his boldest foray from Fort George, and he botched it by allowing the old fox to give him the slip almost at once. Faced by such inspiring examples from Whig politicians of the Argyll faction who seemed reluctant to give him the time of day, Ludovick Grant had every reason to stick to the resolution to live quietly at home which he had formed in 1737. As a result of the upheavals during the rising, the laird of Grant was receiving not a farthing of rent from Glen Urquhart or Glenmoriston and he was receiving precious little from Speyside. To occupy his lands on the other side of Loch Ness effectively, he would have needed a clan regiment of perhaps 800 men. It would have cost a fortune and would have left his far more important regality defenceless. Above all, Ludovick had learned all over again as a result of his re-entry into politics in 1741 that there was nothing in that game for him. His Majesty's Government at Westminster could be relied upon only to welsh on its debts of honour to the Grants for a third time.

The absence of Grant of Grant from the power politics of the Great Glen in 1745–46 helped in a minor way to give the British government a very unpleasant experience, as Grants from west of Loch Ness did eventually fight for Prince Charles at Culloden in significant numbers. From the point of view of that jaundiced Whig Ludovick Grant, and his disillusioned old father Sir James, His Majesty's Ministers had nobody to blame for this fact but themselves. They would not pay the minimum price needed to prevent Urquhart and Glenmoriston getting out of control.

7 Lovat's Approach to Disaster 1737–1745

Simon Fraser's sense of grievance was always one of his best-developed faculties. He was by early 1737 convinced that he had been as ill-used as any man could be. By birth, by the scale of 'my Interest in my countery [i.e. Inverness-shire]', and by what he thought of as his outstanding services to the Hanoverian cause in 1715, services which seemed to grow steadily in retrospect, he was convinced he should have been included in the sixteen representative peers, nominally elected by the Scottish nobility, but in practice nominated by Westminster. Instead he found himself 'forgot and excluded' and, what was worse, incapable of any action to remedy the situation. That was what really rankled him about his failure to obtain a gown for Ludovick Grant. All Simon's huffing and puffing about standing or falling with the Grants was surface posturing. Deep down what hurt was the thought that enemies like Lord Lyon Brodie of Brodie, with whom he had been exchanging salvoes of abusive letters with his usual gusto, were now certainly laughing at him behind his back.[1] The situation was, in terms of Lovatic psychology alone, intolerable. The only relevant question was what might be done about it, and the answer to that conundrum depended on an analysis of the way Lovat had manoeuvred himself into this political cul-de-sac.

He was clear that the rock on which he kept foundering was Duncan Forbes, that conceited 'counterfeit lord', as he saw the Lord President, whose rancour was rooted in repeated electoral rebuffs in county elections.[2] The pyrrhic nature of the Fraser–Grant alliance's victories in Inverness-shire was, from Lovat's point of view, too obvious for words. All they had done was alienate a man whose strategic position as a man of business and adviser to the Argathelians enabled him to manipulate the faction structure at Westminster so as to deprive the Grants and Frasers of the patronage which was the principal, if indeed it was not the sole, objective of their electoral activities. The only interest Simon Fraser ever wanted or intended to represent in any legislature was Simon Fraser. It was therefore an ominous sign when in March 1737 philosophical resignation appeared in Lovat's correspondence with Sir James Grant. A Simon who blessed God that he could live content without so much as sixpence from the administration was either not himself or only too much his old self and finding consolation in thoughts of an alternative strategy.[3] The alternative political ploy was itself obtrusively obvious. It was to ditch the Grants at the next election in order to run a candidate more acceptable to both the administration and the Argyll interest. The odium of so obviously self-centred a performance was something MacShimi could probably just about bear. By the standards of the Scottish upper classes, such an exercise was little more than a routine manoeuvre.

However, Lovat first had to live down the allegation of Jacobite intrigue being broadcast against him by Fraser of Castle Leathers in 1737. Lovat's insistence that the whole fracas derived partly from his own decision to prefer Lieutenant Macpherson to Castle Leathers for the tack or lease of his house and mains* farm of Moniack rings surprisingly true. Inevitably, Lovat raked Castle Leathers with abuse as a false, lying, cheating, cowardly knave and ruffian. Yet verbal drum-fire in Inverness-shire was not likely to concuss eardrums in London, where Castle Leathers was assiduously propagating his allegations, in cooperation with one James Fraser, an apothecary in London who was son to that other Fraser tacksman, Fraser of Phopachy. Lovat needed friends in London. He begged Sir James Grant to stand by him and to concert with Sir Robert Munro in presenting a defence of Lovat to the all-important master of patronage, the Earl of Ilay.[4]

September 1737 therefore saw Lovat, the ardent Grant partisan, in close conference with that other ardent Grant partisan, Sir Robert Munro, making sure that the Forbes interest made no headway in establishing voting rights for its men in the county.[5] The fact was that Lovat was thoroughly frightened by the degree of countenance shown to Castle Leathers by major London politicians. Even Simon registered the message that this was no time to be asking the Court for favours, especially financial favours,[6] though appalling weather, a late poor harvest, and a threat of famine did not suggest that 1738 would be a good year for rent.[7] As it was, Lovat was being told by his own relatives that if he did not mobilise all possible support in London he was likely to be permanently damned in the eyes of Sir Robert Walpole's administration. He tried to stiffen the resolve of Sir James Grant by organising a letter from Inverness burgh in which Lovat's leading supporter there denounced Castle Leathers as a notoriously irresponsible man.[8] Lovat even had to swallow gracefully the bitter pill of Sir James Grant's refusal to support the attack on Provost Hossack and Inverness town council in the affair of

*'Mains' is a common Scots farm name. It implies that the farm once supplied the feudal superior's own household. Hence the derivation of mains from the Latin 'terra mensalis', i.e. the table-land of the estate.

the parliamentary renewal of the boddle tax. Lovat covered his retreat with the usual political smokescreen of an allegation that he would never have stirred in the matter had he not believed the Earl of Ilay entirely approved of a campaign whose sole aim was to win hearts and minds in Inverness for my dear Lord Ilay.[9]

Fawning, cringing, and flattering to the last, Lovat pulled back from another political bout whose sole trophy was a bloody nose. His relations with the Grants of Glenmoriston were becoming as ambiguous as his relations with their Speyside-based chief. They alternated between threats to sue the Glenmoriston men for £10,000 sterling in the High Court of Justiciary in Edinburgh, and love-feasts prior to a negotiated settlement arbitrated by a worried Ludovick Grant of Grant.[10] Instinctively manipulative as ever, Lovat wrote in the dying days of December 1738 to urge Sir James Grant to take action over the dearth of justices of the peace in Inverness-shire. Most of those on the last commission were, according to Lovat, dead or in such remote places as the Isle of Skye. For two years Sir James had been sitting on a list of 'friendly' candidates for the commission supplied by Lovat's henchman Evan Baillie. The time had come, Lovat suggested, for a vigorous approach to the government in Westminster on the subject.[11]

Even Lovat's irrepressible optimism was fading by early 1739. He told Sir James Grant that he found it difficult to believe that Ilay had any remaining affection for Simon Fraser, Lord Lovat. Sir James might swear this was so: Lovat could see no practical effects of this alleged affection. Lovat was also beginning to speak bluntly about the education of his son and heir. His father had jibbed, in the end, at sending him to England, but had kept his word about allowing Ilay to specify his place of education. The upshot was that the boy had been placed with Principal Neil Campbell of Glasgow University, an intimate friend of Argyll and Ilay who treated the Master of Lovat as a perquisite, charging outrageous fees. Lovat was not prepared to have his pockets picked by an academic Campbell indefinitely. Rather he resolved to board the boy in Edinburgh, either with Patrick Cumming, one of the town's ministers, or with Mr John Ker, Professor of Humanity (i.e. Latin), both of them staunch Whigs.[12] By May 1739 Lovat was prepared to tell Sir James flatly that if the sitting MP for Inverness-shire found it troublesome to do my Lord Lovat's business in London, my Lord Lovat would correspond with those that found doing such business less troublesome and embarrassing.[13] Equally, Lovat made it clear that he expected to hear soon that Grant had stood up for him against the campaign of abuse mounted by Castle Leathers and the Frasers of Phopachy. Lovat was himself doing all he could to conciliate Ilay by accepting gracefully the placing of his son in Edinburgh under the wing of the Reverend Patrick Cumming, Ilay's manager and patronage-fixer in the Church of Scotland.[14]

Lovat was surely right in his faith in the healing powers of patronage. As he said to Sir James Grant late in 1739, it was in the government's interest to bring into its network of service and reward the young chiefs of clans whose families were disaffected. When he made this grand generalisation Lovat was seeking a specific concession for his kinsman Clanranald, who wanted a stand of colours in the British army for his eldest son. The boy was being educated in Edinburgh and an ensign's commission for a boy in 1739 might have ensured a different outcome in 1745 when the young man, Ranald MacDonald of Clanranald and Benbecula, joined Prince Charles with all the men he could raise, and mortgaged the family fortunes to finance the Jacobite invasion of England.[15] To give Lovat his due: what he preached, he practised. From his Frasers he demanded deference, but he was not such a fool as to expect it for nothing. He was just as willing to try to drum up work for Donald Fraser, a skilled mill-wright who had worked extensively on MacLeod of MacLeod's mills in Glenelg and the Isle of Skye, as he was to demand political concessions for himself.[16]

Lovat's private life was yet again in shambles. After the annulment of the ceremony with the Dowager Lady Lovat he had contrived to maintain a stable relationship (by his standards) with Margaret, fourth daughter of Ludovick Grant of Grant, until she died in childbirth early in 1729. In 1732 he had tried to marry Marion Dalrymple, daughter of Sir Robert Dalrymple of Castleton, and granddaughter of a Lord President of the Court of Session. However, after the marriage contract was drawn up and the date fixed the girl showed wisdom beyond her years in refusing to go through with the match. On 1 July 1733 he married, under very murky circumstances, Primrose, daughter of the Hon. John Campbell of Mamore. Primrose was therefore a sister of General John Campbell of Mamore, a commander of Whig militia in the '45 and the future fourth Duke of Argyll. Lovat and his new wife had a most tempestuous relationship. He said she was 'a mixture between a devil and a daw', and his correspondence abounds in memoranda accusing her of everything from near insanity to theft.[17] The eventual separation Lovat hailed as an escape from hell at the expense of his pocket. In fact he paid her £30 a year in quarterly instalments, and she outlived him by half a century, dying in Edinburgh in 1796.[18] On top of his political peccadilloes, Lovat did latterly carry this heavy emotional handicap in his frantic bid to ingratiate himself with the ducal house of Argyll.

The way in which he was stripped of his militia company late in 1739 obviously touched Lovat on the quick. When Ludovick Grant tried to cheer him up by minimising the episode's importance, Lovat was quick to point out that with his modest rent-roll and heavy debts, the loss could be ill-afforded.[19] When he surrendered his command to General Clayton, the Fraser Chief boasted truculently that sixty of his ninety-two effectives were Frasers of his name. Clayton probably found the boast pathetic, but gentlemen of his coat were to flee before Fraser broadswords often enough in 1745 and 1746.[20] Lovat had seen the loss of his company coming before the blow fell. He was relieved that the charter confirming him in his estates had passed the exchequer and had run the gauntlet of the Scottish seals before he fell out of favour. Once sealed it was in practical terms irreversible, short of conviction for treason. He knew, of course, that his state of indebtedness made him still politically vulnerable, and with Wade thundering that 'the King knows all our tricks', he also knew that it behoved him to keep a low profile.[21] With hostile Frasers still in London mounting a major propaganda campaign about his Jacobite connections, Simon was profoundly distrusted in high circles and was in a position which he considered 'would vex an apostle'.[22]

Lovat seems genuinely to have believed that the independent companies were being used in a way which deprived the Glen More farmers of effective protection from the thieves of Glengarry and Glenmoriston. Broken up into penny packets, the troops were being used primarily to guard state revenue and property. As Lovat put it 'it is impossible that we can keep the towns, customs houses, excise and the King's roads, and preserve the cows from being stolen at the same time'. However, the reports which 'the two monsters', Phopachy and Castle Leathers were spreading about him in and around Westminster ensured that the government just was not willing to give Lovat control over a compact body of disciplined men. Nobody could be sure what he would use them for in a crisis.

His men were despatched to Inverness to be incorporated in the regiment commanded by 'the gallant earl' of Crawford. John, Earl of Crawford, was about as politically safe a soldier as Westminster could find in North Britain. After service in the British, Austrian and Russian forces this head of a hereditarily Whig and staunchly Presbyterian house had returned home to raise a unit known briefly by his own name, becoming in 1742 adjutant-general and colonel of this newly incorporated Highland Regiment, which encompassed all the existing Highland independent companies plus four additional companies raised for the occasion. The new regiment was shipped off to Flanders almost as soon as it had been formed. Westminster had never been prepared to use the independent companies for much beyond revenue-collection and disarming the Highlanders. The latter function proved impractical because it could only be carried out under warrants from local justices of the peace, which were not forthcoming. As an effective counter to insurgency in the West Highlands, the independent companies could only have been rendered effective by somehow tying the more ambiguous chiefs into a political and patronage relationship with Westminster which meant they had more to lose than gain by failure to cooperate with the Whig ascendancy. As it was, men like Lovat were left sulking, entertaining close allies like Lochiel and his lady, and glorying in that local and clan power which was the only power they had. It was hardly surprising that Lovat was denounced for sending undersized, underaged, or geriatric recruits to Crawford's regiment. Those clansmen were wreaths on another man's brow.[23]

The idea of amalgamating all the independent companies (already popularly referred to in the Highlands as the Black Watch) into one unit had already been mooted in the Highlands for years before the event itself occurred. There exists in the archives of the Grants of Grant a remarkable document which leaves little doubt that as late as 1740 Simon Fraser, Lord Lovat was not without hope that the man responsible for the operation, as colonel of the new regiment, might be himself. The document is a copy of a letter from MacDonald of Scotus to Lovat. The recipient forwarded it presumably to Sir James Grant, who as MP for Inverness-shire might have been able to float the idea in official circles, had he so wished. There is no evidence that he even tried to do so. Lovat's efforts were wasted, despite the care he had taken, care which seems to have included supplying Scotus with appropriate phrases. The whole missive reeks of collusion. After an opening grovel, Scotus wrote that there had been a rumour some years ago in the Highlands to the effect that the companies were to be regimented. At this point his credibility lessens dramatically with the statement that 'all the judicious' were of the view that Lovat should be colonel of the said regiment. From that point the letter degenerates into a dithyrambically written account, or more precisely a gross exaggeration, of Lovat's services to the Hanoverian cause in 1715, culminating in the statement that Lovat and his clan had done more service to government than all the foreign troops brought over on that occasion. Like Lewis Carroll's Bellman in 'The Hunting of the Snark', Lovat tended to believe that if he said a thing often enough it became true. Even in his day this was only the case in British politics if the speaker was, and only as long as the speaker remained, Prime Minister. A willing suspension of disbelief in politics is greatly assisted by the expectation of patronage. Above the level of Inverness-shire, Simon had none.[24]

However, he did have real political clout in his native country, and in 1741 a general election, an event cordially detested by the government and by most politicians, for it meant an expensive disturbance of the even tenor of their ways, was due. Sir James Grant was disturbed to hear rumours that Norman MacLeod of MacLeod was threatening to put up against him in Inverness-shire. The Skye chief, who was not only a local and a powerful figure, but also a close relative of Simon Fraser whose mother was Sybilla, daughter of John MacLeod of MacLeod. At first nothing came back to Sir James from Castle Downie except soothing Lovat soporifics. Of course, Sir James need not worry. Were not the combined interests of Lovat and Sir James more than capable of swaying the wills of the handful of voters? So they were, but Simon could not but notice that his MP fawned on him roughly once every seven years – during a general election. MacShimi was in fact an early discoverer of the thesis that the British voter has meaningful influence over his so-called representative only during an election. In the bleak winter of 1740, with gales, hail and snow, with cattle dying, and grain not sown until late March, Lovat lurked in Castle Downie dreading another famine, and assuring Sir James Grant that he read newspapers only for amusement.[25] Perhaps he did, but there was grimmer amusement in the letters he began to write to Sir James, itemising those areas in which the MP could demonstrate his much-mouthed affection for his most powerful constituent in the hard coin of deeds, rather than in the evaporative medium of words.

Lovat wanted effective defence against 'Major Cracks' (Castle Leathers), a man who had tried to destroy his credit and authority with his kindred, and to divide Clan Fraser. Lovat wanted Grant to make serious efforts to mend Lovatic fences with Lord Ilay. After all, to show his deference to the Argathelians, Lovat, after snatching his heir from the clutches of the Reverend Principal of Glasgow University, had sent the boy to Patrick Cumming, the Edinburgh minister who was not only related to Fraser of Fairfield, and very capable, but was also, to quote Simon 'a thorrow creature of the Earl of Islay's'. Cumming was certainly, from his settlement at St Giles Kirk in 1732 until 1751, the Argyll interests' principal manager for ecclesiastical affairs.[26] Lovat was also disgruntled over marginal aggression on his own territory by Grant clients like Davidson of Achimony, whom he complained had harried his tenants within three miles of Beaufort, at the head of 100 armed men. Nor did Simon take kindly to rumours that Grant of that Ilk's younger brother Colquhoun of Luss was about to attack his own close ally Sir Robert Munro of Fowlis in the Wick burghs he had represented since 1710. The message coming to Sir James from Inverness-shire was plain: if he wanted the seat he had to pay some attention to Lovat's interests and needs.

Two arrogant stiff-necked men were clashing. Lovat made it clear that the time for stringing him along with fair words was over. He might not have any pickings from the government table, but he could stand on his own legs in Inverness-shire. Beneath the unctuous phraseology of the period the snarl in Sir James's voice became unmistakeable when he said that, despite Lovat, he would yet sit at Westminster for another seven years. So he did, but not for Lovat's county. Sir Robert Munro went down in Wick burghs after thirty years' representation. His ally Simon, fighting like an enraged and bad-tempered old bear, mauled Sir James Grant's interest badly enough to drive him out of the Inverness-shire he had held since 1722. Between 1741 and 1747 Sir James retreated into Elgin burghs. Though Lovat expressed the hope that mere political quarrels would in no way disturb the close alliance between the Grants and the Frasers, his rhetoric was unconvincing. What had once been an epistolary torrent on his part became a trickle. The Grants had failed to serve his ends. They had tried to use him, without any kind of return on their part. At vast expense, by his standards, Simon had turned out Sir James. Whether his new love, MacLeod of MacLeod, would prove more enduring remained to be seen.[27]

MacLeod certainly came to the representation of his county with a suitably murky past. In 1739 he and his kinsman Sir Alexander MacDonald of Sleat were alleged to have devised an infamous operation whereby they were deporting some of their tenants, many of them women and small children, to the American plantations as bond servants on trumped-up charges which did not legally carry the penalty of transportation. Threatened with prosecution, MacLeod appealed to Lord President Duncan Forbes to avert the 'multitude of inconveniences' which would follow any prosecution. No more was heard of the matter and MacLeod's loyalty to the Argyll interest was sealed. There were clearly two sides to the tale. Lady Margaret MacDonald furiously denied that Sir Alexander was a kidnapper. Harvest-workers on his Skye estates had indeed been abducted, but she said that this was the work of a freebooter called Norman MacLeod, whom her husband was trying to hunt down. Lady Margaret was however under no illusions about the consequences of legal action for her husband: 'tho' it cannot be dangerouse to him, yett it cannot faill of being both troublesome and expensive'.[28]

A better example would be hard to find of the general point that the most formidable instrument of social control at the disposal of an eighteenth-century magistrate was his known power under certain circumstances to prevent a prosecution process from even starting. Since it was Lovat's basic political policy to cling to the Argyll interest in almost any eventuality, Norman MacLeod's indebtedness to the Argathelians suited the Fraser chief's book well enough. When in May 1740 Sir James Grant conveyed to Lovat the news that the Duke of Argyll had moved into open opposition to Walpole's administration, Lovat did not flinch. He was, he said, with Argyll and Islay 'whether the two brothers be out or be in'.[29] His calculation was, of course, that the Campbell ascendancy in Scottish politics was so massive that any administration would have to make concessions to it. In fact Ilay did not go 'out' with Argyll. He continued to work with Walpole while his brother enhanced their joint bargaining-power with the regime by showing in the general election of 1741 that he could return MPs in Scottish constituencies in his own interest even without government countenance. MacLeod of MacLeod was soon aligned in the House of Commons with a group of MPs known as 'the Duke of Argyll's gang', who habitually voted against government measures in the closing stages cf a deeply troubled and visibly decaying administration saddled with a war with Spain which it did not want and which it managed indifferently.[30]

Yet from Lovat's point of view an Inverness-shire MP in sustained opposition was not likely to be able to produce the favours which Lovat craved, even if Lovat's own behaviour had not made it wildly improbable that any Whig administration would oblige him. By early 1741 Lovat's feud with Ludovick Grant of Grant had reached the point of total and public hostility.[31] In a previous political era Lovat had actively encouraged those Glen More chiefs over whom he exercised considerable influence, like MacDonell of Glengarry, to cultivate good relations with Ludovick Grant of Grant.[32] Now there was no point in sweet-talking the Grants. Sir James, as MP for Elgin burghs, had every reason to be hostile to Lovat after the Inverness-shire election of 1741. He continued to vote with the government, while his eldest son ran the family estates, which centred on Strath Spey, and quarrelled over local issues with the Fraser chief. Ludovick Grant was by 1741 a very jaundiced Whig, but a Whig he was.

Simon had always been ambiguous in his ultimate political loyalties. By 1741, having queered his pitch with the Whigs, he was actively dabbling once more in Jacobite intrigue, dealing with the principal Scottish contact man for the Jacobite court in Rome – John Murray of Broughton, a member of a Jacobite family from Peebles-shire who returned to Scotland from a lengthy spell on the Continent early in 1739. In that year a committee of Scots Jacobite leaders, sometimes known as 'the Concert' was formed to coordinate Highland and Lowland Jacobite efforts towards restoring the Stuarts. It proved a broken reed in practice for only three of its members were 'out' in the '45. One was the Catholic Duke of Perth. The others were Cameron of Lochiel and, very very late in the rising, Lovat. The business manager for 'the Concert' was William Drummond, son of the laird of Balhaldies or Balhaldy in Perthshire. MacGregor being a name proscribed by penal laws, these MacGregors called themselves Drummond for convenience. William Drummond's mother was a daughter of Sir Ewen Cameron of Lochiel, so he was first cousin to the Lochiel of the '45. Scottish Jacobitism tended increasingly to become an affair of intermarried families. However, the lords of 'the Concert' had enough wit to approach Cardinal Fleury, first minister of France, about possible French support for a Scottish rising. Only after receiving a vaguely positive response did they directly contact Murray of Broughton whom they swore to absolute secrecy until the policy of the French court was clarified.

Balhaldy had been sent to France again to try to pin down the elusive diplomacy of the Most Christian King into something like a firm commitment. When he reported progress late in 1742, his report was so vague that the worried Scots lords despatched Murray of Broughton early in 1743 to Paris. Relations between England and Spain had been deteriorating nicely since 1739, when England went to war with the other Bourbon-ruled kingdom of Spain. Formal declarations of war had not been made, but in June 1742 a British army commanded by Lord Stair had landed in the Netherlands for the express purpose of opposing the French conquest of the Austrian Netherlands (the area which was to become Belgium). It is was a blow to Murray to learn before he left London of Cardinal Fleury's death, even though it is wildly unlikely that that master of evasion had ever given firm undertakings to the Scottish Jacobite agents. Once he arrived in Paris, Murray appears to have been shaken by the generally dishonest nature of the negotiations between the French and the two Scottish agents Balhaldy and Lord Sempill. Both sides were lying in an effort to manipulate the other. Balhaldy and Sempill grossly exaggerated the strength and preparedness of the Scottish Jacobites in order to pull France into action, while the French were so shifty that Murray later concluded that they did not really want to restore the Stuarts, but merely to provoke the Scots into active support for a bloody and hazardous civil war.[33]

The exiled Jacobite court was naturally prodigal with gifts of offices and ranks which it did not control to prospective supporters whose loyalty needed a little bolstering. The Old Pretender signed on 14 March 1740 a patent creating Simon Duke of Fraser, Marquis of Beaufort and also an earl, viscount and lord. Balhaldy brought a copy over to Scotland, to waft it under Simon's nose. The original was deposited with Balhaldy's uncle 'Old Lochiel' in Boulogne for safety. In December 1743 the same hand signed a commission to Lovat as 'Lord Lieutenant north of the Spey and to the head of the Spey to the North side of Loch Lochy'. Meaningless as the gesture was, it roughly defined the area in which the Fraser chief aspired to political ascendancy.[34] Loch Lochy marked the northern boundary of Cameron power and even Simon Fraser knew that the redoubtable Clan Cameron had to be treated as an ally and not as a client. In all fairness, it must be said that however pugnacious he might be towards rival territorial powers like the Mackenzies or Grants, who repeatedly crowded the Fraser block at the north end of Glen More, Simon was on the whole successful in cultivating a working relationship with the other Glen More and Glen Spean chiefs. He threatened their position not at all, and he was willing to make their problems his problems.

Thus, early in July 1743 Lovat wrote to Lochiel a letter which started with a long tale of woe about Lovat's health and how only the ministrations of his cousin Dr Fraser of Achnagairn had enabled him to survive a dreadful fever. The letter then went on to say that Cluny had recently visited Lovat and that a council of war had been held between Lovat, Cluny, Lovat's son and heir, Lovat's henchman Ewen Baillie, and Fraser of Gortuleg, Lovat's principal contact with the Duke of Gordon. The duke was expected soon to visit his Badenoch properties, whence he was expected to progress to Lochaber and Lochiel's house. 'Cluny's business', which was the main concern of the meeting at Lovat's seat, was essentially with the duke, but the web of contacts involved defines with some precision the political society in the Great Glen and Glen Spean in which these Highland gentlemen lived.[35] Cluny was a frequent visitor at Downie before and after his marriage to Lovat's eldest daughter. He was certainly there in April 1742, at a time when Lovat was arranging to lend his own Edinburgh house to Lochiel and his family and also busy complaining that as he and the Chisholm bargained with the English Preston company to sell their woods, the Chisholm was cheating him, with the aid of the legal profession, of about £500-worth of timber.[36] It was an Inverness-shire world, riven with feuds, but also full of close alliances between the significant families, and the events of high politics at home and abroad seemed curiously remote. Of course they were not. In retrospect, Lovat's remark to Lochiel in November 1743 that the French were liable to turn insolent after their recent successes against the allied armies, was an ominous forecast of the events of 1744–5.[37]

Later that month Lovat was expressing anxiety about the politics of the county, pressing Lochiel to consult fully with MacLeod of MacLeod on the subject.[38] The whole business of holding together an effective electoral interest in the county was something at which Lovat worked relentlessly and seems to have been the basic motive behind his prodigious hospitality at Beaufort, where the supposedly delicate Fraser chief would sit drinking with his guests until six in the morning. Inevitably, he attracted men like himself who were marginal to the political establishment and locked in assertive rivalry with families more securely reconciled to the Hanoverian regime than themselves. It was significant that to Lovat the Earl of Cromartie, a bankrupt with hopes of ousting the Seaforth family from the leadership of his clan was a boon companion and 'the prettiest Mackenzie alive'.[39] Underneath all this busy politicking, however, lurked the unregenerate Lovat, with all his instinctive Scottish nationalism. The dreadful year 1743 was likely to elicit mere phrases of sympathy from English pens, he told Lochiel. All Scotsmen could do was exercise patience until Providence delivered them from Slavery. Anti-Unionism could hardly be more succinctly put.[43]

Simon's old eyes relentlessly scanned the political horizon. He positively longed for news of the shifting balance of power in a Europe torn with war, and he complained bitterly that Lochiel did not keep him adequately informed from Edinburgh.[41] Because he regularly despatched cattle to Lowland markets, Lovat was in constant touch with his own Edinburgh lawyers, and the Fraser gentry supplemented their Chief's formidable intelligence network. Achnagairn, for example, warned him late in 1743 that there were rumours that John Roy Stuart had been bribed by the government to act as a spy on the Pretender's court in Rome, whence John Roy had had to flee on detection.[42] It is the juxtaposition of local and international pressures that makes Lovat's political life so fascinating. By January 1744 he was desperately worried that his clansmen had exposed him to the venom of 'that little insolent upstart the Provost of Inverness'. By helping a frustrated lover to abduct the daughter and heiress of the late baillie William Fraser of Inverness, the Fraser of Foyers had exposed Lovat's clansmen to endless lawsuits, supported by all those who, like the provost, wished to send Lovat and his clan to hell, at the first opportunity.[43] The antics of his Stratherrick clansmen triggered off a spasm of aggressive hypochondria, no doubt exacerbated by the tensions of correspondence and contact with such notorious Jacobites as the Duke of Perth and 'Drummond' of Balhaldy, who was really the leading member of the proscribed name of MacGregor. Simon had reached the point of refusing to commit his inner thoughts to Lochiel to paper.[44]

Lovat still had to play the political game on both sides of the board. 1744 saw him resolved to visit Edinburgh to see the new Duke of Argyll. Ilay had succeeded his brother in 1743, and it was the duty of any Fraser chief, anxious about his followers, to try to have good relations with him. As it was, Lovat was confident he could save Foyers' estate from penalty despite Foyers' kidnapping of the Inverness baillie's daughter.[45] As the rain poured relentlessly down in the Highland summer of 1744, Lovat's mind ranged further afield again. He knew of the French plans to invade the south of England. He had heard rumours that General Keith, the Jacobite exile from the north-east of Scotland who had risen to high commands in Europe, was to lead a descent on northern Scotland.[46] That same month Lovat expressed his pleasure that Cluny had secured a company in the new Highland regiment, for Cluny was known to need the money, but the Fraser chief added sourly that not a single Fraser or Cameron had secured similar preferment.[47]

The bleak weather of 1744 continued, the worst Lovat had seen for years. The mood of the Fraser chief matched the weather, for he raged at the government as a set of wretches devoid of conscience, honour, and honesty, and threatened to emigrate rather than live to see them wreck the country.[48] He still concerned himself with protecting the interests of Fraser tacksmen upon the Duke of Gordon's Lochaber estates. The commissioners responsible for the ducal debts were anxious to raise rent and encourage industry by urging lesser tenants to bid for their own tacks. Fraser of Gortuleg, strategically placed in Gordon estate administration, promised to give preference to Frasers where bids were even.[49] Lochiel used his good offices in this affair, but in fact enhanced rents, if offered, were unlikely to be paid in a dearth-stricken Highlands where meal was at a premium.[50] Lovat had long ago written off any chance of effective political action through the Argyll interest,[51] and reckoned that the 'fatall Union' was on the verge of completely destroying the identity of Scotland.[52] Both conclusions were arguably sound. Significantly, Lovat deliberately advertised his views to Lochiel, whose political sympathies he clearly assumed were much the same as his own,[53] and whose economic state was equally straitened. As Lovat told Lochiel in December 1742, if they could not raise good prices next year for their cattle after the terrible weather they had suffered, 'all the highlands will be ruined'.[54] Like most Lovatic statements, this one was a shade exaggerated, but clearly money was dreadfully short in the early 1740s. In June 1743 Lovat complained that he, with one of the best estates in the county, could not raise £100 cash to pay a bill which was due.[55]

Lovat's neurosis was heightened by the importunity of creditors since 1743, when his own rents had been very imperfectly paid. Some creditors were already moving to take legal action for recovery of debt from him and Lovat saw behind them 'the venemous asp, John Mackenzie, Delvine's son'.[56] Whether this particular suspicion was valid or not, Lovat was right in believing he lived in a political jungle where the strong ate the weak. The Mackintoshes, for example, disliked intensely Cluny's marriage to Lovat's daughter, for it strengthened both Frasers and Macphersons, at the cost, of course, of ruling out a match with a better-endowed Lowland spouse for both parties. Lovat was clear that power came first, and had the grace to admit that Lord President Duncan Forbes was one of the few who in no way decried the propriety of the alliance.[57] Slightly better weather in the spring of 1743 removed the worst dangers of disasters to crops and cattle, but the seasons themselves seemed to confirm the marginality of a Lord Lovat who cherished few illusions about his failure to secure any significant monetary rewards from either the Jacobite or the Hanoverian courts. He made no bones about his view that a court was worthy of an able man's devotion in so far as, and only in so far as, it offered him meaningful recompense for his pains.[58] He was left full of cynicism in a countryside striken by want and disease, with clansmen dying around him, nursing a far too acute sense of his own impotence.[59]

The old man was quite clear that Scotland's best hope of undoing the Union lay in England's discomfiture in the European power struggle with France. That struggle was peculiarly oblique until 1744, when Britain and

France finally declared war on one another, having acted previously merely as auxiliaries to their allies in Europe, but no informed observer doubted that the sole hope of the Stuarts lay in the decisive vistory of the great military monarchy of France. When in the summer of 1743 it began to look as if the French and their Bavarian allies were facing total defeat at the hands of Austria and her British sponsor Lovat concluded that some malign fate seemed to haunt 'the affairs of poor Scotland', for every opportunity to strike for independence seemed to wither before it bloomed.[60]

Neverthelss, Lovat continued automatically to try to mend political fences within the world of the West Highlands, a world which was, after all, accessible to his own political power. Because he and his allies lay athwart drove routes to southern market for western and island chiefs, cattle-reiving was always a potentially explosive topic. After a visit from Sir Alexander MacDonald and MacLeod of MacLeod, Lovat begged Lochiel to restrain his men from attacking their beasts. He strongly supported a watch to be organised by MacDonell of Barrisdale on behalf of the Mackenzies, Rosses and Munros, for two shillings per pound of their real rent. To Barrisdale this ten per cent was worth £1,000 at least. To Lovat it was a valuable and necessary step to avert civil war. He urged Lochiel to show positive friendship to the Skye chiefs, who in congress in Glenelg were doing their best to stamp out cattle theft in their own isle, as well as on the drove roads south.[61]

At one stage in the summer of 1743 Lovat seems quite seriously to have considered placing his estate in trust under commissioners like those in charge of the Gordon properties, with a view to paying off debt. He himself might take a small income and go to London to pursue his legal feuds with the Chisholm. Predictably, the scheme was soon abandoned.[62] Instead he resumed his ceaseless entertaining of, and intriguing with, local magnates like Lord Cromartie from Ross-shire, MacLeod, and (rather improbably) Mackintosh, who sweetly explained that the reason he and his friends had crowded Lovat a little lately was that they thought him about to die and therefore easy meat.[63] No offence was taken by the tough old gamecock they had failed to feast on. He was rather flattered.

Though the summer of 1743 saw Lovat at a lowish ebb, he still kept the three interlocking circles of activity which so fascinated him under constant scrutiny. First and foremost, he was a great chief of the Gael. His son and heir, the Master of Lovat, was in no doubt that his father valued 'the Earse' (Irish, i.e. Gaelic) well above Latin and Greek. The latter were ornaments for a gentlemen's hand, but Gaelic was an essential tool in preparing a Master of Lovat for the exercise of regional power.[64] Despite having actually threatened to wage civil war with Lochiel in 1736 over cattle-thieving by Camerons, not to mention insults to his own sheriff-depute, Lovat had in fact woven a strong, flexible and increasingly stable relationship with his like-minded neighbours, all of whom ultimately saw the need for coexistence and cooperation, if they were to hold potentially overwhelming predators at bay.[65]

The other two circles were beyond MacShimi's capacity to manipulate. From 1737 his letters had contained admissions that he had possibly burned his boats in British politics to the point where he could never expect anything from the Court of St James. With the irrepressible Simon such a view was always liable to drastic revision but by 1743 even he knew that he not only deserved no further chance from a Hanoverian court partially cognisant with his ambiguous manoeuvrings, but also that he was publicly acknowledged as *persona non grata* there.[66] Such a recognition of permanent exclusion from the warm rays of government favour was likely to increase his interest in the third circle of power – that of the high power-politics of western Europe. In 1737 Lovat could only thinly disguise his glee at rumours that France, Spain, and the Austrian Empire might unite to crush the maritime powers (Britain and the Netherlands) and 'restore the Chevalier'.[67] Relations between the West Highlands and France were close. About this time the Jacobite duke of Perth was asking Lochiel to permit one of Lochiel's kinsmen to recruit for the French service in Cameron country.[68] In the summer of 1743 it looked as if the star of France was fading. Lovat's were not the only well-informed Highland eyes scanning the horizon for signs of its renewal.

In the event it was precisely the inability of France to reverse what appeared at the time to be unfavourable developments in European politics which pushed the French court, late in 1743, into embracing seriously the Jacobite option. The ministers of Louis XV became increasingly afraid that France would be invaded by an English-sponsored coalition of German powers, headed by the old enemy, Austria. To humble England by a sudden invasion, synchronised with Jacobite risings in England and Scotland, became a very attractive notion. Incidentally, there was never any thought of a declaration of war before a French army assaulted London, the main target of the invasion force. A man like Frederick the Great of Prussia was regarded as a cad in the eighteenth century, not because he invaded other realms without warning, for that was standard practice, but because he made no bones about doing what he did. Charles Edward Stuart, the Jacobite 'Prince of Wales', was brought to France to head the invasion and cast over it the glamour of political legitimacy. Early in 1744 a French expeditionary force was assembled, and the government behind it seems to have been in earnest. However, by March 1744 a combination of bad luck, bad weather, and changing circumstances had led to the abandonment of the project.[69]

The prudence displayed by men like Lovat and Lochiel was more than vindicated. They had all along refused to go very far towards rebellion without irreversible French commitment. Now, as the tide of war in Flanders swayed in favour of France the chance of any such French commitment became more remote, as it would have involved withdrawing forces from the victorious armies of the Marshal de Saxe, and would have put at hazard the hard-won gains of French arms. When de Saxe defeated the Duke of Cumberland in the bitterly-fought battle of Fontenoy in May 1745, more British troops had to be sent to the Continent, stripping down garrisons in the British Isles to quite dangerously low levels, but the French obsession with the Flanders theatre of war was simply enhanced. Donald Cameron of Lochiel had offered early in 1745 to cross to France if that would help to precipitate a clear statement of French intentions. Neither the Old nor the Young Pretender had any stomach for that idea. Ambiguity was becoming the best the exiled Stuarts could hope for from the Most Christian King. There always were advocates of the Jacobite cause on one or more of the committees which made high policy decisions for France. The real crunch was what priority the French monarchy was prepared to give to a Jacobite rising. The less clear their devoted Scottish supporters were about this crucial question, the better for the Stuarts.[70]

Fortunately for himself and his clan, Lovat had learned to trust nobody. It irked him that nobody outside his clan and a small circle of allied chiefs really trusted him, but there was good reason for this state of affairs. It did not stop local civil and military authorities from dancing attendance on him in late 1744 and early 1745. Norman MacLeod of MacLeod was assiduous in courteous correspondence with Lovat, a correspondence which stressed the pains the MP was at to try to restore a good relationship between Argyll and the Fraser chief. Nor was Lovat excluded from the bustle which accompanied the business of raising companies for the Earl of Loudon's Regiment. The notable absence of applications from Cameron lairds for commissions did not go unnoticed, but nobody thought that this was a prelude to active rebellion. Young Donald Lochiel was known to have his grandfather's capacity to combine firm Stuart loyalist principles with a canny, pragmatic approach to the political and military realities. It was hoped that Lovat would help his known associate Cluny to make up his company quickly,[71] in order to strengthen Cluny's hand for a majority in due course. A mere three months before the outbreak of the last Jacobite rebellion in August 1745 Lovat was threatening to thrash Rose of Kilravock through the streets of Nairn for saying that Lovat had been deprived of his independent company because of his Jacobite leanings. An equally violent row with the Mackenzie chief politely referred to after the loss of the Seaforth title as Lord Fortrose was averted by a rare Lovatic climb-down.[72] Only the arrival of a royal Stuart in their midst was likely to shake the associated Glen More and Glen Spean chiefs from their sensibly entrenched political positions. In the absence of French support, such a royal apparition was improbable, which is why in the event it came as such a shock.

8 In The Eye Of The Jacobite Hurricane 1745–1746

If acute economic distress was reducing the disposable incomes of the Great Glen chiefs in the early 1740s, it will not do to argue from this fact that the complex and deeply ambiguous political fabric of the region was on the verge of disintegration. The financial straits of certain key local figures did indeed lead to an air of tension and, with the benefit of hindsight, we can see that it was precisely the taut nature of that fabric which ensured that it ruptured spectacularly when subjected to a sharp and unexpected blow from without. The blow was dealt by a psychological rather than a physical weapon, but it was a shearing cut none the less. The arrival of Prince Charles Edward Stuart at Loch nan Uamh late in July 1745 was a mind-blowing experience for the majority of the mainland chiefs within striking distance of his anchorage. It was so unreasonable. He came, self-possessed, totally demanding, and confidently charming, with little money, seven followers, and none of the French aid he had repeatedly been told was a *sine qua non* for a rebellion. His first victim, MacDonald of Kinlochmoidart chanced, shortly after meeting him, to accost Mr Hugh MacDonald, brother of the laird of Morar and Roman Catholic Vicar Apostolic in the Highlands as well as Bishop of Diana *in partibus infidelium*. The good bishop, after ascertaining that Charles brought seven men and little stock of gold or arms, said bluntly that he thought it an ugly business.

He was right. Norman MacLeod of MacLeod and Sir Alexander MacDonald of Sleat, Skye chiefs who rejected Charles's arrogant demand that they instantly throw in their hand with him, never pretended particularly to love the Hanoverian regime. They described the rebellion as 'mad' and its supporters as 'madmen' on the precise grounds that Charles had not met the stipulations laid down by those Scottish politicians, themselves included, with whom he had been in correspondence. Without substantial French aid a rebellion would represent a totally unjustified risk and was likely to end in stark tragedy.

Apart from the high degree of immediate safety guaranteed by a landing in Moidart – an overwhelmingly Roman Catholic area dominated by MacDonald of Clanranald – the whole point about Prince Charles's landfall on the Scottish mainland was that it allowed him a quick and easy access to the strategically central group of clans along the southern end of the Great Glen. The prince came like a thunderbolt from space into a small but complicated world which was still evolving rapidly in response to its own inner needs and the problems and pressures posed by external authority. Indeed, it can be argued that it was evolving on the whole constructively and in a way which made good sense in its own terms and also made a positive contribution to establishing a balance in Scottish and British politics which at least ameliorated the effects of the post-1714 Whig *putsch* in central government.

The presence of weakened regular garrisons in the forts along the line of the Great Glen was, once Charles was known to be in the country, more a provocation than a check to local chiefs, few of whom could cope emotionally with the near presence of a Stuart prince equipped with real charisma, little conscience or scruple and a glibly persuasive tongue. It was too tempting for an excited minor chieftain to cross a vital psychological barrier felt by the whole local community by spilling the blood of regular troops of the British army. That was exactly what Donald MacDonald of Tiendrish or Tirnadrish, son of Ronald Mor of Tirnadrish, second son of MacDonald of Keppoch, did on 14 August 1745 when he pounced on two companies of the Royal Scots. They were easy meat, being recruits raised only in 1744 to supplement the first battalion of the Royal Scots, then serving with distinction under the Duke of Cumberland in Flanders. The second regular battalion of the regiment was in garrison in Ireland. Thus, seasoned Royal Scots at the start of the '45 were everywhere but Scotland – a classic illustration of the Hanoverian state's practice of deploying troops away from their native areas as alien ethnic garrisons. The two newly-recruited companies had been in barracks at Perth, but had then been moved hastily with the Sixth Foot to serve in forts along the line of Loch Lochy and Loch Ness. After serving in Fort Augustus they were marching to reinforce Fort William, which seemed threatened by the presence of Prince Charles on the coast just to the west of it. MacDonald of Tiendrish harried the Royal Scots into surrender, killing two or three men and capturing the rest including Captains Swetenham and John Scott. Tiendrish presented the latter's charger to Prince Charles at Glenfinnan. Captured at Falkirk early in 1746, Tiendrish was subsequently executed. Gay and gallant though he was, he undoubtedly carried a heavy weight of responsibility for the disasters which overwhelmed his people.[1]

The position of most local chiefs in his country on the eve of the '45 was difficult but not intolerable. Of this there is no better example than one of Simon Fraser's sons-in-law, Ewen Macpherson, the close neighbour of the Keppoch MacDonalds and the real leader of his clan long before the death of his father Lauchlan. Simon always assumed that relatives existed to be used, so none of his daughters married without extensive enquiries into the status and prospects of their proposed spouses. When, therefore, on 2 March 1742 young Ewen married Janet Fraser, the nuptials were as much a tribute to the rising influence of the groom as a feast of love. A couple of years later the wily Simon persuaded Lochiel and Ewen Macpherson of Cluny Younger to sign a formal bond of friendship between the Frasers, Macphersons and Camerons, dated 19 April, 17 June and 7 July 1744, binding themselves and their followers, heirs and successors to stand by and support one another. The document included a formal revocation by the Macphersons of the minute of agreement of 1724 with the Mackintoshes whereby they had acknowledged Mackintosh as their rightful chief.[2]

Young Ewen Macpherson of Cluny (his father died three months after Culloden) was by 1745 not only effective head of his clan but, as purveyor of security to the Moray lairds, also a businessman of note. On 21 May he received a positively unctuous missive from three gentlemen of the name of Rose, not to mention Alexander Brodie, Alexander Dunbar, and perhaps most gratifying of all, one Alexander Campbell. They told him that they hoped he was disposed to continue his good offices in preventing depredations into the low countries for they were conscious that they could not be in better hands than his. After expressing a desire to meet him or his plenipotentiary on the second Tuesday in June at Nairn to adjust terms, they rather nervously begged him to give orders to his own people to inflict no damage on them in the meantime.[3] The very next day Alexander Brodie of Lethen penned a letter which sent fresh clouds of incense swirling round Macpherson's chiefly head. Alexander Brodie regretted news from his friend Sir Robert Gordon that the gentlemen of Elginshire were a trifle backward in joining 'your scheme for the protection of the country'. Brodie was clear that the watch organised by the lowland lairds themselves was not adequate and needed to be supplemented by the 'civility' of the Macpherson chief in the form of orders to his own men and indeed 'to those that were not under your protection', to lay off reiving cattle in the Laigh of Moray. Brodie even offered to act as an agent for Macpherson in Elginshire.[4] It was a protection racket, of course, but then so are most modern police forces and all insurance companies.

Cluny functioned very much like a modern insurance company, as a letter dated 23 May 1745 which he received from one of the southern outposts of the Clan Chattan, James Farquharson of Invercauld, showed. Farquharson reported that his own father had only just returned home after spending so long in Aberdeen that he had left it too late to hire captains and soldiers for his own private watches, so he was prepared yet again to participate in Cluny's scheme, not only on his own behalf but also for the Earl of Aboyne and the Earl of Aberdeen, neighbouring Gordon noblemen. Like Brodie of Lethen, he undertook to advertise the advantages of subscribing amongst the landowners of his own high country. Confident of Strathdon, the older Farquharson had doubts about Glenesk and Birse, and thought the precise terms would make all the difference. He urged Macpherson to stick to the previous year's contract and to resist the temptation to ask for a higher cash down-payment from participants. Everything was done in precise legal form. A collector brought round formal insurance proposals whereby Cluny undertook, for a down-payment plus further instalments, to make good any damage suffered by the other contracting party. The 1744 collector, Alexander Charles, and his contracts, had been acceptable to Strathdon, but higher cash payments at the start of the 1745 season were likely to be resisted 'considering the present extraordinary poverty of the countrie, occasioned by the death of cattle and scarcity of victuale'.[5] It was a very fair argument.

Like any modern insurance company, Cluny had to adjust his rates in the light of two main considerations – the ability of the insured to pay and the perceived exposure to risk of any given party. Rather late in the season, on 30 July 1745, he received a highly eulogistic letter from Inchgrundle at the head of Glenesk, itself the most northerly of the Angus glens. In the shadow of that strangely named rocky protruberance, the Shank of Inchgrundle, James Gordon and Alexander Mill sat down to explain away the attempt by the glen folk to withdraw from Cluny's scheme. They had found the 1744 charges stiff, on top of which the winter and spring of '45 had seen heavy losses of cattle. Tenants were poor in Glenesk, farms small, and comparatively few of the surviving beasts were out in fields at the head of the glen where, Cluny's correspondents were far too tactful actually to say, it would be comparatively easy for a raiding band of Macphersons to lift them. However, a mitigation of the charges had clearly always been the fall-back position of the Glenesk folk. In 1744 James Gordon in Inchgrundle, Mr Garden of Mid Strath and Alexander Mill of Glenmark (one of the side-glens) had signed on behalf of the whole community. By 1745 Garden was dead, but after a particularly pressing letter from Cluny, Gordon and Mill summoned the tenants and persuaded them to subscribe. It was impossible, under the circumstances, to set and enforce a specific rate on each. A voluntary contribution produced an offer of £7.00 sterling by Martinmas next (11 November).

It was less than the previous year's payment, but no doubt more than the tenants felt they should pay, which probably means it was about right. Had they not paid they would certainly have been robbed by Macphersons, but paying removed a real risk of being robbed by other Highlanders.[6] The geographical spread of Cluny's insurance business is very impressive, though he was not a pioneer in a field where men like Rob

Roy MacGregor had long before established considerable reputations. Rob Roy, an unsuccessful cattle dealer turned self-appointed constable on the Highland–Lowland boundary zone, was never wholly *persona grata* with the contemporary Scottish ruling class. The support he received from the Duke of Argyll has to be balanced against the lifelong enmity of a Duke of Montrose. In any case Rob suffered from the common MacGregor weakness of living too close to the heartlands of Anglo-Saxon Scotland. Cluny was splendidly remote by comparison, but his tentacles could clearly reach out over great distances. Few chiefs of his day showed such capacity for large-scale business organisation, and it seemed that the head of the Macphersons was well on the way towards honorary membership of the school of basking sharks who manipulated the levers of power and profit in Hanoverian Britain.

Certainly that would seem to be the way the contemporary Scottish Whig establishment saw him, as a remarkable pair of documents sent to him in June 1745 demonstrate. They came from Robert Craigie, the Lord Advocate of Scotland, and concerned the doings of 'Alexander MacDonnel Younger', of Glengarry. This was Alasdair Ruadh, eldest son and heir of the elderly Glengarry. He held a commission in the French army and was an active Jacobite. Indeed he was selected by a group of chiefs to carry a memorial to Prince Charles Edward Stuart in 1745, in which they assured him of their support provided he could obtain sufficient French backing in terms of men and money to justify a rebellion. Subjected to various delays, Alasdair Ruadh arrived in France to find Prince Charles had already sailed on the voyage which culminated in his landing in Moidart. When Alasdair Ruadh wearily turned again and tried to sail back to Scotland his ship was intercepted by two frigates of the Royal Navy and he was lodged, not unreasonably, in the Tower of London until 1747. It was a heart-sickening saga which lay mercifully hidden in the future in the summer of 1745, when Alasdair Ruadh was at home in his own clan country, beating up recruits for his regiment in the French service.

His father John can have seen no harm in the practice. He was himself a peaceable man who had achieved more for his clan by negotiation than with the sword. In August 1724 he had obtained a charter from the Duke of Argyll, the victor of Sheriffmuir, confirming himself and his heirs male in their Knoydart lands, while in 1735 he had signed a bond of friendship and cooperation with the Grants of Glenmoriston.[7] On the other hand, Britain was at war with France in 1745 and the British government was unlikely to look with favour upon the use of part of its territory as a recruiting ground for the army which had so decisively whipped the Duke of Cumberland on the bloody field of Fontenoy in 1745. Certainly the Lord Advocate was a trifle cross with the heir to Glengarry. In a warrant which he despatched to Ewen Macpherson Younger of Cluny he went so far as to describe young Glengarry's enlisting of men for the French service as 'Treasonable Practices' for which he was to be arrested and conveyed under sure guard to Edinburgh, where he was to be proceeded against according to due form of law.[8] An accompanying letter expanded revealingly upon the laconic phrases of the warrant. It explained that the Westminster government looked on Alasdair Ruadh's antics as a threat to its own peace and safety. They were no such thing, of course, but they certainly constituted a severe blow to its prestige in the Highlands. The Lord Advocate then informed Ewen Macpherson that it was precisely in order to discourage this sort of poaching by France that His Majesty's Government had authorised the Campbell Earl of Loudon to raise a regiment in the Highlands, a regiment in which Ewen had been granted a commission as captain. Orders to raise his company would quickly follow. Meantime, if he could execute the warrant against Alasdair Ruadh, his standing with George II would be vastly enhanced. A final paragraph stressed the need for absolute secrecy and admitted that the garrison of Fort Augustus was quite incapable of putting a stop to what was going on in Glengarry's lands, without the active assistance of a powerful local chief.[9]

In many ways young Cluny must have found this a deeply comforting missive. Only a lunatic would have even considered trying to execute the warrant. The consequences, in the Jacobite-charged atmosphere of the Gaelic Highlands, would have been universal execration of a chief willing to act as a tool of the alien Hanoverian dynasty, not to mention guaranteed clan feuds of indefinite duration. On the other hand, the Lord Advocate had a point. If there was to be a stable *modus vivendi* between the British government and the Great Glen chiefs, the latter would eventually have to give up one or two of their more irritating eccentricities, like raising troops for powers formally at war with the British state. Particularly if the Westminster politicians offered alternative outlets for military entrepreneurship, and were not excessively discriminating in selecting holders of commissions to raise companies, this was a not unreasonable long-term policy. The Lord Advocate's information about the impending arrival of a captain's commission for Cluny was in this respect highly encouraging. Like other chiefs, young Cluny was desperate for virtually any supplementary source of income and patronage. Even his far-flung security business was facing shrinking revenues due to the appalling economic climate in the Highlands in the 1740s. Besides, the independent companies attached to Loudon's regiment were to function, like their predecessors, as a rural gendarmerie, and Cluny's delicately balanced blend of blackmail, insurance, and private security service, would be as strengthened by official recognition as it would be weakened by its absence. He naturally solicited a commission, making all the interest he could with chiefs closer to government like Norman MacLeod of MacLeod.

That cautious Whig wrote to Cluny in December 1744 saying that he would do all in his power to serve him, not least because he was married to the daughter 'of my Relation and dear Friend' (a phrase which would have gratified Simon Fraser deeply), but he doubted if it was practical politics to think in terms of a company. There were initially to be only two. One had fallen to a friend of Argyll, and the other was said to be destined for Mackintosh. MacLeod suggested that his young friend might be wise to accept a lieutenancy and bide his time, on the assumption that he would automatically succeed to the first additional company to be raised.[10] Now, in the summer of 1745 as the temper of His Majesty's Government was sweetened by healthy fear of its subjects, Cluny was offered and accepted command of an independent Company.

Words then can hardly express the gravity of the problems posed for Ewen Macpherson by the receipt of a letter dated 'Boradale August the 5th 1745' from 'Charles Prince Regent' in which Charles, characteristically, simply took his loyalty and zeal for the Jacobite cause for granted and summoned him to attend the raising of the royal standard at Glenfinnan 'on munday the 19th instant', adding that if it was not practicable for him to attend, Charles expected him to join the Jacobite army as soon as possible.[11] Ewen Macpherson had taken an oath of allegiance to George II as part of the process of taking his commission in Loudon's regiment. His wife urged him to stand by the established government, and so he did. Lord President Forbes had warned him that he would ruin his own clan if he joined an unsuccessful rising. Cluny in fact was one of the Highland chiefs who duly reported to the Commander-in-Chief Scotland, General Cope, as that unlucky officer marched north hoping to rally the Whig clans and bring Charles to battle in the central Highlands. Arguably both Cluny and Cope were victims of the profound unpopularity of the British government. When they met near Ruthven in Badenoch it was already clear to Cope that he could expect no support. He had resolved to make a dash for Inverness rather than try to force the impossible zig-zags of Corrieyairack Pass against determined Jacobite resistance. The way was clear for Charles to march on Edinburgh virtually unopposed.

Cluny had turned up with an under-strength company. Cope ordered him home to Cluny Castle where he was captured by a Jacobite raiding-party led by Lochiel's brother, Dr Archibald Cameron, after the Jacobite army had turned back from the idea of pursuing Cope and forcing an action. Even after capture Ewen managed to communicate with Lord President Forbes, giving him details of the strength and movements of the 2,000 indifferently armed men who made up the Jacobite army. Only very late indeed did young Cluny throw in his lot with the rebellion – his commission as a Jacobite colonel is dated 7 September 1745.[12] On the same day he was supplied with a document, signed by John Murray on behalf of Prince Charles, authorising him to raise by beat of drum or otherwise a regiment of foot to consist of ten companies, each composed of two sergeants, two corporals, two drummers, and fifty private soldiers, as well as the usual commissioned officers.[13] Despite this authority Ewen Macpherson was unable to carry his entire clan with him. By far the wealthiest and most numerous cadet branch, the Macphersons of Invereshie, remained stubbornly neutral throughout the rebellion, reaping a substantial reward for their wisdom and independent judgement. When Cumberland's troops swept destructively down the Great Glen after Culloden, Mr Blair, the minister of the parish, was able to argue successfully that George Macpherson of Invereshie was a special case entitled to civilised treatment, even from the Duke of Cumberland.

Cluny was at the battle of Prestonpans on 21 September 1745 with 600 men, sharing in the rout of Cope, who had shipped his army down from Aberdeen to just outside Edinburgh. That victory confirmed the Jacobite mastery of most of Scotland. There followed the invasion of England which turned back at Derby. Neither Prince Charles nor Cluny were happy about the decision to retreat, but most of the chiefs were disgusted by the total lack of support from the English Tories, and enraged by the realisation that the assurances they had been given of massive French aid on the way were as bogus as most of the other assurances emanating from Charles, Prince Regent. We have a document which may give us an insight into the soldierly spirit which kept Cluny going, for it records immense pride in the role of the Macpherson regiment in the skirmish at Clifton, where the Jacobite rearguard turned and mauled Cumberland's vanguard. The record says 'this Little action of my Regiment was a most Gallant one and worthie to be Recorded if Done by the Oldest and Best Disciplined Troops'.[14]

Hard fighting is not and cannot be an end in itself. As the Jacobite tide ebbed those Jacobites who understood the military situation, and the way in which the odds were steadily shifting in favour of the Hanoverians the longer the struggle went on, inevitably became desperate and more ruthless as they felt their backs to the wall. Cluny had first gone off to war to fight for King George with most of a volunteer company. By switching sides, however late, he probably tapped a potent vein of Jacobitism and anti-Unionism in his clan, which helped recruit his regiment for Prestonpans. By February 1746 Prince Charles signed and sealed with the royal arms a commission for Cluny to exercise in his own country of Badenoch which he was to enter ahead of the retreating army to press recruits, burning the houses and killing the cattle of any reluctant to serve and punishing deserters, if he saw fit, by death after a court-martial.[15] Ruthless pressures were normal in recruiting at all times in the eighteenth century and Cluny certainly did not alienate the bulk of his clansmen, as their support for him after Culloden showed, but the fact that the Jacobite Prince Regent publicly admitted the need for such methods was a terrible comment on the lack of enthusiasm for his cause among the long-suffering peasantry of Badenoch.

Yet the final phase of the '45 was distinguished by a surprising tendency for Jacobite hopes to revive, in the face of all the evidence. Partly this was due to the fact that, though on the strategic defensive, the Jacobites were able in the course of their retreat repeatedly to assume the tactical offensive. There was their gallant action at Clifton near Penrith as they left England. They occupied the Whig city of Glasgow and held it, in effect, to ransom. They whipped the brutal General Hawley at Falkirk and they not only captured Inverness in 1746, but also chased the Hanoverian forces of the northern Highlands under Loudon and Duncan Forbes from the Dornoch Firth to impotent refuge in Skye.

Of all these offensives none was perhaps more brilliantly conceived than the Atholl Raid which saw the tactical flair and drive of Lord George Murray, the outstanding Jacobite general of the '45, allied to the talents of young Cluny, a first-class regimental commander at the head of his clan regiment. Swooping over the hills from the north early on the morning of 17 March 1746, Lord George and Cluny fell upon the Campbell militia posts in the Braes of Atholl, at the head of Strathtay, and wiped them out, albeit with more prisoners than carnage. It was a brilliant feat of arms. It aroused a blaze of Jacobite optimism,[16] but it raises the interesting question as to what was going on in the Great Glen itself, studded as it was with Hanoverian forts at the start of the '45. (Cluny could press men in Badenoch and throw them into action on the Braes of Atholl only because the Hanoverian garrison at Ruthven, which represented an immediate threat to his clan country, had surrendered to Gordon of Glenbucket and a Jacobite force supported by artillery early in February 1746.

One basic answer is that the '45 was a totally different proposition from the '15. The participants all consciously or instinctively seem to have realised this, and there is no more striking proof of this point than the attitude of the south-western Jacobite mainland clans. In the '15 they had undoubtedly regarded the presence of hostile garrisons near their own territories as sufficient reason to hold back from total commitment to the main Jacobite striking force. In a sense it made no real difference. Mar lacked military capacity, not men. The '15 was a broad-based national rising, while the '45 was an attempted coup d'état by a small minority. Everyone knew that the penalties for failure would be much worse than after the '15, though few grasped just how much worse they would be.

Total commitment to a swift seizure of central power seemed to be the best hope of ultimate security. From the start, the '45 was a desperate gamble.

By early 1746, however, with the failure of the invasion of England the whole focus of Jacobite strategy had shifted to the north. Inverness, though not held by the Jacobites, was by 1 February 1746 clearly their main objective in their grim retreat through vile winter weather. It was the last town capable of forming the pivot of a regular campaign, and its possession opened the option of falling back on guerrilla tactics in the Great Glen. All of this presupposed the elimination of the still intact Hanoverian garrisons. On his march to Inverness Charles stormed and slighted the fortified barracks at Ruthven in Badenoch. Previously when he had passed it, it had bid him defiance, for his army had lacked any cannon. Now he had a few pieces, none heavier than six-pounders, and it was with these, from 18 February, that Charles set the commander of his train, an Irish artillery officer called Colonel Grant, to work against Fort George, basically a modified but still out-of-date Inverness Castle, sitting up on its castle hill beside the river. Colonel Grant was an eminent mathematician who had spent much of his time in Paris labouring in the observatory. It required no advanced mathematics to see that his battery was too light to smash the walls, but Fort George was susceptible to mining under its bastions. The mine was not far advanced when the commander, Major Grant, surrendered at discretion with his force of under 200 men. Lochiel and Keppoch at this point reverted to type and marched off to blockade Fort William, while Brigadier Walter Stapleton, an Irish officer in the French regiment of Berwick who died later of wounds received at Culloden, marched to the south end of Loch Ness to deal with Fort Augustus. It was a miserably-sited and vulnerable structure. Jacobite cannon were too puny to master it, but Stapleton very sensibly used coehorn mortars (named after their Dutch inventor) to destroy all its buildings and blow up its magazine, after which its commander Major Wentworth surrendered with several companies from Guise's regiment.[17]

The operations of Charles's troops were local in scope and probably of little interest to him (during most of this period he was prostrate with a cold and fever) because he knew that only big battles would seat him on a throne in London. He wanted to send the Fort Augustus garrison to France as hostages, to act as insurance in the event of defeat in a general action, but in fact they escaped from prison in Nairn. To the clans who made up the great bulk of the Jacobite army, however, the garrisons were potentially a matter of life and death for their people. Despite the fall of Fort George and Fort Augustus, the strongest of the garrisons, which was also strategically the most threatening, was still very much unconquered. Fort William, its very name a reminder of the revolution which had toppled the Stuarts, was not only a garrison of the regular British army, but also a northern outpost of the reservoir of Whig support represented by the Campbells of Argyll. The link between Fort William and Argyll was one which the Jacobites had no hope of cutting, for it consisted of ships of the Royal Navy which regularly penetrated into the upper waters of Loch Linnhe to assist and supply the fort, itself beleaguered from the start of the rising by irregular bands of Camerons and MacDonalds.

The chief who had an almost umbilical relationship with Fort William was, of course, Lochiel. Ever since 1651 the fortification at Inverlochy had been a major consideration in the political decisions of the Camerons. It is true that by depriving the Great Glen forts of their 'interval troops', and by maintaining only weak garrisons of poor quality in them, the London government had devalued its most important local bargaining counter. It still remains one of the many difficulties in trying to understand why Cameron of Lochiel succumbed to the appeal of Prince Charles to join the rebellion, at their interview at Borrodale in August 1745, that he seems to have made no conscious allowance for the problem of Fort William. Since Lochiel's appearance at the raising of the standard in Glenfinnan saved that event from turning into a fiasco, it is infuriating that his long discussion with Prince Charles remains an enigma wrapped in a mystery. All we know for certainty is that 'he took full security from Prince Charles for the value of his estates', and that Charles made a point later of begging a French regiment for him to honour this well-known pledge to secure Lochiel an income of not less than £700 a year. The fact should be enough to kill any purely romantic interpretation of the deal between the two men, and suggest that Charles used a mixture of threats and cajolery on Lochiel as well as emotional appeal. Charles could reasonably argue that the garrison of Scotland was so absurdly small and of such low calibre that one battle in Badenoch could give him control of the Stuarts' ancient kingdom, while Lochiel obviously feared that the idea of a rising was totally irresponsible, and would cost him all he owned. Certainly many of his Camerons, from heads of cadet houses like Cameron of Callart to Lochiel's hereditary standard Alexander MacLachlan, wadsetter of Coruanan, appear to have been unhappy and reluctant participants in the rising, and Lochiel's uncle Ludovick Cameron of Torcastle faced an acute desertion problem amongst his men immediately after the early victory at Prestonpans.[18]

This was hardly surprising. While Cluny and Lord George Murray were preparing in great secrecy in March 1746 for their attack on the Campbell garrisons in Atholl,[19] the Whig forces in the west were beginning to execute orders from the Duke of Cumberland for ruthless amphibious terrorist attacks on the Macleans, MacDonalds, Camerons, and other Jacobite inhabitants of Morvern and Arisaig. Naval units in Loch

Linnhe coperated with Hanoverian garrisons of western castles such as Castles Stalker and Mingary in what was a mere foreshadowing of the terror to come. It is clear that the Campbell militia commanders from Major General John Campbell of Mamore (who held command at Inveraray) downwards were extremely unhappy about tactics with which they had to cooperate but which they feared would breed untold bitterness.[20] Lochiel was facing a nightmare situation which his rational self must always have known was likely to occur.

Indirect evidence of the turmoil in his mind comes from his correspondence with Cluny in the spring of 1746. He warmly congratulated Cluny, whom he had after all hi-jacked into the rebellion, on the sparkling little campaign in Atholl. Lochiel was particularly pleased about the capture of Campbells whom he, like the other Jacobite chiefs, blamed for the devastation of the Cameron and Maclean farms in Morvern. The Cameron chief raged against the stripping of women and children, the killing of horses, and the burning of cattle in the byres. He believed there were 350 Campbells in Fort William and that it was they who were prime movers in cooperating with the Royal Navy to land parties at Corpach and other points on the shores of Loch Eil to ravage his territory. The wrath of a chivalrous warrior was understandable but misdirected. Cumberland not Campbells lay behind this new scale of savagery. Lochiel's people were fighting back against the raiding parties, but their chief, reverting to that clear-sighted and responsible style of leadership which had always characterised him before the desperate decision at Borrodale, saw that only by knocking out Fort William could this immediate threat be removed. He concluded that the Jacobite forces would soon begin to bombard and cannonade Fort William and made it clear that he thought it a high priority to try to master it at almost any cost.[21]

From the point of view of Lochiel and his Camerons this was a simple recognition of the facts of life. The snag was that they only had a finite time at their disposal to take the fort which had an adequate garrison, communication with the outside world, and a ferociously determined commander in Captain Caroline Frederick Scott. Brigadier Stapleton closed in on Fort William with 1,500 men on 7 March, but his forces were short of food, despite the construction of girnels (or granaries) at Lochiel's house at Achnacarry. They were also chronically short of powerful horses capable of dragging carts and guns down from Fort William, and in any case they lacked the heavy pieces of ordnance essential to mount an effective battery. Captain Scott was undoubtedly a hard-faced, unpleasant man who later acquired a deservedly black reputation for his sadistic punitive expeditions against the lands of the Jacobite Stewart of Ardshiel and others, but he was the right man in the right place in Fort William. He rejected a summons to surrender with contempt. His guns beat down the early Jacobite attempts to form a battery and disabled Colonel Grant, the best Jacobite gunner, leaving the Jacobites only a foppish and ineffective clown, Mirabelle de Gordon, already distinguished by total incompetence at the abortive siege of Stirling Castle, to command their guns. Attempts to employ the mortar attacks which had humbled Fort Augustus were met by obliterative counter-fire from Hanoverian mortar batteries and Scott's garrison had more than enough morale to mount viciously effective sallies which overran Jacobite batteries, some of whose equipment they were amused to see came from the artillery train which Sir John Cope had abandoned at Prestonpans.

The besieged were well aware of the destruction being wreaked by their own sloops of war on Cameron settlements in Morvern, and recorded that this action:

> has, as is reported, produced a kind of manifesto by Lochiel and Keppoch in which they exclaim against the Campbells, for burning houses and corn, killing horses, houghing cattle, stripping women and children, and exposing them to the severity of the weather in the open fields; threaten to make reprisals, if they can procure leave from their Prince, by entering Argyleshire, and acting there at discretion, and by putting a Campbell to death (of whom several had lately been made prisoners in Athol) for every house that should afterwards be burnt by that clan; extol the lenity and moderation of the rebels, notwithstanding the aspersions industriously spread to the contrary; and insinuate, that those who gave orders for the burning, could not answer for it to the British parliament.[22]

This was a substantially accurate account of a document issued by Lochiel and Keppoch from Glen Nevis on 20 March 1746, though the threats of murderous individual reprisals were not there spelled out in detail. The document began with an extraordinary piece of Jacobite rhetoric expounding the view that Campbells, with a history of treason to the House of Stuart stretching back to the reign of James VI were of all men the least entitled to resist Prince Charles. Nay, they ought to be humbly grateful that the Prince Regent had graciously condescended to say that he would turn his back on any inclination to indulge in justified resentment at their past misdeeds, would they but stand neutral in this present quarrel to assert his just rights. Neither Lochiel nor Keppoch was such a fool as to think that the mighty Clan Diarmid would cringe in inactivity while the political balance in Scotland and in Britain was permanently altered to its disadvantage, by violence. Even in the undoubted military decadence initiated by John second Duke of Argyll's attempt to squeeze out his Campbell tacksmen, the vital officer class of a mobilised

clan, the Campbells were too resolute tamely to accept defeat. Besides, the reigning duke had, too late, tried to reverse policies which had weakened his clan without in practice producing higher rents. Far more genuine rings the bitter postscript to the manifesto in which Donald Cameron alone said: 'I cannot omit taking notice that my people were first to feel the cowardly barbarity of my pretended Campbell friends. I shall desire to have the opportunity of thanking them for it in the open field.'[23]
In short, Lochiel saw the terrorist attacks as the final breach in the solidarity of a local community of which both he and his Campbell relatives were part. To political betrayal in the past was now being added physical assault and treachery.

Lochiel had little time left to cultivate his somewhat over-simplified sense of grievance. Cumberland's advance from Aberdeen and the Royal Navy's success in blocking the running of French gold to Prince Charles left that young man few options but battle on the approaches to Inverness. Guerrilla tactics in the Great Glen would have required stores and ammunition to be moved up-country from Inverness much earlier. In any case Fort William was untamed, and would have severely handicapped Jacobite forces trying to manoeuvre in its neighbourhood. By 23 March 1746 Cluny was writing from Blair Atholl to Donald Macpherson of Breakachie ordering him to provide quarters for 1,500 men at Ruthven to facilitate Cluny's march north to join Prince Charles in what was clearly going to be a full-scale general action.[24]

On 16 April 1746 it occurred on Culloden Moor, a few miles from Inverness. Lord George Murray and most of the chiefs were utterly miserable at the prospect of fighting a set-piece battle in a place 'certainly not proper for Highlanders'. Prince Charles seems to have faced his well-deserved nemesis with no tactical plan, just his usual infuriatingly bland confidence that his cause would somehow prevail against all odds. Lord George led the heroic charge of the Jacobite right wing in vain. Keppoch sought and found death with inexpressible gallantry in a single-handed charge against the serried ranks of redcoats moving forward against the ebbing tide of MacDonalds on the Jacobite left wing. Lochiel carried himself with all the courage expected of him, was severely wounded by grapeshot, but was carried off the field alive by his clansmen.

Brave men could do no more. The question on the bleak morning after Culloden was what they should do next. On 13 May 1746 Lochiel, recuperating from his wounds on Loch Arkaigside, wrote to Cluny a letter which certainly displayed an indomitable spirit. It began by flatly stating that 'we are preparing for a summer Campaign' and urged Cluny to assemble and hold together any 'pretty fellows' from Jacobite regiments who straggled into his country. As for food and money, Lochiel assumed Cluny had enough money to pay troops. He had to admit a desperate shortage of meal in the Cameron country. With none available for purchase, he sent two pack horses to Cluny begging him to load them with meal at almost any price (which he would reimburse) and send the grain back to Loch Arkaig. Spies had been sent to Inverness and Edinburgh to seek intelligence.[25] A better summary of the possibilities and problems facing Lochiel after Culloden would be difficult to find. Money and meal were needed to keep troops of any sort in the field. Neither was easily come by. On the other hand, there was a very good case indeed from the point of view of the unambiguously committed Jacobite clans, mostly in or adjacent to Glen More, for fighting on with mobile tactics against Cumberland's inevitable march along the glen from Inverness. Defeated, they could expect, and indeed received from him, absolutely no mercy. By standing together and fighting on they might hope for better terms in the end, especially if over-exposure to peat-reek, dripping roofs and poor food was to persuade Prince Charles to depart for France on a predictably futile search for large-scale reinforcements of men and money. Rid of the appalling incubus of Charles Edward Stuart, Lochiel and his fellows might hope for something better than unconditional surrender.

In a communication to Andrew Stone, Under-Secretary of State in the British government and a loyal servant of the Pelham brothers, Henry and the Duke of Newcastle, who asserted their supremacy at Westminster during the final stages of the '45, John Murray of Broughton, sometime secretary to Prince Charles, gave further information as to the Jacobite leaders' plans after Culloden. It is the case that Murray was writing to save his neck but his account rings true. For example, we know that Prince Charles met 'that Oracle of his country' Simon Fraser, Lord Lovat once, at Fraser of Gortuleg's house where Simon had taken refuge after fleeing from arrest at the hands of Lord Loudon in Inverness. It was the morrow of Culloden and Lovat's advice, expressed in terms of that stalwart Scottish nationalism which was perhaps Simon's strongest emotion next to megalomania, was to fight on. 'Remember', he said, 'your great ancestor Robert Bruce, who lost eleven battles and won Scotland by the twelfth.'[26] Given that Lovat's house and estates were about to be devastated by 900 of Cumberland's men under Brigadier Mordant, it was not lightly given advice.

Murray of Broughton alleged in August 1746 that a few days after Culloden Lochiel, with Cluny and Stewart of Ardshiel, decided to convene a meeting of 'the other gentlemen of the Countrey' at Murlaggan, a couple of miles from the head of Loch Arkaig. The meeting was held and attended by 'the Lord Lovat, Lochiel, Mcdonell of Barisdale, Mcdonnell of Lochgarry, Gordon of Glenbucket, John Roy Steuart, with some others'. It was a gathering of stout-hearted men. Lovat harangued them at length, arguing that they should assemble men for a stubborn defence, otherwise they could not hope to make any terms at all for themselves and their families. He added that if the worst came to the worst it would be better to die fighting than by the ghastly rites reserved for traitors. Murray alleged that there was general agreement to this suggestion and the participants went away promising to meet in a week with their armed men, but that the rendezvous was never kept as the tenantry was unwilling to be called out again. It is typical of Lovat that, although infirmity prevented him offering his active services, he cheerfully committed his son with 400 'picked men'.[27] Whether either the son or the men would have been pleased to hear that he had done so is a nice question.

In most accounts of the aftermath of Culloden there tends to be too much emphasis on the assembly of a substantial remnant of the defeated army at Ruthven in Badenoch and on the message which they received from Charles that every man should seek safety in his own way. Lord George Murray made his way to Ruthven after expressing his contempt for an idiotic order written by an *aide-de-camp* to Prince Charles, Sawnie MacLeod, and sent to Cluny, ordering the Frasers, Camerons, Stewarts, and Clanranald's and Keppoch's people to assemble for a review at Fort Augustus. At Ruthven Lord George was quite clear that in the aftermath of decisive defeat 'there was neither money nor provisions to give: so no hopes were left'. A field army committed to restoring the Stuarts to their three thrones had ceased to be a sane concept. Indeed, from Ruthven on 17 April Lord George wrote a famous, bitter letter to Prince Charles, a letter whose substance was so patently true that it has continued to enrage ultra-Jacobite sympathisers to this day. The novelist and propagandist Compton Mackenzie described it as 'contemptible'. Alas, it was mostly plain fact. The bulk of it was devoted to a withering criticism of the folly of choosing to fight at Culloden, but it started with a supremely cogent remark that 'it was surely wrong to sett up the Royal Standard without having posetive assurance from His Most Christian Majesty that he would assist you with all his might'. In a nutshell, that was the view of the '45 held by its more intelligent participants from start to finish.[28] By 20 April, the curt message from Prince Charles acknowledging the hopelessness of the situation reached Ruthven, and the troops broke up. Had they not, they would have starved.

Charles himself rode down Glen More to Invergarry and then cut across country to Glen Spean on the first stage of that elaborate five-month game of hide-and-seek in the heather which has endeared him to romantic writers ever since. Vastly more significant in human terms was the iron tread of Cumberland and the question of what the chiefs would do as the Hanoverian army systematically devastated Glen More, the heart of the Highlands and indeed of Jacobite support for the '45. A letter from Donald Cameron of Lochiel to Cluny, written at the end of May

1746, gives a fairly clear account of what happened. Lochiel implies that the assembly of forces agreed on at Murlaggan did indeed take place, but it was neither 'so general nor hearty as was expected'. Clanranald's people had retired into their own inaccessible country, from which they refused to budge. A great many of Glengarry's men had opted out by the simple device of surrendering their arms. Only a few of them turned up under Donald MacDonell of Lochgarry, who had succeeded Angus MacDonell of Glengarry in command of the Glengarry regiment in the Jacobite army. He had been appointed chamberlain of the Glengarry estates in 1733 and had bought the bulk of his own landed property from the Duke of Atholl, by whose influence in June 1745 he had been granted a lieutenancy in the Highland regiment being raised by Lord Loudon. Hastening to join Prince Charles after the raising of the standard at Glenfinnan, he showed single-minded devotion to his cause well beyond the point regarded as sensible by most of his comrades in arms. He was, for example, involved in the futile plot organised in the early 1750s by Alexander Murray and his brother Lord Elibank, which envisaged some sort of Jacobite coup in London itself.[29]

As it was, Lochgarry stayed only a day at Invermallie before crossing Loch Arkaig, promising to guard the passes on the north side and return with more men in two days. Neither promise was kept. The Master of Lovat, that much-martyred son whose reluctance to become involved with the Jacobites at all had been resoundingly vindicated by events, simply refused to answer Lochiel's messages, so the Cameron chief was left with a handful of his own faithful clansmen plus a few more warriors under MacDonell of Barrisdale. Together they moved along the west side of the river Lochy to Achnacarry where Lochiel bitterly remarked that they would have been taken by surprise had they relied on Lochgarry's intelligence. Other lookouts fortunately warned the chiefs that Hanoverian forces were moving south from Fort Augustus. Such was the incredible fighting spirit of the 'Gentle Lochiel' that he actually moved north spoiling for battle. Skirmishing ensued between the advance parties of the two sides, but it rapidly became apparent that the Camerons and MacDonells were outnumbered on an absurd scale, and that they were in acute danger of being enveloped and left with the choice between capture or a suicidal last stand. Lochiel deemed it irresponsible to carry war into his own country without enough support to produce results. After retreating twelve miles the last Jacobite battle group thus decided, surely rightly, that dispersal rather than combat was the wise option. Lochiel's letter to Cluny urged him to follow a similar policy by dispersing his men into the hills, keeping all weapons carefully preserved. Astonishingly, Lochiel said he still had great hopes of the French government, though his real thoughts may have been better expressed by the remark that at least they had all better wait and see what His Most Christian Majesty's government meant to do. He concluded by urging Cluny to keep in touch and to urge similar tactics upon his neighbours the MacGregors and Mackintoshes.[40]

Effectively, these events marked the bankruptcy of the policy which Lovat had urged with passionate conviction at the meeting at Murlaggan shortly after Culloden. From the point of view of the chiefs his logic was compelling. It was simply the case that most of them had strained their authority over their people to breaking-point to keep their clans in the field in the latter, dismal stages of an unsuccessful rebellion, and their tenants understandably refused to rally in significant numbers to face what was clearly an overwhelming force of British regulars. Lovat, along with the others, became a hunted fugitive rather than the inspirer of continued irregular warfare, and the problem as to why he, of all men, rallied to the Jacobite cause only in its last hopeless days remains an acute one.

Fortunately there survives a considerable volume of correspondence between Lovat and MacLeod of MacLeod, Lord Loudon, and others during the course of the '45. Carefully examined, it yields convincing evidence as to the evolution of Lovat's attitudes, evidence which can be tested against known facts about his circumstances.[31] In June 1745 General Guest was writing in complimentary terms to Lovat from Edinburgh, assuring him that he was as friendly towards Cluny as Lovat and that if Lovat helped Cluny to complete his company quickly, it might be possible to press for a majority in the regiment for the Macpherson chief. In July Norman MacLeod of MacLeod wrote from his castle at Dunvegan in Skye to say that Cluny owed his captaincy almost entirely to two factors. One was Norman MacLeod's canvassing on his behalf, and the other was the knowledge, assiduously propagated by MacLeod, that Cluny was very closely connected with Lovat. Norman MacLeod regretted the small number of Frasers in the ranks, but remarked that Lovat's eldest son could have had a captaincy for the asking had Lovat not vetoed the idea, and he added that he would continue to press for a commission for Fraser of Foyers. Apart from an evident nervousness on the part of MacLeod at the lack of true cordiality between Argyll and Lovat, the tone of the letters was relaxed. Though MacLeod expressed confidence in August that Lovat's 'Loyaltie and Prudence' would keep him from the 'fatal' consequences of joining the rising of the 'Pretended Prince of Wales', it is clear that the Skye chief was worried. A letter from him of 18 August urged Lovat to send his eldest son the Master of Lovat away from home to complete his education and escape the current crisis. MacLeod also wanted to see Sandy, Lovat's second son, in the British army.

So did another pillar of the Hanoverian settlement, the Earl of Stair, but in September 1745 Lovat wrote to him declining a commission for Sandy in the Earl of Loudon's regiment, on the grounds that he was 'ane extraordinary undergrowth, the next degree to what they call a Dwarf'. More significant by far was the latter part of the letter where Simon moaned that despite his vast services, personally recognised by George I after the '15, Sir Robert Walpole and General Wade had treated him 'like a scoundrell or a banditti', leaving him disgusted with politics and encumbered with debt.

On 15 October 1745 a party of Stratherrick Frasers led by James Fraser of Foyers swooped on Culloden House trying unsuccessfully to seize Lord President Duncan Forbes. MacLeod of MacLeod was blunt in telling Lovat that the affair 'has a very ugly aspect'. Nobody believed that Foyers would have dared launch his attack, which was only beaten off after a brisk exchange of fire, without the tacit appoval of Lovat. Even more transparent was the device whereby Lovat tried to pass off the systematic mobilisation of his clan for the Jacobite army as an act of unfilial insubordination by the Master of Lovat. That Lovat's egotism extended to being a complete domestic tyrant was notorious. Nobody in his household argued with him, let alone defied him. The comic-opera level of behaviour which Lovat indulged in to try to mislead Whig opinion deceived nobody. With as much publicity as he could muster, the masterful Simon 'dispersed' several companies of Frasers on their way to join Prince Charles and then he sat down and wrote an unctuous missive to Lord Loudon, the principal government commander in the northern Highlands, congratulating himself on his loyalty to the House of Hanover. When, however, Loudon heard that the Master of Lovat had left his father's house the very night of the day on which Lovat had written this expression of Hanoverian sympathies, and that the Master had left to lead the 'dispersed' companies into the Jacobite camp, he was furious. A child, Loudon told Lovat, would not be deceived by such mummery. It is hardly surprising that shortly after this Loudon's patience snapped. He believed Lovat had been correct when, three months before he started to wail about his powerlessness, he had boasted of his absolute control over his clan. An anonymous correspondent who wrote to Lovat about this time said that it was commonly believed in the Highlands that the Frasers would rise for or against the government indifferently, depending on the lead they received from Lovat.

On 11 December 1745, Loudon marched to Castle Downie, where Lovat was in residence, and placed him under arrest. Loudon returned to Inverness with his prisoner the next day, but made the extraordinarily foolish decision to hold him temporarily in a private house before transferring him to Inverness Castle. Simon's influence was quite strong enough to ensure escape by the back door, an escape which enabled him to retire to the comfortable house of 'my Chief doer Gortuleg'. Whilst with Fraser of Gortuleg he received the flattering addresses of Lochiel, Cluny, and Murray of Broughton, and also had his first and last meeting with

Prince Charles, on the bitter evening after Culloden.

Whilst there is no question but that the correspondence between Lovat and Loudon and Culloden was, on the side of the Fraser chief, mainly a mass of lies compounded with humbug and cant not quite redeemed by impudence, there is no reason to be sceptical about the passages in which Simon expatiated on his more general sense of grievance. His account of his loss of government favour, and a pension, after the death of George I was just true, as was his expression of his own distress at his breach with Argyll and failure to ingratiate himself with Sir Robert Walpole. Even more significant was the account Lovat gave in a letter he wrote to Loudon on 23 November 1745 of his 'foolishly and madly meddling with Elections'. In retrospect, Lovat could see that his support for his brother-in-law Sir James Grant of Grant against John Forbes of Culloden had cost him much and gained him little. Wade had told him to his face that his hostility to the Culloden interest would cost him his independent company. The Duke of Argyll was at one stage so angry over Simon's sustained campaign against those staunch Argathelians, the Culloden brothers, that he would not even talk to him. When Lovat realised that Grant was not even serving his purpose, he had fallen in with Argyll's wishes in promoting the successful candidature of Norman MacLeod of MacLeod in 1741, but only at crippling financial cost.

Lovat was clear by 1745 that all his electioneering had 'gained to myself a great many Enemys, and by assisting to make those two gentlemen members of Parliament Brought my Estate that was then flourishing into some disorder for I owe to the Bank and to other persons Severall Thousand pounds'. Again, it was an accurate summing-up of a dismally unsuccessful political career. Neither Grant or MacLeod ever did much to repay Lovat's pains and expense. Lovat consciously tied his attitude in the '45 to his financial and political embarrassments. Rather than die a bankrupt nobody, he would fish in muddy waters as in the '15. Detected, he preferred to spit defiance like a wildcat in the heather rather than surrender. What rendered his final defiance futile was the scale of the disaster to Jacobite arms, and the lack of any will to fight among his clansmen and, above all, in the heart of the Master of Lovat.

Of all these chiefs, Cluny Macpherson came nearest to something like successful resistance to the post-Culloden regime. Despite forced marches the Macpherson regiment, headed by its famed 'Bratach Uaine' (the green banner under which the clan claimed never to have fought a losing fight), was six or so miles short of Culloden when the first Jacobite fugitives from defeat met it. Retiring back into Badenoch, Cluny had later to watch Cluny Castle go up in flames and see young Hector Munro camp nearby while his redcoats scoured the countryside for the chief whose person would be some recompense to their commander for two relatives killed at Falkirk. Nevertheless, for nine years Cluny bid defiance to the Hanoverian presence. He was, in fact, in a uniquely important position, for he controlled that substantial sum of money known as the Loch Arkaig treasure. This was a sum of 35,000 Louis d'or sent by the French government on two frigates, the *Bellona* and the *Mars* which dropped into Loch nam Uamh in the first days of May 1746. They also carried food supplies, at least 240 casks of brandy, arms and ammunition. Had such succour reached the Jacobite army a few weeks before Culloden, it might have restored to it some freedom of choice. As it was, much of the stores and a little of the money disappeared into the hands of those cheerful opportunists Coll MacDonell of Barrisdale and his men, who did the unloading. An attack by smaller but pugnacious Royal Navy sloops forced the French vessels to slip away, carrying distinguished refugees such as the Duke of Perth, Lord Elcho, and Sir Thomas Sheridan, leaving the bulk of the treasure to be buried for safety.

Its subsequent fate, after being a matter of sustained historical debate, is now clear, at least in broad outline. About 800 Louis d'or were 'lost' at landing. Murray of Broughton, Charles's secretary, used 4,200 or so to cover outstanding commitments to regiments whose pay was in arrears. He stole 3,000 to assist the flight which ended in arrest and his turning King's Evidence. Prince Charles took some 3,000 to France, leaving some 24,000 which ultimately came under the control of Cluny. Of this some 6,000 were set aside in trust for Lochiel's sons. Dr Archibald Cameron spent 300 of this on a characteristically scrupulous journey to Rome to ask James, the Old Pretender, if he had any objections to the money being used to help Jacobite families. The balance of the Lochiel trust fund was cared for by Cameron of Fassifern who admitted, when a prisoner in Edinburgh Castle in May 1753, that he had placed it in the hands of a Macfarlane who was an Edinburgh lawyer, a Writer to the Signet, who put it out on loan at advantage. It was sensible, prudent management of the least the Stuarts and France could do for Lochiel's boys. What was left became a matter of dispute after 1754 when Prince Charles in his petulant, impoverished, and alcoholic exile had the effrontery to try to recover the money for his own use. Cluny made no attempt to deny that some of it had been employed to meet his own needs in the course of nine desperate years of hunted existence.[32]

The remainder seems to have been used with caution and good sense to meet the more pressing needs of afflicted Jacobites. A good example is Charles Stewart of Ardsheal who told Cluny in September 1746 that he thought he had suffered at least £6,000 of loss and damage. Ardsheal was quite open about his willingness to come to terms with the Hanoverian regime. His trouble was that the local military commander either would not, or could not, 'grant any of us (who bore but the least public station) our peace'. As a result Ardsheal and those few in his area in the same position needed money to flee abroad, as well as money to sustain their families in their absence. Cluny sent this leading victim of Captain Scott £100.[33] There survives a receipt from Lochiel's uncle, Ludovick Cameron of Torcastle, for £100 to help him go abroad.[34] All in all, the scraps of receipts which survive confirm the tenor of the account Cluny furnished when he went to France in 1755, in which he made it clear that the money was given to deserving sufferers for the Jacobite cause such as Glengarry, Lochgarry and the latter's brother Angus – 'a valuable officer in the 1745 and was a great sufferer in consequence'. One is left with the satisfaction of knowing that the money went mainly to those who most needed it, and not to their ungrateful lord and master, Prince Charles.

Ardsheal's remark about the impossibility for leading Jacobites of coming to any terms other than the scaffold with the British government is deeply significant. They were in exile because they had all gone too far. Quite clearly even that very large section of English and Scottish opinion which disliked Whig government without being positively Jacobite reckoned that the '45 was inexcusable. On top of the trauma and chaos, the exploitation of the episode by France rankled deeply. Lochiel and his brother Archibald escaped to France with Prince Charles in September 1746. Once fully recovered from his wounds, Lochiel was made colonel of the regiment of Albany in the French service. Prince Charles was Count of Albany. Lochiel attended him, during his brief period of acceptability at the French court at Versailles, as his Master of the Horse. Lochiel's father died in exile in 1748, in which year the 'Gentle Lochiel' himself tragically and prematurely died. His sons John (died 1762) and James (died 1759) followed him in the French service. Cluny, who had been gazetted a lieutenant-colonel in the regiment of Albany in 1746 found when he reached France in 1755 that it was an absolute rule of the French army that officers earned pay only at the head of troops. Penniless, he found that he could only touch a gratuity of 6,000 livres, much of which he had already spent, when at last he secured a commission as a lieutenant-colonel of the Royal Scots regiment, and was received at the head of his troops. So, by 1756 the wearisome process of begging his active commission was over.[35] His wife joined him in 1757 and he died, still in exile, in 1764.

In one of the interminable begging memorials which he had to address to the French court, Cluny explained the source of all his troubles in the following terms:

> il avoit herite de Ses ancetres un inviolable attachement a la maison de Stuart, et avait dedaigne des offres tres avantageuses pour lui, sa famille et sa tribe, qui lui furent faites par le gouvernement avant l'arrivee de Son Altesse Royale en Ecosse en 1745, il prit les armes et l'accompagna

a la tete de sa tribe pendant tout son expedition.[36]

It was, as it had to be, admirably calculated to appeal to the official mind of Bourbon France, which ever since the late sixteenth century had been using the congenial culture of Counter-Reformation Catholicism plus its own formidable propaganda and patronage machine to foster a cult of authority in general, and royal authority in particular. Yet it was by no means an accurate account of realities in pre-1745 Scotland. Cluny claimed an inviolable attachment to the House of Stuart, yet he had sworn and to some extent honoured allegiance to the House of Hanover. He had by no means disdained the advantageous offers of the British government, and some he had accepted with alacrity. Nor had he seized his arms and led his people to fight by the side of Prince Charles as soon as he heard of his arrival, but had marched off to fight for Cope. In France Cluny found it impossible to live on his meagre army pay. Thomond admitted in 1759 that he deserved a better fate and described the Cluny family's position as dismal.[37] Yet another barrage of petitions had to be organised, and it is hardly surprising that his wife in 1764 refused to let the French government bury with military honours a man they had kept in dire poverty for years.[38]

Cluny's over-simplified retrospective view does provide an opportunity to assess what really went on among the closely inter-connected group of chiefs in the Great Glen and the strategically linked Glen Spean in the years 1745–6. One thing is clear – these men were moving into still loose but always closer bonds with one another. They all shared an anxiety to control cattle-reiving, and their private watches were only one aspect of a zeal to assert and define property rights. However, they were as anxious to cooperate at the political level as at the level of simple law and order. All were marginal, not just economically, but politically, and Simon Fraser was perhaps the one who saw clearest of all, behind the inevitable reams of verbiage which he generated like a smokescreen, that they would stand far stronger if they stood together. Hence his loose confederal agreement with Lochiel and Cluny in 1744. Into this empirical and evolving world came in the late summer of 1745 the one person none of them wanted to see, at least if he came unaccompanied by soldiers arms and money – Charles Edward Stuart.

The resulting strain on the local political system was simply appalling. Almost all the clans and their chiefs had a vein of Jacobite loyalism as part of their cultural heritage. Much of it was tied up with their religion. In the case of young Ewen Macpherson of Cluny there was no particular reason, economic, political or religious, strong enough to propel him into the Jacobite camp, though he must have held ambiguous private views to make the transition so effectively. The fact remains that Lochiel, who seems to have joined Charles in a spirit of desperation, since he envisaged losing everything, had to kidnap Cluny to bring him into the Jacobite fold. Cluny and Keppoch, both Episcopalian Protestants by persuasion, acted throughout as brothers in arms, though the fact that Keppoch's people were predominantly Roman Catholic must have given edge to their zeal to fight for a prince at least nominally of their religion.

John MacDonell of Glengarry produced, admittedly after the rebellion was over, a most intriguing account of what happened to him in the course of the whirlwind of events in which he was swept up from late August 1745. According to Glengarry, when he heard that the Young Pretender was landed and joined by Lochiel, Keppoch and other chiefs of clans, he did his best to dissuade his tenants and dependants from joining the Jacobite army but found to his chagrin that his arguments were ineffectual, for his people not only joined the Pretender but 'threatened to take himself Prisoner if he did not likewise join them'. As a result, he left his own country, going to Dunkeld in Strathtay to put himself under the protection of the Duke of Atholl. The day after he reached Dunkeld he went with the duke to consult with Sir John Cope at Crieff. He offered that officer all the information he had about the Jacobite army. However, Prince Charles soon 'came to Blair of Athole within sixteen miles of Dunkeld'. The Duke of Atholl was determined to retire first to Edinburgh, then to London, and Glengarry was all for accompanying him to avoid suspicion of disaffection to the government. From this course he was dissuaded by Atholl who urged him to go home, live quietly, and try to minimise his clan's involvement in the rising. This Glengarry claimed to have done, even to the point of regularly visiting the officers of the Hanoverian garrison at Fort Augustus and doing all the services he could, as he was sure they would testify. Even when leading Highland and French officers of the Jacobite army visited his family during the siege of Fort Augustus, Glengarry claimed he refused to meet them.

After Culloden Glengarry went to Inverness to wait on Cumberland, but Lord President Forbes sent him back to his own country with a pass from Cumberland's military secretary Sir Everard Fawkener, with a view to prevailing on his own tenants to surrender at once. Persuading them to do so was made more difficult by the news that the people of Urquhart and Glenmoriston, who had come in to surrender arms, had all been imprisoned, but Glengarry eventually persuaded all but fourteen of his tenants to surrender to the humane Campbell commander Lord Loudon. After giving up their arms, they were released with certificates of surrender from Loudon. The next event was predictable.

Cumberland's troops swept down and burned all the houses and stole all the cattle and effects, with absolutely no distinction between rebels and non-rebels. Captain Loftus of the Old Buffs distinguished himself by pillaging Glengarry's own house and leaving the chief's family almost as little means of subsistence as the tenants had. Inevitably, Glengarry had difficulty in persuading his Morar and Knoydart tenants to throw themselves on Cumberland's mercy but as he was threatened with a Hanoverian firing squad if he failed, he worked hard at the job and succeeded, only to have some of them poached by his wadsetter MacDonell of Barrisdale, who was trying to put together an impressive number of men to surrender arms to the army post at Bernera. Surrendering had become a competitive business. Next, Glengarry was forced to accompany Hanoverian forces as they lifted all the cattle on his Knoydart properties,, after which he was arrested and lodged at his own expenses in Edinburgh Castle from 1746 to 1749. The only charity he received to sustain himself, his wife, and their numerous children was £25 from Lord Justice Clerk Milton, Argyll's man of business. As there were no charges against him, his lawyer was able by using *habeas corpus* to spring him from jail in October 1749, when he emerged to face many debts and no assets.[39] He was buried in the Chapel Royal of Holyrood House on 3 September 1754, at a total cost of £17 5s. 1½d., including £5 11s 1½d. to the poor of the parish, and 5s. 0d. 'to the Common poor'. At least he was interred with dignity.[40]

There is surely some element of truth in Glengarry's tale of woe. He would have been very happy to come to terms with the victorious Hanoverian forces at the first opportunity, and had carefully manoeuvred throughout the earlier stages of the rising to keep that option open to himself. Yet he was not the injured innocent of his own post-Culloden painting. He has been described as 'that slippery individual' by two leading historians of Jacobitism.[41] Equivocation was part of his nature. It is typical of him that when John Murray of Broughton, Prince Charles's secretary, discussed Glangarry's relationship with his Jacobite son-in-law Gordon of Glenbucket, he could not be sure just how far Glengarry was behind Glenbucket's visit to Rome in 1738 to establish contact with the Pretender.[42] What is clear is that nobody believed that Glengarry's clansmen could possibly have been mobilised on the scale they were for the Jacobite army without some measure of tacit approval by Glangarry himself. And mobilised the MacDonells of Glengarry certainly were, for they served Prince Charles as a clan regiment throughout the rising. After his arrest, witnesses came forward to say that Glengarry had been seen 'in arms marching at the head of a body of rebels, and that he was called their Colonel, and was wearing a white cockade'. On the other hand, he was not 'out' in any meaningful sense, and the Earl of Albemarle, the Duke of Cumberland's successor as Commander-in-Chief Scotland, assured the

Duke of Newcastle in September 1746 that Glengarry had indeed co-operated with the Fort Augustus garrison during the rising, and with Albemarle after Culloden. Glengarry's second son, Angus, led the Glengarry regiment until he was accidentally killed after the battle of Falkirk in January 1746.

Thereafter the regiment was commanded by Coll MacDonell ('Young Barrisdale') eldest son of Archibald MacDonell ('Old Barrisdale'), who was an uncle of John of Glengarry. 'Young Barrisdale' and his son Archibald, known as 'youngest Barrisdale', had an incredibly confusing career after Culloden, an action they managed to miss. Arrested by the victorious Hanoverian forces, they were released and then promptly arrested by the Jacobites, on the not unreasonable suspicion of double-dealing, and transported to France where they were jailed. Excluded, like Glengarry, from the Act of Indemnity in 1747, they returned to Scotland in 1749 only to be arrested by the British government. Coll died in Edinburgh Castle in 1750. 'Youngest Barrisdale' was released in 1753, rearrested, sentenced to death, reprieved in 1754, and finally freed in 1762. He became an officer in the Queen's Highlanders, a move which was a demonstration of his complete reconciliation with the Hanoverian dynasty, to which he took oaths of allegiance.[43]

The truth as to what went on in Glengarry's country during the '45 is probably irrecoverable due to an excess of totally contradictory evidence. Glengarry was in fact committed to Edinburgh Castle in 1746 as the result of information formally sworn against him by Coll of Barrisdale and six other gentlemen, all of whom alleged that Glengarry had forced them out into rebellion by using his powers as feudal superior. They then went on to say that he cheated their reasonable expectation by failing to come out himself, though he did pocket appreciable sums of money from Prince Charles. The information went on to say that by offering rent rebates to tenants who joined Prince Charles, and savagely harrying the farms of Jacobite deserters, Glengarry kept his clan regiment better up to strength than most of those under the Stuart banner.[44] The Lord Justice Clerk, Andrew Fletcher, knew Barrisdale well enough and reckoned him so much the sharper of the two that he 'could sell Glengarry in a mercat'. Fletcher concluded sagely that Barrisdale and his shady allies could be telling the truth, but that equally 'this may be another fetch of his to save his Sweet Bacon'.[45]

What does emerge quite clearly from a detailed examination of the minds of the Great Glen chiefs and their outlying allies during the '45, is that most of them seem to have had grave reservations about the rising, as well as deep-seated ambiguities in their relationship with the Whig regime at Westminster. Lochiel turned his back on his doubts early and went manfully forward with Keppoch at his side. Cluny had to be kidnapped into the Jacobite cause he then served so magnificently. The northernmost of the major Great Glen chiefs, Glengarry and Lovat, both tried to cling to profoundly ambiguous political positions long after it had become clear that Westminster was not prepared to tolerate such behaviour. Glengarry at least saved his neck, if not his fortune. Simon Fraser undoubtedly considered that his own fortunes, financial and political, were at such a low ebb that it was worth hazarding all by impudently transparent double-dealing, for which he duly paid the supreme penalty.

It was the misfortune of Lovat and the group of chiefs with whom he had deliberately linked the fate of the Frasers after he rescued them from the danger of becoming a mere appanage to the northern and predominantly Whig clans, that the guerrilla tactics and military inaccessibility of their home territories which had minimised the consequences of failure in several previous rebellions simply did not apply in the '45. After Tiendrish blooded the rising with his initial guerrilla attack on the Royal Scots, events moved at great speed and in unexpected ways. The local clans were initially very reluctant to march on Edinburgh leaving an undefeated Cope behind them. In the event they ended up marching to Derby. Their greatest victories they owed to the shock tactics and rapid movements of irregular warfare. By the time they fell back on their home territories early in 1746 they increasingly and instinctively wanted to take measures which might have enabled them to mount a sustained guerrilla resistance pivoting on the Great Glen and achieve some sort of compromise settlement. Such a settlement was incompatible with the presence, let alone the ambitions of Charles Edward Stuart. It is highly significant that though Lovat urged Charles to fight on after Culloden, he actively discouraged any suggestion of a second meeting between himself and the Jacobite Prince Regent when both were skulking in the heather and Charles wanted to spend a day fishing with him.

Yet by then the game was up. For the Jacobite chiefs of the area the post-Culloden situation spelled the irremediable loss of an ancient and cherised autonomy as, with an unconquered Fort William behind them, they faced a redcoat juggernaut rolling down from Inverness which their clansmen no longer had the will to oppose. The one odd exception to all this was Simon Fraser, Lord Lovat, the man of whom an anonymous correspondent during the '45 said that he had in his lifetime recovered his estate 'from almost nothing' and rescued his clan 'from bondage and slavery'. The aged fox of the Gaelic Highlands had indeed been a great chief of the Frasers, but a lifetime of wheedling, plotting, planning, manoeuvring, bullying, bribing and grovelling had left him impotent and bankrupt, with nothing more to lose after he had failed to extract any advantage out of the rising. Hence the great roar of defiance from Lovat at Murlaggan. The fox's skin fell away and the old lion within stared at utter ruin and was not afraid. With all lost, Simon was his own man, at last. For him alone final defeat was liberation.

9 *The Way Back – From Culloden to Yorktown*

For an unfortunate few, among whom Lord Lovat was numbered, military defeat was followed by pursuit, capture, condemnation, and the bloody ritual of the scaffold. Retreat to an islet on Loch Morar, in the far western recesses of Inverness-shire availed him not. Cumberland was determined to show that there was no area out of reach of the long arm of King George. When a party of the military from Fort William finally dragged the Fraser chief out of Morar, the victor of Culloden was cock-a-hoop, writing to the Duke of Newcastle that:

> . . . the taking of Lord Lovat is a greater humiliation and vexation to the Highlanders than anything that could have happened, as he is dignified with great Titles and Ranks high in command: and they had such confidence in his cunning and the strength of the country, that they thought it impossible for anyone to be taken who had these Recesses open, as well known to him, to retire to, especially as they had a high opinion of his skill to make the best use of these advantages.[1]

The heroic courage with which Lovat met death in London on 9 April 1747 made a great impression. His *sangfroid* in the short period he passed in the Tower of London between sentence and death was turned into a living legend by a Jacobite pamphleteer whose impact all the invective of Whig counter-propaganda failed to blunt.[2] Nevertheless, Cumberland was right in that the greatest impression of all was the one made on Highland minds by the mere fact that Lovat had been seized by Hanoverian forces.

Brutal though the actions of Cumberland's punitive columns were in the Highland glens, and ruthlessly though the policy of fire and sword was sustained by his friend and successor as Commander-in-Chief Scotland, William Anne, second Earl of Albemarle, there is a great deal of evidence that it was not the activities of blundering redcoats which broke the will to fight in the Jacobite areas. The Highlanders were used to hard times, and they had guns and spirits for another round when circumstances might be more favourable.[3] What does seem in the long run to have entirely destroyed any serious or widespread zeal for another rising in the Central

Highlands was disillusionment with France. Scholars to this day disagree as to exactly where the Jacobites came in the list of priorities of the French government in 1745–6, and it is clear that in the complex of committees which hammered out the policies of the French monarchy there were strong advocates of the Jacobite cause. However, no historian has made a convincing case for the view that after 1744 the exiled Stuarts were sufficiently high on the Bourbon scale of priorities to make a rising in Scotland a sensible venture,[4] and few Scots Jacobites had any illusions left on that score after Culloden. One or two of the more sophisticated ones resented the perfidy of Prince Charles, who had repeatedly assured them that massive French help was on the way. Most simply resented what they saw as a French betrayal of the Highlanders. Nearly all were resolved not to sacrifice themselves again to the ultimate benefit only of France.

That meant that there was no absolute barrier, in many cases, between Highland Jacobites and the House of Hanover, except the latter's understandable suspicion of recent rebels. Common interests, as usual, proved the bridge across which enemies could pass into the land of reconciliation. For a few, the process started early. Simon Fraser, Master of Lovat, the eldest son of Lord Lovat, was a precocious example. Whilst imprisoned and condemned for high treason in 1747, he discovered himself to be the man who held the balance in a contested Inverness-shire election. Ludovick Grant of Grant put up against MacLeod of MacLeod. The latter was the government candidate backed by the Duke of Argyll, Duncan Forbes of Culloden, and the Prime Minister, Henry Pelham, a man best described as a cleaned-up version of Walpole. Grant was the Master's uncle, and he bid fair to make a fight of it until Forbes, knowing that the Master alone could save the government man from defeat, sent emissaries to interview the Master in his place of detention, Edinburgh Castle. Of course, any attempt to bargain over a pardon, let alone for a restoration of the estates would have been the height of bad breeding. Everyone therefore admired to distraction the 'genteel' manner in which the Master agreed unconditionally, albeit in hopes of future favour, to sell his uncle down the river. It was done with a charm and dignity worthy of a conservative North British gentleman. Grant of Grant threw in his hand when he heard the news that his nephew had made this friendly gesture to the British Establishment.[5]

That Lord Lovat had pressured an unwilling elder son into leading Clan Fraser in the rebellion was common knowledge in Scotland. Petitions on the Master's behalf showered in. One from 'the northern ministers', i.e. Presbyterian incumbents in Inverness-shire, Ross-shire, and Nairn, waxed eloquent about the misfortunes of this 'raw and unexperienced youth'. They depicted one raised in 'Protestant and Revolution Principles' seduced against 'his real Principles' into the frenzy of rebellion. Here, these reverend petitioners exclaimed, was a clear case for 'the Royal Clemency'. The campaign worked. Simon Fraser had surrendered in August 1746. He was kept in Edinburgh Castle until after his father's execution, but then the Duke of Newcastle obtained a warrant for his release provided he lived in Glasgow. Simon had the wisdom to reject outright the offer of a regiment in the French army, a patent device to commit him indefinitely to the hopeless Jacobite cause. Instead he took up the study of law at Glasgow University and in 1750 was granted a complete pardon, and indeed a small pension by the British government. *Persona grata* once more, he confirmed Argyll's good opinion of him by accepting a government veto on his candidature for Inverness-shire in 1753, and was practising at the English bar in 1756 when a military crisis in the opening stages of a world-wide war between Britain and France gave him his chance. The war had really begun in America by 1754, and in 1756, through Argyll's influence with the Elder William Pitt, Simon Fraser was offered the command of one of the first two regiments to be raised in the Highlands for American service.[6]

Even a native-born American possessed of great talent and considerable property could find the raising of troops in the British American colonies a difficult business. That may be why one of the earliest recorded suggestions that Jacobite groups in the Highlands might provide recruits to serve the Hanoverian dynasty in North America came from Sir William Pepperrell. This remarkable New Englander had inherited a great merchant house from his father in 1734. As head of the militia of Maine and president of the Massachusetts council he was a natural choice to command the expedition which Governor William Shirley of Massachusetts persuaded the New England colonies to launch against the French fortress of Louisbourg on Cape Breton Island in 1744. When Britain declared war on France in that year the weak French garrison of Louisbourg made the grave error of drawing attention to themselves by harassing New England fishermen in the Gulf of St Lawrence. Their reward was to be overwhelmed by a somewhat amateurish colonial expeditionary force of 3–4,000 men under Pepperrell, who was not only commissioned a colonel on 1 September 1745, with authority to raise and command a foot regiment of the regular British Army, but who also became the first native American to be created a baronet (in November 1746).[7] Governor Shirley and Pepperrell were expected to raise their regiments from amongst the colonials stationed at Louisbourg, but the prospect of service in the regular British line, under officers of whom half were intended to be British regulars by origin, appealed so little to the New England militia that neither regiment could be completed before they both had to be broken when peace came in 1748.

On 24 June 1746 Pepperrell wrote to Shirley's kinsman and lifelong patron, the Duke of Newcastle, suggesting that a couple of hundred of the 'Rebell prisoners, who may have been unwarily seduced' into participation in the '45 might with advantage be sent across the Atlantic to help make up the muster rolls of his own and Shirley's regiments.[8] At the particular time, given the paranoid attitude of the English Establishment towards Scotsmen in general, and Highlanders in particular, it was wildly improbable that Newcastle would embrace the suggestion, but the fact that the suggestion had been made, and by a non-Scottish source, was significant.

Two bridges existed to help power-wielders in Hanoverian Britain make the mental transition to the point where they were willing to envisage heavy recruiting from former Jacobite areas, or perhaps more precisely heavy recruiting through aristocratic families in the Highlands which had been tainted with Jacobitism. One was simply the extent to which aristocratic Scottish families had already established a distinguished tradition of service in the British army, often at the very highest levels. The modern British army was largely created in the Continental wars of William of Orange after 1688, and Scots Whigs were well entrenched in William's military and political entourage. John Campbell, second Duke of Argyll and Duke of Greenwich (1678-1743), the man who more than any other foiled the Jacobite rising of 1715, is perhaps the best example of the sort of career made possible by these circumstances. A colonel of horse under William, he rose in the reign of Queen Anne to be Britain's most distinguished soldier after the great Marlborough, of whom he was latterly a jealous rival. More significant, perhaps, was the case of John Dalrymple, second Earl of Stair (1673–1747), a general under Marlborough who went on to be British ambassador in Paris under George I, and who fought as a field-marshal under George II at the battle of Dettingen in 1743. Stair's brother-in-law was a dashing cavalry officer, General Sir James Campbell, third son of the second Earl of Loudon. Sir James was killed at the battle of Fontenoy, but his son eventually succeeded as fifth Earl of Loudon. John Campbell, fourth Earl of Loudon (1705–1782), whose own mother was a daughter of the first Earl of Stair, was the military commander whose lengthy career after he joined the British army in 1727 pulls together so many of the key themes in the relationship between the Hanoverian dynasty and the Scottish aristocracy.[9] Here was a man who fought throughout the '45 on the Hanoverian side, and who by 1756 was British Commander-in-Chief in North America where he had under his command a formidable force of Highland soldiers, many of them commanded by officers whose political antecedents were not as impeccably Whig as his own.

The second bridge to the acceptance of such a state of affairs was the existence of one Highland regiment, the Black Watch, which paraded as early as May 1740 at Aberfeldy in Perthshire. It was numbered originally as the 43rd regiment of the line, but later re-numbered as the 42nd. It had fought with outstanding heroism at Fontenoy in 1745, and had survived the traumas of the subsequent Jacobite rising to maintain its place in the line. The confidence with which the British government regarded it must, however, not be exaggerated. When eleven regiments were recalled from Flanders in October 1745 to cope with the crisis caused by the Jacobite rebellion the Black Watch was indeed one of them, but whereas the other ten were ordered north for Scotland under General Hawley, the Black Watch was kept south of the Thames, as part of a force poised to repel any French thrust across the Channel. The British government had not forgotten that in 1743 the Black Watch had mutinied *en masse* in protest at the bland impudence with which His Majesty's Government proposed to violate their terms of enlistment (which were for home service only), by sending them to serve as cannon or fever-fodder abroad. Three men were shot as a warning after the mutiny was crushed. Intriguingly, Lord John Murray, later colonel of the regiment, had portraits of the three hung in his dining-room. It was an ambiguous gesture.

The two bridges could facilitate, but were in fact too slender to bear the weight of, a major reversal of policy. For that to come, necessity rather than willing choice had to be the compelling factor. By 1756 the British government had to try the Highlands, and more particularly the former Jacobite Highlands, as a recruiting ground. The Elder Pitt, who assumed control of the British war effort late in that year, claimed in retrospect that the raising of Highland troops on a large scale during his period in power was a moral revolution carried through because of his own greatness of soul. It was in fact more an act of desperation, and a very cursory examination of the relations between France and England in the years following the Peace of Aix-la-Chapelle of 1748 will show why this was so. That peace terminated what was known in America as King George's War, in Europe as the War of the Austrian Succession. In the New World it became clear almost at once that France did not intend to treat the peace as more than a mere truce. As early as 1750 the French were pushing forward and building forts in the territory they called Acadia, the British Nova Scotia, a territory with a French population but legally British since 1713. By July 1754 the young Virginian Lieutenant-Colonel George Washington had been forced to surrender his command of colonial troops after a fierce action against a besieging French force at Fort Necessity in the head waters of the River Ohio. Finally, on 9 July 1755 General Braddock, who had brought out two regular British regiments to stiffen the colonial volunteer forces, was himself catastrophically beaten and killed by the French and their Indian allies on the Monongahela River in the same region. The action was a prelude to a world war.[10]

There were Scots in Braddock's regular ranks, ranging from Commissary Robert Leake, a Lanarkshire man who had received a commission from the government as a lieutenant in an independent company during the '45, and who went out to America as Braddock's Commissary of Provisions, surviving to die a respected citizen of New York in 1773,[11] to Colonel Sir Peter Halkett of Pitfirrane, a Fife laird who laid down his life alongside Braddock. However, the large-scale introduction of Highland troops into North America, which was a feature of the British response to disaster on the Monongahela was almost entirely due to the difficulties the Westminster government faced in raising adequate forces in the Americas. Cadwallader Colden (1688–1776), an immigrant Scots physician and future lieutenant-governor of New York, held no illusions on the score of American will to fight even the Indians. In 1727 he published *The History of the Five Indian Nations Depending on the Province of New York*, a work occasioned by a legal dispute. In 1756 he was a refugee in New York, having fled his home on the Hudson with his wife and daughters because of the chaos reigning on the frontiers of the province. To a London correspondent he deplored English newspaper emphasis on American martial spirit. In his view Americans belonged to a society obsessed mainly with material gain, and few Americans had any skill at, let alone aptitude for frontier warfare. New York had its problems but Colden groaned at the way the Quaker politicians of Pennsylvania ignored Indian raids, and fell into civil confusion. In general, Colden argued, soldiers could only be raised in America by offering cripplingly high pay or by impressment, and he knew the latter was politically unacceptable. He was clear that military salvation for North America could come only from Great Britain.[12]

Although colonial or, as they preferred to be known, provincial troops were raised in North America in significant numbers and on a bewildering variety of footings, there is no reason to doubt the soundness of Colden's conclusion. Provincial forces were not capable of holding off an aggressive France and her Indian allies. Nor was it possible to raise significant numbers of men from the supposedly friendly or allied Indian tribes. This fact became a matter of bitter controversy, especially after Lord Loudon was replaced as commander-in-chief in America by Major-General James Abercromby. The British superintendant for the northern Indians was Sir William Johnson, a man reputed to have exceptional influence with the 'Six Nations' Indians, and more particularly with his closest neighbours in northern New York, the Mohawks. The particular confederation of tribes to which the Mohawks belonged seems to have been formed about 1570, by five tribes, but after the admission of the Tuscarora in 1722 it expanded to become the Six Nations or League of the Iroquois. Strategically placed in northern New York, with settlements along the shores of Lakes Erie and Ontario, the Six Nations might have rendered outstanding service to

Britain in the Seven Years War, known in America as the French and Indian War, between 1756 and 1763. In practice they rendered very little aid to the British during hostilities which in their part of the world went on from 1754 to 1763.

Contemporary critics of Johnson within the administration of the colony of New York waxed bitter about the contrast between his pretensions to great influence with the Indians, and his inability to control them. Abercromby asked Johnson to mobilise a force of several hundred Iroquois as a matter of urgency. Sir William failed to deliver the goods. Those few who did attach themselves to British forces, as some did, especially when the balance of advantage could be seen to be swinging relentlessly against the French, were less than staunch in battle, provoking the comment: 'Nor indeed was their assistance expected, by those who knew their boasted fidelity was a mere delusion, and that Mr Johnson's so much magnified influence, what it has since appeared to all men, the grossest imposture. They even declared before their march, they intended not to engage, but to be witnesses of the gallantry of our troops.'[13]

Sir William Johnson survived such criticism relatively unscathed, dying in 1774 to leave behind a reputation for intelligence, loyalty, generosity and rectitude which has only recently been seriously qualified. He was intelligent and he had powerful influence in government circles. With the Indians he was intimate, in every sense of the word, for decades. He was therefore in a very strong position to exploit his office to his own financial advantage, and to exploit the Indians ruthlessly, if urbanely. He allowed few of the accounts he rendered to the Crown to be checked. He was deep into the disreputable business of stripping the Indian nations of their lands, accumulating hundreds of thousands of acres for himself from tribes like the Creeks and Oneidas, and acting as intermediary and agent for many other land sharks. It is true that he proved to be far more willing to contemplate a solution by appeasement to the great Indian rising of 1763–4 than the then Commander-in-Chief Major-General Jeffrey Amherst, and that Amherst's recall enabled Johnson to have his way, but Sir William was not, from an Indian point of view, worth dying for. When he killed Indians with the rum he sold to them in destructive quantities, he did not even pay for his customers' burials. He charged the Crown.[14]

John Stuart, a Scot who emigrated to America around 1748 and who became, somewhat to his own surprise it seems, superintendent of the southern Indian department in 1762, was another of the same kidney as Johnson. He knew the major tribes of his superintendency – Creeks, Cherokees, Choctaws, Chickasaws, Catawbas and so on – well. Nevertheless, his principal positive achievement was his own enrichment, and it is significant that virtually all of his handsome personal fortune was amassed after he became superintendent. One Gavin Cochrane, who forwarded a

'Treatise on the Indians of North America Written in the Year 1764' to the Earl of Halifax in the hopes that it might reach the royal eye, had no illusions about the basic attitudes of the Indian tribes to the Anglo-French confrontation. Cochrane was clear that the French, with their more lavish presents and their fur-based economy, were less alarming to the Indians than the British, with their masses of land-hungry, Indian-hating settlers.

Yet the Indians had the perception to understand that with the alarming fall in their own numbers, and the inexorable rise in those of the white settlers, Indian hopes for survival depended upon a balance between the French and the British. Only that balance would leave space for the much weaker Indian nations between the rival powers. Thus during the war years the Indians tried to avoid strife between themselves, and few of them joined either the British or the French armies with any degree of zeal. The endless debates in which the policies of major Indian groups were formulated had reached logical conclusions. The expulsion of France from North America after 1763 was from an Indian point of view a disaster. Nor was it at all easy for the British imperial government to relate to the egalitarian structures of Indian tribes. It is no accident that worried Britons were given to citing the Roman author Sallust's comments on the Getuli and aborigines of his day, that they were '*genus hominum agreste, sine legibus, sine imperio, liberum atque solutum, qui neque moribus, neque lege aut imperio cujusquam regibantur*' ('a species of man, rural, without laws or authority, free and unrestrained, who are ruled by nobody's customs, laws or command'). It was a gross over-simplification, for the Indian nations had their own intricate patterns of law and social control, not to mention their own elaborate procedures for decision-making. We must translate these criticisms based on classical tags into a simple statement that the absence of a hereditary Indian aristocracy made it difficult for Britain to relate to and manipulate Indians.[15]

If the 10–12,000 souls who were believed to make up the Six Nations and their colonies in the mid-eighteenth century[16] therefore constituted no available pool of military manpower at the disposal of the British government, it was a different story when it came to those Highlanders whom the British establishment had as recently as 1745–6 been only too happy to classify in the same 'savage' category as the Choctaw or Mohawk. For a start, the Highlands held a much larger population within a much smaller compass than the League of the Iroquois. In 1755 the Reverend Dr Alexander Webster of the Tron Kirk in Edinburgh conducted an enumeration of the population of Scotland which has stood up well to modern probing, and which gave a total figure of roughly 550,000 for the Gaelic-speaking parts of the Highlands and Islands. This learned and social divine was a devoted adherent of Hanover. He had refused to flee from Edinburgh when Prince Charles occupied it late in 1745, and he made no secret of his sympathies during the occupation.

Particular interest therefore attaches to his estimate of 59,563 people for Inverness-shire, the county of the Jacobite heartland in the '45. His survey was commissioned by the British government through Lord President Dundas of the Court of Session, and modern demographers, excited by the quality of his aggregate calculations, have perhaps failed to see the importance of an exercise in dis-aggregation which Webster performed for every county. He carefully calculated the number of fighting men, whom he defined as males between 18 and 56 years of age. This was a more restricted view than the 16 to 60 norm usually adopted in Webster's day, but he was clear that at 16 a boy was too immature for war, and at 60 most men were 'too Crazy and Infirm'. Allowing for the halt and the blind, Webster reckoned military effectives at one-fifth of total population. Inverness-shire therefore contained about 12,000 effectives.[17] It has always been difficult to understand why the British government wanted to have Webster's enumeration. No comparable data existed for England before 1801, nor did Webster's work have any forward administrative uses. However, on the eve of a world war in 1755 one explanation was clearly a desire to know roughly the manpower potential of a country likely to be disproportionately important as a recruiting area.

For reasons which are not far to seek, the Black Watch or 42nd regiment, after its prominent role at Fontenoy and its carefully sheltered role during the '45, had been sent to Ireland where it was stationed for the seven years from 1749 to 1755. Using troops of one nationality on police duty over another nationality is a standard, and indeed perhaps a necessary device for any multi-national polity, especially when there is no such thing as an effective police force. To make assurance doubly sure the 42nd was commanded in Ireland by a Campbell lieutenant-colonel whose hard-core Whiggery may be deduced from the fact that he was a future Duke of Argyll. The political waters were still muddied by swirls of sediment stirred up by the last Jacobite rebellion and in 1753 the last man to be executed for high treason in the '45 suffered his ghastly death with great heroism. This was Archibald Cameron, younger brother of the Gentle Lochiel of the '45. This estimable physician was seized in 1753 by a party from the small garrison at Inversnaid near Loch Lomond. He was apparently gathering funds for the Pretender but his execution on 7 June was mainly due to a widespread conviction in Hanoverian court circles that he was testing the water in the Western Highlands on behalf of Frederick the Great of Prussia, who was quarrelling with the Elector of Hanover and saw in Jacobitism what most European monarchs saw in it – a means of harrying the Elector's *alter ego*, the King of Great Britain and Ireland, by encouraging endless trouble in the Highlands.[18]

Before the 42nd embarked for America, there was an interesting change in its command. Lieutenant-Colonel Campbell was promoted to the command of the 54th regiment and Major Francis Grant was promoted to succeed him. It was a popular promotion in the regiment. When the men heard of the vacancy they actually raised money to purchase the lieutenant-colonelcy for Major Grant. Fortunately the money was not required, for the purchase system so common in the peacetime army was here waived in favour of promotion by merit. Francis Grant was a younger brother of Ludovick Grant of Grant, so that family, whose unenthusiastic Whiggery and rebellious Glen More tenantry had so irritated Westminster in 1745–6, was by 1756 poised to recover on American soil the government favour it had forfeited on Scottish soil. In addition to a change in command the 42nd also experienced a major expansion. Before its departure from Ireland officers were sent with recruiting parties to Scotland, where their efforts were so successful that in June 1756 a second battalion of 700 recruits for the Black Watch was embarked at Greenock on the Clyde for America. From the point of view of the new regimental commander, it was significant that the second-in-command under Loudon was a near neighbour, James Abercromby of Glasshaugh Banffshire, a member of a cadet branch of the Abercrombys of Birkenbog. Promoted to major-general for the American expedition, Abercromby had an impeccable political track-record. After being active in local government he had become MP for Banffshire in 1734 and held the seat for twenty years whilst climbing the ladder of military promotion. A close friend of the Whig philosopher David Hume, Abercromby was to assume supreme command of British forces in North America when Loudon was recalled in March 1758.[19]

The second Highland corps raised primarily for North American service was, like the Black Watch, raised under stolidly Whig auspices, or more precisely under the auspices of the Honourable Archibald Montgomerie, who later succeeded to the great Ayrshire estates of his house as Earl of Eglinton. Though a Lowland Whig, Archibald Montgomerie had one sister married to Sir Alexander MacDonald of Sleat in Skye, and another married to the Laird of Abercairney on the southern borders of the Highlands. By choosing officers who were themselves men of property and influence in the Highlands, Montgomerie had no difficulty in raising a regiment of 1,460 effectives, who were needed so badly in the line of battle that after being embodied at Stirling they were shipped out of Greenock for the British naval base of Halifax in Nova Scotia before they had had time to master basic arms drill.[20]

From the point of view of the formerly Jacobite chiefs of Glen More and Glen Spean this pressure to raise Highland troops was a crucial opportunity to set a seal on their reconciliation with the Hanoverian dynasty. Absolutely central to that process were the letters of service issued to

Simon Fraser, sometime Master of Lovat, to raise a Highland corps. A reluctant Jacobite, he had worked very hard at the task of establishing his loyalty to the government after his full and free pardon passed the seals in 1750. He became an advocate in 1752, and was one of the counsels for the pursuers (or prosecution) in the notorious trial of James Stewart of Aucharn at Inveraray on 21 September 1752, before Lords Elchies and Kilkerran and Archibald Campbell, third Duke of Argyll (acting as Lord Justice General) as judges.

Politically the trial was extremely significant. Steward stood accused as art and part in the murder of Colin Campbell of Glenure, factor on the forfeited estate of Ardsheal. It was an unusual circuit trial in that both the Lord Advocate and the Lord Justice General participated. Steward was convicted and hanged. The justice of the sentence has been a matter of passionate debate ever since, but the social function of the trial was never in doubt. It was a decisive step in crushing the possibility of a rising tide of guerrilla warfare in the Highlands against the post-Culloden order. Such agrarian violence might well have involved progressive politicisation of the lower orders, so it was vitally important not only that the arch-Whig Argyll, MacCailean Mor, sat in judgement, but also that Simon Fraser prosecuted and thereby underlined the fact that violent resistance would be in no way condoned by the former Jacobite proprietors.[21]

The sons of Lord George Murray, the Jacobite general of the '45, were in the van of those who sought to reintegrate the former Jacobite families fully into the British ruling class. It was an objective in which they were much assisted by their predominantly Protestant episcopal faith, and by the refusal of the Scottish aristocracy to treat the Whig–Jacobite division (which often ran through families), as grounds for social ostracism. Lord George Murray's second son James, who eventually became a British general, was commissioned captain in the Black Watch in July 1757. He was wounded in the attack on Ticonderoga in 1758, again in an expedition to Martinique in the Caribbean in 1763, and eventually was wounded a third time so severely that he could never afterwards lie down. Francis Grant, Murray's commanding officer at Ticonderoga, married his daughter Anne Charlotte in 1780 to the Honourable and Right Reverend George Murray, fourth son of the third Duke of Atholl and Bishop of St David's. Ticonderoga was an action in which the Highland troops gave bloody proof of their fidelity to the white horse of Hanover, and in which Abercromby lost his reputation by an ill-judged assault upon a heavily-defended French-held fort. The 42nd alone lost 8 officers, 9 sergeants, and 297 men killed, as well as 17 officers, 10 sergeants, and 306 soldiers wounded. At once steps were taken to raise seven more companies for the 42nd in the Highlands. A few Irishmen recruited in Glasgow under slightly modified names were the only non-Highland soldiers in this

840-strong battalion embodied at Perth in 1758.[22]

The fate of Fraser's Highlanders, the old 78th regiment, was militarily far happier than that of the older 42nd. Simon Fraser raised it on the forfeited estate of his own family, which was vested in the crown, as well as on the properties of his kinsmen. He himself raised 800 men, to which the local lairds added over 700 more, making a very strong corps of 1,460 men. Numbers were vital, for Lord Barrington, the long-serving Secretary at War, had been clear from 1757 that the scale of reinforcements required for the campaigns of 1758 would constitute 'a number much too large to be got in America'. He accepted the need to raise Highland troops, using the Duke of Argyll to vet the names of those to whom letters of service to raise men would be given. Thereafter Barrington was emphatic that 'The only business I shall have with these Companies is to see that they be well accoutred etc. and sent out of Scotland as soon as possible'. Barrington stuck relentlessly to his chosen theme, stressing that 'I have no doubt but that the additional Highland Companies will be sent to America as soon as they are raised; and that none will be suffered to remain in the Country, on any pretence'.[23] Certainly, Fraser's Highlanders were shipped out of Greenock as fast as possible, along with Montgomerie's, to reach Halifax in July 1757. Thereafter the experience of the two corps diverged.

Montgomerie's Highlanders were attached to an expedition mounted in 1758 under an ailing but iron-willed Lowlander from Fife, Brigadier-General John Forbes, against the main French post in the Ohio Valley, Fort Duquesne. The enterprise to some extent retraced Braddock's steps, but with a much happier conclusion, for Forbes built a road and fought his way through until the French abandoned their untenable position, which was duly re-christened Pittsburgh. The campaign cost Montgomerie's Highlanders 104 dead and 220 wounded, despite the absence of any costly final assault. Fraser's Highlanders campaigned more spectacularly, but at a lower cost. They were first despatched to Louisbourg under Brigadier James Wolfe, an English officer who had served at Culloden and then in garrison and road-making duties in Scotland for several years, learning by the admittedly depressingly wet summer of 1749 to be 'quite out of conceit with Scotland'.[24]

After the fall of Louisbourg, the strategic key to the St Lawrence, Wolfe led the decisive British thrust up that river, striking at Quebec, the very heart of French Canada. Fraser's Highlanders were involved both in Wolfe's first unsuccessful attempt to bring on a general engagement by forcing the French lines on the Montmorency River, and in the climacteric battle on the Heights of Abraham where both Wolfe and his opponent the Marquis de Montcalm were mortally wounded, and after which Quebec fell. Wolfe's little army blasted its way to victory with two disciplined, lethal volleys, the first of them perhaps the most perfect fired on an eighteenth-century battlefield. When it boomed out like a single cannon shot, it tolled the knell of New France. The second volley completed the destruction of the French line, but the devastating and bloody charge which shattered any hopes of a rally by the French troops was spearheaded by Fraser's Highlanders, whose broadswords wreaked exactly the sort of havoc which had turned shaken British ranks into a ghastly shambles at Prestonpans and Falkirk during the '45. However, the ironies of that fatal day outside Quebec bit deeper still. Montcalm's *aide-de-camp* was an exiled Scots Jacobite, the Chevalier James de Johnstone, who had fought at Culloden, and who was extremely nervous at the thought of falling prisoner to English line regiments whose predecessors he had himself helped to capture at Prestonpans.

When a French officer called Jean-Baptiste Roche de Ramezay surrendered Quebec to the British, he sealed the final demise of the Auld Alliance, that precarious and often bad-tempered alliance between Scotland and France which had persisted, off and on, and latterly more off than on, since the Middle Ages. Under its auspices his own Ramsay family appears to have emigrated to France around 1600, and his father had emigrated from Burgundy to New France in 1685. One of Jean-Baptiste's sisters, a strapping six-footer of a nun, was so passionately patriotic and given to cooperating with and informing the French army that she provoked James Murray, Wolfe's successor and governor of Quebec, into a waggish threat to conscript her into a grenadier company. Her stature would have been appropriate for a unit always composed of the biggest and strongest men in any given regiment, and she would only have been fractionally more reluctant to serve than many others of her comrades-in-arms.

Quebec in 1759–60 was a curious microcosm of Scots–French relations, at a moment when events were setting a final seal on important and irreversible changes in them. The Chevalier James de Johnstone and the de Ramezays represented dead or dying options.[25] The fate of New France was not finally seen to be settled until September 1760, when overwhelming British forces compelled surrender, on generous terms, of the entire French civil and military establishment at the gates of Montreal. Indeed in the spring of 1760 Fraser's Highlanders suffered their heaviest battle losses of the war when Murray was defeated by de Levis in the Sillery woods outside Quebec. Fifty-nine dead and 156 wounded represented a far more serious blood-letting for Fraser's Highlanders than the 18 dead and 148 wounded they had suffered at Wolfe's triumph. However, in November 1759 Sir Edward Hawke's naval victory at Quiberon Bay off the Breton coast had destroyed the last French plan for invading Britain with a view to restoring the Stuarts, and by the end of 1760 it was becoming clear that Britain was emerging triumphant in her worldwide struggle with France.

The British rather than the French state represented the future.

The men who served in Fraser's Highlanders were often perfectly conscious of their place in world history. One elderly volunteer, Malcolm Macpherson of Phoiness, who distinguished himself by a skilled and murderous use of the broadsword against the French at Louisbourg made no bones about his two reasons for following the fortunes of war at so mature an age. One was to recoup fortunes damaged by an unlucky lawsuit. The other was to revenge himself on the French for what he saw as the treacherous promises which had led him to come out in the '45. Many officers of Fraser's, apart from their commanding officer, had been active Jacobites several of whom had, unlike their lieutenant-colonel, been present at Culloden. Charles Stewart, for example, had been severely wounded in Stewart of Appin's Jacobite regiment on that dismal April day in 1746, when many Jacobites quite unfairly blamed their defeat on Lord George Murray, rather than on their incompetent prince. As a lieutenant in Fraser's the same Charles Stewart was gravely wounded in the action at Sillery woods outside Quebec in April 1760, being provoked to remark as he convalesced: 'From April battles, and Murray generals, good Lord deliver me!' To give James Murray his due, the witticism was taken in good part when reported to him.[26]

Simon Fraser's 78th regiment of foot was in fact the vehicle not only for his own political strategy, but also for that of neighbouring families in the Great Glen and Glen Spean, especially if they were of high social status and bore once disaffected names. The roll of officers' names is itself a political document of high significance. At the head of the list of captains stood John Macpherson, brother of Cluny of the '45. Ewen Macpherson of Cluny had died in France in 1756, leaving by his wife Jane (daughter of Lord Lovat) a son, Duncan, and daughter, Margaret. Many other famous names followed John Macpherson. Donald MacDonald, brother to Clanranald, held a captain's commission and fell at the gates of Quebec in 1760. Amongst the lieutenants, Roderick MacNeill of Barra was killed on the Heights of Abraham in 1759, alongside his fellow lieutenant Alexander MacDonell, son of MacDonell of Barrisdale. A lieutenant of Fraser's Highlanders who survived the war was Charles Stewart, son of the stout-hearted and poetic Inverness Jacobite Colonel John Roy (from the Gaelic *ruadh* meaning red). That proud singer of a lost cause, who had fought for the French at Fontenoy and throughout the '45, had died in exile in 1752, but his son followed the road to political and social survial marked out by the heir of Lovat.

Amongst the captains of the 78th was John MacDonell of Lochgarry, heir to a title and house brought low indeed by the troubles of the '45. He was in fact a classic example of how a man could use military service as a springboard to political and social recovery. Having soldiered through the

French and Indian war, he was a veteran major by December 1777, when letters of service were issued to Lord MacDonald to raise a regiment in the Highlands and Islands. As his lordship did not wish to assume a field command, he used his influence to have Major John MacDonell of Lochgarry appointed lieutenant-colonel in command of the regiment. Lochgarry thereby acquired his regiment, without losing the quite essential support which Lord MacDonald could supply when it came to raising recruits. In practice Lochgarry lost his chance to lead the 76th regiment, or MacDonald's Highlanders, because he was captured as he crossed the Atlantic to assume his new command. Under a different lieutenant-colonel, his men shared his fate in 1781, when they were part of the British army which surrendered to the French and Americans at Yorktown. After repatriation, the regiment was disbanded at Perth in 1784. It was hardly a lucky career for this excellent unit, and Lochgarry was a colonel when he died in 1789, but in the last analysis the sustained display of political reliability by both officers and men (despite energetic American attempts to win them over when they were incarcerated) helped set the seal on the total reconciliation between the Highland aristocracy and the House of Hanover.

One factor which might conceivably have obstructed the earliest stages of this rapprochement was the strategic position which the Duke of Argyll held in vetting those to whom letters of service for the raising of regiments might be issued. The tightness of the stranglehold held by the Argyll interest on the distribution of patronage had had a great deal to do with political discontent in Inverness-shire in the 1730s and 1740s. On the whole, the Campbell grip on the regiments raised in the period 1757–60 was fairly tight. Simon Fraser clearly had to work very hard to ingratiate himself with Argyll before he could obtain letters of service for the raising of Fraser's Highlanders. Montgomerie's Highlanders were equally sound politically, and two small corps, Keith's and Campbell's Highlanders, raised in 1759 and despatched to serve in Germany under Duke Ferdinand of Brunswick, were no exceptions to this rule. Numbered the 87th (Keith's) and 88th (Campbell's) regiments, these units did, it is true, boast one commanding officer who was a relative of one of the best-known of Scottish Jacobite exiles. Major Robert Murray Keith, who assumed command of three companies of 105 men each when they were embodied as the 87th, was related to James Francis Edward Keith, brother of the tenth Earl Marischal. The Keith brothers fought as Jacobites in both the '15 and the '19, but by 1740 were clearly trying to mend fences at Westminster. They kept clear of the '45. James Keith died a hero's death as a Marshal of Prussia at the battle of Hochkirch in October 1758. The Earl Marischal received a full pardon from George II in May 1759, it is said partly for forwarding intelligence of Franco-Spanish intrigues of which he became cognisant as Frederick the Great's ambassador to Madrid. Withall Robert Murray Keith had long been an officer in the Scots Brigade in the United Netherlands, that most Protestant and Whiggish of units. He was as reliable as John Campbell of Duntroon, lieutenant-colonel of the 88th, whose officers included such nominees of the Campbell Earl of Breadalbane as Captain Archibald Campbell of Achallader and John Campbell of Auch.[27]

There was, however, one outstanding and vital exception to the generalisation that the Highland regiments of this vintage were essentially raised within the boundaries of the political power of the various branches of the Campbell name, and under the overall supervision of Argyll himself. In the north-east the ducal house of Gordon had long maintained a powerful independent interest, and had contrived to emerge from the '45 with enhanced rather than diminished stature. Cosmo George, third Duke of Gordon was made a Knight of the Thistle for his loyalty to Hanover in the last Jacobite rebellion. He died in 1752, leaving a young son and heir born only in 1743, Alexander, fourth Duke of Gordon. That Argyll relished the idea of somehow gaining control of the Gordon interest during the young duke's minority was only too obvious to the widowed duchess, who promptly remarried Major (later General) Staates Long Morris, a member of a distinguished New York family. His grandfather was Lewis Morris (1671–1746), chief justice of New York and royal governor of New Jersey. In 1697 his New York estate had been erected into the manor of Morrisania, and Staates Long was one of the half-brothers of Gouverneur Morris (1752–1816) the American statesman and diplomat, who was himself a son of the second lord of the manor of Morrisiana by a second wife. The Morris family of New York were wealthy landed aristocrats and though Gouverneur Morris staunchly upheld the cause of American independence after 1776 he did so reluctantly, and from the most conservative point of view possible. Staates Morris was therefore a perculiarly appropriate custodian of Gordon interests at a time when it was becoming clear that any Scottish political dynasty which wished to maintain a high level of visibility to the ultimate dispensers of power and patronage at Westminster would be well-advised to raise troops for overseas service.[28]

The importance of the independent Gordon initiative for several ex-Jacobite families in the Great Glen was considerable. The Duke of Gordon held extensive landed property in Lochaber. In bygone days this may have made him a menace to the independence of the region, but by the late eighteenth century it meant that he offered the families in the area which were on reasonable terms with his house a possible alternative sponsorship into the good graces of His Majesty's Government, a sponsorship which did not involve compulsory enlistment in the praetorian guard of the Argathelians. Of course, the Gordons simply had to make a success of their first regiment. The Duchess of Gordon contrived to obtain letters of service for Major Morris by exercising her ducal prerogative of direct access to the monarch. She made it quite clear to George II that she dreaded the possibility of Argyll trying to take control of her son's political interest during his minority. No Hanoverian sovereign, or English minister, was ever favourable to the pretensions of an over-mighty Scottish subject when he could find a viable rival, so the letters of service were forthcoming, and the ducal house and Gordon gentry made an all-out effort to ensure that the regiment was raised promptly and efficiently. Staates Long Morris was the lieutenant-colonel in command. To underline the commitment of the ducal house, its sons, though very young, were given commissions. Alexander, Duke of Gordon headed the list of captains, Lord William Gordon headed the lieutenants, and Lord George Gordon the ensigns. The symbolic nature of these commissions was underlined by the role of Duke Alexander, who was still at Eton and was very firmly told by George II to remain there. The duchess was herself a formidable figure in local politics, being born the Lady Catherine Gordon, only daughter of the second Earl of Aberdeen, so the lairds and noblemen of the Gordon connection did indeed exert themselves to the utmost. In a matter of weeks 960 men assembled at Gordon Castle. Thence they marched to Portsmouth for shipment to India, reaching Bombay late in 1761.

In India detachments of the 89th did outstanding service under the command of Major Hector Munro, who had once hunted Cluny in the Highlands. Hector Munro won the battle of Buxar in October 1764, a battle which set the seal on the British conquest of Bengal. Because of its distant postings, the 89th was reduced only in 1765. Most of the other Highland regiments raised in this period were disbanded in 1763 or 1764 after the Peace of Paris had confirmed the dizzy ascent of the British political complex to world power and imperial ascendancy. A by no means insignificant element in that sudden rise had been the availability of a large new reservoir of military manpower in the Highlands of Scotland, a reservoir which started to overflow when many other sources of troops were running dry. The role of the Highland aristocracy and gentry as the entrepreneurs in this military industry was crucial, and the decision by Westminster to ignore, in appropriate cases, the taint of a Jacobite past amongst the Highland military enterprisers was also fundamental to the success of the operation. Shrewd observers had guessed, almost immediately after Culloden, that the decisive nature of that Jacobite defeat would probably create a scramble to board the Hanoverian bandwagon on the part of many members of the ruling class whose previous record of support for that dynasty was less than spotless.

In sermons preached at the Tolbooth Kirk in Edinburgh on 23 June

1746, celebrating the crushing of the Jacobites at Culloden, the Reverend Alexander Webster, ultra-Whig and future pioneer demographer, was unctuously anxious to confine the fruits of victory to those who had truly laboured in the Hanoverian vineyard. He respectfully dedicated the published version of his sermons 'to all those whose concern for the welfare of our Jerusalem, And Zeal for the British Israel, commenced before the Battle of Culloden'.[29] Like most of his contemporaries, Webster seems to have seen the rebellion primarily in terms of disaffection amongst the upper orders of society. It was a universal prejudice amongst the powerful and educated classes in the eighteenth century, (and earlier) that the lower orders were incapable of purposeful action without a lead from above. It was an unbalanced view, of course, but when all is said and done it contained more truth than falsehood when applied to Scottish Jacobitism. Even Webster admitted that a firm political line adopted by a Highland chief was usually accepted by the bulk of his followers. Modern scholarship would suggest that when this was not so, there were usually divisions amongst the chiefly family or clan gentry. This is not to say that the Highland peasantry lacked opinions; merely that their social superiors could and did set the political course.[30] Having brought men out to fight for Prince Charles in 1745–46, Simon Fraser was by the late 1750s doing the same office for the House of Hanover. What, it may be asked, did the men he raised think of it all in 1757 or thereabouts?

Unfortunately the historical record is thick with rhetoric on the subject, and thin on evidence from private soldiers, most of whom were non-literate Gaelic-speakers. In 1763, when the 'Great War for the Empire' was at an end, the politicians at Westminster found themselves burdened with a national debt whose explosive wartime growth horrified them. As early as 1761 the annual charge upon it had risen to £19.5 million, a figure three times the pre-war sum. George Grenville, premier from April 1763, embarked on draconian retrenchment, cutting the army from 120,000 men to 30,000, and the navy even more drastically. William Pitt was incensed by the severity of the army cuts, saying that they sent 'the bravest men the world ever saw' to 'starve in country villages and forget their prowess'. In 1766, during the Rockingham ministry, when relations with America had become a major issue, Pitt spoke, at the end of a speech that was mainly about the need for reconciliation with the American colonies, of his own achievement in reconciling Highlanders. He said:

> I sought for merit wherever it was to be found; it is my boast that I was the first minister who looked for it and found it in the mountains of the north. I called it forth, and drew into your service a hardy and intrepid race of men, who, when left by your jealousy, became a prey to the artifice of your enemies, and had gone nigh to have overturned the State

> in the war before the last. These men in the last war were brought to combat on your side; they served with fidelity, as they fought with valour, and conquered for you in every part of the world.

An anonymous Chatamite pamphleteer, industriously puffing his leader's image and current line, said of the formerly Jacobite clans that 'their chiefs or connections obtained commissions, the lower class, always ready to follow, . . . with eagerness endeavoured who should be first enlisted'.[31]

The same vein of euphoria can be found in Scottish gentry sources. A comment on recruiting in 1760 for Johnstone's Highlanders or the 101st regiment is an example of such contemporary comment. The regiment itself was little more than a recruiting device, a framework within which lairds like Gordon of Knockespick, Campbell of Balliveolin, or the Grants of Rothiemurchus might beat up their individual companies in the shires of Argyll, Ross and Inverness for export to the German wars. 'A respectable veteran' who served as a lieutenant in one of the companies recalled later that: 'It was not necessary, in those days, to go to manufacturing towns to bribe with whisky and high bounties the idle and the profligate; we got plenty of young men in the country.'[32] At least the entrepreneurs in this particular trade bent to their task with a self-righteousness worthy of a modern 'Captain of Industry'. Hesitation or self-doubt they seldom displayed, and that was just as well.

In practice the whole business of decanting Highland peasants into North America as soldiers was shot through with ironies, but perhaps most ironic of all was the situation in which they were deployed against native American Indian peoples. To the Anglo-Saxon world this was a case of deploying one sort of 'savage' against another. Yet the very antithesis of 'savage' and 'civilised' had been beaten out and given its peculiar Anglo-Saxon resonances on the frontier between first Anglo-Norman, and then Anglo-Saxon, power and the Celtic peoples of the British Isles. This intellectual baggage had then been taken across the Atlantic to provide a convenient 'cant of conquest' for the Euro-Americans who fell with predatory intent upon the disease-ravaged, but quite sophisticated native American cultures of the Antlantic seaboard.[33] By the 1750s few Indians had many illusions left about Europeans of any kind. Sir William Johnson forwarded in August 1756 a statement made by representatives of the Onondagas, one of the Six Nations, as evidence of the need not to inflame during the war Indian sensitivities about settler encroachments. The translation ran as follows:

> We are informed the English are building a fort at Shamokin. We cannot comprehend the method of making war which is made use of by our brethren the English; When we go to war, our manner is to destroy a

nation and there's an end of it. But the English chiefly regard building forts, which looks as if their only scheme was to take possession of the lands.[34]

That perception goes far to explain Iroquois lack of enthusiasm for the British in the French and Indian war, but in fact tensions between British settlers and Indians were far more explosive in the late 1750s to the south of the Iroquois, in the Cherokee country threatened by the expansion of the Carolina colonies, to the point where the French at one point seriously hoped for formal alliance with the Cherokee.[35] By August 1756 Highland troops were already being moved by Loudon into garrisons in the Mohawk section of Six Nation country.[36] The first large-scale deployment of Highland troops in punitive operations against Indians came, however, as the result of the major Cherokee rising in 1759 against the endless encroachments of the Carolina settlers. The rising was led by Aganstata, known to his British opponents as Oconostota, and it gave rise to a bloody little frontier war. Amherst detached Colonel Montgomerie of Montgomerie's Highlanders, with 700 men of his regiment, reinforced with 400 other regulars and a strong force of provincial troops. Proceeding south with all due despatch, Montgomerie embarked on a policy of destroying Cherokee villages, only to find after a few easy successes that the Cherokee were more than capable of harassing his own columns. One single sally aimed at an Indian village cost him 2 officers and 20 men killed and 68 wounded. Nor did Montgomerie prove capable of preventing the surrender of the British garrison in Fort Loudon, a small stronghold on the boundary of Virginia. After their surrender on terms all the men of the garrison were massacred except for John Stuart, who in 1763 was to be appointed general agent and superintendant of Indian affairs for the southern department by the British government. This 'war carrying on by the Cherokees against the Southern Colonies'[37] proved difficult to finish. By August 1761 Amherst was convinced that his new commander in the south, Lieutenant-Colonel James Grant, had brought the Cherokee to the verge of defeat by means of tactics not dissimilar to those employed against Highland clans in 1746. First Grant defeated the Indians at Etchoe in June 1761, then he ravaged their lands. Amherst boasted that: 'Colonel Grant has not only destroyed Fifteen of their Towns . . . but also 1400 acres of corn, pease, and beans, and has driven near 5000 men women and children into the woods, where, if they do not make a proper Submission, they cannot fail of starving in the winter.'[38]
Grant's 2,600 troops had more than redeemed the defeat of Colonel Archibald Montgomerie.

Underneath the endless conflict on the Cherokee frontier lurked a political problem which kept recurring in white-Indian relations. The

Cherokee were before 1730 no more than a loose association of independent and equal individuals and settlements. The creation of an explicit tribal structure was largely the result of European pressure and demands. Indeed it was an eccentric Scotsman, Sir Alexander Cuming, who persuaded some, but by no means all Cherokee villages, to recognise a sort of embryo 'government' headed by the warrior Moytoy. This potential tyranny of warriors who might be able to preserve peace by creating a climate of fear among their own people in order to restrain them from attacks on whites was, however, so contrary to Cherokee cultural traditions that it failed to survive. By the 1750s the amorphous Cherokee 'government' was dominated by religious leaders who swayed their people by charisma and rhetoric, but who lacked the power to check the retaliations against settlers and traders which led to war in 1759–61. Reluctant to face all-out war against the Carolinas and Virginia, whose aggressive settlers massively outnumbered even this most numerous of the southern tribes, Cherokee leaders after 1762 introduced warriors into their central councils, primarily in order to endow the councils with power to coerce Cherokees. The new order, barely stabilised by 1775, disintegrated during the War of American Independence. Only in the early nineteenth century did the Cherokee evolve something like an aristocracy and a formal constitution. Predictably, this development did not stop the Americans from stealing their lands and expelling them.[39]

With the acceptance of quite mild peace terms in 1762, the 12,000 or so Cherokee, with their 2,500–3,000 fighting men, ceased to present any immediate problem and resumed their role as important suppliers of deerskins and absorbers of trade goods.[40] The French were already broken for ever as an independent power in North America. The Highland soldiers, raised and commanded by an aristocracy which Englishmen could understand and manipulate, and which the British political establishment was prepared to accept as a junior partner, ceased to be instruments of survival and became another ethnic minority in a polyglot pre-modern political structure – a ramshackle planetary complex rather than a state. Individual Highland noblemen were by 1763 well integrated into the British political élite. While serving in Canada, where he was wounded in both the attack on and in the subsequent British defence of Quebec, Colonel Simon Fraser had been elected the MP for Inverness-shire, a position which he occupied until his death in 1782. It was an impressive achievement, especially in the light of his father's failure to secure decisive influence over previous MPs.

More impressive still were the signs of continuing favour for Simon. From serving in Canada in 1761 he moved to Portugal as a brigadier-general in the expeditionary force sent to bolster England's old satellite when Spain entered the war in 1762 and promptly invaded Portugal. Simon Fraser became a temporary major-general in the Portuguese service but by 1771 he had achieved a permanent British rank of major-general and had the political and social clout to try to recover his estates. After due petition, it was announced that his military services entitled him to 'some particular act of grace'. By a special piece of legislation (24 Geo. III, c.37) he recovered the properties and lordships (though not the Lovat peerage which was only revived in 1837) in exchange for a payment of £20,983 to cover debts paid off by the government. He was a good decade ahead of all the other families forfeited in the '45. This polished, brave and hard man had shown, from the moment he set his face against an offer of a French commission, the only practical road to political recovery for the old Jacobite aristocracy of the Central Highlands. It was a path of blood – that of the Highland peasantry and, be it said, his own. It was also a path full of political cronyism. Simon had as a younger man been intimate with Alexander Wedderburn, that able and shameless Scots legal careerist who clawed his way up to power and patronage as a parliamentary agent of Robert, Lord Clive, the conqueror of Bengal.[41]

Humbler Highlanders were by the 1750s already forming a steady stream in the great flood of migration across the Atlantic, fitting flexibly into the interstices of the British imperial framework like the 'two respectable, intelligent old Indian Traders' George Galphin and Lachlan MacGillivray, who traded mainly with the Creek Indians south of Cherokee country in South Carolina and Georgia. Their enterprises can be traced back to the 1730s, and Lachlan's half-Indian son Alexander MacGillivray became an immensely influential and wily chief of the Creeks.[42] What craft and diplomacy could do for a doomed people facing endless American pressure, Sandy MacGillivray did. Well educated by his father's brother, a Presbyterian clergyman in Charleston, MacGillivray grasped that ambiguity is the armour of the weak, so this polygamous Indian chief was at one time the proud holder of a colonel's commission from the British, as well as general's commissions from the Spaniards and the Americans. Having fought against the birth of the United States, he showed that he could live with the new state and even hold it at a safe distance, by exploiting the need of Spanish Florida for an Indian alliance to protect itself from the depredations of American frontiersmen. Economically, MacGillivray was heavily involved with the firm of Panton, Leslie and Company, whose principals were Aberdeenshire men and strong Tories during the American Revolution. Like him, they survived the debacle of British arms by sheltering under Spanish protection in Florida when it was over.[43] Obviously, Scots traders and American Indians could and did coexist, cooperate, and interbreed. It is interesting that the two best known Scottish novelists of the later eighteenth century, Tobias Smollet and Henry Mackenzie, both used American Indian society as a means of criticising their own. In his last, and probably his best novel *The Expedition of Humphry Clinker* (1770) Smollet wallowed in the usual horrific torture scene when his hero the Scots Lismahago survives the death of his fellow-captive, but Smollet then contrasts Indian good sense on matters of religion with European bigotry and intolerance. Mackenzie in his *The Man of the World* (1773) also has the mandatory torture scene, but then contrasts the stern simplicity of the Indian with the duplicity and corruption of civilisation. Neither writer knew what he was talking about. God knows what Mackenzie would have made of Alexander MacGillivray.[44]

Yet Scottish Highlanders, as settlers, were also among the supplanters of the Indians, and had been for a long time before 1763. The earliest and largest of the Highland settlements was in North Carolina in what was then known as Bladen County, now Cumberland County, about a hundred miles up the Cape Fear River. There were certainly Highlanders there when North and South Carolina separated in 1729. Under the governorship of the Scotsman Gabriel Johnston between 1734 and 1752, Highland immigrants were strongly encouraged, and critics insisted that Johnston rather favoured than discriminated against men with records of active Jacobitism. Very substantial emigration from the mainland and islands of Argyllshire was well established after 1739, the year in which Neil MacNeil from Kintyre led a shipload of 350 people to Cape Fear. The volume of emigration undoubtedly increased sharply after 1746–7. It was a heterogenous population including Campbells and other leading Argyllshire names like MacNeil, Maclean, MacDougal, and MacLachlan. Another province with significant numbers of Highland settlers, though nothing like as many as the 5,000 or so who may have been concentrated in Cumberland County as early as 1753, was Georgia. That colony was founded by the imperial philanthrophist James Edward Oglethorpe, himself a former Jacobite who had spent time at the court in Saint-Germains, but who turned his back on that cause for ever after 1719. When he secured his charter in 1732 Oglethorpe had in mind two main groups of potential migrants; the alarmingly large class of people imprisoned for long periods in England for petty debt, and German Protestants harassed and driven out by a still aggressive Counter-Reformation spirit in their homelands. However, he also needed a warlke population for a province designed as a buffer against the pretensions of Imperial Spain.

For the marches of the new province, his agents recruited heavily from the notoriously Jacobite landward area at the head of the Great Glen, within a ten-mile radius of Inverness. In October 1735 a first contingent of 160 people sailed from Inverness to establish a new town on the border of Spanish Florida. Every effort was made to underline the pro-Hanoverian tone of the enterprise. The Whig magistrates of Inverness made

Oglethorpe a freeman by proxy, while the fiercely anti-Jacobite Society in Scotland for Propagating Christian Knowledge paid an annual stipend of £50 to the minister who accompanied the emigrants, the Reverend John MacLeod from Skye. John MacLeod was a strong personality and no ordinary Skianach, for he was related to the chiefly MacLeods of Dunvegan. The settlement of Darien, which these Scots established, had a mixed history, including much violence during the war with Spain which lasted from 1739 to 1748. Equally troubled, though mainly by disputes over land rights, was the history of the small settlement of less than two hundred souls which was set up in the northern parts of New York by Captain Lachlan Campbell, a Campbell laird from Islay who from 1738 disposed of his Islay estates and moved several shiploads of settlers from his native isle to lands north of the Huron which Governor Clarke of New York assigned to him, partly in hopes of consolidating the threatened northern frontier of the province.[45]

It was therefore quite natural that when the Highland regiments raised for the French and Indian war were nearly all disbanded at its conclusion in 1763, a fair proportion of the soldiers preferred to settle permanently in America rather than return to the rigours of their homeland. Contacts between Highland officers and men like Sir William Johnson greatly assisted the process. Himself an Irishman, Johnson had always shown partiality for scions of the Irish gentry. Like himself, such men were Protestant and Hanoverian, as they mostly had to be to maintain minimal political coherence in the imperial archipelago. However, the great majority of Highland officers qualified on similar grounds, and British regiments moved through Johnson's Mohawk Valley domain in very large numbers during the war. Elements of the 42nd, 44th, 46th, 55th, 60th, 78th and 80th British regiments were at various times in the area. Johnson made social contact with their officers and regularly incorporated young officers of good breeding but slender interest into his own patronage empire. The post-war development of the Mohawk Valley needed an influx of docile white tenants to work the estates of Johnson and his clients. Lieutenant Hugh Fraser of the 78th, for example, struck a deal whereby he arranged for Highland soldiers thoughtfully mustered out of the British Army at Quebec in 1763 to settle on Johnson properties with their families, while Johnson helped Fraser and his father-in-law Lieutenant Jonathan MacTavish, also of the 78th, to obtain grants of military bounty lands for themselves in northern New York. Sir William was even willing to buy an officer like Donald Fraser, a relation of Hugh Fraser, out of Fraser's Highlanders in exchange for a pledge by the said Donald that he would come with a tail of dependents to settle on Johnson's Kingsborough land grant.[46]

Through a son, Johnson was in 1767 in continuing contact with Lord

Adam Gordon, himself the fourth son of Alexander, Duke of Gordon. Lord Adam had commanded a regiment in the Americas, and had indeed visited Johnson Hall, Sir William's seat on the Mohawk. Like most ambitious career officers with political connections Lord Adam deemed it wise to keep a seat at Westminster. He was MP first for Aberdeenshire and later for Kincardineshire. Johnson offered to obtain for him a 10,000 acre grant in northern New York, an offer which Lord Adam accepted, on condition that 'the Duke of Atholl, my very worthy neighbour (and a friend to your son too) . . . go halves'. Atholl, one of the very greatest of Highland noblemen, saw in American land a relatively cheap appanage for a younger son. By 1767, however, New York had already experienced major rioting against the British attempt to tax the American colonies by means of the Stamp Act. The dream of an Atlantic empire on a semi-militarised basis in which the American provinces would be run by a junior branch of the aristocracy which manned the central legislative autocracy at Westminster was wearing very, very thin. Lord Adam was utterly unyielding on the central issue of the subjection of America to the absolute theoretical power of Westminster. He refused 'to vote away for ever Dependancy of that country on Great Britain – I could not have done it – had a regiment of Guards been the Bribe.'[47] It was an interesting view of the ultimate satanic temptation to a military wheeler-dealer in the corridors of power in eighteenth-century Westminster.

Lieutenant Hugh Fraser, who under Johnson's patronage was carving for himself a very junior role in an incipient Anglo-American aristocracy, had by 1765 not only settled his military followers from Fraser's Highlanders on the Mohawk, but had also persuaded some of their kinsfolk from the Highlands to come over and join them.[48] These hardy and clannish people became increasingly willing to cross the Atlantic. In 1773 Harry Munro, rector of St Peter's Church in Albany, New York, who acted as a contact between Sir William Johnson and Scots emigrants vouched for by their parish ministers, reported that 'by letters from Scotland it appears that the lower class of people are generally discontented, and the spirit of Emigration prevails greatly'.[49] Discontent with a bleak lot in Scotland did not, however, imply lack of docility in North America. The whole point about this particular group's migration is that social control by aristocracy and clergy formed the very framework of their translation across the ocean. The forty or so Highland families who settled on Johnson's estates in 1773–4, in the last months of his life (he died in 1774) gave him nothing but satisfaction.[50] It was to be the supreme tragedy in the history of these industrious, frugal people, that the same sort of leadership which had led them to defeat at Culloden, and catastrophe at Ticonderoga, was by 1776 poised to use them as a praetorian guard for Westminster in the shameful, and from a British point of view, totally sterile debacle of the War of the American Revolution.

It is notorious that American opinion became inflamed against the Scots in the course of that long and bitter struggle. Nor was American fury unreasonable. If the retrospective myth-mongering of nationalist historians in both England and America be stripped away, the fact is that only a tiny minority in the American colonies wanted complete independence as late as 1775, and that minority dared not openly express its views for fear of political isolation. The conflict was essentially one within the British Atlantic community over the English political tradition (any separate Scottish tradition was snuffed out in 1707). At Westminster a more and more conservative and minimalist interpretation of the Glorious Revolution of 1688 had become predominant, transferring the absolutist prerogative power to which James VII and II aspired to a redefined sovereign – the King, Lords and Commons. In America a more radical Whig view persisted and flourished, holding that if 1688 meant anything at all, it had to mean that government ultimately derived its powers from society, and not *vice versa*, as in the modern British tradition.

Americans might be paranoid about corruption and plots against their liberties, though there was plenty of the former, but they had a firm grasp of a central truth – the politicians at Westminster were fanatically determined to uphold a theory which endowed them in the last analysis with total, absolute and arbitrary power. To critics of this development, British politicians gave the reply they always give: that they were such reasonable chaps that nobody should worry their head about purely theoretical issues of no real importance. The stubbornness of their own stance belied their words. None of them was willing to budge on the central issue. Opposition groups were just as mulish, and this fact should not be obscured by the rhetorical humbug of Edmund Burke, who tried at the time to suggest that all would have been well if only his own paymasters, the Rockingham Whigs had monopolised power. Neither sympathy, nor vision, nor one single positive political proposal (such as American MPs at Westminster) characterised the approach of the 'moderate' and 'reasonable' government of Lord North to the central crisis of British history. Most Americans, anxious to renegotiate a relationship on a sane basis, were left with nowhere to go. Westminster was the greatest friend of American independence.[51]

And the Scottish ruling classes supported Westminster almost to a man. Only the odd Lowland peer (often very odd) was an exception. Support for Westminster was the logical culmination of a policy which the Jacobite families had been pursuing since the failure of the '45, a policy triumphantly vindicated by the return of Simon Fraser's estates in 1774, on the eve of the American war. Besides, articulate opinion in Scotland was overwhelmingly anti-American once war had come. From burghal patriciates to country gentry, to the Kirk by Law Established, one theme rang out far louder than the few dissenting voices. Dr Alexander Gerard, Professor of Divinity in King's College, Old Aberdeen, summed it all up in a sermon which he preached on 26 February 1778 in Old Aberdeen. Quoting the inevitable St Paul in Romans 8, he urged everyone to render unto Caesar in matters secular whatever Caesar said was his. In his capacity as Church of Scotland fugleman for the English Establishment, Gerard even paraded the disreputable theory of virtual representation, whereby those not represented at Westminster were assured they really were, concluding with a call for a return to purity of manners as the only solution to the crisis. Allowing for some modernisation of language, it was a sermon which could well have served as a model for the strident appeals for political passivity and 'a return to those qualities which once made Scotland great' which echoed from many a Scots pulpit in the disastrous last part of the twentieth century.[52] And Gerard spoke what his influential listeners wanted to hear.

The Stamp Act crisis of the mid 1760s had exhausted what sympathy there was for American complaints in the British legislature, and the local rulers of North Britain were absolutely committed, with few exceptions, to automatic support of official policy, the more so because radical critics of government in favour with Americans like Wilkes, were offensively anti-Scottish. The Reverend Doctor John Witherspoon, head of the College of New Jersey (the ancestor of Princeton University) and the best-known Scottish voice championing American independence, knew full well how hostile the North British oligarchs were to American aspirations. Like so many independent-minded Scots of ability since 1707, he had emigrated rather than spend all his life in futile conflict with the conservative local establishment. In his case the conflict had been with the Moderate rulers of the Kirk, men dedicated to reaching a *modus vivendi* with the aristocratic politicians at Westminster who had already harnessed the secular rulers of Scottish society to their chariot. Witherspoon knew that his compatriots were likely to acquiesce in the demand for submission without any rational constitutional accommodation, but he appealed to them to see that most Americans by 1776 were moving towards, and would achieve, independence.[53]

Witherspoon's opinions were not shared by the British ruling classes. Long wars against rebels are fought by men who think they can defeat a rebellion, and the military effort sustained by George III's Britain between 1776 and 1783 was impressive. The old tradition of blaming defeat on military and naval incompetence is simply part of the politicians' cover-up for failure. Strategically disadvantaged against a coalition of hostile powers, the soldiers and sailors of Britain fought as well as they could be expected to fight. The high command was not significantly less competent than in the French and Indian war. The overall performance was not worse than was to be seen in the French Revolutionary wars. Miscalculation and failure were common, but they always were. It was North and his fellow political oligarchs, so convinced that 'the people' (however defined) were dangerous and stupid, who lost the war, first by having no policy to avert the danger of a great civil war in the British world, and secondly by stupidly pulling their punches in the early stages of the conflict and thereby encouraging rather than daunting the irreconcilable hard-core American Whigs. The upshot was a long and bloody war.

The automatic loyalty of the older Highland Jacobite aristocracy to Westminster was demonstrated early in the war. John Murray, fourth Earl of Dunmore (1732–1809), was on his mother's side a Nairne, a grandson of the staunchly Jacobite William Lord Nairne. His own father, descended in the female line from the royal Stuarts, was 'out' in the '45. As a boy, John Murray had been a page to Prince Charles at Holyrood. The third earl obtained a pardon and there was no problem over succession when he died in 1756. The fourth earl was politically reliable enough to be nominated and, of course, elected a 'representative' Scottish peer in 1761. After cultivating the Great and the Good in London he was nominated to the governorship of New York in 1770 and in 1771 promoted to the gubernatorial plum of Virginia. At first he charmed the Virginian planter gentry, and led in 1774 a successful punitive expedition against the Shawnee Indians, albeit with insufficient severity wholly to please his provincial militia. But by 1775–6 Dunmore was at odds with most of the colony. Taking refuge on a warship, he harried the coasts of Virginia, and committed political suicide by urging negro slaves to revolt. Defeated, he retired to England, resumed his seat in the Lords, became governor of the Bahamas between 1787 and 1796, and died, appropriately, in Ramsgate, a seaside resort in Kent.[54]

Once again British ministers faced the problem of mobilising effective manpower for a war which required them to keep nearly 60,000 men in the field thousands of miles from home in theatres of war which produced a high wastage rate. Once again, the potential sources of recruitment for the British Army in North America proved disappointing. American Loyalists were hardly adequately catered for or encouraged, but British leaders still managed to develop a deep sense of resentment at their failure to rally on a sufficient scale to Westminster's banners. As for the Indians, the assumption at Westminster at the start of the war was that they would be available to fight for the British. The British government had tried, by establishing a provisional settler frontier in 1763, to slow down if not stop the expansion of white settlers. The Indian Department under John Stuart in the south and Guy Johnson – Sir William's nephew, son-in-law and successor in the north – had intricate contacts with the tribes. By 1779 parliamentary opinion was as disgruntled with Indians as with Loyalists.

The Indians were on the whole more suspicious, and rightly so, of Americans than of the British government, but they were too canny and astute to be simply used by others, while their consultative techniques and factional politics provided an ideal mechanism for delay. British policy was to restrain Indian allies until they could operate with regular troops. Under Joseph Brant, a Mohawk chief, the bulk of the Iroquois did take the British side, but Oneidas and Tuscaroras split the unity of the confederacy by allying with the rebels. By 1779 all the Iroquois tribes were suffering appallingly from civil war, massive American punitive strikes, and hideously severe weather.[55] The southern Indians were an even more interesting case. Stuart had an elaborate network of fellow Scots as deputies: Alexander Cameron with the Cherokees, David Taitt with the Creeks, Charles Stuart among the Choctaws, and Farquhar Bethune among the Chickasaws. Cameron could not restrain the Cherokees from violence in response to settler land-grabbing. The result was the Second Cherokee War in which massive American forces struck so savagely in 1776 at the Cherokee lands that most of the southern tribes became frightened to fight without allies. Intricate factional politics ensured that the American Whigs never had to face a combined assault by the southern tribes. Alexander MacGillivray did eventually swing majority Creek opinion round to active cooperation with the British, but Creek reinforcements came too little and too late for Westminster's cause.[56]

Once again, Highland regiments, like Hessian mercenaries, looked like a necessary instrument of military survival for the harassed politicians at Westminster. At the outbreak of war the total land forces available on the Irish and English establishments (the Scottish establishment was abolished in 1707) came to about 48,000 men. Roughly 15,000 were in England, 12,000 in Ireland, and 8,000 in America. The remaining troops were scattered over Africa, the West Indies, Minorca, Gibraltar, and Scotland. By 1781 no less than 110,000 regulars were on the books, despite massive losses by death, disease and desertion. Of these some 56,000 were in the Americas, ranging from Canada to the Caribbean. This feat of recruiting was only made possible by strenuous efforts. England was almost comically barren as a recruiting ground. Adjutant General Edward Harvey moaned in December 1775 of 'sad work everywhere in recruiting' and called for unprecedented zeal 'in these damned times'. The reason why such a high percentage of English recruits between 1775 and 1783 were convicted criminals given a choice between the lash, jail, or gallows and His Majesty's Service was not far to seek. Army pay was miserable. A nominal 8d. a day for a private was reduced by a whole range of charges for food clothing and 'servis', to 2d. or 3d. a day. Labourers lived well by comparison, and were free of the ferocious discipline of the Articles of

War. Junior officers were so penurious that skilled tradesmen in England lived better.

Ireland hardly proved more productive. Technically, Roman Catholics were excluded from the British Army's ranks, on either establishment. By 1775 it was clear that the government had no interest at all in enforcing such restrictions, at least for private soldiers. However, in July 1775 it was reported that seventeen British regimental recruiting parties were rounding up a total of less than two dozen recruits a week in Ireland. As the war proceeded from bad to worse His Majesty's Government leaned backwards frantically to find conciliatory gestures which might stimulate recruiting of Roman Catholics in the whole of the British Isles. By 1780 their proposed Roman Catholic relief legislation had drawn upon them the terrible scourge of massive riots in London stimulated by the eccentric pro-American radical MP Lord George Gordon, who asked a not unreasonable question of a ruling clique whose explanation for their own tenure of power under a much-vaunted 'Protestant Constitution' was little more than an assertion of Divine Right. Lord George wanted to know why God should prefer them to any other self-satisfied and unsuccessful group of oligarchs when there was reason gravely to doubt their Protestant commitment. He was crushed. Recruiting hardly improved.

Regiments had to be hired from the rulers of the German principality of Hesse and many other German soldiers had to be recruited into British regiments. Perfectly serious, if unsuccessful, attempts were also made to hire 20,000 Russians for the British service. In the British Isles Scotland alone offered recruiting solace to the Modern Carthage as it lurched towards its well-earned nemesis at the hands of Americans who increasingly saw themselves as Ancient Romans. Lord John Murray wrote to Lord Barrington, the reigning secretary at war, in January 1776, saying that 'the present ardor of the Highland Gentlemen is great to be employed in His Majesty's Service'. It was so employed, especially in the shires of Inverness and Argyll. There was also enthusiasm among the Scottish burghal patriciates for His Majesty's service. As a result, of the roughly 15,000 men raised for that service by the efforts of towns and individuals in 1778, no less than two-thirds came from Scotland. By then it had proved necessary to provide for legal impressment of the able-bodied unemployed among the lower orders. The measure marginally encouraged 'voluntary' enlistment in England, but also created grave jurisdictional problems, spectacularly highlighted by pitched battles between naval and army press-gangs in the streets of some seaports.[57]

The granting of letters to specific Highland noblemen authorising them to raise a new regiment was not something George III regarded as ideal. He could see the element of patronage in the system, especially when bounty money was available to encourage recruits, and commissions were at the disposal of colonels. He would have preferred men to labour with disinterested zeal to make up or augment existing units, but it is doubtful if anyone who mattered would have stirred a little finger on such a basis. The Highland aristocracy was consciously assimilating to the predominantly English ruling class of Britain. Beneath the unctuous rhetoric about His Majesty's Service, which helped secure acquiescence from the lower orders as well as to bolster self-esteem in the élite, men raised regiments to lay the foundations of future wealth and influence. Predictably, the pace in the Highlands was set by General Simon Fraser who 'was farther countenanced' by receiving letters of service in 1775 for raising a regiment of two battalions. He himself now possessed the direct territorial power he had lacked in 1757, but it was as true in 1775 as in 1757 that the colonel with letters of service was essentially the chairman of a board of directors consisting of noble chiefs, barons, and gentlemen tacksmen, and that at grass-roots level it was the entire board which rounded up the recruits. That was why a forfeited man with an ancient name could raise a regiment – he was an ideal rallying point for the other aristocrats without whom he would have been helpless.

Fraser's Highlanders of 1775, numbered the 71st regiment, had an officer corps which was a drumroll of ancient names from Glen More and Glen Spean. The majors of the first battalion were John MacDonell of Lochgarry, who died a colonel in 1789, and Duncan Macpherson of Cluny, who eventually retired from His Majesty's Guards in 1791. The captains of that battalion included young Duncan Chisholm, Norman MacLeod of MacLeod, and Charles Cameron of Lochiel, whose career was sadly cut short by death in 1776. The officers of the second battalion were a less glittering galaxy, but Captain Aeneas Mackintosh of Mackintosh at least ensured that the second battalion had Mackintosh to offset the Chisholm, MacLeod, and Lochiel in the first. In addition, the second battalion had two very interesting younger sons amongst its officers. Charles Cameron, a son of Cameron of Fassfern, was a captain. He was killed in action during the siege of Savannah in 1779. Among the lieutenants was a Ludovick Colquhoun, a son of Luss.

Of all these names, perhaps the most significant was that of Lochiel. For all the brevity of his service, the fact that he was wearing King George's coat marked a decisive and long overdue turning-point in the history of his ancient house. The 'Gentle Lochiel' of the '45 had been well provided for with a French regiment, but when two of his sons who died in 1759 and 1762 respectively followed him in the same service, there was a real danger that the countenance of the Most Christian King would consign successive Lochiels to exile and to exclusion from the mainstream of Highland developments. With the granting and acceptance of the British commission to his third and only surviving son that possibility no longer existed. The Cameron gentry raised 120 men on Lochiel's forfeited properties in order to equip him with a company. That Lochiel himself was on what proved to be his deathbed in London hardly mattered at the highest political level, though the soldiers themselves were extremely upset about the state of his health prior to their embarkation at Glasgow. It required considerable Gaelic oratory from General Simon Fraser to persuade Lochiel's men to board ship. Two factors proved decisive. One was the placing of Cameron of Fassfern at the head of the company. The other was the perfectly correct argument from their colonel that Lochiel's interests were best served by willing obedience to orders by his men, even if he could not accompany them.

The outset of the American War was no time for an ex-Jacobite house to be seen to be backward when all others were crowding forward to offer their services to the Hanoverian dynasty, in the certain knowledge that the government could not afford to spurn their offers. From Sweden, eager to participate in the process of re-integration, came no less a person than Lord MacLeod, heir to the forfeited Earl of Cromartie, the Mackenzie chieftain who had tried to exploit the Hanoverian leanings of Seaforth during the '45 so as to replace him as the chief of the Mackenzies. Cromartie was lucky to be spared his life, at the cost of perpetual confinement to the county of Devon. His heir, also out in the '45, retired to Sweden, entered its army, and in thirty years of service rose to be a lieutenant-general. By 1777 the hour was ripe for his return, especially after the example of Simon Fraser had shown how forfeited estates could be recovered. Lord MacLeod presided over the raising of MacLeod's Highlanders, or the 73rd regiment. Interestingly, he could obtain only 840 of his 1,100 men in the Highlands, and Lowlanders, as well as a few English and Irish, had to make up the ranks. The Central Highlands had been not only the main source of officers, but also the most fertile source of private soldiers for the boom in Highland military entrepreneurship. Very interestingly, contemporaries recognised that, while the gentry of Argyll were very forward in matters military, the lower orders in that county were far from sharing their enthusiasm. Partly this may have been due to a strong seafaring tradition in a land deeply interpenetrated by the sea, and including many islands, but it certainly deeply affected the structure of the 74th regiment, or Argyll Highlanders, which Colonel John Campbell of Barbreck was authorised to raise by letters of service dated December 1777. Barbreck was himself a living tribute to the seminal role of the original Fraser's Highlanders, disbanded in 1763. With them he had served as a captain and a major. All the officers save four were Highlanders, but only 590 of the men were from the Highlands. The rest came from Glasgow and the western Lowlands, and made it up to 960 rank and file. Shipped out of Greenock for Halifax, the great British naval and military base in Nova Scotia, the 74th was soon divided when its élite flanking companies were ordered to New York. Of these the grenadier company was commanded by Colquhoun of Luss. Even at this apogee of Highland recruiting, when Highland regiments were relatively speaking more important than ever before or since, it is clear that the will of the gentry was stronger than the basic available human resources in the region.

One reason for this was the number of theatres in which His Majesty's Government saw fit to deploy Highland troops. Fighting a world war against Bourbon powers free of Continental commitments and able to concentrate all their energies on a multi-theatre global struggle was a recipe for over-extension of British resources. Two Highland regiments raised in 1778 spent the war in Ireland on garrison duty. These were the Atholl Highlanders (the 77th) and the Aberdeenshire Highland Regiment (the 81st). The former had the distinction of being commanded by Colonel James Murray, son of Lord George, the greatest Jacobite general. Both regiments, to their credit, mutinied when the government tried to ship them to India in 1783 in flat violation of their terms of enlistment, which entitled them to a discharge. Like several Highland fencible regiments they were raised originally for home security duties.

However, although two Highland regiments successfully resisted shipment to India, others did serve there. The 78th regiment or Seaforth's Highlanders, despite a mutinous episode in Edinburgh when they occupied the hill known as Arthur's Seat near Holyrood Palace, soldiered for a protracted period in India. The Earl of Seaforth had in theory forfeited his lands and title for participation in the '15 and '19. In practice the state was incapable of dispossessing him of his lands, though it did deprive him of his title. By 1730 that Seaforth was effectively reconciled to Hanover. His grandson Kenneth Mackenzie was allowed to repurchase a title to the estate, and was made an Irish peer as Viscount Fortrose. In 1771 he even recovered the Seaforth earldom. With the Cromartie Mackenzies cutting themselves back into the power game after 1777, it was no time for Seaforth to hang back. Besides, troops were desperately needed in southern India where the British provoked the Marathas and Haidar Ali, the soldier ruler of Mysore, only to suffer severely at Haidar's hands, and later at the hands of his son and successor Tipu. The Seaforth Highlanders served in many arduous and costly Indian campaigns, but not under Kenneth, Earl of Seaforth, for he died on the voyage out, and his successor in the estate and title, Colonel Humberstone Mackenzie, fared little better, being killed by wounds received in an action against the Angria, the hereditary Maratha admiral, off the Malabar Coast. The politico-military world of Hanoverian Britain was no place for men with faint hearts or weak stomachs.[58]

In the central theatre of war in the Americas Highland troops were an almost ideal weapon for the Hanoverian aristocracy and the Westminster political machine it dominated. By no means all Highland regiments were composed exclusively of Highlanders. Seaforth's was yet another example of a unit made up with Lowlanders, Irish and English. Nevertheless most of these regiments had a hard core of 4–500 monoglot Gaelic speakers, totally sealed off by definition from the great political issues tearing the English-speaking world apart. Officers who did not have the Gaelic often felt the need to learn it. Most Highland gentlemen were bilingual and so assured of their social status that they could be both affable and effective commanders, much preferred by their men to English officers. Where Highland gentry had a similar relationship with Highland settlers in America, it proved possible to raise Highland battalions in America to fight for Westminster. Men discharged after 1763 from the 42nd or from Fraser's or Montgomerie's, and who had settled in America or Canada, mainly made up the two battalions embodied in 1775 and regimented in 1778 as the 84th or Royal Highland Emigrant Regiment. The uniform was Highland dress, with sporrans made of racoon skin. Those Highlanders who had settled in the patriarchal empire of the Johnsons in the Mohawk Valley predictably rallied to Sir William's successor, Guy Johnson, and his brother-in-law, Sir John Johnson, in opposing the Whig radical junta organised as the Tyron County Committee of Safety. The upshot was that the Highlanders had to leave with the Johnsons for the superior security of Canada.

The most celebrated single episode of Highland participation in the War of American Independence, which seemed incomprehensible to fervently nationalistic American scholars of a previous era, fits neatly into this general pattern. The Highland settlements in North Carolina had, immediately before the outbreak of war in 1776, been overlaid with a recent wave of predominantly MacDonald emigration led and organised by gentlemen tacksmen like Allan MacDonald of Kingsburgh, the husband of the Flora MacDonald famed (and indeed possibly overrated) for her part in the escape of Prince Charles in 1746. Kingsburgh crossed the Atlantic in 1774, settling on the Cape Fear River well away from his financial embarrassments at home and surrounded by MacDonald tenants from Skye and Raasay. When Governor Martin of North Carolina sent commissions to Loyalist leaders in the back country, it was hardly surprising that Allan MacDonald accepted a major's commission in what was effectively a Highland army raised under Brigadier General Donald MacDonald. Official British opinion was fatuously confident that half-measures would suffice to bring the war against the rebels to an early and successful conclusion. General MacDonald's force was a victim both of that delusion, and of the paradox that while British policy by the end of the war placed wholly excessive reliance on the Loyalists' support, at the start it made no serious allowance for them. The Highland army was smashed at the battle of Moore's Creek Bridge in 1776 by superior Whig forces. With its gentry leadership killed or imprisoned and confiscated, the Highland community gave the revolutionaries no further serious trouble.[59]

It must be stressed that the Highlanders who fought so stubbornly against American independence on behalf of Westminster were primarily those Highlanders who were integrated into and controlled by the aristocratic and commercial institutions of Hanoverian Britain. By the 1750s most of the old Jacobite aristocratic Highland families were particularly anxious to come to terms with the politico-economic structures dominated by Westminster, and these families naturally carried their tenants and other clients along with them on the road they were determined to ride. Highland Jacobites who emigrated to America before this crucial switch of objectives among the Jacobite leadership were not nearly so likely to calculate that their balance of advantage lay in upholding the unbridled sovereignty of King, Lords and Commons. From the '15 through to the wave of emigrants who escaped immediately after the '45, many old-fashioned Jacobites of good family who still believed in the central plank of active Scottish Jacobitism – repudiation of the incorporating Union of 1707 – reached the colonies. Their descendants were just as likely to take a revolutionary role as a loyalist one after 1775, even if like the Garden family of South Carolina they came to America as Episcopal clergy. The colonies were a bolt-hole for the usually fiercely Jacobite Scottish Episcopal ministers. The Reverend Alexander Garden for example, emigrated to Charleston South Carolina around 1720 and he died there in 1756. Of his two sons, Alexander the celebrated naturalist became a loyalist and was a panegyrist of Lord Cornwallis, the British commander who eventually surrendered at Yorktown. Confiscation of property and exile were this Alexander's fate, but the property was simply transferred to his son Alexander Garden (1757–1829), who returned from Europe in 1780 to fight for American independence.[60]

Much better known as a revolutionary soldier was another Highland Scot, Lachlan Mackintosh, son of John Mor Mackintosh of Darien, one of the Highlanders settled in South Georgia in 1736. An ardent supporter of the revolutionary movement, Lachlan rose to be a controversial general officer in the American Continental Army. Almost all the descendants of John Mor seem to have been staunch American Patriots in 1775–6.[61] Even more intriguing is the example of a branch of the most fanatically ultra-Jacobite family of them all – the Oliphants of Gask. David Olyphant (as he spelled his name) was a physician, born in 1720, who emigrated to South Carolina after Culloden. He had been an active Jacobite and became a strong supporter of American independence, serving the revolutionary armies in the southern colonies as director of hospitals. After 1783 he was a member of the General Assembly of South Carolina, moving to Rhode Island due to failing health in 1785. Quite unexpectedly, he married there, fathering a son who became a leading American merchant in the China trade and the progenitor of a great New York business dynasty whose interests spanned the China trade, coal-mining, canals, steamers, and railroads.[62] Even among the Creek Indians the pro-British Alexander MacGillivray must be balanced against William Mackintosh (1775–1825), a chief of the Lower Creeks noted for collusion with the Americans and more particularly with his kinsman George M. Troup, Governor of Georgia. This particular Indian leader had been fathered on a Creek woman by Captain William Macintosh, a British regular officer and agent to the Creeks. The son was given an American commission as a brigadier-general after the war of 1812 and was killed in 1825 by his fellow tribesmen for his self-seeking betrayal of his people to a state government unscrupulous, greedy and racist even by the standards of the time.[63] Among the many tragedies of a bad British peace settlement with America in 1783 was Westminster's thinly-veiled desertion of its Indian allies.

The surrender of Cornwallis to Washington and his French ally the Comte de Rochambeau at Yorktown on 18 October 1781 broke the will of the British political classes to continue fighting in America. Fraser's Highlanders were among the units which marched out to pile their arms to the melancholy tune called 'The World Turned Upside Down'.[64] Their colonel, Simon Fraser, had not accompanied them to America and his world was by no means turned upside down. The shedding of the radical part of the British community by the surgery of American independence reinforced the conservative political ideology ascendant in the imperial archipelago itself, and the old Jacobite families of Glen More and Glen Spean confirmed their integration into that ascendancy by their support for the war. Fort George at Ardersier, built to daunt the clans, became between 1775 and 1783 the great drill square where they were prepared for service. Highland gentlemen assumed command in Fort William, Fort Augustus, Fort George. From Culloden to Yorktown, disasters both, the wheel of political fortune in the Central Highlands had spun half round. In 1746 the local aristocracy had been 'out' and down at the foot; by 1781 they were in the ascendant.

10 *Conclusion: Most Loyal of North Britons*

From the point of view of the ruling class in Inverness-shire between 1747 and 1815 there could hardly be such a phenomenon as a surplus population. Landlords had two overriding and interlocked ambitions. One was to gain the good will of the Westminster government, which carried with it access to vitally important favours and patronage. Such favour was particularly necessary for that large proportion of the local aristocracy who had gambled with their future by actively supporting the '45, and who had, of course, lost. The other ambition was simply a burning desire to become richer. Apart from rationalised estate management, usually involving the massive extension of sheep-grazing, the only two alternative techniques for achieving their ambitions easily available to the lairds were both labour-intensive.

By the late eighteenth century and through to 1815, kelp-making had become an enormously important source of revenue to all estates which, like Clanranald's estate, contained a high proportion of sea-coast and island properties. Kelp is the calcined ashes of seaweed, valued in commerce for the carbonate of soda, iodine, and other chemicals which they contain. Until totally undercut by imports and a new inorganic chemical industry after 1815, kelp was a major source for the industrial alkali required in large quantities for the manufacture of soap and glass. To make one ton of kelp, twenty tons of weed were required, cut by unskilled labour, with simple iron tools, often by the laborious and bone-chilling procedure of standing up to the waist in freezing water whilst cutting it off rocks. The other technique available to local élites was longer lived and just as labour intensive. Recruiting was a very important politico-economic activity for the landowners right through from 1756 to 1815. Miss Mary Grant of Grant described a neighbour in 1775 as the busiest man in the county with his 'farming, road-making, and recruiting'.[1] The activities were all natural and expected.

Emigration from such a society was regarded with extreme hostility by its leaders. But significant emigration did manifest itself in the early 1770s, often led by disgruntled tacksmen and involving those non-aristocratic members of Highland society best endowed with vigour, enterprise, and a little capital. Emigration to America was not cheap, but was about the only effective criticism the bulk of the population could level at the social and political system they lived under. To stay and protest was both futile and likely to attract persecution. By 1775 it was pretty clear that rebellion was on the way in the American colonies and emigration was merely likely to reinforce the radical streak in the thirteen colonies, which were emerging as the least deferential part of the British Atlantic community. Inverness-shire landlords were quick to assemble in September 1775 as justices of the peace to listen to a letter from the Lord Advocate announcing that he wished every possible legal obstacle to be placed in the way of emigration from the county during the present disturbances in America. The response from the lairds was enthusiastic. They resolved to cooperate with the sheriff of the county and the board of customs to block this pernicious flow. Copies of the resolution were to be transmitted to every parish in Inverness-shire that the ministers might acquaint the people with the resolution and the accompanying measures. Within a couple of days even Glen Urquhart had a visitation from a deputation of lairds determined to see the parish minister perform his duties as political and moral policeman to the British Establishment.[2] Further to tighten the net, the Lord Advocate closed all Scottish harbours to emigrant ships from 21 September by executive order for the duration of the war.

Male tenants aged between sixteen and forty-five were by definition potential recruits. Recruits were the essential foundations on which a colonel could rear a whole structure of patronage in the shape of commissions available primarily to his 'Friends', that splendid eighteenth-century term which covered relatives, allies, and clients of sufficient social standing. Even an officer's death 'upon the affair at Boston', otherwise known as the Battle of Bunker Hill, could offer a commanding officer a second chance to play with the patronage of a commission.[3] The early stages of the American war were something like a politico-military bonanza for the Highland aristocracy. One curious side-effect was the repeal of the penal laws forbidding anyone to use the name MacGregor. That much-harassed clan had ensured that these penal laws would be upheld by producing two companies of MacGregors from Balquhidder to fight for Prince Charles in 1745–6. By 1774 the penal laws were not being enforced. John Murray-MacGregor (nephew of the MacGregor of Glencarnoch who had fallen at the head of his men at Culloden) made a fortune in business in London, and helped secure an act of parliament repealing the suppression of the Name in November 1774. Predictably, he accompanied his success with a barrage of appropriate propaganda, talking about bringing '500 MacGregors to assist in reducing the Americans to order'.[4] In 1795 John Murray-MacGregor was recognised by the Lord Lyon (Scotland's supreme heraldic authority) as MacGregor of that Ilk. When, in 1822 and again in 1953, the Honours of Scotland (the crown jewels symbolic of the ancient kingdom abolished in 1707) were paraded before the titular head of the United Kingdom, the MacGregors had a place of honour in the escort. Political reliability in 1774–5 had reaped a long harvest of symbolic reward.

Surviving passenger-lists make it clear that in the early 1770s there was emigration from Glen More lands administered by the Board of Annexed Estates. Apart from social tension between landlord and tacksman, a series of bad harvests, which had reduced cattle stocks and still left an expensive shortage of grain for man and beast, stimulated widespread discontent. 176 tenants on former Lovat properties petitioned the Board for a reduction in rent, arguing that otherwise they might be tempted to follow their neighbours to America. It was a shrewd threat, and people from Glengarry were certainly leaving for America. But between 1775 and 1783 the war in America effectively closed the door on Highland migration. The good sense of the Highland people warned them of the hazards of privateers on the Atlantic routes and of a bitter, bloody civil war in the colonies. It was no time to move families across.[5]

On the other hand, for the recruiter the closing-off of emigration was an unqualified blessing. The Inverness-shire lairds were still an extremely close-knit group. The magnates knew one another intimately, and were often related. Lesser lairds were equally inclined to intermarry. Cameron of Glen Nevis, for example, married Grant of Glenmoriston's daughter in September 1775.[6] They were the justices of the peace for the shire, and though they deprecated recruiting techniques which too openly resembled forcible kidnapping, and were prepared to rescue specific individuals from them, they made no bones about leaning over backwards to support recruiting, on the grounds that the necessity of the state required this.[7] There is no need to question the sincerity of their belief that this was so. It was an attitude wholly consistent with their politics, though it also coincided with self-interest, for a justice might very well be one of those trying to raise enough interest to secure a commission in General Fraser's new regiment for a friend or kinsman, and without recruits there would be no regiment.[8]

Highlanders were undoubtedly propelled into regiments by a complex of pressures. Hard times were always a persuasive recruiting-sergeant. The survival of martial and clan spirit from the days of the '45 has been advanced as another reason, but even in the 1790s amongst clergy of the Church of Scotland it was quite fashionable to express scepticism about this factor. It is debatable just how enthusiastic many Jacobite rankers were in 1745–6, and it is clear that in the late eighteenth century landowners often had to offer substantial bounty payments on enlistment to fill the ranks. They also had direct powers of coercion over families who were their tenants, powers which allowed them to bargain for the lives of sons or fathers in exchange for fixity of tenure. For Gordon estates, which included properties in Lochaber, there survives unambiguous evidence of bargaining for land and bounties in exchange for military service. The once-mighty ducal house of Gordon was trying in the late eighteenth century to climb back from long-term decline and virtual bankruptcy. Raising regiments was a central element in its recovery programme, which required a close link with the Westminster government. It was natural for the Duke of Gordon to keep a detailed list of men of military age on his Lochaber properties. He was, among other things, a military entrepreneur, and they were his potential work force. As with most enterprises, engaging a work force was a complex bargaining game.

Some landlords in the Glen More and Glen Spean country were more ruthless than others. In November 1794 Alexander MacDonell of Glengarry wrote to his agent in Inverness:

> Sir, enclosed you have a list of small tenants belonging to my Knoydart property – their leases being expired by Whitsunday first – and having refused to serve me, I am fully determined to warn them out, and turn them off my property, without loss of time.

Little wonder that the Highlands and Islands made a disproportionate contribution to British military manpower during the French Revolutionary and Napoleonic Wars. Estimates vary, but from a population of about 300,000, one estimate reckoned that between 1793 and 1813 37,000 Highlanders were raised for regular battalions and militia regiments. Volunteer regiments are excluded from this estimate, and at least one calculation adding them in would more than double it, though this seems unduly high.[9]

However, as military enterprisers Highland landlords were subject to violent fluctuations in their market, and to gradual long-term obsolescence. The American war boom collapsed spectacularly with the acknowledgement of defeat in 1783. Savage retrenchment came almost at once, with regiments being broken faster than they had been raised. The consolation which the former Jacobite families enjoyed at precisely this moment when the military bubble burst was, however, no mean one. Their estates were restored to them. The precedent had been clearly set by the 1774 act which restored the Lovat estates to Simon Fraser. That act recited some very unusual circumstances in the forfeiture. It had been held at the time that the deed of entail which settled succession to the estate effectively obstructed the forfeiture procedure. This view the Court of Session had rebuffed by only one vote, and yet there had been no appeal. Evidence had been available by 1747 of the undue pressures placed on the young Simon Fraser to lead out his father's clansmen. The young man had then rejected a French commission, dedicated himself to the service of the House of Hanover, in which he achieved a major-general's rank, and had in the Seven Years War distinguished himself 'by calling forth, from a corner of the kingdom, many thousand soldiers'. Little wonder that the statute concluded that 'his case appears to be peculiarly distinguished'. Nevertheless, it was clear that where young Simon led others could follow and in 1784 an act generally known as the Disannexing Act restored all the other properties. It referred to the annexation and continued:

> . . . and whereas, by the experience of many years since that time, it has been found, that no subjects in any part of His Majesty's Dominions are more loyal or dutiful, or better affected . . . many of whom, of all ranks and descriptions, have performed signal services to their country in the late wars . . . and more particularly the heirs and families of all or most of the said attainted persons have been employed in the service of their lawful sovereign.

Certified as ultra-loyal North Britons by unswerving support for Westminster's catastrophically unsuccessful American policies, such men were truly worthy of a signal mark of the royal esteem.[10]

Furthermore, they could reasonably expect that, as Westminster recovered both its nerve and its prestige, and occasions arose which called for the rapid expansion of British military strength, they might resume their key role as military entrepreneurs. The policy of reduction adopted in 1783 in fact survived for only some four years. In September 1787 the government of the Younger Pitt was faced with a crisis in the long-standing duel between France and Britain for influence in the independent Netherlands. Faced with a threat of armed French intervention in the affairs of the United Provinces (the old Dutch republic) Pitt and his colleagues decided to place the armed forces on an effective war footing. The Dutch crisis was defused when the French backed down within six weeks, but the weaknesses in British imperial defence structures revealed by the crisis led on to a drastic reorganisation of the army, a reorganisation without precedent in time of peace. The two most exposed bastions of empire proved to be the West Indies, starved of troops since 1783, and India, which had been weakened by the recall of four royal regiments in 1785. By the time the West Indies had been reinforced the dearth of troops was such that an augmentation of four new regiments for India was authorised. Two were to be raised as Highland corps by Sir Archibald Campbell and Robert Abercromby.

The 74th regiment was raised not by Sir Archibald Campbell, who was in Madras, but by his agents, who regarded the Secretary at War as an interfering upstart, and who insisted on turning the operation into an exercise in Campbell gentry solidarity. It was perhaps the last British regiment raised in the old way. A Pay Office Act of 1783 had deprived colonels of many of their financial powers and the development of Chatham Barracks in England and Duncannon Fort in Ireland centralised the inspection and training of recruits.[11] The Secretary at War was becoming part of a very gradual but unmistakeable trend towards bureaucratisation and centralisation which was part of the Establishment's attempt to refurbish its administrative image after the American fiasco.

The outbreak of war between Britain and Revolutionary France in 1793 opened an era which proved to be, in effect, the twilight of the old-style colonel-entrepreneur in the Highlands. With one short intermission these French wars raged until 1815. The need for troops was acute. However, by 1790 severe social conflict had already come to the Highlands, and it could not but hinder recruitment. In that year there had been a brief war scare when Britain successfully forced Spain to abandon her unrealistic claims to prevent settlement on the west coast of North America in the area known as Nootka Sound. It was a region far beyond effective Spanish colonisation and was destined to become part of British Columbia. The contested settlement was in fact on Vancouver Island. Without allies, Spain had to back down, but before she did so an augmentation of the army was proposed in Britain. Attempts to recruit additional companies for the Black Watch proved unsuccessful in the face of seething resentment in the Highlands over large-scale evictions of tenants to make way for specialist sheep farms of vast size. The Black Watch spent much of 1792 marching and counter-marching in Ross-shire, acting as a rural gendarmerie to put down widespread rioting against the spread of extensive sheep-farming with its attendant evictions. It was not the case that the Highland landlords were bent on expelling their tenants from the country. On the contrary, they wanted to retain the evicted ones as crofters, to provide a pool of labour for kelping and military service. Yet Sir Walter Scott recalled later that when, as a boy, he accompanied his father and a military detachment to enforce a Highland eviction in the 1780s, they found the people already fled – to America.

Under the circumstances, it is less surprising that there was considerable delay in raising the first Highland regiment for the renewed French wars after 1793, than that it was raised at all. It was raised under the aegis of Colonel F.H. Mackenzie, afterwards Lord Seaforth, and was the 78th Foot.* Even more traumatic, due to political in-fighting, was the raising of the second new Highland regiment for this war, the 79th or Cameron Highlanders. The Camerons were not raised, as might have been

*The number is explained by a pre-war establishment of 77 regiments.

expected, by Cameron of Lochiel, but by a rival family represented by Alan Cameron of Erracht. This big and aggressive man, after an adventurous life in Scotland and the southern British colonies in North America, where he was an active Loyalist during the revolutionary period, made his fortune by marrying a West Indian heiress. His family had, since the early sixteenth century, claimed to be legitimate heirs to the Lochiel succession. Even so, Alan of Erracht's behaviour once he had the money behind him to fund his social pretensions was extraordinarily injudicious, going to the length of matriculating Lochiel's arms the Lord Lyon and thereby unleashing an unpleasant legal battle which he lost. The one trump Erracht had was his wife's money, which enabled him to offer to raise a Highland corps without benefit of bounty money, and under obligation to receive his officers from those on half-pay, rather than nominating them in the usual fashion. It was an expensive bid for government favour which necessarily totally alienated Lochiel's interest and ensured that the young Cameron chief put his support behind the Duke of Gordon who was also recruiting in Lochaber.

Lord Adam Gordon happened to be Commander-in-Chief Scotland. He had cooperated with Erracht on a committee of the Highland Society of London which had in 1782 secured the repeal of the by then unenforced legislation barring the wearing of Highland dress by anyone not in a Highland regiment. However, in the bitter military politics of the 1790s Lord Adam knew where his family loyalties lay. The newly raised Camerons served first in an unsuccessful campaign in the Low Countries and were then posted to the West Indies, a posting which everyone knew was a virtual death sentence. His regiment destroyed by fever, Erracht had o raise it all over again. The Gordon Highlanders had by this time so denuded Lochaber of recruits, that the second embodiment of the Camerons contained slightly more English, Welsh and Irish than Scots by 1798. The balance redressed, the regiment went on to distinguished service in Spain under the Duke of Wellington, and Erracht died Lieutenant-General Sir Alan Cameron KCB.[12]

The price of such glory, in blood and money, was very heavy. It was bought by many a laird, including Erracht, at the price of a son's blood. For the Highlands and Islands as a whole the army was a means of outdoor support for economically surplus young males, but by the end of these wars it was clear they were in increasingly short supply. Most of them would have fared better by emigrating to America, and it was to block this possibility that Highland landlords used their immense political pull with Westminster to obtain the Emigration Act of 1803 which quite deliberately tried to impose such severe restrictions and regulations on emigrant ships as to make the cost of a passage well beyond the means of the average Highlander. The Act was sponsored by the Highland and

Agricultural Society founded in Edinburgh in 1784 and denounced by Lord Selkirk, a Lowland peer interested in emigration to British North America, as representing 'one class of men' – the lairds.[13] This humbugging obstruction is in fact a much more serious charge against Highland proprietors than their subsequent encouragement of emigration after 1815. Kelping collapsed after the peace of 1815 and never again were the Highlands to be so important as a reservoir of soldiers. As the economy of the Highlands and Islands changed, emigration became inevitable, though whether the eventual conversion of so large a proportion of North Britain to wet deserts inhabited mainly by grouse and deer was a desirable outcome is another question.

Some of the techniques of the military entrepreneurship which was such an important part of upper-class politics in the Highlands between 1756 and 1815 had a curiously protracted after-life. During the Boer War Simon Fraser, Lord Lovat and chief of Clan Fraser raised in 1899–1900 his own regiment, the Lovat Scouts, officered mostly in the old style by neighbouring lairds, and a fine regiment it proved.[14] Nevertheless, the most important exponent of regiment-raising in Highland history remains his ancestor of the latter part of the eighteenth century who, though the son of a man beheaded for treason, learned how to use the British Army as a means whereby the old Jacobite families were reconciled with Westminster. That process made them part of the British ruling classes, which is what they remain. It is a far cry from that distant day in 1654 when the Cromwellian garrison came to Inverlochy to daunt the clans.

Notes

1 THE ENVIRONMENT AND THE CLANS

1. Chalmers M. Clapperton, 'Scotland's Geological Evolution', in C. M. Clapperton (ed.), *Scotland: A New Study* (Newton Abbot and North Pomfret, 1983), pp. 15–27.
2. H. H. Read, *British Regional Geology : The Grampian Highlands*, 2nd ed., revised by A. G. MacGregor (Edinburgh, H.M.S.O., 1948).
3. Moray McLaren, *The Shell Guide to Scotland* (London, 1973), p. 456.
4. ibid., p. 102.
5. Valerie Haynes, 'Scotland's Landforms', in Clapperton (ed.), *Scotland: A New Study*, pp. 28–63.
6. This point is most emphatically established by G. W. S. Barrow in 'The Highlands in the Lifetime of Robert the Bruce', conveniently reprinted in his *The Kingdom of the Scots* (London, 1973), pp. 362–83.
7. James N. M. Maclean, *The Macleans of Sweden* (Edinburgh, 1971), p. 11.
8. The best brief introduction to the growth and evolution of clanship is still W. R. Kermack's *The Scottish Highlands: A Short History (c.300–1746)* (Edinburgh, 1957).
9. Duncan C. MacTavish (ed.), *The Commons of Argyll: Name-Lists of 1685 and 1692* (Lochgilphead, 1935).
10. David Stevenson, *Alasdair MacColla and the Highland Problem in the Seventeenth Century* (Edinburgh, 1980).
11. Andrew McKerral, *Kintyre in the Seventeenth Century* (Edinburgh, 1948), Chs. V–VII.
12. Jean Munro, 'When Island Chiefs Came to Town', in *Notes and Queries of the Society of West Highland and Island Historical Research*, No. XIX, December 1982, pp. 11–19.
13. The best introduction to the Gaelic verse sources for the detailed history of the clans is John A. Maclean, 'The Sources, particularly the Celtic Sources, for the History of the Highlands in the Seventeenth Century', Aberdeen University Ph.D. Thesis 1939. I am deeply indebted to this basic work.
14. Deposition of Colin Campbell of Llangreg and his son to Marquis of Atholl, 1684, summarised in *Historical Manuscripts Commission*, Twelfth Report, Appendix, Part VIII (London, H.M.S.O., 1891), p. 13.
15. C. I. Fraser of Reelig, *The Clan Fraser of Lovat* (Edinburgh, Johnston's Clan Histories, 1952) – a most perceptive little book.
16. Sir Arthur Mitchell (ed.), *Geographical Collections Relating to Scotland made by Walter Macfarlane*, Vol. II, Scottish History Society, Vol. LII (Edinburgh, 1907), pp. 549–50.
17. The best introduction to the many strands in Celtic chieftainship is *The Highland Clans* (London, 1967), by Sir Iain Moncreiffe of that Ilk and David Hicks, a book at once learned and attractive.
18. D. F. (Duncan Forbes of Culloden) to the fourth Earl of Loudon, 7 January 1746, Huntington Library, San Marino, California, MS LO 7180.
19. I. F. Grant, *The Clan Grant* (Edinburgh, Johnston's Clan Histories, 1955).
20. *Macfarlane's Geographical Collections*, Vol. II, p. 171.

21. ibid., p. 169.
22. Alexander Mackenzie, *The MacDonalds of Glengarry* (Inverness, 1881).
23. Maclean, 'Celtic Sources', p. 244.
24. The standard history of Clan Cameron is John Stewart of Ardvorlich, *The Camerons: A History of Clan Cameron* (Glasgow, the Clan Cameron Association, n.d.). Somerled MacMillan, *Bygone Lochaber: Historical and Traditional* (privately printed, Glasgow, 1971), is strongly prejudiced against the Lochiels, but is important because it provides an introduction to the elements which were pressed together to make the historical Clan Cameron.
25. Rev. Alexander D. Murdoch (ed.), *The Loyall Dissuasive and Other Papers Concerning the Affairs of Clan Chattan: by Sir Aeneas Macpherson, Knight of Invereshie 1691–1705*, Scottish History Society, Vol. XLI (Edinburgh, 1902).
26. Alexander Mackintosh Shaw, *Historical Memoirs of the House and Clan of Mackintosh and of the Clan Chattan* (London, 1880), pp. 441–7, and A.M. Mackintosh, *The Mackintosh and Clan Chattan* (Edinburgh, 1903), pp. 314–16.

2 THE CLANS AND THE WIDER WORLD

1. D. Meek and J. Kirk, 'John Carswell, Superintendant of Argyll: a reassessment', *Scottish Church History Society Records*, Vol. XIX (1975), pp. 1–22.
2. D. Stevenson, *Alasdair MacColla and the Highland Problem in the 17th Century* (Edinburgh, 1980), and *Scottish Covenanters and Irish Confederates* (Belfast, 1981).
3. J. Correia-Afonso (ed.), *Indo-Portuguese History : Sources and Problems* (Bombay, 1981), p. 46, quoting Artur B. de Sá.
4. I have sought illumination on these problems from Mary McHugh's excellent thesis 'Kirk, State and the Catholic Problem in the Western Highlands and Islands of Scotland, 1690–1760', unpublished M.Litt., University of Strathclyde, 1982, especially chapters 1 and 2.
5. B. Lenman, 'The Scottish Episcopal Clergy and the Ideology of Jacobitism', in Eveline Cruickshanks (ed.), *Ideology and Conspiracy: Aspects of Jacobitism 1689–1759* (Edinburgh, 1982), pp. 36–48.
6. Mary McHugh. op. cit. chs 3 and 4.
7. William Ferguson, 'The Problems of the Established Church in the West Highlands and Islands in the Eighteenth Century', *Scottish Church History Society Records*, Vol. XVII (1972), pp. 15–31.
8. William Mackay (ed.), *'Chronicles of the Frasers' by Master James Fraser*, Scottish History Society, Vol. XLVII (Edinburgh, 1905), pp. 394–5.
9. A. J. Youngson, *After the Forty-Five* (Edinburgh, 1973), p. 20.
10. Henry Hamilton, *The Industrial Revolution in Scotland* (Oxford, 1932), pp. 151–3.
11. Thomas Pennant, *A Tour in Scotland 1769* (London, 5th ed., 1790), p. 229, 'Trade of Lochaber'.
12. Sir John Sinclair (ed.), *The Statistical Account of Scotland*, Vol. XXI, pp. 258–9, 'Additional Information from the Reverent Mr Ross'.
13. 'J. Stewart Appine' to 'The Laird of Locheill Younger', London, 13 September 1711, Lochiel MSS, No.24, West Highland Museum, Fort William.
14. Colm O. Baoill (ed.), *Poems and Songs by Sileas MacDonald c.1660–c. 1792*, Scottish Gaelic Text Society (Edinburgh, 1972), pp. 16–19 and note 208 on p. 129.
15. 'An Unpublished Document of the '45', *Clan Chisholm Journal*, No. 19 (1976), pp. 1–5.
16. 'Culloden', and 'Army Surgeon in the '45', ibid., No. 8 (1965), p. 12 and No.25 (1982), p. 5, resp. For these and the previous reference I am indebted to their unacknowledged author Mrs Jean Munro.

17. Andrew McKerral, 'West Highland Mercenaries in Ireland', *Scottish Historical Review*, Vol. XXX (1951), pp. 1–14.
18. G. A. Hayes-McCoy, *Scots Mercenary Forces in Ireland (1565–1603)* (Dublin, 1937), p. 340.
19. James Ferguson (ed.), *Papers Illustrating the History of the Scots Brigade in the Service of the United Netherlands 1572–1782*, Scottish History Society, Vols. XXXII, XXXV and XXVIII (Edinburgh, 1899–1901).
20. James A. Fallon, 'Scottish Mercenaries in the Service of Denmark and Sweden 1626–1632', University of Glasgow, Ph.D. Thesis, 1972.
21. M. V. Hay, *The Blairs Papers (1603–1660)* (London, 1929), p. 246.
22. I am grateful to Professor Alan G. Macpherson of the Memorial University of Newfoundland for drawing my attention to his important article 'Order Book of the Appin Regiment: Some Discrepancies Corrected', *The Stewarts*, Vol. IX, No.3 (1953), pp. 263–74.
23. Quoted in Jean Munro, 'The Local Clans and Jacobitism', in *The Hub of the Highlands: The Centenary Volume of the Inverness Field Club 1875–1975* (Edinburgh, 1975), p. 184.
24. George P. Insh, *Scottish Colonial Schemes 1620–86* (Glasgow, 1922), and John G. Reid, *Acadia, Maine, and New Scotland: Marginal Colonies in the Seventeenth Century* (Toronto, 1981.)

3 THE FIRST FORTS – FROM INVERLOCHY TO FORT WILLIAM

1. Cited from Gilbert's *Contemporary History of Affairs in Ireland*, II, p. 468, by C. H. Firth in his article on Oliver Cromwell in the *Dictionary of National Biography* (D.N.B.), Vol. XIII, ed. L. Stephen (London, 1888).
2. *Calendar of State Papers, Domestic Series* (C.S.P.D.), 1654, ed. M. A. E. Green (London, 1880), p. 339.
3. ibid., pp. 261–2 and 408–9.
4. ibid, pp. 367 and 472.
5. C.S.P.D., 1655, ed. M. A. E. Green (London, 1881), p. 193.
6. C.S.P.D., 1654, p. 261.
7. ibid., p. 317. There is a plan of Inverlochy which shows very clearly the disposition of the cannon in the projecting bastions printed in C. H. Firth (ed.), *Scotland and the Protectorate*, Scottish History Society, Vol. XXXI (Edinburgh, 1899), at p.xxxviii.
8. C.S.P.D. 1655, p. 161 and p. 425.
9. General Monck to the Protector, 7 July, 1654, printed in C. H. Firth (ed.), *Scotland and the Protectorate*, pp. 143–4.
10. 'Treaty with Euan Cameron of Lochiel', ibid., pp. 276–80.
11. S. S. Webb, *The Governors-General: The English Army and the Definition of the Empire, 1569–1681* (University of North Carolina Press, Chapel Hill, 1979), pp. 52–55 and 167–72. It will be clear that despite my admiration for this fine book, I think it underestimates the strength of the influence of the non-military local ruling classes in the British Isles, not least on those of their number, like Oliver Cromwell, whom fate placed at the head of armies.
12. C. H. Firth (ed.), *Scotland and the Protectorate*, pp. 384–5.
13. ibid., pp. xliii–xlvii, with a plan at p. xliv.
14. C.S.P.D., 1655, p. 125.
15. W. L. Sachse, 'The Migration of New Englanders to England, 1640–60', *The American Historical Review*, Vol. 53 (1947–48), pp. 251–78. For Stephen Winthrop see C. H.

Firth, *Scotland and the Protectorate*, pp. 45, 105 and 308, as well as P. J. Pinckney, 'The Scottish Representation in the Cromwellian parliament of 1656', *Scottish Historical Review*, Vol. 46 (1967), pp. 95–114.

16. David Stevenson, *Alasdair MacColla and the Highland Problem in the 17th Century* (Edinburgh, 1980), Ch. 11. Balhaldy's *Memoirs of Sir Ewen Cameron of Locheill, Chief of the Clan Cameron* were eventually printed by the Maitland Club (Edinburgh, 1842).
17. C. Dalton, *The Scots Army 1661–88: With Memoirs of the Commanders-in-Chief* (London, 1909).
18. A. Robertson, *The Life of Sir Robert Moray: 1608–1673* (London, 1922), pp. 124–35.
19. *The Register of the Privy Council of Scotland*, (R.P.C.S.), 3rd Series, Vol. I, 1661–4, ed. P. Hume Brown (Edinburgh, 1908), pp. 6, 125–6, 149, 220 and 279.
20. R.P.C.S., 1665–9, ed. P. Hume Brown (Edinburgh, 1909), pp. 406–7.
21. R.P.C.S., 1661–4, pp. 55–6.
22. ibid., pp. 72, 81 and 596–7.
23. J.R. Elder, *The Highland Host of 1678* (Glasgow, 1914).
24. R.P.C.S., 1661–4, p. 256.
25. ibid., pp. 410–16. For Restoration power-politics in Lochaber see John Stewart of Ardvorlich, *The Camerons* (Glasgow, 2nd ed., 1981), pp. 69–78.
26. R.P.C.S., 1665–9, pp. 140–1.
27. R.P.C.S., 1673–6, ed. P. Hume Brown (Edinburgh, 1911), pp. 205–6.
28. R.P.C.S., 1669–73, ed. P. Hume Brown (Edinburgh, 1910), pp. 236, 341, 367, 373 and 375.
29. R.P.C.S., 1665–9, pp. 150–52, and D. Warrand (ed.), *More Culloden Papers, Vol. I : 1626 to 1704* (Inverness, 1923), p. 166 for extract act of council of Inverness, 24 September 1666.
30. ibid., pp. 170–4.
31. R.P.C.S., 1661–4, p. 638.
32. See Edward Gibbon to the Principal Officers of the Ordance, 11 April, 1 May, 10 May and 20 May, 1689, Blathwayt Papers, Huntington Library, San Marino, California, HM28623.
33. S. S. Webb, 'William Blathwayt, Imperial Fixer: Muddling Through to Empire, 1689–1717', *The William and Mary Quarterly*, 3rd Series, Vol. 26 (1969), pp. 373–415.
34. Report from Marshal de Schomberg, Lord Mordaunt, and Lord Churchill, 25 February 1689, and enclosed returns, Blathwayt Papers, HM28623.
35. C. S. Terry, *John Graham of Claverhouse* (London, 1905), and Hugh Mackay, *Memoirs of the War Carried on in Scotland and Ireland* (Edinburgh, Bannatyne Club, 1833).
36. C.S.P.D., 1690–91, ed. W. J. Hardy (London, 1898), pp. 286–7.
37. ibid., pp. 298–9.
38. 'Great Britain Army Account Book 1692.' This is a MS Establishment of the Forces of William and Mary, with the charges per diem and per annum. It is the official copy with the signatures of the Ministry: 'Godolphin, R. Hampden, H. Fox, E. W. Seymour'. MS G 7872Z, A 172, 1692, William Andrews Clark Library, University of California at Los Angeles.
39. R.P.C.S., 1690, ed. E. W. M. Balfour-Melville (Edinburgh, 1967), pp. 563–5.
40. ibid., p. 564.
41. ibid., p. 565.
42. 'Memoir of a Plan for preserving the Peace of the Highlands: written a short time after the Revolution', *Culloden Papers* (London, 1815), No. XX, pp. 14–18.
43. There is an excellent account of all this in John Prebble, *Glencoe* (London, 1966).
44. Philip Aubrey, *The Defeat of James Stuart's Armada 1692* (Leicester, 1979).
45. For Mackay's views and Highland politics in 1689–90, see the Appendix of original correspondence in Mackay's *Memoirs*.

4 THE NADIR OF GOVERNMENT

1. *The Register of the Privy Council of Scotland* (R.P.C.S.), 3rd Series, Vol. XIV (1689), ed. H. Paton (Edinburgh, 1933), pp. 272–3 (for Inverness and its ransom); and pp. 584, 602 and 606 (for Maclean of Duart and his prisoners).
2. R.P.C.S., 3rd Series, Vol. XV (1690), ed. E. W. M. Balfour-Melville (Edinburgh, 1967), p. 264.
3. ibid., pp. 179–80, 182 and 185.
4. For the 'Dartmouth' episode I have drawn heavily on a splended article by my colleague Colin Martin : C. J. M. Martin, 'The *Dartmouth*, a British Frigate Wrecked off Mull, 1690 : 5. The Ship', *The International Journal of Nautical Archaeology and Underwater Exploration* (1978), 7, 1 : pp. 29–58.
5. J. Prebble, *Glencoe* (London, 1966).
6. W. Ferguson, *Scotland 1689 to the Present* (Edinburgh, 1968), pp. 19–26.
7. *Memoirs of Sir Ewen Cameron of Locheill, Chief of the Clan Cameron*, Maitland Club, Vol. 59 (Edinburgh, 1842), pp. 322–3.
8. Jane Garrett, *The Triumphs of Providence: The Assassination Plot, 1696* (Cambridge University Press, 1980).
9. *Memoirs of Sir Ewen Cameron*, pp. 112–13.
10. Audrey Cunningham, *The Loyal Clans* (Cambridge, 1932), pp. 411–12.
11. *Memoirs of Sir Ewen Cameron*, pp. 332–6.
12. The best account of the complexities of the Fraser succession is in Alexander Mackenzie, *History of the Frasers of Lovat with Genealogies of the Principal Families of the Name* (Inverness, 1896), Chs. XV–XVIII.
13. W.C. Mackenzie, *Simon Fraser, Lord Lovat: His Life and Times* (London, 1908), pp. 21–3.
14. P. W. J. Riley, *King William and the Scottish Politicians* (Edinburgh, 1979), Introduction and pp. 119–23.
15. The letter is printed in A. Mackenzie, *History of the Frasers of Lovat*, pp. 219–21.
16. The evidence of the female servants is conveniently reproduced in a pamphlet entitled *A True Copy of the Depositions taken by Order of the Lords of Secret Council, before the Lord Justice General, and other Lords of Justiciary, in the Crimes of Rebellion and Violence, committed by Capt. Simon Fraser, upon the Person of my Lord Mungo Murray, Son to John Marquis of Athol, and on the Person of my Lord Salton; and of the horrid Rape committed upon the Person of Lady Emillia Murray, Lady Dowager of Lovat etc.* which pamphlet is conveniently reprinted in *A Collection of Scarce and Interesting Tracts – Selected from the Somers-Collections* (London, printed for R. Edwards, 1795), pp. 595–602. For the apparel of a lady of ducal rank in the late seventeenth century (and for the point that any form of drawers was deemed 'not quite nice'), see R. K. Marshall, *The Days of Duchess Anne: Life in the Household of the Duchess of Hamilton 1656–1716* (London, 1973), pp. 90–91.
17. W. C. Mackenzie, *Simon Fraser*, p. 28.
18. James Steuart of Ardvorlich to Lord Murray, 18 January 1694, *Historical Manuscripts Commission* (hereafter H.M.C.), *Twelfth Report, Appendix, Part VIII: The Manuscripts of the Duke of Athole, K. T. and of the Earl of Home* (London, H.M.S.O., 1891), pp. 46–7.
19. Colon John Hill to Lord Murray, 14 July 1694, summarised as No. 122, ibid., p. 48.
20. The quotation is from a letter from Simon Fraser to Colonel John Hill, cited in the summary of Earl of Marchmont to Earl of Tullibardine, 13 November 1697, No. 143, ibid., pp. 56–8.
21. Viscount Tarbat to Earl of Tullibardine, 1 March 1698, No. 146, ibid., pp. 58–9.
22. A. Mackenzie, *History of the Frasers of Lovat*, pp. 253–4.
23. A. Fergusson (ed.), *Major Fraser's Manuscript*, Vol. 1, pp. 133–4.
24. Mackenzie, *History of the Frasers*, pp. 290–93.
25. David McRoberts, 'The Scottish Catholic Archives, 1560–1978', in *The Innes Review*,

XXVIII, No.2 (Autumn, 1977), pp. 79–80.

26. *An Account of Capt. Simon Frazer of Beaufort, Who has been carrying on a Plot in the Highlands of Scotland, against the Government: And at the same Time, was engaged in another wicked Design, to suborn Witnesses against several Great Families in Scotland, as if they were in a Correspondence with the Courts of France and St. Germains. Printed 1704,* reprinted in *A Collection – Selected from the Somers-Collections*, pp. 591–594.
27. Sir James Balfour Paul (ed.), *The Scots Peerage*, Vol. 1 (Edinburgh, 1904), p. 479.
28. *Correspondence of Colonel N. Hooke, In the Years 1703–7*, ed. Rev. William Dunn MacRay, 2 Vols. (London, for the Roxburghe Club, 1870–71), Vol. 1, pp. 372–427.
29. *Secret History of Colonel Hoocke's Negotiations in Scotland in 1707 Written by Himself* (Edinburgh, 1760), p. 89.
30. The scheme is touched on in Claude Nordmann, 'Louis XIV and the Jacobites', in Ragnhild Hatton (ed.), *Louis XIV and Europe* (paperback ed., London, 1976), pp. 82–111. However, it will be greatly illuminated by a forthcoming monograph by Mr John Gibson, author of a classic study of the naval side of the '45. I am most grateful to Mr Gibson for his kindness in showing me drafts of what promises to be a highly original contribution to the literature, and for being willing to discuss these matters with me.
31. This section is based on a summary of a substantial selection of Lovat's French correspondence preserved in the National Library of Scotland (N.L.S.) MSS. 147–81. It is basically correspondence in French, but with several royal decrees signed by Louis XIV and Colbert de Torcy. The very latest documents relate to a period after Lovat's return to Britain (see for example note 34 below).
32. Robert Chambers, *Domestic Annals of Scotland*, Vol. III (Edinburgh, 1861), pp. 254–6.
33. This account is based on Mackenzie's, *History of the Frasers*, and the first volume of *Major Fraser's Manuscript*.
34. Lovat to George I (draft), 19 January 1721. This letter is in French, but that would be a perfectly natural language to use in addressing a former German princeling, who would regard it as the polite court language. It is the last individual document in the collection described in note 31.

5 THE 'DISAFFECTED CLANS' FROM THE '15 TO THE ERA OF GENERAL WADE

1. For Argyll on the Peerage Bill see Argyll to Grange, 25 May 1721, printed in: Historical Manuscripts Commission, *Report on the Manuscripts of the Earl of Mar and Kellie* (London, H.M.S.O., 1904), pp. 522–3. For the general background to the '15 see B. Lenman, *The Jacobite Risings in Britain 1689–1746* (London, 1980), chs. 3–6.
2. Atholl to Montrose, 26 July 1715, SRO/GD220/5/460/2.
3. Same to same, 3 January 1715, SRO/GD220/5/460/1.
4. For this comic relationship see Reay to Atholl, 3 January, 15 January, 15 March, 26 July, and 3 August 1715, SRO/GD220/5/459/1–5.
5. Sir William Gordon to Montrose, 12 January 1715, SRO/GD220/5/482/1.
6. Copies, Montrose to Jean de Robethon, 12 February, and 1 March 1715, SRO/GD220/5/511/1 and 4 resp.
7. Sir William Gordon to Montrose, 24 April 1715, SRO/GD220/5/482/11.
8. Same to same, 6 May 1715, SRO/GD220/5/482/12.
9. Pollock of that Ilk to Montrose, and enclosed return of effectives, 17 June 1715, SRO/GD220/5/568/1–2. For the reply see Montrose to Pollock of that Ilk, 21 June 1715, SRO/GD220/5/568/3. For the indefensibility of the outposts see Pollock to Montrose, 14 July 1715, SRO/GD220/5/568/5.

10. For the extensive correspondence between Pollock and Montrose on the signs of a coming rising in July and August 1715, see SRO/GD220/5/568/6–12.
11. Same to same, 24 and 28 September, and 28 October 1715, SRO/GD220/5/568/17–19.
12. Mar to 'the Lairds of Glengary, Lochiel, Clanranald, Keppoch, Apin, Glenco, McDougal, and Glenmoriston', 1 September 1715, Lochiel MSS., West Highland Museum (hereafter WHM), No. 96.
13. Mar to 'Laird of Lochyeal younger', 2 September 1715, Lochiel MSS., WHM, No.50.
14. Clanranald to Lochiel younger, 15 September, 1715, Lochiel MSS., WHM, No.20.
15. 'Maidrane' to Lochiel younger, and J. C. (John Campbell?) to same, 17 and 19 September 1715, resp., Lochiel MSS., WHM, Nos. 27 and 4 resp.
16. Mar to Lochiel younger, 27 September 1715, Lochiel MSS., WHM, No.95.
17. For Sir Robert Pollock's reports from 28 November to 31 December 1715, see SRO/GD220/5/568/21–6.
18. Alan Cameron to John Cameron of Lochiel younger, 17 January 1716, Lochiel MSS., WHM, No.29.
19. Contemporary accounts of military activity in the west during the '15 are conveniently reprinted in C. S. Terry (ed.), *The Chevalier de St. George and the Jacobite Movements in his Favour 1701–1720* (London, 1901), pp. 242–59.
20. Mar to Lochiel younger, 27 and 31 January 1716, Lochiel MSS., WHM, Nos.97 and 101 resp.
21. Mar to Sir William Gordon, 16 January 1716, Lochiel MSS., WHM, No.100.
22. For Sir Robert Pollock's reports on the last stages of the rebellion in Glen More, and on Keppoch's heroic implausibilities, see SRO/GD220/5/615/1–18.
23. Second Earl of Stair to Duke of Montrose, Paris 18/29 February 1716, SRO/GD220/5/624/2. For the systematic proscription of the English Tory party by the Whigs see E. Cruickshanks, *Political Untouchables: the Tories and the '45* (London, 1979).
24. 'Coppy of pairt of a letter from Sir Robert Munro of ffowlis, 15th inst., to Captain Robert Munro' undated but clearly late 1715 or early 1716, SRO/GD220/5/630/6.
25. Sir Robert Munro of Foulis to Montrose, 28 January 1716, SRO/GD220/5/630/1.
26. John Hope, later Sir John Bruce of Kinross and Craighall, to Montrose, Aberdeen, 8 February 1716, SRO/GD220/5/631/4a.
27. Same to same, 'Blair in Athole', 1 April 1716, SRO/GD220/5/631/9.
28. Same to same, Inverness, 6 April 1716, SRO/GD220/5/631/10a.
29. Same to same, 7 April 1716, SRO/GD220/5/631/11.
30. Same to same, 19 April 1716, SRO/GD220/5/631/15.
31. Sir William Gordon to Montrose, 1 March, 13 April, 1 June 1716, SRO/GD220/5/663(1–3).
32. Duke of Montrose to Mungo Graham of Gorthie, 14 July 1720, SRO/GD220/5/833/17a.
33. David Murray, *The York Buildings Company* (Bratton reprint, Edinburgh, 1973), esp. the Appendix.
34. Inversnaid 1715 Forfeited Estate Papers, SRO/E636.
35. Montrose to Mungo Graham of Gorthie, 24 February 1715, SRO/GD220/5/817/32.
36. Gorthie to Montrose, 20 and 26 December 1715, SRO/GD220/5/817/30 and 33 resp.
37. Montrose to Gorthie, 4 March 1718, SRO/GD220/5/824/19.
38. Same to same, 17 April 1719, SRO/GD220/5/829/6.
39. Lochiel 1715, Forfeited Estates Papers, E663.
40. Bundle marked, 'No.5 Factors' Accounts 1715–22', Glenmoriston 1715, Forfeited Estates Papers, E663.

41. Bundle marked, 'Papers connected with sale of Estate, c.1722–32', esp. 'Filled Accott. of the purchase money of the Estate of Glenmoriston 1732', ibid.
42. For the Grants of Corrimony and Sheuglie see Francis J. Grant, *The Grants of Corrimony* (privately printed, Lerwick, 1895).
43. Montrose to Gorthie, 7 March 1718, SRO/GD220/5/824/20.
44. For the details of this brief campaign see W.K. Dickson (ed.), *The Jacobite Attempt of 1719*, Scottish History Society, Vol.XIX (Edinburgh, 1895).
45. Montrose to Gorthie, 21 April 1719, '2 in the afternoon', SRO/GD220/5/824/7.
46. Lovat's memorandum is printed as an appendix to Burt's *Letters from a Gentleman in the North of Scotland to his Friend in London* (5th ed., London, 1818), pp. 254–67.
47. Wade's 1724 report is printed in Col. James Allardyce (ed.), *Historical Papers Relating to the Jacobite Period 1699–1750*, Vol.1, the New Spalding Club (Aberdeen, 1895), pp. 131–49. For his interest in Gaelic culture see Mackenzie of Coul to John Mackenzie of Delvine, 7 October 1725, National Library of Scotland MS.133. Delvine Papers. I owe this reference to Jean Munro.
48. Wade's 1727 report can be found in ibid., pp. 150–165.
49. W. Taylor, *The Military Roads in Scotland* (Newton Abbot, 1976).
50. Col. David Stewart, *Sketches of the Character, Manners, and Present State of the Highlanders of Scotland* (2nd ed., Edinburgh, 1822), Vol. 1, pp. 244–246. Stewart's statement that the regiment was only embodied in May 1740 is incorrect and must be modified in the light of the War Office correspondence printed by H.D. MacWilliam. *The Black Watch Tartan* (Inverness, 1932), pp. 27–30. I am deeply grateful to R.W. Munro for drawing my attention to this piece of evidence.

6 THE ALIENATION OF GRANT OF GRANT AND ITS CONSEQUENCES

1. P. Lawson, 'Grenville's Election Act, 1770', *Bulletin of the Institute of Historical Research*, Vol. LIII, No.128, November 1980, pp. 218–28.
2. G. Menary, *The Life and Letters of Duncan Forbes of Culloden*, pp. 97–8.
3. Lovat to Sir James Grant of Grant, 10 November 1729, S.R.O., GD248/97/1/41 Seafield Pps.
4. Lovat to Ludovick Colquhoun of Luss, 16 September 1729, S.R.O., GD248/97/1/38.
5. Same to same, 7 October 1729, S.R.O., GD248/97/1/40.
6. Lovat to Sir James Grant of Grant, 27 October 1727, S.R.O., GD248/97/1/43.
7. Same to same, 24 October 1727, S.R.O., GD248/97/1/45.
8. Memorandum by Patrick Grant dated 14 October 1727, S.R.O., GD248/97/1/46.
9. Lovat to Sir James Grant of Grant, 25 October 1732; and 2 November 1732 (with undated draft of recipient's reply); also Lovat to Ludovick Colquhoun of Luss, 27 October 1732, S.R.O., GD248/97/1/29, 26 and 28 respectively.
10. R. Sedgwick, *The History of Parliament: The House of Commons 1715–1754*, Vol. I (London, 1970), p. 387.
11. Lovat to Sir James Grant of Grant, 7 and 31 March 1733, S.R.O., GD248/97/1/47 and 56 resp.
12. Same to same, 11 December 1733, S.R.O., GD248/97/1/39.
13. Same to same, 6 May 1734, S.R.O. GD248/97/1/63–4.
14. Same to same, 25 October 1732 and 13 December 1734, S.R.O., GD248/97/1/29 and 6 resp.
15. For an excellent discussion of these issues see W. Speck, 'Whigs and Tories dim their glories: English political parties under the first two Georges' and the colloquy by

Geoffrey Holmes in J. Cannon (ed.) *The Whig Ascendancy: Colloquies on Hanoverian England* (London, 1981), pp. 51–76.

16. Lovat to Ludovick Colquhoun of Luss, 5 February 1734, S.R.O., GD248/97/1/62.
17. Lovat to Sir James Grant of Grant, 23 January 1733, S.R.O., GD248/97/1/68-9 Seafield Pps.
18. Same to same, 5 January 1734, S.R.O., GD248/97/1/70 Seafield Pps.
19. Same to same, 27 December 1734, S.R.O., GD248/97/1/72.
20. Copy Lovat to Sir Robert Walpole, 27 December 1734, S.R.O., GD248/97/1/73.
21. Lovat to Ludovick Colquhoun of Luss (later Sir Ludovick Grant of Grant Bart), 27 December 1734, S.R.O., GD248/97/1/74.
22. Lovat to Sir James Grant of Grant, 20 December 1734, S.R.O., GD248/97/1/75.
23. Same to same, 29 November 1734, S.R.O., GD248/97/1/78.
24. Same to same, 6 December 1734, S.R.O., GD248/97/1/77.
25. Same to same, 2 November 1734, S.R.O., GD248/97/1/83.
26. Same to same, 10 October 1734, S.R.O., GD248/97/1/84.
27. R. Sedgwick, *The House of Commons 1715–1754*, Vol. I, pp. 386–7.
28. Sir James Balfour Paul, *The Scots Peerage Vol. VI* (Edinburgh, 1909), pp. 323–5.
29. 'Copy James Steuart of Pitrindick's letter to Roben Urquhart of Birdyards', S.R.O., GD248/97/1/104.
30. 'Copy of Captain Urquhart of Birdyard's Letter to the Lord Lovat, 12 January 1734', S.R.O., GD248/97/1/105.
31. Lovat to Sir James Grant of Grant, 28 March 1734, S.R.O., GD248/97/1/92.
32. Same to same, 9 March 1734, S.R.O., GD248/97/1/96.
33. Same to same, 3 November 1733, S.R.O., GD248/97/1/109.
34. Lovat to Ludovick Colquhoun of Luss, 27 August 1733, S.R.O., GD248/97/1/114.
35. 'Excerpt letter of Simon Lord Lovat to Archibald Earl of Ilay – October 1734,' S.R.O., GD248/97/1/85.
36. 'Copie of Belnain's Letter to the Lord Lovat, 11 May 1734,' S.R.O., GD248/97/1/88.
37. Lovat to Sir James Grant of Grant, 16 March 1734, S.R.O., GD248/97/1/94.
38. Lovat to Ludovick Colquhoun of Luss, 10 January 1735, and to Sir James Grant of Grant, 31 January 1735, S.R.O., GD248/97/2/4 and 5 resp.
39. B. Lenman, *The Jacobite Risings in Britain 1689–1746* (London, 1980), pp. 163–4.
40. Earl of Findlater to Lovat, copy, n.d., S.R.O., GD248/97/2/1.
41. The strange saga of the Grants of Grant in eighteenth-century politics may be followed in R. Sedgwick, *The House of Commons 1715–1754*, Vol. I, pp. 399–400 and Vol. II, pp. 77-81.
42. Lovat to Sir James Grant of Grant, 24 January 1735, S.R.O., GD248/97/2/6.
43. Same to same, 16 May 1735, S.R.O., GD248/97/2/30.
44. Same to same, 27 December 1735, S.R.O., GD248/97/2/63.
45. Same to same, 17 December 1736, S.R.O., GD248/97/2/115.
46. There is a vast and extremely repetitious correspondence by Lovat on these themes with members of the Grant family in S.R.O., GD248/97/2.
47. Lovat to Sir James Grant, 22 January 1736, S.R.O., GD248/97/2/85.
48. 'Copy of My Lord Lovat's letter to Major General Moyle', 21 February 1736, S.R.O., GD248/97/2/98.
49. Lovat to Sir James Grant, 7 March 1735, S.R.O., GD248/97/2/17.
50. Same to same, 14 January 1737, and enc. copy of Lovat's letter to Sir Robert Munro of Fowlis, S.R.O., GD248/97/3/3.
51. Same to same, 4 February 1737, S.R.O., GD248/97/3/8.
52. Lovat to Ludovick Grant, 14 February 1737, S.R.O., GD248/97/3/14.
53. Same to same, 27 January 1737, 28 January 1737, and 8 April 1737; and Lovat to Sir

James Grant of Grant, 30 June 1737, S.R.O., GD248/97/3/7, 10, 29 and 43 resp.

54. There is a collection of revealing, if very repetitive letters between Lovat and Sir James and Ludovick Grant in S.R.O., GD248/97/3/30–40, dating from May and June 1737
55. G. W. T. Omond, *The Lord Advocates of Scotland*, Vol. 1 (Edinburgh, 1883), pp. 350–55. Lovat's views are nowhere more pungently expressed than in Lovat to Sir James Grant, 7 April 1737, S.R.O., GD248/97/3/23, where Lovat compares the proceedings at Westminster to those high-handed acts of tyranny whereby Edward I of England drove his own nominee John Balliol, King of Scots, to rebellion.
56. Lovat to Sir James Grant, 16 July 1737, 9 September 1737, and 23 September 1737, S.R.O., GD249/97/3/45, 47 and 48 respectively.
57. There is a vast correspondence in 1737 and 1738 on this topic. It can be studied in S.R.O., GD248/97/3 and especially items 58, 59, 60, 61, 66, 69, 70, 74, 78, 79 and 80.
58. Lovat to Sir James Grant, 21 April 1738, and 13 May 1738, S.R.O., GD248/97/3/81 and 84 resp.
59. Same to same, 17 October 1738, S.R.O., GD248/97/3/88. For the erection of Beauly into a burgh of regality see G.S. Pryde, *The Burghs of Scotland* (London, 1965), p. 79.
60. Same to same, 23 June 1737, and 28 September 1737, S.R.O., GD248/97/3/40 and 49 respectively.
61. Same to same, 29 December 1738, S.R.O., GD248/97/3/95.
62. Lovat to Ludovick Grant of Grant, 18 March 1737, S.R.O., GD248/97/3/22.
63. Same to same and Lovat to Sir James Grant, 14 December 1738, and 15 December 1738 respectively, S.R.O., GD248/97/3/92 and 93 resp.
64. Lovat to Sir James Grant, 10 November 1738, S.R.O., GD248/97/3/89.
65. W. Mackay, *Urquhart and Glenmoriston* (Inverness, 2nd ed., 1914), Chs. XIV and XV; Rev. A. Sinclair, *Reminiscences Historical and Traditional Of The Grants Of Glenmoriston* (Edinburgh, 1887), pp. 28–34.
66. Sedgwick, *The House of Commons*, Vol. II, pp. 79–80.
67. John MacDonell of Glengarry to Sir James Grant, 31 June 1740, and Donald Cameron of Lochiel to Ludovick Grant of Grant, 17 December 1740, printed in W. Fraser, *The Chiefs of Grant*, Vol. II (Edinburgh, 1883), p. 142.
68. Deskford to Ludovick Grant of Grant, 10 March 1741, ibid., p. 143.
69. Alexander Brodie of Brodie to same, 18 August 1745, ibid., p. 145.
70. Deskford to same, August 1745, ibid., pp. 151–2.
71. Ludovick Grant's 'official version' of his own behaviour and motives can be found in 'A short narrative of the conduct of Ludovick Grant of Grant during the rebellion', printed in W. B. Blaikie (ed.), *Origins of the Forty-Five*, Scottish History Society, 2nd series, vol. II (Edinburgh, 1916), pp. 269–309. Quotations are all from this source.
72. *Vide*, 'A note on Mackintosh of Mackintosh', in D. Warrand (ed.), *More Culloden Papers*, Vol. IV (Inverness, 1929), pp. 76–80.
73. Duncan Forbes of Culloden to Ludovick Grant of Grant, 22 September 1745, 24 September 1745, 12 October 1745, 27 October 1745, and 5 November 1745, in *The Chiefs of Grant*, Vol. II, pp. 160–1, 171, 180 and 183 respectively.
74. Lord Lewis Gordon to same, 3 November 1745, and 16 December 1745, ibid., pp. 182 and 196–7 respectively.
75. Norman Macleod of Macleod to same, 19 December 1745, ibid., p. 200.
76. The Reverend John Grant's *apologia* may be found, along with those of Shewglie and his son in 'The case of the Rev. John Grant, Minister of Urquhart; and of Alexander Grant of Sheugly in Urquhart, and James Grant, his son', in Blaikie, *Origins of the Forty-Five*, pp. 313–32.

77. *Vide*, two letters by the leading Grants of Urquhart and Glenmoriston to Ludovick Grant of Grant, 26 January 1737, and 14 March 1737, in *The Chiefs of Grant*, Vol. II, pp. 132–5.
78. John Grant, factor of Urquhart, to same, 12 September 1745, ibid., pp. 156–7.
79. Ludovick Grant of Grant to his tenants of Urquhart, 6 October 1745, ibid., pp. 166–7.
80. Alexander Grant of Corrimony to Ludovick Grant of Grant, 15 October 1745, ibid., pp. 173–4.
81. John Grant, factor of Urquhart, to same, 20 December 1745, ibid., pp. 201–202.
82. Ludovick Grant of Grant to the above, 10 October 1745, ibid., pp. 169–170.
83. Major Robert Grant to Ludovick Grant of Grant, 12 December 1745, ibid., pp. 192–3.

7 LOVAT'S APPROACH TO DISASTER 1737–1745

1. Lovat to Sir James Grant, 18 February 1737, SRO/GD 248/97/3/15.
2. Same to same, 25 February 1737, SRO/GD 248/97/3/18.
3. Same to same, 18 March 1737, SRO/GD 248/97/3/21.
4. Copy same to same, 22 April 1737, SRO/GD 248/97/3/27.
5. Same to same, 23 September 1737, SRO/GD 248/97/3/48.
6. Same to same, 7 October 1737, SRO/GD 248/97/3/55.
7. Same to same, 4 October 1737, SRO/GD 248/GD 248/97/3/56.
8. Same to same, and enclosure from Evan Baillie, 2 December 1737, SRO/GD 248/97/3/61–63.
9. Same to same, 31 March 1738, SRO/GD 248/97/3/79.
10. Same to same, 10 and 15 December 1738, SRO/GD 248/97/3/92 and 93.
11. Same to same, 29 December 1738, SRO/GD 248/97/3/95.
12. Same to same, 19 January and 16 March 1739, SRO/GD 248/97/4/1 and 12–13X.
13. Same to same, 4 May 1739, SRO/GD 248/97/4/16.
14. Same to same, 11 May 1739, SRO/GD 248/97/4/17. For Ilay and Patrick Cumming see H. R. Sefton, 'Lord Ilay and Patrick Cumming: A Study in Eighteenth Century Ecclesiastical Management', *Records of the Scottish Church History Society*, Vol. XIX, pp. 203–216.
15. Same to same, 6 September 1739, SRO/GD 248/97/4/27–8X. For Ranald of Clanranald see *Burke's Landed Gentry*, 17th ed. (London, 1952), p. 1611.
16. Same to same, 28 May 1739, SRO/GD 248/97/4/18.
17. See the memo on Lady Lovat in SRO/GD 248/97/4/23.
18. Lovat to Sir James Grant, 11 September 1739, SRO/GD 248/97/4/31–2X. For the latter-day matrimonial vicissitudes of Simon Fraser see Sir James Balfour Paul (ed.), *The Scots Peerage*, Vol. 5 (Edinburgh, 1908), pp. 539–40.
19. Lovat to Ludovick Grant of Grant, 8 November 1739, SRO/GD 248/97S/4/35.
20. 'Copy of My Lord Lovat's Letter to Generall Clayton', 4 January 1740, SRO/GD 248/97/4/40X.
21. Lovat to Ludovick Grant of Grant, 30 July 1738, printed in W. Fraser, *The Chiefs of Grant: Vol. II Correspondence* (Edinburgh, 1883), pp. 369–70.
22. Same to same, 18 December 1738, ibid., p. 373.
23. This section is based on an extensive correspondence printed in ibid., pp. 373–404. For 'the gallant earl' see Sir James Balfour Paul (ed.), *The Scots Peerage*, Vol. 3 (Edinburgh, 1906), pp. 39–40.
24. Copy of 'Aeneas Mackdonell of Scothouse letter to the Lord Lovat Feb 10 1740', SRO/GD 248/97/4/52.
25. Lovat to Sir James Grant, 27 March 1740, SRO/GD 248/97/4/47.

26. Patrick Cumming was also Professor Church History in the University of Edinburgh between 1737 and 1762, 'taking as his text-book *Jo. Alphonsi Turrentini Compendium Historiae Ecclesiasticae*, but very few students attended him'. *Vide* Sir Alexander Grant, *The Story of the University of Edinburgh*, Vol. II (London, 1884), pp. 308–309.
27. The whole business of the 1739–40 break between Lovat and Sir James Grant is recorded in a characteristically repetitious correspondence, in which most major points including the contradictory ones are made six times over, in the Seafield MSS, SRO/GD 248/97/4/45–67.
28. Lady Margaret MacDonald to Lord Milton, Justice Clerk, 1 January 1740, printed in *Culloden Papers* (London, 1815), pp. 154–5.
29. Lovat to Sir James Grant, 16 May 1740, SROS/GD 248/97/4/55.
30. Romney Sedgwick (ed.), *The House of Commons 1715–1754*, Vol. II, Members E-Y (London, H.M.S.O., 1970), p. 237.
31. Lovat to Sir James Grant, 31 January 1741, SRO/GD 248/97/5/4.
32. Copies of Glengarry to Lovat, and Lovat to Glengarry, 7 May 1734 and 11 May 1734 resp, SRO/GD 248/97/5/9 and 10.
33. These events are summarised in the Introduction to W. B. Blaikie (ed.), *The Origins of the Forty-Five*, Scottish History Society, 2nd Series, Vol. 2 (Edinburgh, 1916). For Murray of Broughton's jaundiced retrospective view of the 1743 negotiations in Paris see R. F. Bell, *Memorials of John Murray of Broughton Sometime Secretary to Prince Charles Edward 1740–1747*, Scottish History Society, Vol. XXVII (Edinburgh, 1898), pp. 41–5.
34. W. C. Mackenzie, *Simon Fraser, Lord Lovat: His Life and Times* (London, 1908), pp. 316–17.
35. Lovat to Lochiel, 3 July 1742, Lovat letters Achnacarry House.
36. Same to same, 28 April 1742, ibid.
37. Same to same, 5 November 1743, ibid.
38. Same to same, 12 November 1743, ibid.
39. Same to same, 19 November 1743, ibid.
40. Same to same, 25 November 1743, ibid.
41. Same to same, 28 October 1743, ibid.
42. Same to same, 30 November 1743, ibid.
43. Same to same, 26 January 1744, ibid.
44. Same to same, 2 February 1744, ibid.
45. Same to same, 20 June 1744, ibid.
46. Same to same, 3 July 1744, ibid.
47. Same to same, 10 July 1744, ibid.
48. Same to same, 26 January 1744, ibid.
49. Thomas Fraser of Gortuleg to Lochiel, 17 November 1743, ibid.
50. Lovat to Lochiel, undated postscript, ibid.
51. Lovat to MacLeod of MacLeod, 10 December 1742, copy, ibid.
52. Same to same, 2 December 1742, copy, ibid.
53. Lovat to Lochiel, 11 December 1742, ibid.
54. Same to same, 17 December 1742, ibid.
55. Same to same, 4 June 1743, ibid.
56. Same to same, 21 May 1743, ibid.
57. Same to same, 27 May 1743, ibid.
58. Same to same, 15 April 1743, ibid.
59. Same to same, 12 June 1743, ibid.
60. Same to same, 21 June 1743, ibid.
61. Same to same, 2 July 1743, 8 July 1743, 20 August 1743, ibid.
62. Same to same, 29 July 1743, and 2 October 1743, ibid.
63. Same to same, 17 September 1743, and 8 October 1743, ibid.

64. Master to Lovat, 22 May 1740, ibid.
65. Lovat to Lochiel, 28 October 1736, ibid.
66. Same to same, 12 May 1737, ibid.
67. Same to same, 9 February 1737, ibid.
68. Duke of Perth to Lochiel, 21 May 1736, ibid.
69. F. J. McLynn, *France and the Jacobite Rising of 1745* (Edinburgh, 1981), Chs. 1 and 2.
70. ibid., pp. 29–30.
71. See correspondence from Norman MacLeod of MacLeod to Lovat dated 23 September 1744, and 19 July 11 and 18 August 1745 printed in 'Unpublished correspondence between Lord Lovat, MacLeod of MacLeod, Lord Loudon, and others, in connection with the rebellion of 1745', in *Transactions of the Gaelic Society of Inverness*, Vol.XIV (1887–8), pp. 2–7.
72. Mackenzie, *Simon Fraser*, pp. 317–18.

8 IN THE EYE OF THE JACOBITE HURRICANE 1745–1746

1. C. Wilkinson, *Bonnie Prince Charlie* (London, 1932), pp. 67–9. L. Weaver, *The Story of the Royal Scots* (London, 1915), chs. VII and VIII.
2. W. Cheyne-Macpherson, *The Chiefs of Clan Macpherson* (Edinburgh, 1947), p. 32 and Appendix VI, pp. 96–8.
3. Alexander Campbell, James Rose, J. Rose, Alexander Brodie, Alexander Dunbar, and Hugh Rose to Ewen Macpherson of Cluny Younger, 21 May 1745, W.H.M., MS D.1.
4. Alexander Brodie of Lethen to same, 22 May 1745, W.H.M., MS D.2.
5. James Farquharson of Invercauld to same, 23 May 1745, W.H.M., MS D.3.
6. James Gordon and Alexander Mill to same, 30 July 1745, W.H.M., MS D.7.
7. D. J. MacDonald, *Clan Donald* (Loanhead, 1978), pp. 357–8.
8. Robert Craigie, Lord Advocate, to Ewen Macpherson of Cluny Younger, warrant dated 24 June 1745, W.H.M., MS D.5.
9. Same to same, 24 June 1745, W.H.M., MS D.4.
10. Norman MacLeod of MacLeod to Ewen Macpherson of Cluny Younger, 8 December 1744, cited in W. Cheyne-Macpherson, *The Chiefs of Clan Macpherson*, p. 39.
11. Charles Prince Regent for Cluny Macpherson, 6 August 1745, W.H.M., MS D.8.
12. W. Cheyne-Macpherson, *The Chiefs of Clan Macpherson*, pp. 40–45.
13. Commission from Prince Charles by John Murray, dated Perth 7 September 1745, W.H.M., MS D.9.
14. 'Information of the Skirmish near Penrith, 16 December 1745', W.H.M., MS D.10. Internal evidence and provenance leave little doubt as to Cluny's authorship of the original version.
15. Commission of fire and sword by Prince Charles to Cluny, Fairntoun 3 February 1746, W.H.M., MS D.11.
16. Sir James Fergusson of Kilkerran, *Argyll in the Forty-Five* (London, 1951), pp. 127–134.
17. David Lord Elcho, *A Short Account of The Affairs of Scotland in the Years 1744, 1745, 1746*, ed. the Hon Evan Charteris (Edinburgh, 1907), pp. 389–95.
18. S. MacMillan, *Bygone Lochaber* (privately printed, Glasgow, 1971), pp. 163–71.
19. Lord George Murray to Colonel Macpherson of Clunie, 11 March 1746, W.H.M., MS D.14.
20. Fergusson of Kilkerran, *Argyll in the Forty-Five*, ch. 7.
21. Donald Cameron of Lochiel to Ewen Cameron of Cluny, 20 March 1746, W.H.M., MS D.13.
22. There is an admirable contemporary account of the siege in *The Scots Magazine*, Vol. VIII (1746), pp. 139–41 and pp. 181–3. The quotation is from p. 141.

23. The manifesto is convenintly printed in N. H. MacDonald, *The Clan Ranald of Lochaber* (privately printed, n.d.), pp. 43–4.
24. Ewen Macpherson of Cluny to Donald Macpherson of Breakachie, 23 March 1746, W.H.M., MS D.15.
25. Donald Cameron of Lochiel to Ewen Macpherson of Cluny, 13 May 1746, W.H.M., MS D.16.
26. W. C. Mackenzie, *Simon Fraser, Lord Lovat*, pp. 330–331.
27. John Murray to (?) Andrew Stone, Tower of London, 27 August 1746, printed in *Memorials of John Murray of Broughton*, ed. R. F. Bell, *Scottish History Society*, Vol. XXVII (1898), pp. 415–16.
28. W. Duke, *Lord George Murray and The Forty-Five* (Aberdeen, 1927), pp. 190–96.
29. Revs. A. and A. MacDonald, *The Clan Donald*, Vol. III (Inverness, 1904), pp. 328–29.
30. Ewen Cameron of Lochiel to Cluny Macpherson, 25 May 1746, W.H.M., MS D.17.
31. These letters are conveniently printed in W. Mackay, 'Unpublished Correspondence between Lord Lovat, MacLeod of MacLeod, Lord Loudon and others, in connection with the Rebellion of 1745', *Transactions of the Gaelic Society of Inverness*, Vol. XIV, 1887–8, pp. 1–39.
32. The relevant documents from the Stuart Papers in Windsor Castle are reprinted by Marion F. Hamilton in 'The Locharkaig Treasure' *Scottish History Society Miscellany Vol. VII* (Edinburgh, 1941), pp. 131–68.
33. Charles Stewart of Ardsheal to Ewen Macpherson of Cluny, 24 September 1746. The receipt for £100 for Ardsheal is signed by William Stewart and written on the tail of Ardsheal's letter, W.H.M., MS D.18.
34. Receipt from Ludovick Cameron dated 2 April 1746, W.H.M., MS D.19.
35. It is documented in Thomond to Cluny, 31 October 1755; 1 February 1756; and 11 February 1756, W.H.M., D.22–24. W. Cheyne-Macpherson is erroneous in *The Chiefs of Clan Macpherson*, p. 54, in suggesting no place in the French military establishment was found for him.
36. There are two copies of this Memoir, obviously dating from 1755, in W.H.M., MS D.26.
37. Thomond to Cluny, 7 November 1759, W.H.M., MS D.29.
38. One of the later petitions dated March 1760 is in W.H.M., MS D.31.
39. 'Memorial for John MacDonell of Glengarry, 1750' compiled by 'Glengarry's Doer' (his Edinburgh lawyer) and preserved in W.H.M., Lochgarry Papers, bundle A.
40. 'Note of Dues for Burying in the Royal Chapell of Holyroodhouse The remains of John MacDonell Esq[r] of Glengarry 3 September 1754', W.H.M., Lochgarry Papers, bundle A.
41. A. and H. Tayler, *1745 and After* (London, 1938), p. 39.
42. 'John Murray's Papers', in *Origins of the '45*, ed. W. Biggar Blaikie, Scottish History Society, 2nd Series, Vol. II (Edinburgh, 1916), p. 25.
43. The best brief account of Glengarry and the three Barrisdales in the '45 can be found in Vol. III of Sir Bruce Seton and J. G. Arnot (eds.), *The Prisoners of the '45*, Scottish History Society, 3rd Series, Vol. XV (Edinburgh, 1929), pp. 48–51 and 65.
44. Lord Justice Clerk to Duke of Newcastle, 9 August 1746, and Enclosure I, in *The Albemarle Papers*, ed. C. S. Terry (Aberdeen, New Spalding Club, 1902), Vol. II, pp. 404–6.
45. Lord Justice Clerk to Earl of Albemarle, 9 August 1746, ibid., Vol. I, pp. 86–9.

9 THE WAY BACK – FROM CULLODEN TO YORKTOWN

1. Quoted in W. C. Mackenzie, *Lovat of the Forty-Five* (Edinburgh, 1934), pp. 167–8.
2. *Vide, A Candid and Impartial Account of the Behaviour of Simon Lord Lovat* (London, 1747),

and *An Answer to a Dangerous Pamphlet Entitled a Candid and Impartial Account of the Behaviour of Simon Lord Lovat, Fully Detecting the Clandestine Views of that Writer and Interspersed with Reflections on the Principles and Practices of the Jacobites* (London, 1748).

3. This is clear from the material printed in C. S. Terry (ed.), *The Albemarle Papers*, 2 vols. (Aberdeen, the New Spalding Club, 1902).
4. F. J. McLynn, *France and the Forty-Five* (Edinburgh, 1981), argues at length that the French government missed a great opportunity in 1745–6, whereas the evidence deployed suggests rather that it preferred to back a sure winner in Flanders, and to encourage a diversionary side-show in Britain.
5. R. Sedgwick (ed.), *The House of Commons 1715–1754*, Vol. 1 (London H.M.S.O., 1970), pp. 386–7.
6. 'Testimony in favour of Simon Fraser, Lord Lovat's eldest son, by the northern ministers (no date), in handwriting of Mr Donald Fraser, who signs it', printed in W. Mackay, 'Unpublished Correspondence between Lord Lovat, MacLeod of MacLeod, Lord Loudon, and others, in connection with the Rebellion of 1745', in *Transactions of the Gaelic Society of Inverness*, Vol. XIV (1887–8), p. 37. For Simon's political career see Sir Lewis Namier and John Brooks (eds.), *The House of Commons 1754–1790* (London, H.M.S.O., 1964), pp. 470–472.
7. There are useful entries for Sir William Pepperrell, and William Shirley in *The Dictionary of American Biography*, Vols. 14 and 17 (New York, 1934 and 1935 resp.).
8. S. M. Pargellis, *Lord Loudon in North America* (Yale, London and Oxford, 1933), p. 16 footnote.
9. The D.N.B. has convenient articles on the second Duke of Argyll and the second Earl of Stair, and is the best place to pursue the complexities of Dalrymple–Campbell intermarriages.
10. L. H. Gipson, *The Great War for the Empire: The Years of Defeat 1754–1757* (New York, 1946).
11. *Commissary Wilson's Orderly Book: Expedition of the British and Provincial Army under Major General Jeffrey Amherst against Ticonderoga and Crown Point, 1759* (Albany, N. Y., and London, 1857), p. 6.
12. Cadwallader Colden to Peter Collinson, New York, 23 April 1756, Newberry Library, Chicago, Ayer Collection MS 178. For Colden see *Appleton's Cyclopedia of American Biography*, ed. J. G. Wilson and J. Fiske, Vol. 1, pp. 683–4 (New York, 1888).
13. *A Review of the Military Operations in North America, from the Commencement of the French Hostilities on the Frontiers of Virginia in 1753, to the Surrender of Oswego, on the 14th of August, 1756; in a Letter to a Nobleman*, reprinted in the *Collections of the Massachusetts Historical Society for the Year 1800* (Boston, 1801), pp. 67–163. The original is dated New York, 20 September 1756, and the quotation comes from p. 109. Governor Livingston and two New York lawyers have been suggested as possible authors of this anonymous work.
14. The most important recent critique of Sir William Johnson is Julian Gwyn's long and perceptive article on him in *Dictionary of Canadian Biography, Vol. IV, 1771 to 1800* (Toronto, 1979), pp. 394–8.

    Milton W. Hamilton's *Sir William Johnson and the Indians of New York* (Albany, 1975), and his magisterial *Sir William Johnson Colonial American, 1715–1763* (Port Washington, New York, 1976), with all their virtues, both take an excessively rosy view of Sir William's dealings with Indians.
15. Gavin Cochrane, 'Treatise on the Indians of North America Written in the year 1764', Newberry Library, Chicago, Ayer Collection MS 176.
16. F. W. Hodge, *Handbook of American Indians North of Mexico* (reprinted New York, 1959), Part 1, p. 619. Almost certainly contemporary observers underestimated Iroquois numbers substantially.

17. J. G. Kyd (ed.), *Scottish Population Statistics including Webster's Analysis of Population 1755*, Scottish History Society, 3rd Series, Vol. 44 (Edinburgh, 1952), pp. 7–81.
18. There is a good account of Dr Archie's life and death in the D.N.B.
19. For Francis Grant see *Commissary Wilson's Orderly Book*, footnote p. 3. The *Dictionary of American Biography*, Vol. 1 (New York, 1928), pp. 28–9, has a useful entry on General James Abercromby.
20. Col. David Stewart of Garth, *Sketches of the Character, Manners, and Present State of the Highlanders of Scotland; with Details of the Military Service of the Highland Regiments* (Edinburgh, 2nd edn., 2 vol., 1822). Accounts of the raising of the 77th (Montgomerie's) and 78th (Fraser's), will be found in Vol. 2, pp. 14–16 and 18–23.
21. For the 'Appin Murder' see D. M. Mackay (ed.), *Trial of James Stewart (the Appin Murder)* (Edinburgh, Notable British Trials Series, 1931).
22. Stewart of Garth, *Sketches of the Highlanders*, Vol. 1, p. 308.
23. Barrington to Cumberland, 8 July and 16 August 1757, printed in S. Pargellis (ed.), *Military Affairs in North America 1748–1765 : Selected Documents from the Cumberland Papers in Windsor Castle* (New York, 1936), pp. 380–2 and 394–5 resp.
24. F. E. Whitton, *Wolfe and North America* (London, 1929), p. 189.
25. For Johnstone see *Memoirs of the Chevalier de Johnstone*, translated by Charles Winchester, 3 vols. (Aberdeen, 1870–1. For the de Ramezay family see *Dictionary of Canadian Biography, Vol. II, 1701 to 1740* (Toronto, 1969), pp. 545–9, and *Vol. III, 1741–1770* (Toronto, 1974), pp. 543–4; and *The Campaign of 1760 in Canada : A Narrative Attributed to Chevalier Johnstone* (Quebec, Literary and Historical Society of Quebec, 1887). This last appears to be an earlier account than that in the *Memoirs*. It was written in English and deposited in the Archives de Guerre in Paris. The anecdote on Murray and the nun is in a footnote on pp. 13–14 of the published text.
26. Stewart of Garth, *Sketches of the Highlanders*, Vol. 1, pp. 332–6.
27. Regimental details for units raised between 1757 and 1760 are drawn from the two volumes of Stewart of Garth, supplemented by the D.N.B.
28. The best introduction to Staates Long Morris's American background and family is a group of articles in the *Dictionary of American Biography*, Vol. XIII (New York, 1934), pp. 209–215, on the first and second lords of the manor of Morrisania, and on Gouverneur Morris.
29. Alexander Webster, *Heathens professing Judaism, when the fear of the Jews fell upon them. The substance of two sermons preached in the Tolbooth church Edinburgh, on occasion of the thanksgiving, June 23 1746, appointed for the victory obtain'd over the rebels at the Battle of Culloden, April 16 1746*, (Edinburgh, 1746).
30. ibid., p. 50. For a recent analysis of the social structure of active Jacobitism see B. Lenman, *The Jacobite Risings in Britain 1689–1746* (London, 1980).
31. The anonymous follower of Chatham is cited in Stewart of Garth, *Sketches of the Highlanders*, Vol. 2, p. 19.
32. The veteran's words are cited in ibid., p. 41, presumably from correspondence with Stewart of Garth.
33. F. Jennings, *The Invasion of America* (Norton paperback ed., New York, 1981), Ch. 1.
34. Extracts from Indian Papers, August 1756, in *The Papers of Sir William Johnson* [hereafter Johnson Papers], ed. A. W. Lauber (Albany, N.Y., 1939), Vol. IX, pp. 517–18.
35. *Vide*, Contemporary Copy, Kerlerec to the French Ministry, 13 December 1756, ibid., pp. 569–73.
36. Loudon to Johnson, 31 August 1756, ibid., pp. 516–17.
37. G. Croghan to Johnson, 13 January 1761, ibid., Vol. III, p. 301.
38. Amherst to Johnson, 11 August 1761, ibid., pp. 516–17.
39. Fred Gearing, *Priests and Warriors: Social Structures for Cherokee Politics in the 18th Century*, Memoir 93, the *American Anthropological Association*, Vol 64, No.5, Part 2, October 1962.

40. D. H. Corkran, *The Cherokee Frontier: Conflict and Survival, 1740–1762* (University of Oklahoma Press, Norman, Oklahoma, 1962).
41. The most convenient biography of this Simon Fraser is still the D.N.B. Vol. VII entry. For the electoral history of Inverness-shire 1761–1782 see Sir Lewis Namier and John Brooke, *The House of Commons 1754–1790*, Vol. 1 (London, H.M.S.O., 1964), pp. 484–5.
42. [James] *Adair's History of the American Indians*, edited Samuel Cole Williams (Johnson City, Tennessee, 1930), pp. 288–9 inc. footnote.
43. For MacGillivray's business connections see William Panton (1742?–1801) and John Forbes (1769–1823), *Dictionary of American Biography*, Vols. XIV (N.Y., 1934), pp. 199–200, and VI (N.Y., 1931), p. 506, resp. For Alexander MacGillivray himself see J. W. Caughey, *MacGillivray of the Creeks* (Norman, Oklahoma, 1938).
44. B. Bissell, *The American Indian in English Literature of the Eighteenth Century*, Yale Studies in English Vol. LXVIII (New Haven, 1925), pp. 104–7.
45. J. P. MacLean, *An Historical Account of the Settlements of Scotch Highlanders in America Prior to the Peace of 1783* (Cleveland, 1900), Chs. V–VII.
46. John C. Guzzardo, *Sir William Johnson's Official Family: Patron and Clients in an Anglo-American Empire, 1742–1777*, Syracuse University, Syracuse, New York, unpublished Ph.D., 1975, esp. Ch. IV 'Towards an Anglo-Irish Countryside: 1761–6'.
47. Lord Adam Gordon to Johnson, 10 January 1767, *Johnson Papers*, Vol. XII, pp. 248–52.
48. Johnson to Cadawallader Colden, 15 August 1765, ibid., Vol. IV, pp. 823–4.
49. Harry Munro to Johnson, n.d., and 21 May 1773, ibid., Vol. VII, p. 1026, and Vol. XII, pp. 1023–4 resp.
50. Johnson to John Donell, 28 June 1774, ibid., Vol. XII, pp. 1111–1112.
51. J.P. Kenyon, *Revolution Principles* (Cambridge, 1877). For a devastating, because utterly factual, exposition of the role of His Majesty's Government as the midwife of American Independence, see M. Jensen, *The Founding of a Nation: A History of the American Revolution 1763–1776* (New York and London, 1968).
52. Alexander Gerard, D.D., *Liberty the Cloak of Maliciousness, both in the American Rebellion, and in the Manners of the Times: A Sermon Preached at Old Aberdeen, February 26 1778, Being the Fast-Day Appointed by Proclamation on Account of the Rebellion in America* (Aberdeen, 1778, sold by Alexander Thomson, Aberdeen; T. Cadell, London; and W. Creech, Edinburgh).
53. John Witherspoon, D.D., *An Address to the Natives of Scotland Residing in America Being an Appendix to a Sermon Preached at Princeton on a General Fast* (London, printed for Fielding and Walker, 1778). For Witherspoon's career see *Dictionary of American Biography*, Vol. X, pp. 435–8.
54. ibid., Vol. III, pp. 519–20.
55. Barbara Graymount, *The Iroquois in the American Revolution* (Syracuse, N.Y., 1972).
56. Helen L. Shaw, *British Administration of the Southern Indians 1756–1783* (Bryn Mawr, 1931); James H. O'Donnell, *Southern Indians in the American Revolution* (Knoxville, Tennessee, 1973); and David H. Corkran, *The Creek Frontier 1540–1783* (Norman, Oklahoma, 1967).
57. Edward E. Curtis, *The Organisation of the British Army in the American Revolution*, Yale Historical Publications Miscellany XIX (New Haven, Connecticut, 1926), esp. Ch. III.
58. The evidence, though not the interpretation, advanced in the discussion of these regiments, will be found in Stewart of Garth, *Sketches of the Highlanders*, Vol. 2.
59. For Flora MacDonald see J. P. MacLean, *Flora MacDonald in America* (Lumberton, North Carolina, 1909), and the very interesting re-assessment of her role in 1746 in A. Maclean, *A MacDonald for the Prince* (Stornoway, 1982). For the Loyalists in general and the North Carolina Highland Loyalists in particular see Paul H. Smith, *Loyalists*

and Redcoats: A Study in British Revolutionary Policy (Chapel Hill, North Carolina, 1964); Robert McC. Calhoon, *The Royalists in Revolutionary America 1760–1781* (New York, 1973); and Robert O. De Mond, *The Loyalists in North Carolina During the Revolution* (Durham, North Carolina, 1940).

60. For the botanist and Loyalist Alexander see *Dictionary of National Biography*, Vol. VII, pp. 846–7. For the Patriot soldier see *Dictionary of American Biography*, Vol. VII (New York, 1931), pp. 133–4.
61. ibid., Vol. XII (New York, 1933), pp. 69–70.
62. The best introduction to the American Olyphants is in ibid., Vol. XIV (New York, 1934), pp. 34–5. On these and allied matters I have benefited greatly from the correspondence and conversation of Mrs Sylvia Bennet of San Francisco, the publication of whose researches will, I hope, redress a long-standing (and Harvard-based) bias in American historiography.
63. ibid., Vol XII, pp. 70–71.
64. Piers Mackesy, *The War for America 1775–1783* (Cambridge, Mass., 1964), p. 427.

10 CONCLUSION: MOST LOYAL OF NORTH BRITONS

1. Miss Mary Grant of Grant to Sir James Grant of Grant, 1775, SRO/GD 248/52/1/8.
2. James Grant to Sir James of Grant, September 1775, SRO/GD 248/52/1/23.
3. Francis Grant to Sir James Grant of Grant, 30 July 1775, SRO/GD 248/52/1/22.
4. Colquhoun Grant to Sir James Grant of Grant, 11 September 1775, SRO/GD 248/52/1/52.
5. J. M. Bumstead, *The People's Clearance: Highland Emigration to British North America 1770–1815* (Edinburgh, 1982), Ch. 3.
6. Ludovick Grant to Sir James Grant of Grant, 28 September 1775, SRO/GD 248/52/1/72.
7. For the recruiting activities of Peter Mackenzie of the 42nd regiment and the resulting legal uproar see Ludovick Grant to Sir James Grant of Grant, 4 November 1775, and consequent correspondence and memoranda, SRO/GD 248/52/1/95–9.
8. For an example of attempts to obtain a commission from General Fraser for a son see Robert Grant to Sir James Grant of Grant, 7 November, 1775, SRO/GD 248/52/1/100.
9. E. Richards, *A History of the Highland Clearances: Agrarian Transformation and the Evictions 1746–1886* (London and Canberra, 1982), Ch. 5, 'Emigrants and Soldiers'. The quotation is from the extract of the chief's letter printed on p.152. I must thank Mrs Ann MacDonell of Speanbridge for drawing my attention to a MS list in her possession of all the able-bodied men aged 16 to 60 on the Duke of Gordon's property in 1778.
10. Lovat's 1774 Act is 14 George III, c. 22, while the Disannexing Act is 24 George III, c. 57.
11. J. M. Pimlott, 'The raising of Four Regiments for India, 1787–8', *Journal of the Society for Army Historical Research*, Vol. 52 (1974), pp. 68–84.
12. Loraine Maclean of Dochgarroch, *The Raising of the 79th Highlanders* (Inverness, 1980).
13. Bumstead, *The People's Clearance*, p. 144.
14. For the life of this remarkable man see Sir Francis Londley, *Lord Lovat* (London, n.d.).

Index